Coterminous Worlds

*Magical realism and contemporary
post-colonial literature in English*

Cross /Cultures

Readings in the Post/Colonial Literatures in English

39

Series Editors:

Gordon
Collier
(Giessen)

Hena
Maes-Jelinek
(Liège)

Geoffrey
Davis
(Aachen)

Amsterdam - Atlanta, GA 1999

Edinburgh University Library

Books may be recalled for return earlier than due date;
if so you will be contacted by e-mail or letter.

Due Date	Due Date	Due Date

Coterminous Worlds

————— ☙ • ❧ —————

Magical realism and contemporary post-colonial literature in English

Edited by

Elsa Linguanti
Francesco Casotti & Carmen Concilio

∞ The paper on which this book is printed meets the requirements of "ISO 9706:1994, Information and documentation - Paper for documents - Requirements for permanence".

ISBN: 90-420-0448-7 (bound)
©Editions Rodopi B.V., Amsterdam - Atlanta, GA 1999
Printed in The Netherlands

Table of Contents

———————————————————————— ℬ

Acknowledgements   / vii
Introduction
ℬ   ELSA LINGUANTI   / 1

Notes on Spanish-American Magical Realism
ℬ   TOMMASO SCARANO   / 9

The Magic of Language
in the novels of Patrick White and David Malouf
ℬ   CARMEN CONCILIO   / 29

Salman Rushdie's Special Effects
ℬ   SHAUL BASSI   / 47

Worlds, Things, Words
Rushdie's style from *Grimus* to *Midnight's Children*
ℬ   CARMEN DELL'AVERSANO   / 61

Representing the Worlds
Sanskrit poetics and the making of reality
ℬ   ALESSANDRO MONTI   / 71

The Ragged Edge of Miracles
or: A word or two on those Jack Hodgins novels
ℬ   LUCIA BOLDRINI   / 83

Bees, Bodies, and Magical Miscegenation
Robert Kroetsch's *What the Crow Said*
ℬ   LUCA BIAGIOTTI   / 103

Myth, Magic, and the Real
in Gwendolyn MacEwen's *Noman*
ℬ   BIANCAMARIA RIZZARDI PERUTELLI   / 115

Bewildered With Nature
The magical-realist in Joe Rosenblatt
ℬ   ALFREDO RIZZARDI   / 125

vi

Coterminous Worlds
ઠ   ROBERT BRINGHURST   / 139

The Magic Reality of Memory
Janet Frame's *The Carpathians*
ઠ   ISABELLA ZOPPI   / 151

Re-Dreaming the World
Ben Okri's shamanic realism
ઠ   RENATO OLIVA   / 171

Reality and Magic in Syl Cheney–Coker's
The Last Harmattan of Alusine Dunbar
ઠ   PAOLO BERTINETTI   / 197

"History never walks here, it runs in any direction"
Carnival and magic in the novels of Kojo Laing and Mia Couto
ઠ   PIETRO DEANDREA   / 209

Magical Realism Beyond the Wall of Apartheid?
Missing Persons by Ivan Vladislavic
ઠ   VALERIA GUIDOTTI   / 227

Wilson Harris
A case apart
ઠ   ELSA LINGUANTI   / 245

Works Cited   / 269
Contributors   / 281

ଓ • ઠ

Acknowledgements

We gratefully acknowledge the permission granted by Faber & Faber (London & Boston) to reproduce the four graphs used in the essay "Wilson Harris: A case apart."

The painting by Lorenzo Canale used on the cover is reproduced by kind permission of the artist.

Introduction

———————————— ❧

FOR YEARS NOW, the literary phenomenon discussed here[1] has fascinated, even mesmerized me; at the same time, I felt a certain distaste for a parallel phenomenon, the literary postmodern. I don't wish to go into detail about this here (complex matters of definition and personal idiosyncracy); suffice it to say that I have found the postmodern to be an ambiguous attraction at best. There is doubtless a ludic aspect to postmodernism – something appealing that seems to legitimate the project, insofar as it makes itself out to be disinterested, disenchanted and perhaps even liberating. Yet it is often also a purely intellectual, sometimes ambitious and complacent, nihilistic game, ultimately expressing despair, as distinct from the deep, diffused sense of melancholy that characterizes modernism.

Texts in English that can be placed under the umbrella of the term 'magical realism' reveal certain formal affinities with postmodernism, but seem tuned to a different wave-length, one sufficiently difficult and enticing to excite interest, if not fascination. What is this wave-length precisely, and why has it manifested itself in such a large variety of forms across so many anglophone cultures? How do these texts function? What elements do they actually have in common?

The variants are in fact numerous and quite distinct. There are destabilizing tendencies within the still dominant mode of narrative realism itself – in the unusual yokings of the 'ordinary' and the 'extraordinary' in the language of Patrick White, for instance, where wholly separate worlds seem impelled to undergo forms of osmosis; or there is the occasional glimmer of the marvellous in David Malouf, who, in a measured, reflective tone, reveals "undisclosed connections" and "limitless possibilities," an "expanding beyond us," a refusal to accept inherited oppositions as irreconcilable.[2] Or

---

[1] That is, in the present volume, which is a selection of papers from a conference on "Il realismo magico e le letterature di lingua inglese," held at Pisa, 21–22 November 1996.

[2] See Elsa Linguanti, "Sequenze e ritmi in *A Fringe of Leaves* di Patrick White," in *Australiana*, ed. Paolo Bertinetti & Claudio Gorlier (Rome: Bulzoni, 1982): 209–21; Malouf,

again, *naturalia* and *mirabilia* coexist peacefully in the novels of Jack Hodgins and in the epic writing of Syl Cheney–Coker, or uncannily in Janet Frame, closely mirroring her world-view and mode of writing. And then there is the Rushdie phenomenon – and, finally, Wilson Harris, going "beyond the novel" to annihilate conventional realism.

ଓ • ଐ

This looks like a renewal of literature – what Wendy Faris calls "a new youth of narrative."[3] Realist–naturalist aesthetics give way to a new vision of 'reality' which does not embody merely a postmodernist dynamic of dispersal or a bricolage of Derridean traces, but is mutable and heterogeneous, its heartbeat requiring auscultation by means of some new form of stethoscope. Realism, naturalism, social realism, psychological realism and surrealism make way for 'magical realism,' which interrogates the very idea of literary 'realism' as the conventionally accepted way of encoding 'reality.' Here the factual coexists and interacts with the imaginary and with the paradoxes of the world of man, in a form of symbiosis.

Neighbouring areas include not only the postmodern but also the postcolonial (both sub-groups of the general category of contemporary literature). The magical-realist impulse did not, of course, originate in Europe (though it has found its way there in Günter Grass's *Tin Drum* and Patrick Süskind's *Perfume*, and in the occasional interesting hint in Golding, Murdoch and Spark). Most of the writers considered in the present selection were formed less by the literature of modernism than by the Great Tradition of the nineteenth century, and by intimate suspicion of the complacent nihilism of postmodernism. They come from countries which have occupied a 'marginal' position, not only in the geographical sense, but also in the sense of being kept on the periphery of the cultural system by its central forces, though destined nevertheless to converge towards/at the centre, as a result of the dynamics at work in every system, or, in the structure of present-day societies, to become part of the polysystem.[4] The books consid-

---

12 *Edmonstone Street* (London: Chatto & Windus, 1985): 51; and Elsa Linguanti, "Too Narrow a Body: Reading David Malouf," *Africa, America, Asia, Australia* 3 (1988): 19–36.

[3] Wendy B. Faris, "Scheherazade's Children: Magical Realism and Postmodern Fiction," in *Magical Realism: Theory, History, Community*, ed. Lois Parkinson Zamora & Wendy B. Faris (Durham NC/London: Duke UP, 1995): 163.

[4] On 'marginality,' see esp. Jeanne Delbaere, "Magic Realism: The Energy of the Margins," in *Postmodern Fiction in Canada*, ed. Theo D'Haen & Hans Bertens (Postmodern Studies 6; Amsterdam & Atlanta GA: Rodopi/Antwerp: Restant, 1992): 75–104.

ered here are fully representative of the post-colonial world, whether we mean by this the literature of the British Commonwealth (a geographical distinction within what remains of a unitary idea of the English World), expressions of (erstwhile or lingering) subject-status and subjectivity within a wider range of cultures such as the Third World or ethnic minorities scattered throughout the First World, or literary manifestations of anti-colonial resistance in their broadest forms.

From the periphery, seen for a long time as the place of the Other, these texts often embody their very own encounter with otherness; where the Other is everything that is not at its ease within monolithic structures, everything outside the order, rules and logic of the West and therefore regarded not infrequently as lower on the scale of eurocentric values.

ෆ • ಬಂ

It should, of course, be remembered that the oxymoron 'magical realism,' as used to define the texts in English that we are dealing with here, was first employed long before to describe a movement in painting (during the Twenties: Franz Roh in Germany, Massimo Bontempelli in Italy) and, later, a literary movement in South America (in 1927 and again in 1945). In its applications, it is a term that is perhaps not wholly satisfactory. Nevertheless, the designation 'magical realism' retains its charm, while the variants that have been proposed – 'mythic realism' (Michael Ondaatje), 'grotesque' and "psychic realism' (Jeanne Delbaere–Garant), or, within the group of those contributing to the present volume, 'miraculous realism' (Lucia Boldrini) and 'shamanic realism' (Renato Oliva), etc – seem less comprehensive.

The critical literature on magical realism, at least as far as texts in English are concerned,[5] is unsatisfactory. At times it focuses on magical elements rather than literary aspects, or on explaining connections with local geographical, religious or anthropological questions (the 'geographical fallacy'), or on the emergence of a general need for the supernatural and the religious as a popular phenomenon, such as in current 'new age' thinking. Zamora and Faris's recent *Magical Realism* deals mainly with texts in English, and contains some essays that represent honest attempts to define the specific nature of this form of narrative writing, together with others that apply the

---

[5] A higher standard is maintained by Irlemar Chiampi's semiotic study of South American magical realism, *El realismo maravilloso: Forma y ideología en la novela hispano-americana* (tr. from *O realismo maravilhoso: Forma y ideologia no romance hispano–americano* [1976; São Paulo: Editora Perspectiva, 1980]; Caracas: Monte Avila Editores, 1983).

label indiscriminately, thus increasing the confusion, above all in their attempt to include British and American texts in which anti-realist elements are not coextensive with the magical-realist mode.

It is true that we have to account for national variants. Australia, Canada and New Zealand, for example, with their heritage of Western order, are more strongly influenced by Pascal's *"esprit de géometrie,"* even if they inevitably have to come to terms with what Susan Musgrave calls a "tap root":[6] ie the Indian culture in Canada, the Aborigine in Australia and the Maori in New Zealand: all examples of cultures of the Other. African writers seem to share what Wilson Harris calls "a shamanic yearning for a break-through from a predatory coherence or stasis."[7] Writers from the Indian subcontinent defuse binary oppositions by releasing the vision of a hybrid, transformative and metamorphic reality, as does Harris, drawing on Guyanese resources. And it is also true that the magic of reality and the reality of magic are something poets have always known, a negotiation with other worlds. "Poetry has to do with crossing borders, carrying precious loads," as the poet Robert Bringhurst says.[8]

It is also true that dissatisfaction with inherited concepts, suspicion of received ideologies, increase in scientific knowledge, and common anxiety over the state of the planet have combined to open up problems in the later twentieth century which have influenced the cultural typology of the global village, independently of place.

Yet is it not to be expected that perspectives that are not drily documentary but, rather, capable of incorporating ignored or forgotten, excluded or marginalized aspects of the world should originate on the periphery? 'Threshold art,' 'interstitiality' and the 'transcultural' are key concepts, and we know that hybridity and syncreticity are constituent elements of post-colonial literature which, according to Harris, moves freely on a middle ground between opposites.

ଓଃ • ৪৩

A hypothesis has begun to take shape in tentative and partial answer to the questions indicated above. After the crises of the subject and of authority, after the death of God and of the Logos, the birth and management of new

---

[6] Susan Musgrave, *Songs of the Sea Witch* (Vancouver: Sono Nis, 1976).

[7] Wilson Harris, "The Open Door," *Journal of Modern Literature* 20.1 (1996): 7.

[8] Robert Bringhurst, *Pieces of Map, Pieces of Music* (Toronto: McClelland & Stewart, 1987): 99.

cultural typologies entails attacking inherited dichotomies such as man/
nature, centre/margin, myth/history, and real/marvellous (rather: real/
imaginary) and "philosophical pairs,"[9] such as realistic language = true/
rhetorical language = false. Semiotically speaking, we now encounter inclu-
siveness, the non-disjunction of contradictory elements, and above all the
encounter with Otherness (not so much as intended by Jacques Lacan as by
Martin Buber and Emmanuel Levinas).[10]

Foundational concepts of twentieth-century science – the principles of indeterminacy and complementarity (identical phenomena are susceptible of
alternative theoretical explanations and alternative theory-bound descriptions) and the theories of quanta and parallel universes – and such contemporary extrapolations as chaos mathematics, fluid dynamics and the
'butterfly effect' interact with general thought, encouraging alternative
modes of thought and changing our attitudes about how the world is/was
supposed to work.

The fact that the wondrous never resolves into the supernatural in these
texts is an indication that the whole literary operation of magical realism is
instrumental; it is a form that is considered suitable for the presentation of
ways of reconciling other modes of opposition that are experienced as
intolerable. "Relief from the implacable polarization within history" is what
Wilson Harris advocates; the calling into question of reality by means of
otherness, or the "bursting of bonds"; the attempt to salvage an organic
image of the world as a "seamless whole."[11]

ᛃ • ᚵ

However, these are literary texts in which we are searching for constants. It
is necessary to devise conceptual instruments that make it possible to

---

[9] The term is used by Chaïm Perelman & Lucie Olbrechts–Tyteca in *The New Rhetoric:
A Treatise on Argumentation,* tr. John Wilkinson & Purcell Weaver (*Traité de l'argumentation.
La nouvelle rhétorique,* 1958; Notre Dame IN: U of Notre Dame P, 1969).

[10] That is to say, the Other not as revealed from the splitting through of the Ego but as
a presence, an inflowing world, penetrating and fructifying the world of the I: "a turning
to, a dynamic facing of, the other, from *I* to *Thou.*" Martin Buber, *To Hallow This Life,* ed.
Jacob Trapp (New York: Harper, 1958): 122. For Levinas, see *Totality and Infinity: An Essay
on Exteriority,* tr. Alphonso Lingis (*Totalité et infini,* 1961, Pittsburgh PA: Duquesne UP,
1969) and *Time and the Other and Additional Essays,* tr. Richard C. Cohen (*Le temps et l'autre,*
Pittsburgh PA: Duquesne UP, 1987).

[11] Wilson Harris, *Tradition, the Writer and Society: Critical Essays* (London/Port of
Spain: New Beacon, 1967): 15 and *Explorations* (Mundelstrup/Sydney: Dangaroo, 1981):
78.

explore unfamiliar logic (capable, that is, of explaining the new textual
reality before us, as always in the study of literary texts) and to investigate
the organization of the significance assumed by the structures of meaning
within texts (a task which comes before any search for links with external
systems). In any case, we will have to deal with new cultural models on the
one hand, and with manifestations that are variously idiolectal, national and
personal, on the other.

As regards the exploration of unfamiliar logic, we find isotopies based on
the non-disjunction of contradictory elements (myth/history, *naturalia/
mirabilia*) – not either/or, but both/and. Textual axiologies are often undefinable because of a challenging of socio-cognitive codes. Another still
more common feature is censure of the principle dictating the reality of the
social order. Cultural typologies are renewed by memory and by an awareness of new against old cosmologies, thus entailing acknowledgment of the
persistence of myth. Lastly, metaphors built on analogical links with quantum theory, the theory of chaos, and fluid dynamics replace the modernist
metaphors of fragmentation and segmentation and the postmodern ones of
dispersal and dissemination. All these elements display a tedency to connect
rather than separate, to recover and salvage rather than scatter or deconstruct, in order to form osmotic, metamorphic models.

As regards structures of meaning, even if some of the formal techniques
are common to postmodernism (problematic enunciation, explicit and
implicit meta-diegesis, the loss in mimetic function of conventional dialogue,
alteration of temporal order, the anti-conventional treatment of space in
textual construction), it is also true that in these texts the data include
aspects of the world that have generally been marginalized or excluded from
literary treatment, but are here shifted to the centre. The emphasis is on the
'thereness' of the non-human, the counterfactual, otherness. Spaces are
hybrid: opposite properties coexist. The temporal regime is mainly one of
regressiveness and simultaneity. Characters are not single and central, but
come in groups of two or more, or form communities. The story-line is
rendered problematic, freed from logical connections, and working only by
means of internal causality. Dominant themes centre on process-formation
and carnivalization: routes, journeys, growth, initiation, death and rebirth,
mutation, metamorphosis. Lastly, the language is both lexically and syn-
tactically inventive and frequently has recourse to the multiplication of
signifiers (lists), plays on words, polysemy, paradoxes, and a constant
literalization of 'figures' – metaphor, oxymoron, hyperbole, and antonomasia – which seems to confirm the overturning of the dichotomy realistic

language=true/rhetorical language=false (endorsed by recent work in linguistics and neurobiology on mental representations and cognitive semantics). Yet perhaps this is not so great a novelty. I am prompted to recall a fragment, quoted twice by Plutarch, in which Gorgias of Lentini says of literature (a privileged place for the exercise of language: ie, rhetoric) that it is a form of deceit in which the deceiver is *dikaioteros* – more direct, more honest, more accurate, more in the right – than the non-deceiver, and where the person deceived is *sophoteros* – more intelligent, more prudent, more astute – than the one who remains undeceived.

I should like, in closing, to thank Robert Bringhurst and Wilson Harris for the approval they showed towards our venture. Bringhurst gave his permission to publish excerpts from his books; Harris very kindly gave encouraging support to my reading of one of his most difficult – and beautiful – books. All of the Italian contributors on anglophone literatures in this collection have reason to be grateful to Claudio Gorlier for starting us all on our journey. And all of the contributors have reason to be grateful to Gordon Collier for the competence, patience, and good humour with which he helped 'iron out the bumps.'

ELSA LINGUANTI

ᔥ ● ᔥ

Notes on Spanish-American Magical Realism

————————————— ℘ —————————————

Tommaso Scarano

I N HIS OPENING PAPER at the first congress entirely dedicated to *realismo mágico*,[1] Emir Rodríguez Monegal pointed out that (far from offering a fruitful basis for critical discussion) the label had turned out to have a paralyzing effect and might be compared to a cul-de-sac, or labyrinth with no centre; at best, tautological, at worst, pleonastic.[2]

Rodríguez Monegal meant, of course, to be provocative (and in this he was successful). Yet his conclusions were not (and in my opinion, are still not) completely unfounded. Behind the apparent transparency and clarity of the formula, there is, in reality, an excessive vagueness, above all owing to the adjective '*mágico*.' And this explains the multiplicity of definitions that have been given, which in some cases present striking contrasts. It also explains the continual adaptations and adjustments that the content of the formula has been forced to undergo, depending on the texts referred to.

In the course of the debate, various links, influences and divergences have been alleged or refuted in an equally peremptory manner. The influence of surrealism has been denied by some and acknowledged by others. *Realismo mágico* has been compared to, or else clearly differentiated from, the fantastic. The Latin American *real maravilloso* theorized by Alejo Carpentier

---

[1] XVI Congreso Internacional de Literatura Iberoamericana (East Lansing, Michigan, 1973).

[2] Emir Rodríguez Monegal, "Realismo mágico versus literatura fantástica: un diálogo de sordos," *Otros mundos, otros fuegos: Fantasía y realismo mágico en Iberoamérica*. Proceedings of the XVI Congreso Internacional de Literatura Iberoamericana (East Lansing, 1973; Latin American Studies Center, USA: Michigan State University, 1975): 25–37.

has been considered a variant of *realismo mágico*, or something quite different, or again substantially the same. Mythology and folklore continually have come into, and passed out of, the discussion. Lastly, the *mágico*-element for some scholars resides in the particular way in which the writer perceives what is real, whereas for others it is a question of a way of writing, and for yet others an aspect typical of the American reality-referent.

The discussion has inevitably spawned new formulas such as *real imaginario, realismo artístico, realismo integrador, realismo fantástico, realismo mitológico* and *realismo maravilloso*. Each of these in turn has been considered the formula best able to summarize the main aspects of this narrative technique, but none has yet succeeded replacing the original formula, not even the last-cited, *realismo maravilloso*, which is undoubtedly the most correct, in that it unites two well-codified literary categories, the realist and the anti-realist *par excellence*.[3]

Yet, as is well known, formulas die hard, and as they have been consecrated by tradition, in whatever way, they command a certain respect. It is thus understandable that the formula *realismo mágico* continues to be used. It is sufficient to be aware, in using it, that it is no more than a simple formula – that is to say, a model that "in itself is poor in meaning."

      ℭ • ℛ

I want to say something about certain aspects of *realismo mágico*, but, given the complexity of this literary phenomenon, I will only be able to deal with the topic in a fragmentary manner. The first fragment, which might be entitled "Three Americans in Paris," opens on the terrace of a Parisian café, where three young Latin Americans used to meet in the late Twenties and early Thirties to hold interminable discussions about politics and literature. Each of them had his own dictator to describe, Estrada Cabrera, Machado, or Gómez; each had his own literary project to accomplish and had discovered a fundamental aspect of American reality which had formerly been ignored, his own hidden face of American culture. The three young men were Miguel Ángel Asturias, from Guatemala, Alejo Carpentier, from Cuba, and Arturo Uslar Pietri, from Venezuela. Writing in the Eighties, Uslar Pietri summarizes the interests of this group of Americans in Paris as follows:

---

[3] I refer to Irlemar Chiampi's contribution, which remains of fundamental importance, *El realismo maravilloso: Forma y ideología en la novela hispano-americana* (tr. from *O realismo maravilhoso: Forma y ideologia no romance hispano–americano* [1976; São Paulo: Editora Perspectiva, 1980]; Caracas: Monte Avila Editores, 1983).

Asturias gave expression, in an almost obsessive manner, to the vanished world of the Maya culture, in a fabulous mixture in which there appeared, like the extravagant characters in a *grand guignol*, the Dictator's police, the unlikely contrasts of situations and convictions, and an almost supernatural vision of an almost unreal reality. Carpentier was fascinated by the negro elements of Cuban culture. He could speak for hours on end about *santeros, ñáñigos,* voodoo rites, and the magic mentality of the average Cuban in the presence of the various heritages of the past. As for myself, I came from a country where the dominant element was neither the Indio or the negro, but the rich undefinable mixture of a contradictory cultural crossbreed.[4]

In 1924, Asturias moved to Paris, where he came into contact with such Surrealists as Aragon, Breton and Tzara, and where he met Picasso and Braque. He thus came to know all the leading exponents of French avant-garde Surrealism. In 1927, he completed (with J.P.M. González de Mendoza) a Spanish translation of the *Popol Vuh*, the sacred book of the Quichua Indians, based on the French version of Georges Raynaud, who held courses at the Sorbonne on the myths and pre-Columbian religions of Meso-America and with whom Asturias worked closely. This was followed in 1928 by a translation of the *Anales de los Xahil*. As he recalled in later years, under the guidance of Raynaud and other French anthropologists and ethnologists, Asturias became an enthusiastic and voracious student of these cultures, with the aim of tracing the *disjecta membra* of the Mayan Empire.[5] The year 1930 saw the publication of the *Leyendas de Guatemala*, the great work which laid the foundations of Asturias' later production, made up of *indio* folklore, stories heard from children, memories and fantasies. Paul Valéry, who read the translation by Francis de Miomadre, was enthusiastic about these "story-dream-poems," with their "bizarre mixture of beliefs, tales and customs, representing all the stages of development of all the ages of a composite people," from "a land where nature, botany, indigenous magic and theology

---

4 Arturo Uslar Pietri, "Realismo mágico," in *Godos, insurgentes y visionarios* (Barcelona: Seix Barral, 1986): 135: "En Asturias se manifestaba, de manera casi obsesiva, el mundo disuelto de la cultura maya, en una mezcla fabulosa en la que aparecían, como extrañas figuras de un drama de guiñol, los esbirros del Dictador, los contrastes inverosímiles de situaciones y concepciones y una visión casi sobrenatural de una realidad casi irreal. Carpentier sentía pasión por los elementos negros en la cultura cubana. Podría hablar por horas de los santeros, de los ñáñigos, de los ritos del vudú, de la mágica mentalidad del cubano medio en presencia de muchos pasados y herencias. Yo, por mi parte, venía de un país en el que no predominaban ni lo indígena, ni lo negro, sino la rica mezcla inclasificable de un mestizaje cultural contradictorio."

5 See Pietro Raimondi, "Miguel Ángel Asturias," in Asturias, *Opere*, ed. & intro. Raimondi (Turin: UTET, 1973): xiv.

combine to compose the most delirious of dreams."[6] In other words, here was a *surrealistic* "reality." Valéry's expression requires us to say something about the surrealism of Asturias.

It is undeniable that Asturias' experience of Surrealism in Paris was fundamental for the definition of his language and for the dreamy atmosphere that pervades his writings. However, his own surrealism is less intellectual, and more vital, existential, and magical, than French Surrealism. Asturias himself likens it to the primitive or infantile mental attitude of the *indio*, who mixes reality and imagination, reality and dream.

> Life in Guatemala, which is what pervades my novels, mixes together the real and the fantastic in such a way that it is impossible to separate them. I believe that this might be explained by what may be defined as 'American magical realism,' in which the real is accompanied by a dream-world reality so full of details that it turns into something more than reality itself, as in the native texts (*Popol Vuh, Anales de Xahil, El Guerrero de Rabinal*). The reality in which my characters move is a mixture of the magical and the real. The magical is a kind of second, almost complementary language used to penetrate the universe that surrounds them. They live, we live (because the novelist lives with his characters) in a world in which there are no barriers between the real and the fantastic, in which any episode, when narrated, becomes a part of something unworldly and where, in the opinion of the people, that which is born of the imagination takes on the substantial nature of reality.[7]

Carpentier arrived in Paris a few years after Asturias, in the spring of 1928, after a short period in prison, where he started writing a novel entitled *Ecué-Yamba-O*, a Lucumí–Ñáñigo formula ("God be praised") sung at initiation ceremonies. He had managed to escape from Cuba thanks to his friend, the French poet Robert Desnos, who had lent him his own passport. Desnos now introduced him to the group of Surrealists, with whom he

---

6 Raimondi, "Miguel Ángel Asturias," xxvii.

7 "En la vida guatemalteca [he wrote in 1959] que es la que invade mis novelas, están mezclados la realidad y lo fantástico, que es imposible separarlos. Por eso creo que cabría dar como explicación lo que podría llamarse el 'realismo mágico americano,' en el que lo real va acompañado de una realidad soñada con tantos detalles que se transforma en algo más que la realidad, como en los textos indígenas (*Popol Vuh, Anales de Xahil, El Guerrero de Rabinal*). Es una mezcla de magia y realidad en la que mis personajes se mueven. La magia es algo así como un segundo idioma, como una lengua complementaria para penetrar el universo que los rodea. Viven, vivimos, porque el novelista vive con sus personajes, en un mundo en que no hay fronteras entre lo real y lo fantástico, en el que un hecho cualquiera, contado, se torna parte de un algo extraterreno, y lo que es hijo de la fantasía cobra realidad en la mentalidad de la gente"; "Quince preguntas a Miguel Angel Asturias," in *Revolución de Cuba* (Havana; 17 August 1959).

remained in close contact until his return to Cuba in 1939, and, through Desnos, he also met Asturias.

In a sort of parallel between his own cultural experience in Paris and that of his friend from Guatemala, Carpentier, too, soon "ardently felt the desire to express the American world," and eagerly set about trying to learn about his continent. "For eight years," he wrote in 1964, "I believe I have done nothing other than read American texts. America appeared to me like a sort of enormous nebula that I endeavoured to understand, because I had the vague awareness that my work [...] would be deeply American."[8]

When the first edition of *Ecué-Yamba-O* was published in Madrid in 1933, the nature of Carpentier's America was already clear. *Ecué-Yamba-O* is the first stage of a complex discourse about the black element and Afro-Cuban culture and religion. The novel describes the life of Cuban blacks in the sugar plantations, suggestively presenting their beliefs, religion and culture in an atmosphere full of magic, surprise and mystery. The language shows clearly the influence of Carpentier's avant-garde experience, above all in its bold metaphors and Cubist description of the countryside.

However, the crisis was already brewing which was to detach Carpentier from the Surrealist group, and, again like Asturias, this Surrealist phase proved to be a stage in the growth of a deeper and more lasting commitment to American *real maravilloso*. His return to Cuba in 1939, when he discovered *La Habana Vieja* (Old Havana), and his visit to Haiti in 1943 were decisive in leading him to compare the authentically marvellous element in American reality with the avant-garde's claim to arouse wonder, in Carpentier's view an unjustified one.

In an article published in *El Nacional* in April 1948, later re-used as the prologue to *El reino de este mundo*, Carpentier fiercely attacked the conjuring tricks performed by former Surrealist thaumaturges who had now become pure bureaucrats, and whom poverty of imagination had reduced to learning by heart "codes of the fantastic, based on the principle of the donkey

---

[8] "ardientemente el deseo de expresar el mundo americano"; " Por el espacio de ocho años creo que no hice otra cosa que leer textos americanos. América se me presentaba como una enorme nebulosa, que yo trataba de entender porque tenía la oscura intuición de que mi obra [...] iba a ser profundamente americana"; Carpentier, "Confesiones sencillas de un escritor barroco" (interview with César Léante, 1964), in *Homenajes a Alejo Carpentier: Variaciones interpretativas en torno a su obra*, ed. Helmy Giacomán (New York: Las Américas, 1970): 21.

devoured by a fig, proposed by [Lautréamont's] *Les Chants de Maldoror* as the supreme inversion of reality."[9]

Carpentier's experience in Haiti was decisive in helping him recognize at last in reality the American essence that he had sought in literature. He said in this connection: "I stand here, before the prodigies of a magic world, a syncretic world, a world where I found a living condition, in a primeval state, already made, prepared, revealed, everything that the surrealists, it must be admitted, invented, all too often artificially."[10] Carpentier's message is quite clear: American reality is a compendium of natural, cultural and historical prodigies, and the unusual, the portentous and the marvellous are components that are typical of American reality. In other words, he proclaims the authentically marvellous character of the real, as opposed to the false marvels of what is unreal. This is Carpentier's theory of the American *real maravilloso*.

03 • ಐ

Arturo Uslar Pietri arrived in Paris in the middle of 1929. The previous year he had published a collection of stories, *Barrabás y otros cuentos*, sixteen texts which broke with the picturesque and affected realism in fashion at the time. Domingo Miliani sees this and the following collection, *Red* (1936), as the forerunners of the texts of *realismo mágico*.[11] And Uslar Pietri was indeed the first writer in the field of Latin American criticism to speak of *realismo mágico*, in an essay on the Venezuelan short story published in 1948. Referring to a group of young *cuentistas* who were influenced by certain avant-garde magazines of the mid-Twenties (the models were above all French Cubism and Spanish Ultraism), and in particular by his own *Barrabás*, Uslar Pietri expresses their novel way of telling stories as follows: "What came to

---

[9] "códigos de lo fantástico, basados en el principio del burro devorado por un higo, propuesto por los *Cantos de Maldoror* como suprema inversión de la realidad"; Carpentier, "De lo real maravilloso americano" (1949), in *Tientos y diferencias* (1964; Montevideo: Arca, 1973):·115–16.

[10] Carpentier, "Un camino de medio siglo," in *Razón de ser* (Caracas, 1976). (This is the text of a lecture held at the Universidad Central de Venezuela in 1974). I quote from Alexis Márquez Rodríguez, *Lo barroco y lo real maravilloso en la obra de Alejo Carpentier* (Mexico City: Siglo XX, 1982): 44: "Me hallo ahí ante los prodigios de un mundo mágico, de un mundo sincrético, de un mundo donde hallaba al estado vivo, al estado bruto, ya hecho, preparado, mostrado, todo aquello que los surrealistas, hay que decirlo, fabricaban demasiado a menudo a base de artificios."

[11] Domingo Miliani, *Arturo Uslar Pietri, renovador del cuento venezolano* (Caracas: Monte Avila, 1969).

predominate in the story was the tendency to consider man as a mystery surrounded by realistic data. A poetic divination or a poetic negation of reality. Something that, for want of a more suitable term, might be called magical realism."[12]

In Uslar Pietri' s view, *realismo mágico* was essentially the perception of the mystery, or magical element, in man and reality – a revaluation and use of myths and popular legends in the conviction that it is in the conscience of the people that "a broad channel of communication between the mythical and the real" is created.[13]

Las lanzas coloradas, a mythicized epic of the wars of Venezuelan independence, was published in Madrid in 1931 (though Uslar Pietri only left Paris in 1934). The choice of subject is not without significance. As with Asturias and Carpentier, it was in France that Uslar Pietri discovered the peculiar condition of the American world and its difference from European reality, hence also the special role and task of the Latin American writer: "to reveal, to discover, to express, in all its unusual fulness, the almost unknown, almost hallucinatory reality which was Latin America, in order to penetrate the great creative mystery of the cultural crossbreed."[14] For Uslar Pietri too, this is a kind of *redescubrimiento* of Spanish America, which leads him to recognize the most obvious and significant (but also the least known and valued) aspect of its identity: namely, a cultural peculiarity which was the result of a complex series of encounters between different cultures and epochs.

Thus the moment had come for Uslar, too, to take his leave of Surrealism, which had been an important creative game, but had finally revealed its true character, that of "the autumnal game of an apparently exhausted literature."[15] The game played by the new Latin American writers, on the other hand, was quite different: not a game of imagination, "but rather a realism

12 Arturo Uslar Pietri, "El cuento venezolano," in *Letras y hombres de Venezuela* (Mexico City: FCE, 1948); repr. Madrid: E.M. Edition, 1978): 287: "Lo que vino a predominar en el cuento fué la consideración del hombre como misterio en medio de datos realistas. Una adivinación poética o una negación poética de la realidad. Lo que a falta de otra palabra podría llamarse un realismo mágico."

13 Uslar Pietri, "Tio tigre y Juan Bobo," *Letras y hombres de Venezuela*, 250: "un ancho canal de comunicación entre lo mítico y lo real."

14 Uslar Pietri, "Realismo mágico," *Godos, insurgentes y visionarios*, 137: "revelar, descubrir, expresar, en toda su plenitud *inusitada* esa realidad casi desconocida y casi alucinatoria que era América Latina *para penetrar el gran misterio creador del mestizaje cultural*."

15 Uslar Pietri, "Realismo mágico," 137: "el juego otoñal de una literatura aparentemente agotada."

that faithfully reflected a reality till then unknown, contradictory and rich in peculiarities and alterations, which made it unusual and surprising, as compared with the categories of traditional literature."[16]

The three Americans in Paris, then, had similar cultural experiences, which led them from Surrealism to *realismo mágico* as the most authentic expression of their Latin American condition. I believe that this element in the lesson of Surrealism is to be underlined. Clearly, *realismo mágico* is not Surrealism, but it undoubtedly incorporated several of its elements, especially some found in late Surrealism, following Breton's second manifesto of 1930, which developed the conception of the immanence of the super-real in the real, and the reconciliation of contradictory aspects of the world.

For example, it has been rightly noted[17] that Carpentier's theory of the *real maravilloso* borrowed various ideas from Pierre Mabille, the author of the famous Surrealistic anthology *Le miroir du merveilleux* (1940), which gathered texts concerning the perception of the marvellous from a range of different cultures. These ideas included those of the origins of the marvellous in folklore, in popular mythology, and in religious syncretism, as well as the hypothesis according to which fringe cultures are the privileged site of the marvellous.

If I had to indicate where and when the coagulation of the elements destined to become the generative nucleus of *realismo mágico* first took place, I would say in Paris, while Surrealism was in full flower; but I would have to add: through an interest in the New World, and in opposition to Surrealism.

ය • ಚಿ

I should like now to consider the critical debate over 'magical realism' – the notoriously partial, generic and erroneous interpretations of Ángel Flores and Luis Leal. I do so for three reasons. The first is to revive discussion of the relationship between *realismo mágico* and the fantastic, which in my opinion critics have not yet fully elucidated, preferring as they do the simplicity of separation to the more productive complexity of probable contaminations. Secondly, I wish to question the all too widely – but, in my view, mistakenly – accepted differentiation between *realismo mágico* and *real*

---

[16] Uslar Pietri, "Realismo mágico," 138: "sino un realismo que reflejaba fielmente una realidad hasta entonces no vista, contradictoria y rica en peculiaridades y deformaciones, que la hacían inusitada y sorprendente para las categorías de la literatura tradicional."

[17] Chiampi, *El realismo maravilloso*, 39.

maravilloso (the former *creates* a marvellous reality and integrates it into objective reality, whereas the latter *represents* the nature of a certain reality). Lastly, I also wish to show (and this might offer a suitable title for this second part) that "some critics' mistakes may be a blessing in disguise."

I begin with the famous lecture given by Ángel Flores at the MLA in 1954.[18] This was the first time that the expression *realismo mágico* was used in an academic context to define a trend in Spanish-American literature. Flores used the formula 'magical realism' to define a way of story-telling that had developed in the Forties and had rejected the stereotyped models of indigenous, regionalistic, creole realism, preferring a more complex image of reality, based, as Flores said, on "the amalgamation of realism and fantasy."

The works mainly referred to in his analysis were Kafka's *Metamorphosis*, De Chirico's metaphysical paintings, and Borges' *Historia Universal de la infamia* (*Universal History of Infamy*) and "El Jardín de senderos que se bifurcan" ("The Garden of Forking Paths"). These last two were said to represent moments of change and renewal in Spanish-American literature.

This was sufficient for many critics to affirm that by 'magical realism' Flores in fact meant the fantastic; which appeared to put an end to the whole question. This must have seemed correct even to Flores himself, given that a few years later, in presenting an anthology of Spanish-American narrative that included many of the authors quoted in his 1954 lecture, he no longer spoke of 'magical realism,' but of the fantastic.

Yet, though inaccurate, Flores' interpretation nevertheless contains two remarks that could be applied – and this is what always made him a subject of interest for me – to writings of magical realism, as this was to be defined in works not yet published in 1954. The first highlights the fact that in these works "the unreal happens as part of reality," and the second, that they share "the same transformation of the common and the everyday into the awesome and the unreal."[19] For the "amalgamation of realism and fantasy" takes place, for Flores, by means of two procedures: the realistic narration of the unreal; and the unrealistic narration of the real (or if you prefer, the naturalization of the unreal, and the supernaturalization of the real).

In my view, both procedures, whether combined or not, are fully relevant to a large number of 'magical-realist' texts, both when they narrate the marvellous as natural, or as an integral part of reality, or as the hidden face

---

[18] Ángel Flores, "Magical Realism in Spanish American Fiction," *Hispania* 38.2 (1955): 187–92.

[19] Flores, "Magical Realism in Spanish American Fiction," 190–91.

of the real, and when they use techniques such as alienation, deformation or exaggeration to narrate the real as marvellous, prodigious, and magical.

It is interesting, however, to note that these two procedures also apply to certain contemporary forms of the fantastic, as in some stories by Cortázar or Silvina Ocampo, in which the non-natural or absurd event is not rejected as a stumbling-block to reason, as in 'classic' forms of the fantastic, but is accepted, together with all its mystery, as an integral part of reality. In these stories the fantastic aspect is provided by an altered perception of the natural, which transforms (or deforms) it into the alarmingly unreal. This suggests the undoubtedly stimulating hypothesis that certain points of contact, and maybe even reciprocal influences, may exist between *realismo mágico* and this form of 'neo-fantastic' (as Jaime Alazraki calls it)[20] or post-fantastic (as others prefer).[21]

Ten years later, Flores' analysis was attacked by Luis Leal,[22] who accepted neither the criteria followed in the selection of works, nor the position of leader attributed to Borges. For Leal, the chief exponent of *realismo mágico* was not Borges, the creator of imaginary worlds, but Carpentier, the theorist of the *real maravilloso*, who, in his *El reino de este mundo*, tells the story of French rule in Haiti, the revolt of the negro slaves, and the bloody reign of the fanatical Henri Christophe.

Leal's contribution was not particularly important in itself, but it had the undeniable merit of highlighting the realist component of *realismo mágico*, both through reference to post-expressionism,[23] and through the emphasis it placed on Carpentier's conception of American reality. This element still needs stressing, insofar as the marvellous component of *realismo mágico* has perhaps been over-emphasized vis-à-vis the realist.

The great novels of the tradition of *realismo mágico* are first and foremost stories about the cultural, social, historical and economic reality of Latin America. It is therefore correct to claim that, among the great texts of *realismo mágico*, it is the Spanish-American works that make the greatest effort to

---

[20] Jaime Alazraki, *En busca del unicornio: los cuentos de Julio Cortázar* (Madrid: Gredos, 1983).

[21] On contemporary Argentinian fantastic literature, see Tommaso Scarano, "Raccontare l'assurdo: Il fantastico di Silvina Ocampo, Julio Cortázar e Bioy Casares," in *Modelli, innovazioni, rifacimenti: Saggi su Borges e altri scrittori argentini* (Viareggio: Mauro Baroni Editore, 1994): 165–98.

[22] Luis Leal, "El realismo mágico en la literatura hispanoamericana," *Cuadernos Americanos* 63.4 (1967): 230–35.

[23] As interpreted by Franz Roh in his *Realismo mágico: Problemas de la pintura más reciente*, an essay (published in *Revista de Occidente*, 1927), well-known in Hispanic circles.

recover and recognize an American identity, which is the keenest problem that 'discovered' colonial peoples have to face. For example, Gabriel García Márquez's Macondo is the mythical space where the history of the colonization and under-development of the whole of Latin America is written. On the other hand, Abancay, in *Los ríos profundos* by José María Arguedas, is a micro-hell where the positive myths of the indigenous culture clash with the negativity of the imposed Hispanic culture. Or again, Comala, in Juan Rulfo's *Pedro Páramo*, though wholly immersed in a climate of unreality, is a place that reveals the roots of the Mexican revolution and its failure.

Yet Luis Leal's analysis also suffers from a serious weakness, that of choosing Carpentier's narrative as the sole model for *realismo mágico*. As a result of its specificity, Carpentier's concept of the *real maravilloso* hardly represents the manifold aspects of the writing in the great magical-realist texts. It is sufficient to consider how restrictive it proves to be if used to describe the complexity of works such as *Pedro Páramo* or *Cien años de soledad*.[24]

I believe we have to give up the idea of recognizing model authors, much less model texts; we should, rather, carry out a more systematic and refined examination of the narrative procedures, technical choices, and expressive and linguistic peculiarities which are at the basis of magical-realist texts. This has not yet been done in a satisfactory manner (perhaps the only serious attempt has been that of Irlemar Chiampi). This sort of study would at least counter the presumed but misleading opposition between Carpentier's *real maravilloso*, seen as an ontological concept, and the *realismo mágico* of García Márquez, seen as an aesthetic concept.[25]

I tend to think that among the elements that make up the *real maravilloso* as defined by Carpentier are also those we generally call by the name *realismo mágico*, which is a far richer, more complex mode of narration.

ೞ • ಐ

---

[24] Referring to the specificity of his *real maravilloso*, Carpentier himself says in the above-mentioned lecture held at the University of Caracas in 1974: "lo que yo llamo lo real–maravilloso [...] difiere del realismo mágico y del surrealismo en sí" ("what I call *real maravilloso* is different from both 'magical realism' and from surrealism"). See Alexis Márquez Rodríguez, *Lo barroco y lo real maravilloso*, 44.

[25] One of the most firmly convinced supporters of this diversity is Márquez Rodríguez; see his *Lo barroco y lo real maravilloso* and "Alejo Carpentier: Teorías del barroco y del real–maravilloso," in *Ocho veces Alejo Carpentier* (Caracas: Grijalbo, 1992): 55–91.

I wish now to define and exemplify certain aspects of the magical-realist text, by referring not only to the writers already cited, but also to a story by Gabriel García Márquez, which gives me the theme of the third and final section of my paper: "Magical realism and jumping beans."

Let us start with Carpentier, and affirm that one of the aims of the magical-realist text is to recount the marvellous or prodigious 'typical' of reality: in other words, to narrate the real, but privileging those aspects that are unrealistic, or beyond the bounds of the normal. In order to recount the unrealistic aspects of reality, the narrative discourse has to overcome two difficulties. The first is to make the inprobable object or event narrated seem real; for, paradoxically, the more the discourse succeeds in representing and adhering to the real, the more it undermines its character as realist discourse. The second difficulty is to find a language that succeeds in saying what cannot be said. García Márquez writes: "It is necessary to create a whole system of new words constructed for our reality."[26] For many magical-realist writers, above all Carpentier, this meant a form of neo-baroque writing.

There is a frequently quoted passage in *Los pasos perdidos* which offers a magnificent example of the problem of describing and authenticating the unrealistic aspect of reality:

> Beyond the gigantic trees rose masses of black rock, enormous, thick, plummet-sheer, which were the presence and the *testimony* of *fabulous* monuments. My memory had to recall the world of Bosch, the *imaginary* Babels of painters of the *fantastic*, the most *hallucinated* illustrators of the temptations of saints, to find anything like what I was seeing. And even when I had hit upon a similarity, I had to discount it immediately because of the proportions. What I was gazing upon was *something like* a Titans' city – a city of multiple and spaced constructions – with Cyclopean stairways, mausoleums touching the clouds, vast terraces guarded by *strange* fortresses of obsidian [...]. There, against a background of light clouds, towered the Capital of the Forms: an *incredible* mile-high Gothic cathedral, a mile high, with its two towers, nave, apse, and buttresses situated on a conical rock of *rare* composition touched with dark iridescences of coal [...] there was something about it *so not of this world* [...] that the bewildered mind sought no interpretation of that *disconcerting* telluric architecture, accepting *without reasoning* its vertical, inexorable vertical beauty.[27]

---

[26] Gabriel García Márquez, "Fantasia y creación artística en América Latina y el Caribe," *Texto crítico* 14 (1979): 6; "sería necesario crear todo un sistema de palabras nuevas para el tamaño de nuestra realidad."

[27] Carpentier, *The Lost Steps*, tr. Harriet de Onís (1956; Harmondsworth: Penguin, 1968): 154–55 (my emphases); "Allá, detrás de los árboles gigantescos, se alzaban unas moles de roca negra, enormes, macizas, de flancos verticales, como tiradas a plomada,

Here is an example (on which my emphases are sufficient comment) of American *real maravilloso* narration as intended by Carpentier, and it is also an example of the natural (for it is authentically natural) narrated as if it were non-natural.

With regard to the marvellous aspect of American reality, both Uslar Pietri and Carpentier point to an element which needs particular emphasis: namely, syncretism. In Carpentier's reflections, this concept is contained within the broader notion of 'synchronism,' in the sense of the simultaneous presence of different times. Syncretism and synchronism are thus seen as the 'marvellous' simultaneity of widely different cultures, races, religions, and histories, or as the incongruous coexistence of autochthonous and allogenic, archaic and modern. Yet they are also, and above all, constituent elements of the *mestizo* identity of Latin American, and primary characteristics of its diversity with respect to other histories and cultures.

Uslar Pietri is quite clear about this when he argues that the identity of Latin America lies in the "very fact of a peculiar and unique cultural situation, created by a vast process of crossbreeding of cultures and heritages, mentalities and attitudes, which is revealed in all manifestations, both of collective life and individual character."[28]

Carpentier's *El reino de este mundo* represents a sort of triumphal celebration of syncretism as a marvellous aspect of American reality. All the stories, set in a particular period of the history of Haiti (about fifty years, starting from 1760), contain unusual or incredible elements. Everything seems out of place and unreal: the presence of Pauline Bonaparte and her court at Cap

---

que eran presencia y *verdad* de monumentos *fabulosos*. Tenía mi memoria que irse al mundo del Bosco, a las Babeles *imaginarias* de los pintores de lo fantástico, de los más *alucinados* ilustradores de tentaciones de santos, para hallar algo semejante a lo que estaba contemplando. Y a un cuando encontraba una analogía, tenía que renunciar a ella, al punto, por una cuestión de proporciones. Esto que miraba era *algo como* una titánica ciudad – ciudad de edificaciones multiples y espaciadas – , con escaleras ciclópeas, mausoleos metidos en las nubes, explanadas immensas dominadas por *extrañas* fortalezas de obsidiana. [...] Y allá, sobre aquel fondo de cirros, se afirmaba la Capital de las Formas: una *increíble* catedral gótica, de una milla de alto, con sus dos torres, su nave, su ábside y sus arbotantes, montada sobre un peñon cónico hecho de una materia estraña, con sombrías irisaciones de hulla.[...] había algo *tan fuera de lo real* [...] que el ánimo, *pasmado*, no buscaba la menor interpretación de aquella *desconcertante* arquitectura telúrica, aceptando *sin razonar* su belleza vertical y inexorable" (*Los pasos perdidos* [1953; Madrid: Cátedra, 1985]: 223).

28 Uslar Pietri, "Realismo mágico," 139; ".... hecho mismo de una situación cultural peculiar y única, creada por el vasto proceso del mestizaje de culturas y pasados, mentalidades y actitudes, que aparec[e] rica e inconfundiblemente en todas las manifestaciones de la vida colectiva y del carácter individual"

Français, the black women dressed in the latest Versailles fashion, with feathered crowns on their heads, the black ministers wearing white stockings and wigs, and the insignia of the Sun King decorating the enormous gilt carriage of the black ex-cook, Henri Christophe, who has become a fanatical slave-driver king.

But the improbability of the historical reality described is only the most macroscopic, and, ultimately, superficial form of syncretism present. It is more interesting to observe the way the plural character of syncretic reality pervades the narrative discourse, producing not only the simple representation, albeit strange and mystifying, of the simultaneous presence of dimorphic elements, but also the blending of real and non-real, one of the central aspects of *realismo mágico*.

El reino de este mundo is based on the coexistence of two contradictory visions of the world: the educated, rational and empirical vision of the white dominators – the French colonizers – as against the mythic, supernatural and magical vision of the black slaves. These two visions logically exclude one another, but coexist in the historical, cultural, and racial reality of Haiti. At the level of the story, and the organization of its discourse, this syncretism is signified by and reflected in a complex strategy of focalization. The black men's vision, permeated by magic and the supernatural, is confirmed by the black focalizer, Ti Noël, and refuted by the white focalizer, Lenormand De Mezy. At the same time, but vice versa, the rational, empirical vision of the white men is confirmed by the white and refuted by the black focalizer.[29]

So far, there is nothing new: the simultaneous presence of distinct focalizers makes the various interpretations of reality problematic. But the play of perspectives and different readings of reality becomes complicated and ambiguous when the educated and europeanized narrator recounts these two antithetical realities, authenticating each and thus determining the fusion of real and non-real. A good example is offered by the following passage, which, in an openly contradictory fashion, narrates the death and the survival of the black *houngan* rebel Mackandal at the stake:

> Macandal was now lashed to the post. The executioner had picked up an ember with the tongs [...]. The fire began to rise toward the Mandingue, licking his legs. At that moment, Macandal moved the stump of his arm, which they had been unable to tie up, in a threatening gesture which was none the less

---

[29] In this connection, see Amaryll Chanady, "La focalización como espejo de contradicciones en *El reino de este mundo*," *Revista Canadiense de Estudios Hispánicos* 12.3 (1988): 446–58.

terrible for being partial, howling unknown spells and violently thrusting his torso forward. The bonds fell off and the body of the Negro rose in the air, flying overhead, until it plunged into the black waves of the sea of slaves. A single cry filled the square:

"Macandal saved!"

Pandemonium followed. The guards fell with rifle butts on the howling blacks, who now seemed to overflow the streets, climbing toward the windows. And the noise and screaming and uproar were such that very few saw that Macandal, held by ten soldiers, had been thrust head first into the fire, and that a flame fed by his burning hair had drowned his his last cry.[30]

The white colonizers are only able to read this second version of reality; for this reason, they lose the colony. The narrator, on the other hand, perceives both of them, thus succeeding at the end of the novel in reading reality as the black men read it, and in using the authority that his role of omniscient narrator confers on him to authenticate the reality of the non-real.

Ti Noël was astonished at how easy it is to turn into an animal when one has the necessary powers. In proof of this he climbed a tree, willed himself to become a bird, and instantly was a bird. [...] The next day he willed himself to be a stallion, and he was a stallion [...]. He turned himself into a wasp, but he soon tired of the monotonous geometry of wax constructions. He made the mistake of becoming an ant, only to find himself carrying heavy loads...[31]

This last passage leads us back to Flores' suggestion that the naturalization of the unreal entails an amalgam between real and marvellous. Here,

[30] Carpentier, *The Kingdom of This World*, tr. Harriet de Onís (New York: Alfred A. Knopf, 1957): 35–36; "Mackandal estaba ya adosado al poste de torturas. El verdugo había agarrado un rescoldo con la tenazas [...] El fuego comenzó a subir hacia el manco, sollamándole las piernas. En ese momento, Mackandal agitó su muñón que no habían podido atar, en un gesto conminatorio que no por menguado era menos terrible, aullando conjuros desconocidos y echando violentamente el torso hacia adelante. Sus ataduras cayeron, y el cuerpo del negro se espigó en el aire, volando sobre las cabezas, antes de hundirse en las ondas negras de la masa de esclavos. Un solo grito llenó la plaza. *Mackandal sauvé!* Y fue la confusión y el estruendo. Los guardias se lanzaron, a culatazos, sobre la negrada aullante, que ya no parecía caber entre las casas y trepaba hacia los balcones. Y a tanto llegó el estrépito y la grita y la turbamulta, que muy pocos vieron que Mackandal, agarrado por diez soldados, era metido en el fuego, y que una llama crecida por el pelo encendido ahogaba su último grito" (*El reino de este mundo* [Barcelona: Seix Barral, 1978]: 40–41).

[31] Carpentier, tr. Harriet de Onís, 143–44; "Ti Noël se sorprendió de lo fácil que es transformarse en animal cuando se tienen poderes para ello. Como prueba se trepó a un árbol, quiso ser ave, y al punto fue ave [...] Al dia siguiente quiso ser garañón y fue garañón [...] hecho avispa se hastió pronto de la monótona geometría de las edificaciones de cera. Transformando el hormiga por mala idea suya, fue obligado a llevar cargas enormes... " (139).

Carpentier does not narrate or 'represent' the marvellous as real, because that is how his characters see it. Rather, he accomplishes the more complex operation of presenting the magical world of myths and popular legends by consigning it to an omniscient narrator, who communicates it to the reader as real, absorbing the reader into a fictive reality in which he cannot help perceiving the incredible as credible, and the unrealistic as real.

In the sixth chapter of Asturias' *Hombres de maíz*, the narrator alludes ten times, in the space of a hundred or more pages, to the popular belief that when Nico Aquino, the courier, crosses the mountains, he turns into a coyote. Then he abandons the point of view of the characters who believe in the truth of the *náhual*, a belief he does not share:

> He had been turning the color of a thorn. He cast off his human shell, a rag-doll with dripping eyes, his tragic human mourning inseparable from the memory of his woman [...]. He cast off his human shell and leaped up on to a sandbank warm but rough beneath his four extremities of howl with hairs [...] with teeth from a cob of white maize, his far-fetching body like a handsaw sawing, pitched forever forward, four paws of running rain, blazing eyes of liquid fire, his tongue, his panting – as he panted, he went suffa, suffa, suffa, suffa – his intelligence, his itching.[32]

This is an example of how the magical-realist text narrates the supernatural event without any ambiguity, removing all mystery, and presenting it as an event that is not in conflict with reality. This aspect of the non-conflictual coexistence of contrary elements is undoubtedly one of the central traits of *realismo mágico*, the one that differentiates it most strikingly from classic fantastic narrative. Where the latter, through its characters and narrator, conveys doubt, anxiety and crisis, the magical-realist narrative insinuates the absence of doubt, and relates a perception of the non-natural as organic and consistent with reality; in so doing, it is quite similar to the kind of neo-fantastic mentioned above.

In *Cien años de Soledad*, there is only one supernatural event, if I am not mistaken, that is doubted by a character – the appearance of the ghost of

---

[32] Asturias, *Men of Maize*, tr. Gerald Martin (New York: Delacorte/Seymour Lawrence, 1975): 296–97; "Se había ido poniendo color de espina. Dejó su caparrazón de hombre, muñeco de trapo con ojos goteantes, su trágico duelo de hombre inseparable del recuerdo de su mujer [...] Dejó su caparazón de hombre y saltó a un arenal de arenitas tibias y de lo más arisco bajo sus cuatro extremidades de aullido con pelos [...] con sus dientes de mazorca de maíz blanco, su alargado cuerpo de serrucho serruchando, echado siempre hacia adelante, sus cuatro patas de lluvia corredora, sus quemantes ojos de fuego líquido, su lengua, su acecido (al acezar hacía sufulufulufú ...), su entendimiento, sus cosquillas " (*Hombres de maíz*, in *Obras completas* [1949; Madrid: Aguilar, 1968], vol. 1: 756).

Prudencio Aguilar. José Aureliano Buendía does not believe Úrsula when she says she saw him on the patio, intent on treating his wounded throat, and answers her, "Los muertos no salen." He then changes his mind. But this is less important than the fact that, from now on, the appearances of Prudencio are no longer narrated as seen by Úrsula or by José Arcadio Buendía, but as seen by the narrator.

> Almost reduced to dust by now, by the profound decrepitude of death, Prudencio Aguilar visited him twice a day. They talked about cockerels. They planned to set up a breeding farm of magnificent animals [...] It was Prudencio Aguilar that washed him, fed him, and brought him fascinating news about an unknown figure named Aureliano, who was a colonel in the war.[33]

But the *naturalization of the non-real* in García Márquez is usually more subtle. When Father Nicanor realizes that he cannot convince the people of Macondo, whether by exhortation or in his sermons, to give him the money he needs to build the church, he exhibits himself in a demonstration of levitation, which, as if by magic, makes his mean parishioners generous:

> The boy who had served mass brought him a cup of creamy, steaming chocolate, which he drank at one gulp. Then he wiped his mouth with a handkerchief that he took out of his sleeve, stretched out his arms, and closed his eyes. Then Father Nicanor rose twelve centimetres above the floor level. It was a convincing stratagem. He continued to go from house to house for several days, repeating the levitation experiment, while the altar-boy collected so much money in a sack, that the building of the temple started in less than a month.[34]

In this case, the miraculous phenomenon is normalized not only by the realist narration of the event, and by the assertive form, but also by the detail of the cup of chocolate. A formula, prayer, or invocation would have made a

---

[33] García Márquez, *Cien años de soledad* (Madrid: Cátedra, 1991): 243–44; "Ya casi pulverizado por la profunda decrepitud de la muerte, Prudencio Aguilar iba dos veces al día a conversar con él. Hablaban de gallos. Se prometían establecer un criadero de animales magníficos.[...] Era Prudencio Aguilar quien lo limpiaba, le daba de comer y le llevaba noticias espléndidas de un desconocido que se llamaba Aureliano y que era coronel en la guerra" (my translation here and elsewhere; Gregory Rabassa's 1970 English version is too imprecise).

[34] García Márquez, 178; "El muchacho que había ayudado a misa le llevó una taza de chocolate espeso y humeante que él se tomó sin respirar. Luego se limpió los labios con un pañuelo que sacó de la manga, extendió los brazos y cerró los ojos. Entonces el padre Nicanor se elevó doce centímetros sobre el nivel del suelo. Fue un recurso convincente. Anduvo varios días por entre las casas, repitiendo la prueba de la levitación mediante el estímulo del chocolate, mientras el monaguillo recogía tanto dinero en un talego, que en menos de un mes emprendió la construcción del templo."

break between normal and non-normal; whereas the cup of chocolate forms a link between realistic and unrealistic; it is the banal touch of realism that domesticates and lends reality to the supernatural event.

At other times, the non-natural event is so embedded in the narration of other events, or is so casually introduced, that it loses all importance.

> [Úrsula] asked to be helped to carry José Arcadio Buendía into his bedroom. Not only was he as heavy as ever, but during his prolonged stay under the chestnut–tree, he had developed the capacity to increase his weight wherever and whenever he wanted, with the result that seven men were not able to lift him up, and they had to drag him to his bed.[35]

Procedures of this kind are generally associated in the magical-realist text with their overturning: that is to say, with the narration of the ordinary real as portentous and supernatural (Flores' second insight). It is sufficient to think of the inappropriate degree of amazement and disconcertedness shown by the characters of Cien años de soledad in the face of objects believed to be magical and marvellous (ice, false teeth, a pianola, etc), and above all of the frequency with which García Márquez uses the procedure of exaggeration in order to shift an object or event from the plane of the real to that of the supernatural, without it being necessary to give them properties different from their own. On the contrary, Márquez operates hypertrophically: that is to say, he increases the quantity in order to obtain a change in quality, thus projecting the object or event into an unreal dimension. Given the extremely high frequency with which this procedure is used, it ends up by representing the normality of the fictive universe of Macondo, thus characterizing it in its entirety.[36] Everything is ordinarily enormous, extreme, and hyperbolic at Macondo, with the result that the overall reality turns into total unreality.

There is no space here to investigate this point in detail, but I give one example for the sake of illustration. It is perfectly normal for a little girl to invite friends to her house, but Meme invites seventy-two. The number makes the event and all its consequences unrealistic, although these are narrated in terms that are perfectly realistic:

---

[35] García Márquez, 243; "[Úrsula] pidió ayuda para llevar a José Arcadio Buendía a su dormitorio. No sólo era tan pesado como siempre, sino que en su prolungada estancia bajo el castaño había desarrollado la facultad de aumentar de peso voluntariamente, hasta el punto de que siete hombres no pudieron con él y tuvieron que llevarlo a rastras a la cama."

[36] In this connection, see Mario Vargas Llosa, García Márquez: Historia de un deicidio (Barcelona: Seix Barral, 1971): 565.

It was necessary to ask the neighbours for beds and hammocks, to establish nine eating shifts, to fix times for the bathroom and to borrow forty stools so that the girls in the blue uniform with men's boots would not wander around the place all day. The invitation was a disaster, because hardly had the noisy college girls finished their breakfast than it was already time for the lunch shifts, and then for dinner [...]. On the evening of their arrival, the schoolgirls created such chaos, trying to go to the toilet before going to bed, that the last ones were still going in at one o'clock in the morning. Consequently, Fernanda bought seventy-two chamber-pots, but she only succeeded in transforming the nocturnal problem into a matutinal one, because there was a long queue of girls in front of the toilet from the earliest hours of daylight, each with her chamber-pot in her hand, waiting for her turn to wash it.[37]

Using this same procedure, magical-realist texts overturn history by turning it into myth, either by using popular tradition, or else by means of a form of narrative that renders the real consituent elements extreme and hyper-trophic.

I would like to conclude by underlining the fact that the particular character of magical-realist writing stems from all the above elements taken together, from the narration of the marvellous aspect of reality as true and incredible, and from the intertwining of a naturalized supernatural and a supernaturalized natural. The deep meaning of this combination lies in the representation of a wholly fictive reality – as Vargas Llosa defines it[38] – in which the principle of non-contradiction is not valid, and the isotopes of the natural and the non-natural are not in conflict.

ભ • ෆ

In the article quoted above, "Fantasía y creación artística en América Latina y el Caribe," García Márquez says of Mexico:

---

[37] García Márquez, 379–80; " Fue preciso pedir camas y hamacas a los vecinos, estable-cer nueve turnos en la mesa, fijar horarios para el baño y conseguir cuarenta taburetes prestados para que las niñas de uniformes azules y botines de hombres no anduvieran todo el día revoloteando de un lado a otro. La invitación fue un fracaso, porque las ruidosas colegialas apenas acababan de desayunar cuando ya tenían que empezar los turnos para el almuerzo, y luego por la cena [...] La noche de su llegada, las estudiantes se embrollaron de tal modo tratando de ir al excusado antes de acostarse, que a la una de la madrugada todavía estaban entrando las últimas. Fernanda compró entonces setenta y dos bacinillas, pero sólo consiguió convertir en un problema matinal el problema nocturno, porque desde el amanecer había frente al excusado una larga fila de muchachas, cada una con su bacinilla en la mano, esperando turno para lavarla."

[38] Vargas Llosa, *García Márquez*, 565.

Many volumes would need to be written in order to explain its incredible reality. After living here for almost twenty years, I can still spend whole hours, as I have often done, contemplating a pan of jumping beans. Benevolent rationalists have explained to me that their movement is due to the fact that there is a live larva inside them, but the explanation seems a poor one to me: the wonder is not that the beans move because they have a live larva inside them, but that they have a live larva inside them which makes them move"; García Márquez, "Fantasia y creación artística en América Latina y el Caribe.[39]

This is much more than an amusing story. The jumping bean encapsulates everything I have been trying to say. It is, in itself, both true and incredible, real and marvellous; it can be perceived and represented as either natural or non-natural. Above all, it exemplifies the attitude that the magical-realist narrator adopts before the real, when his reading of the world is not exclusively directed by the poor canons of rationality.

ᘓ   •   ᘓ

---

[39] García Márquez, 7; "habría que escribir muchos volúmes para expresar su realidad increíble. Después de casi veinte años de estar aquí, yo podría pasar todavía horas enteras, como lo he hecho tantas veces, contemplando una vasija de frijoles saltarines. Racionalistas benévolos me han explicado que su movilidad se debe a una larva viva que tienen dentro, pero la explicación me parece pobre: lo maravilloso no es que los frijoles se muevan porque tengan una larva dentro, sino que tengan una larva dentro para que se puedan moverse."

The Magic of Language
in the Novels of Patrick White and David Malouf

&

Carmen Concilio

> Toad, all the roads from a man to a woman,
> a man to a man, woman to man, woman to woman
> lead through the non-human. This
> is the reason, toad, for musicians.
> [...]
> We speak to each other by means
> [...]
> of the bones and the horns and the bodies
> [...]
> and bowels of dead animals... [1]

> to give a sense to Being means to go from the Same to the Other, from I to *Autrui*, it means to draw a sign, to free the structures of language.[2]

R AWDON WILSON illustrates the emergence of magical-realist fiction in South America with a parable by Jorge Luis Borges about two brothers.[3] The first brother began questioning the linear conception of time and geometry. His new, anti-rational logic was based on the

---

[1] Robert Bringhurst, "Conversation with a Toad," in *The Calling: Selected Poems 1970–1995* (Toronto: McClelland & Stewart, 1995): 23.

[2] Emmanuel Levinas, *Totality and Infinity: An Essay on Exteriority*, tr. Alphonso Lingis (*Totalité et infini: Essai sur l'extériorité*, 1961; Pittsburgh PA: Duquesne UP, 1969).

[3] Rawdon Wilson, "The Metamorphoses of Fictional Space: Magical Realism," in *Magical Realism: Theory, History, Community*, ed. Lois Parkinson Zamora & Wendy B. Faris (Durham NC/London: Duke UP, 1995): 209.

principles of differential geometries, whereby worlds became imaginable (Tlön) and the very fact that they could be imaginatively perceived was a guarantee of their existence. In a similar way, the second brother grew tired of the laws of gravity, the solidity of substance and the relation of cause and effect, and began imagining a world in which things floated together, like quicksilver, where the sky could be made of flowers and the wind of light.

By subverting traditional realism, Borges and Gabriel García Márquez undoubtedly revolutionized the realm of fiction. But there is another kind of magic that emerges from the attempt to give the world a new shape through words: the magic of language. To communicate without the use of words, to grasp the potentiality of a language that is free from the constraints binding world to word and self to world: this seems to be the underlying aim of the works of Patrick White and David Malouf. These two writers have never been seen as magical-realist novelists, and Malouf has recently denied ever having thought of himself as writing in this mode. Nevertheless, he has admitted that, as compared with film, the novel has the advantage of enabling the writer to let silence speak, by creating a new though unspoken reality. This affirmation by Malouf should serve to reinforce, rather than discourage, the following speculations about the magical function of language in the works of the two Australian writers.[4]

In his autobiographical essay "The Prodigal Son" (1958), Patrick White wrote that when he returned to Australia he became aware of a new necessity: "I wanted to discover the extraordinary behind the ordinary, the mystery and poetry which alone could make bearable the lives of such people." Commenting on his novel *Voss* (1957), he further wrote:

> Always something of a frustrated painter, and a composer *manqué*, I wanted to give my book the textures of music, the sensuousness of paint, to convey through the themes and characters of *Voss* what Delacroix and Blake might have seen, what Mahler and Liszt might have heard. Above all I was determined to prove that the Australian novel is not necessarily the dreary, dun-coloured offspring of journalistic realism."[5]

---

[4] In a brief conversation I had with David Malouf in London, on the occasion of the International Symposium "Enigmas and Arrivals: Writing Now" (29–30 April 1997), the author confirmed his distance from writers such as García Márquez, by expressing special appreciation of the latter's *Love in the Time of Cholera*, a novel which has little to do with the acclaimed magic realist *One Hundred Years of Solitude*. Nevertheless, Malouf also admitted that the medium of the novel allows a certain kind of work on language, particularly on the language of silence, which other mediums, such as film, do not permit.

[5] Patrick White, "The Prodigal Son" (1958), in *Patrick White Speaks* (London: Jonathan Cape, 1990): 15–16.

This aesthetic goal thus favoured the disruption of the narrative modes imposed by classical realism. It is striking that this melting of words into music and painting, this defence of synaesthesia, also informs the narrative of the Guyanese writer Wilson Harris, who, in turn, affirms:

> When I first travelled into the rain forest [...] I was aware of something peculiar to myself, which I can only describe as the afflatus coming up from the unconscious. [...] Language began to secrete into itself metaphoric images to do with architecture, to do with painting, to do with music, whatever."[6]

Language becomes metamorphic and therefore highly metaphoric, as the two epigraphs to this essay demonstrate – Robert Bringhurst asserts that all communication between human beings runs through the non-human, while, for Emmanuel Levinas, the road from one man to another is built on the liberation of the structures of language, in face-to-face dialogue between the *Same* and the *Other*.[7]

Reality, that which we take to be normal in daily life, ordinary characters and common experiences. is seen through the magic of White's language. I do not wish to look in detail at affinities between White's *Voss* and Wilson Harris' *The Palace of the Peacock* (1960), though Harris has dedicated essays to the Australian writer.[8] Yet if the attempt to break out of realism was already evident in White's belief that "It is all mutual,"[9] the far more radical narrative practice adopted in Harris's novel, where everything seems to be metamorphic, confirms a common strategy, a common interest in alchemical narrative forms, capable of combining in a 'seamless whole' the ordinary and extraordinary, *naturalia* and *mirabilia*, the real and the magical.[10]

---

6 Mark Williams & Alan Riach, "Reading Wilson Harris," in *The Uncompromising Imagination*, ed. Hena Maes–Jelinek (Mundelstrup/Sydney: Dangaroo, 1991): 58.

7 Emmanuel Levinas, *Totality and Infinity: An Essay on Exteriority*, tr. Alphonso Lingis (*Totalité et infini*, 1961; Pittsburgh PA: Duquesne UP, 1969); and *Time and the Other and Additional Essays*, tr. Richard A. Cohen (*Le temps et l'autre*; Pittsburgh PA: Duquesne UP, 1987).

8 Wilson Harris, "Fossil and Psyche," in *Explorations*, ed. Hena Maes–Jelinek (Mundelstrup/Sydney: Dangaroo, 1981): 68–82; Harris, "Paradoxes of Form," in *The Womb of Space. The Cross-Cultural Imagination* (Westport CT: Greenwood, 1983): 66–78. See also Mark Williams, "Containing Continents: The Moralized Landscapes of Conrad, Greene, White and Harris," *Kunapipi* 7:1 (1985): 34–45, and Jeffrey Robinson, "The Aboriginal Enigma: *Heart of Darkness*, *Voss* and *Palace of the Peacock*," *Journal of Commonwealth Literature* 20:1 (1985): 149–55.

9 Patrick White, *Voss* (1957; Harmondsworth: Penguin, 1960): 188; further page references are in the text.

10 See Elsa Linguanti's "Foreword" to this volume.

Since White's language, like that of Harris, is pictorial, musical, metamorphic and metaphoric, I will be focusing primarily on *elocutio*, or syn-
tactical, semantic and lexical invention, in order to detect the germs of
magical realism, starting with *Voss*. For one of the expressive modalities of
magical-realist literature is to be found in a language's managing to
articulate the unspeakable.

"Mutual. It is all mutual." Here is the epiphanic illumination of the
necessity of reciprocity, of an exchange, an osmotic flow, or a progressive
shifting – as Levinas would say – between Self and Other, in language; of a
being together or "*zusammen*,"[11] of universes which only appear incompatible: the female and the male universes, to begin with.

To communicate without words: this was the starting-point. In *Voss*, the
longed-for communion concerns two deserts: Voss is an explorer imprisoned "in his own brilliant desert" (90), while Laura Trevelyan's reality is
fixed in an unfinished diary, epitomized by "a blank page, [...] far more
expressive than [her] own emptiness" (91). First presented as non-
communicating monads, Voss and Laura – both authors of letters that the
other will never read – attain progressively higher forms of mutual comprehension: "'I can understand him'," Laura says, "'if not with my reason'"
(161). Writing of Malouf's adaptation of the novel as an opera libretto, Annie
Patrick says:

> Malouf perceives their communion by letter as "one of the book's most daring
> moves [...] in some spiritual dimension where space, time and the barriers of
> the individual soul are immediately dissolved." In fictional terms this daring
> manifests itself in its non-realist challenge of narrative conventions.[12]

This anti-realist challenging of narrative conventions, this bold dis-
closure of the magical intrinsic in language, swings between suspicion of
words and aspiration towards "an ideal state in which the official tongue
was music" (30), as the music master, Mr Topp, says. As far as suspicion of
words is concerned, it is not surprising that Laura experiences comprehension, but "not in words" (108), and that during his voyage of exploration
Voss should exchange "dry communications" (123) with his companions,
since "it is necessary to communicate without knowledge of the language"
(169). Similarly, with the Aborigines he wishes to communicate "by skin and
silence" (170). The bridge joining the Self and the Other – be it woman, mate,

---

[11]   Patrick White, *Voss*, 188.

[12]   Annie Patrick, "David Malouf the Librettist," in *Provisional Maps: Critical Essays On
David Malouf*, ed. Amanda Nettlebeck (Nedlands: U of Western Australia, 1994): 137.

or Aborigine – consists of non-verbal language, because words are invariably "pebbles" (20), "great round weights" (63), "wooden" (128), "stones" (136). Moreover, Voss himself affirms: "*Wörter haben keine Bedeutung. Sinnlos!*" (Words have no meaning. No sense!; 190).

"Writing," White explains in *The Prodigal Son*, "became a struggle to create completely fresh forms out of the rocks and sticks of words" (16). The power of words to fix a meaning by the mere act of naming is called into question here. Thus, though names are still believed to shape reality – "Names should be charms [...] I used to hope that, by saying some of them often enough, I might evoke reality" (106), Voss says. The act of naming reality is felt to obliterate its magic. Better, then, to forget the names of the stars, and surrender to the enchantment of their various combinations of forms: "he could draw a line through certain stars, and create figures of constellation [...] for the stars themselves are more personal than their names" (193), and "to understand the stars would spoil their appearance" (137). Verbal language is thus stretched, or suspended, in order to achieve that merging of contradictory terms which is the necessary condition for the emergence of magical realism.[13] Moreover, what White borrowed from Jung and Buber is precisely the idea that illumination is accompanied by the joining of apparent opposites, "of irreconcilable halves."[14]

Another subversive factor in the creation of an ideal musical language is the juxtaposition of adjectives and nouns from heterogeneous semantic groups. It is as though metaphors, oxymora and synaesthesia were the means of stitching incompatible universes together. Of Laura Trevelyan, who is significantly sewing at the beginning of the novel, it is said she is "happiest shut with her own thoughts, and such was the texture of her marble, few people ever guessed at these" (7), while her skirt is variously described as stiffly adding "several syllables to her decision" (8), or again:

---

13 "Finalmente, el discurso realista maravilloso se define por la no disyunción de los términos contradictorios [...]. [la no disyunción] demuestra que las dos especies discursivas diferenciadas se subsumen a una misma estructura de combinatoria de los contradictorios"; Irlemar Chiampi, *El realismo maravilloso: Forma y ideología en la novela hispano-americana* (tr. from *O realismo maravilhoso: Forma y ideologia no romance hispano–americano* [1976; São Paulo: Editora Perspectiva, 1980]; Caracas: Monte Avila Editores, 1983): 185–86 [Ultimately, magic realist discourse is defined as the non-disjunction of contradictory terms [...]. [The non-disjunction] demonstrates that the two differentiated kinds of discourses are subsumed under a single structure which combines the contradictory terms] (my translation).

14 Karin Hansson, *The Warped Universe: A Study of Imagery and Structure in Seven Novels by Patrick White* (Lund: CWK Gleerup, 1984): 97.

"her skirt, which was of a pale colour and infinite afternoon coolness, streamed behind her" (120). Voss's clothing is presented in a similar way: "Voss, too, was translated. The numerous creases in his black trousers appeared to have been sculptured for eternity" (171). The allusion here is literal, for, after the explorer's death, a statue will fix his presence in that place for ever.

Eager to bond differences, Laura embroiders her nuptial blanket with the word *together*, a word translated by Voss into sensual images of anthropomorphized Nature:

> Written words take some time to thaw, but the words of lilies were now flowing in full summer water, whether it was the water or the leaves of water, and dark hairs of roots plastered on the mouth as water blew across. Now they were swimming so close they were joined together at the waist, and were the same flesh of lilies, their mouths, together, were drowning in the same love-stream. [...] You will, she said, if you will cut and examine the word. *Together* is filled with little cells. And cuts open with a knife. It is a see seed. (187)

This image of bodily communion, in which Nature is humanized and words are naturalized to the point of blooming, entails a revisiting of the myth of the Hermaphrodite, as narrated in Ovid's *Metamorphoses*. This image of the dual become one without loss of difference, this mythic–mystical union of the male and female universes ("a psychical marriage," as Wilson Harris defines it[15]), this initiation into alterity, is another of the features of magical-realist literature. Here, the solitary hero of the Western tradition (central to the story, self-conscious and transparent to himself) is replaced by doubles, twins or pairs of characters, alone capable of mirroring the plurality of biological and psychological combinations.

Voss and Laura are complementary figures, as well as projections of the author's psyche, as White states in his autobiography, *Flaws in the Glass*.[16] Yet Laura also reminds us of the muse who inspired Petrarch's poetry. Laura is therefore also the Jungian *anima*, the guide in the spiritual voyage undertaken by Voss. The union of the male and female principles, of Voss and Laura, the stranger (foreign) and the strange (peculiar), corresponds to the encounter with other universes that often occurs in a Blake-like "marriage of light and shadow" (190), or mystical "union of earth with light" (213),

---

[15] Harris, "Fossil and Psyche," 72.

[16] "Driving away from the convent [of St. John Kalyvitis], it occurred to me from knowing Voss–Laura to be myself, that the abbess was another aspect of Laura Trevelyan"; Patrick White, *Flaws in the Glass: A Self-Portrait* (Harmondsworth: Penguin, 1981): 197.

while "the world of fire and the world of ice were the same world of light" (251), and "the world of semblance communicated with the world of dream" (259). Similarly, a poem written by Voss's companion Frank Le Mesurier reads: "the silky seed that fell in milky rain from the Moon was raised up by the Sun's laying his hands upon it" (251).

Examples of inversion and synaesthetic confusion are innumerable. What is ethereal and insubstantial becomes tactile; what is only visible becomes musical and audible, too; sounds become colours. What belongs to Nature becomes anthropomorphized, while human beings undergo natural metamorphoses. Thus, it is possible to drink from "the evening air" (71), or "from the great arid skies of fluctuating stars" (89), or you can simply "drink the wind" (156). The "light is ironical" (15), the "spring sun is lyrical" (110), but its "beams are knives and swords" (247; 364). The morning is "glassy" (93) or "pearly" (99), the sky can be "blue" but "hateful" (95), or "blood red" (166). Darkness can be "nihilistic" (85) or "woollen" (86), "spongy" (87) or "furious" (89). A valley is composed of rocks of "sculptural red and tapestries of musical green" (197). The sky "is flowering" (213), and "waters are challenging," while "the light of dawn is water of another kind" (282). Conversely, "the flesh of roses becomes personal" (158), human words become "wooden" (128), and the human voice is either "white" (117) or "very red" (60), while "Laura's glistening, green laughter was threaded through the days" (158). On the other hand, "Voss is jubilant as brass" and also "particoloured like truth" (144).

In White's novels, then, the idiolectal use of lexicon and paradoxical combinations is not merely literary metaphor, but, rather, attempts to liberate language from any possible constraint, through lexical and semantic choices that tend to upset any impression of realism. Thus, within a single paragraph or syntactic unit, language mimetically metamorphoses together with the named object, as the adjectives and nouns referring to the moon in the following passage demonstrate:

> There was a golden moon, of placid, swollen belly. There were the ugly, bronze, male moons, threateningly lopsided. One night of wind and dust, there was a pale moonstone, or, as rags of cloud polished its face, delicate glass instrument, on which the needle barely fluttered, indicating the direction that some starry destiny must take. The dreams of men were influenced by the various moons [...]Their dreams eluded them, however, under the indicator of that magnetic moon. (176)

Accepting the belief that the various strategies adopted by magical-realist literature include the treatment of extraordinary events as if they were ordinary facts, the incursion of magical realism into White's narratives is also significant from a thematic point of view. Leaving aside the various episodes of telepathy between Voss and Laura, it is again towards the stars that we must turn our gaze.

Voss's expedition is tragically terminated by the appearance of a comet. This "unearthly phenomenon [...] too beautiful to ignore" for the white men of the expedition is saluted by the Aborigines as a bad omen coinciding with the arrival of "the Great Snake, the grandfather of all men, that had come down from the north in anger" (378). In her study of White and Jung, in which she also documents White's extensive use of Judaeo-Christian symbolism, Karin Hansson comments: "One fact that would support the idea of the Comet as a symbol of unity is the notion of bisexuality related to the Great Serpent in Aboriginal tradition, according to Mircea Eliade [*Australian Religion*] an impressive image of divine totality and of *coincidentia oppositorum*."[17]

In its threatening closeness to the earth, the comet foreshadows the possible end of the world, both in fantasy literature (as in H.G. Wells's short story "The Star") and in magical-realist narratives such as Janet Frame's novel *The Carpathians*, where it also assumes the form of a linguistic apocalypse. A similar event is also at the heart of a novel by the Aboriginal writer Sam Watson, *The Kadaitcha Sung* (1990), where Halley's comet represents the Eye of Biamee to the Aborigines and is therefore endowed with a magical and mythic quality. Watson and the novelist Mudrooroo are thus recognized by critics as representatives of a magical-realist movement, insofar as they try to revitalize the traditional cosmology and the cultural heritage of the Aborigines. Their contribution to magical-realist literature is understood as a post-colonial project of emancipation from the rationalistic and historicist (realist) categories of the Western world.[18]

However, an apocalyptic image, not foreshadowing the destruction of the world but in accordance with the proper meaning of the term *apocalypse* as signifying the revelation of revelations, or "darkest side of magic realism,"[19] is also at the core of White's novel *Riders in the Chariot*.[20] Here,

---

[17] Hansson, *The Warped Universe*, 202.

[18] "I use the term 'postcolonial' to imply a position occupied by the Aborigines from which to speak out against the oppressive and tyrannical reign of colonialism – past and present – in Australia"; Suzanne Baker, "Magic Realism as a Postcolonial Strategy: *The Kadaitcha Sung*," *SPAN* 32 (April 1991): 55–63.

[19] "Apocalypse is merely the darkest side of magical realism, in which the magic and the realism are most completely fused, in which the most unimaginable event is the most inevitable"; Brian Conniff, "The Dark Side of Magical Realism: Science, Oppression, and

magical elements are found not only in lexical and semantic choices, but also in the visionary aspects of the narration. Here, too, oxymora and literalized metaphors abound: light is "pearly" (7), "gold. Or red" (23), or "metallic" (78), while "whole towers of green remained unclimbed, rocks unopened" (11–12). The sky "quickens" and afterwards is blue (12), but can also become "marbled" (71); and the moon is "the pale fossil of a moth" (71). Moreover, in the darkness "a little milky flower" forms "falls of moonlight" (23). The human voice is frequently "rose and violet" (44), while Miss Hare's smiles "weave like shallow water over pebbles" (71).

Similarly, the four protagonists of *Riders in the Chariot* show meta-morphic characteristics and have symbolic names, another feature of the subversion of realism.[21] Though from a realist point of view Miss Mary Hare is the embodiment of the white colonial madwoman, this stereotype is undermined by various contradictory peculiarities. With her skirt caught in the twigs of the bush, "she" is "part woman, part umbrella" (7); but she is also "a particle" (8) in perfect harmony with the landscape and all its details, "alive, changing, growing, personal, like her thoughts, which intermingled, flapping and flashing, with the leaves, or lay straight and stiff as sticks, or emerged with the painful stench of any crushed ant" (15). She speaks with the animals and her movements are those of a leaf. Lying in the grass, she understands "what it feels like to be a dog" (22), while she is also "familiar with the core of rock" (53). Her name is Mary, but her iconography is that of an innocent *Protestant* Madonna; her surname is an allusion to the figure of the hare which is sometimes visible on the surface of the moon, "the sacrificial animal" (93).

Like Voss, Miss Hare is also "translated: she was herself a fearful beam of the ruddy, champing light" (24), and like Voss, she awaits a final revela-tion in life, which will take the form of an "illumination [which] is syn-onymous with blindness" (24). If Laura in *Voss* believes "in wood, with the reflections in it, and in clear day-light, and in water" (9), Miss Hare is afraid of abstractions and prefers tactile experience ("if she could have touched something – moss, for instance – or smelled the smell of burning wood"; 36) to non-verbal comprehension ("not in words"; 36). Miss Hare lives in

---

Apocalypse in *One Hundred Years of Solitude*," *Modern Fiction Studies* 36:2 (Summer 1990): 178.

[20] Patrick White, *Riders in the Chariot* (1961; Harmondsworth: Penguin, 1974). Page references are given in the text.

[21] "In Jung anything fourfold, such as the four principal characters in *Riders in the Chariot*, would denote wholeness and unity"; Hansson, *The Warped Universe*, 102.

communion with Nature and outside of time – at Xanadu there are no clocks: "light told all that was ever necessary" (39). She is both a mythic and a historical character. Her colour is a glowing red (signifying the life force).

When Miss Hare meets the young Aboriginal painter, Alf Dubbo (the dark man), whose name announces that he is a half-caste (Half Abo), the two "illuminates" do not communicate in words, but silently exchange "a token of goodness" (63). Mrs Godbold, moreover, the personification of that "lovingkindness" (121) which White's questers seek, and whose name is an allusion to the mystic dimension as well as to the colour of gold, is described as "discreet, uncommunicative" (65). Finally, Mordecai Himmelfarb is the victim of History (his name contains the word *Mord* = murder), but he is also the Wandering Jew (Mordecai is a biblical character, who acknowledges obedience only to God and not to the King). He is the symbolic sacrificial victim of the Holocaust, but he is also, realistically, a worker in a bicycle factory in the Australian provinces. His surname literally means 'the colour of the sky' in German. His colour is therefore Blue (the void).[22]

As with Laura and Voss, the encounter between Himmelfarb and Miss Hare takes place in the realm of Nature, under a huge tree. It is what Levinas calls a *face-to-face* dialogue with the Other. It is a dialogue between two people who are both considered "different," between the outsider ("Miss Hare is *different*"; 7) and the Other: "I, too, am different," Himmelfarb says, adding, "that would appear, mathematically and morally, to make us equal" (94). Himmelfarb represents the unassimilated Jew, the opposite of the owner of the factory, who had anglicized his name by translating it from Rosenbaum into Rosetree on his arrival to Australia. However, if Miss Hare and Himmelfarb are complementary figures (both of them are defined as "scapegoats"; 93), there are many other pairs of characters in the novel. Himmelfarb, for example, is the orthodox Jew, while Rosenbaum represents the westernized Jew. Furthermore, Mrs Jolley is opposed to Miss Hare, since they embody the principles of good and evil; and Miss Hare, whose name is an anagram of Reha (which, as Karin Hansson explains, is a variation on *aher* meaning 'different' or 'other' in Hebrew), is the reincarnation of Himmelfarb's dead wife. Lastly, Mrs Jolley is a friend of Mrs Flack, whose name in German (*Fleck*) means 'stain.'

---

[22] "Jungian quaternity also applies to White's colour symbolism and the pertinent mandalic images. According to Jung, the three principal ones, gold, red and green, can also represent God the Father, God the Son and the Holy Ghost, respectively. In Mandalic contexts the missing blue is higly significant"; Hansson, *The Warped Universe*, 112.

The struggle between good and evil – alluded to in a goat's burning to death in its den, in a snake's being fed with bowls of milk in Miss Hare's kitchen, as well as in the constant references to the historical as well as personal Holocaust of Himmelfarb, who fled from concentration camps only to end up crucified by the factory workers – prepares the ground for the final vision of the Chariot of Redemption. The Chariot is an image from the *Book of Ezekiel* in the Old Testament. The prophet describes four creatures, each with four faces, those of a man, a lion, an eagle and a bull. Each has two pairs of wings, one covering its body and another whose movement causes the Chariot to move, as it travels according to God's will in a whirlwind of fire and brightness.[23]

The biblical text does not describe the faces; similarly, Himmelfarb cannot sketch the faces of the four figures in the Chariot. Only Alf Dubbo manages to paint the mysterious group with the faces of the four pro-tagonists of the novel as he saw them around Himmelfarb's death-bed. This last moment of communion also implies the common achievement of the Revelation they were all seeking. After this magical moment, Miss Hare mysteriously disappears, while there are rumours of a "miracle" ("some-thing of a supernatural kind"; 484) at Barranugli, an otherwise barren-and-ugly suburb.

In his novels White expresses a form of secular religiosity (to use another oxymoron) or elective communion of souls. He also pushes language and the creations of the imagination towards new expressive possibilities, using Blakean dramatic imagery and biblical visions and epiphanies to represent the reality of the Australian outback, where *naturalia* and *mirabilia* can co-exist. As later in postmodern literature, and as in magical-realist literature (I am thinking here of García Márquez and Wilson Harris), White too abstracts the realist elements from landscapes of apocalypse and holocaust.

The difference between the aesthetic projects of postmodernism and magical realism, however, is clearly stated by Wilson Harris:

> The way I diverge from the post-modernists – I must insist on this – is that the post-modernists have discarded depth, they have discarded the unconscious, thus all they are involved in is a game, a kind of game, whereas what I am saying is not just a game. I am convinced that there is a tradition in depth

---

[23] "The quaternity is of course closely related to Ezekiel's vision of the Chariot, its four wheels, the Four Living Creatures, each with four wings and four faces. [...] The Chariot also belongs to Jewish Merkabah symbolism, significant of the relationship between man and God and a means of redemption. The Talmud forbade discussion of it"; Hansson, *The Warped Universe*, 197.

which returns, which nourishes us even though it appears to have vanished, and that it creates a fiction in the ways in which the creative imagination comes into dialogue with clues of revisionary moment.[24]

He further explains:

> The concept of 'marvellous realism' constitutes for me an alchemical pilgrimage, a ceaseless adventure within the self and without the self in nature and beings that are undervalued or that have been eclipsed or imprisoned by models of conquest.[25]

Emmanuel Levinas then helps us to circumscribe these catastrophic obsessions of our modernity. In 1976 he writes:

> The world wars (and local ones), National Socialism, Stalinism (and even de-Stalinization), the camps, the gas chambers, nuclear weapons, terrorism and unemployment – that is a lot for just one generation, even for those who were but onlookers.[26]

Holocaust and apocalypse are thus inevitable features of our time; they are historical disruptions questioned by postmodernism, but also disruptions that are points of departure, starting from which magical-realist narratives aspire to re-create the world in accordance with new possibilities and combinations, not substituting order for chaos, but, rather, favouring the chameleon-like mutability of the world itself.

Levinas is critical of the Western concept of totality (the discovery of the whole and of God as Whole, which means deafness to the Other), to which he prefers a concept of infinity involving various forms of alterity. The path followed by Western philosophy, says Levinas, remains that pursued by Ulysses, whose adventures were ultimately nothing but a return to his homeland – complacency in the Same, misconstruction of the Other. The same fault is also attributed to modernism by Jean–François Lyotard, when he says that Joyce's *Ulysses* is not the story of a return, since the hero never leaves home – Bloom does not return to Dublin; a *flâneur*, he simply walks and wanders through Dublin.[27] Levinas can thus be said to counter the myth of Ulysses with the story of Abraham and of his final exile.

---

[24] Wilson Harris, "Literacy and the Imagination," in *The Literate Imagination: Essays on the Novels of Wilson Harris*, ed. Michael Gilkes (London: Macmillan, 1989): 27.

[25] Michel Fabre, "Recovering Precious Words: On Wilson Harris and the Language of Imagination," in Maes–Jelinek, ed., *The Uncompromising Imagination*, 48.

[26] Emmanuel Levinas, *Proper Names*, tr. Michael B. Smith (*Noms propres*, 1976; Stanford CA: Stanford UP, 1996): 3.

[27] Jean–François Lyotard, "Going Back to the Return," in *The Languages of Joyce: Selected Papers from the 11th International Joyce Symposium* (12–18 June 1988), ed. Rosa Maria

A final exile, an endless journey into Nature, is also the destiny of the poet Ovid in David Malouf's *An Imaginary Life*. Exiled from the Latin language, Ovid becomes a stranger to himself. Incapable of communicating with the Getae in Tomis, he identifies his own aphasia with the language of the spiders – weavers of silence. The path that takes Ovid from aphasia to self-translation into another language does not pass through culture, but through Nature and cultivation of a different kind. For the poet must learn the name of a local seed, *korschka*. He repeats the magic word to himself, but no spell can revive his memory of the Latin name corresponding to this absolutely new taste. The tongue savours the word, exploring the new linguistic sense, by virtue of the impossibility of translation.

Himself translated (in the sense of the Latin verb *tradere*) or transposed into a new language, Ovid is a literalized metaphor. From that of being an Augustan poet, his meaning translates into that of being an exile. Yet in this land without flowers, trees or ornamental gardens, on this barren earth devoid of the buds and blooms of *elocutio*, and ignorant of poetry, Ovid suddenly sees a poppy. And if previously the seed was tasted by the tongue though not pronounced in the language of culture, now the flower is seen and spoken in Latin, as if it were a "magic word on the tongue to flash again on the eye,"[28] The magic of nomination implies the magic of vision and vice versa. Furthermore, if the seed was previously an emblem of the untranslatability of the past into the present, now the poppy, born from a seed which has been transported by the wind (*metapherein*), epitomizes a translation. Having taken root in this foreign land, while originating in Ovid's infancy, the poppy might be seen as a metaphor of the progressive sense of rootedness experienced by Ovid even in his condition of existential alterity. Ovid is that poppy. And this is the central image of the novel, since in it Ovid's infancy and his old age, two marginal episodes of his life, coincide, as if the frame had become the centre of the painting.

After the epiphany of the poppy, Ovid learns another language, that of the Getae, in addition to the pre- or non-verbal language of the wolf-child. Finally, he dedicates himself to the cultivation of local flowers, thus displacing culture into Nature. In this magical world, the metaphor of translation, transplantation and transposition, of a language that synaesthetically involves senses other than that of hearing, such as sight and taste, forms a link

Bosinelli, Carla Vaglio Marengo & Christine van Bhoeemen, tr. Madeleine Burt Merlini (*L'écrit du temps*; tr. 1988; Venice, 1992): 193–210.

[28] David Malouf, *An Imaginary Life* (1978; London: Picador, 1980): 31. Further page references are in the text.

between the episode of the poppy and two important lyrical moments in the novel: the oneiric encounter with the Barbarians, and the encounter with the Child.

Far from the imperial centre, Ovid heads for the bush in successive waves of dreams of exploration, and here strange figures mounted on centaurs whisper a mysterious word to him from the sky: "it was the tune, that I recognised. As if, having no language of my own, now I had begun to listen for another meaning" (24). This encounter with the Other, bringing new meanings, anticipates the three subsequent appearances of the Child. The first time, he appears in the form of an hallucination – "was the vision real?" (49), asks Ovid – since to name what one sees, this act of synaesthetic translation, can magically produce reality. The wild boy, says Ovid, lies "beyond human imagining" (149); he has no equal in Ovid's poetry and he is therefore not the fruit of *poiesis*. He is neither a product of the imagination nor wholly real. He belongs, rather, to the world of magic, fable and folklore.

His appearance, however, causes a dream-like metamorphosis:

> We have all been transformed, the whole group of us, and become part of the woods. We are mushrooms, we are stones [...] I am a pool of water. I feel myself warm in the sunlight, liquid [...] A breeze shivers my surface. (61)

This magical transformation carries the literalization of the metaphor to an extreme, since the Child drinks from that pool, breaking its surface. As in the earlier episodes of the seed and the poppy, what the encounters with the Barbarians and with the Child reveal, respectively, is the linguistic impossibility of repeating the word heard in the dream, and the possibility of an osmotic exchange between Self and Other, or between the man of culture and the son of Nature, which passes through taste and encounters Narcissus in the optical illusion of the double in the pool of water.

The natural double represents another metaphoric shift in the cultural Self, a new form of translation: guided by the boy in this wasteland, Ovid meets his final metamorphosis in death. "I am there" (152) are the last words binding Ovid to that land. Their meaning not only refers to the Heideggerian concept of *da-sein*, but also to a final sense of belonging that is implied and sought for in post-colonial literature. These words also refer to ultimate communion with Nature and its elements, as total acceptance (as Levinas would say) of endless exile, abandoning the ideal of totality here represented by the borders of the Roman Empire, and accepting the infinity of space.

The character of Ovid, who is translated into a new language and chooses Nature over community, is then reversed in *Remembering Babylon*

(1993), where the English protagonist, Gemmy, is shipwrecked on the Australian coast, lives for a while with the Aborigines, and finally tries to re-enter the white community of Queensland. Like the Child, Gemmy speaks a pre-verbal, Babel-like and stammering language, and like his predecessor he has a deep knowledge of the world of Nature. Again like Ovid, he is bilingual, suspended between English (already half-forgotten) and the languages of the Aborigines. Half-white and half-black, Gemmy is a new sort of acrobat. In falling over the fence which introduces him into the white world – but also into the text – and shouting his words of surrender, "Do not shoot – I am a British object,"[29] Gemmy innocently denounces his linguistic status, as a subject of the British Empire and of its colonial discourse.

The possibility of the existence of other languages, as well as of the Aborigines, and the presence of a huge void in the landscape are the main causes of terror for the white settlers, the reality of whose world depends on the words they use to name it. The reality of the settlement, for instance, is signalled by the name printed on the map in the Government Office in Brisbane. However, the settlers complain that there is something unbearable about the places, the vast empty spaces and silence between those names on the map and surrounding the settlements scattered along the coast.

Gemmy's arrival means the intrusion of the marvellous and the mysterious: the children who first meet him see him as "something extraordinary" (1) and stand "spellbound" (2). To the white people, if not to himself, he remains an enigma, a figure of speech which Paul Ricœur likens to metaphor, hyperbole and proverb, or to those tropes involving the substitution of a translated for a literal sense.[30] Like Ovid, Gemmy is a living metaphor, one in which the translated or superimposed second sense turns out to be truer than the original.

The enigmatic thus breaks into the ordinary, for Gemmy's story is still full of gaps. Translated into the tales of the Aborigines, his story remains

---

29 David Malouf, *Remembering Babylon* (1993; London: Vintage, 1994): 3. Further page references are in the text. – This narrative incident calls to mind the story of "James Morrill, sole survivor of the barque *Peruvian*, lost in 1846, who spent seventeen years with the tribes of North Queensland. Such was his confusion at being confronted by a white shepherd with a gun that he shouted, 'Do not shoot, I'm a British *object!*'"; see Michael Alexander, *Mrs. Fraser on the Fatal Shore* (New York: Simon & Schuster, 1971): 73 (Alexander's emphasis).

30 Paul Ricœur, "An Enigma: Metaphor and Simile (eikôn)," in *The Rule of Metaphor. Multi-Disciplinary Studies of the Creation of Meaning in Language*, tr. Robert Czerny, Kathleen McLaughlin & John Costello (1975 *La Métaphor vive*, tr. 1977; Buffalo/Toronto: U of Toronto P, 1993): 24–27.

incomplete. Similarly, the account written down by the schoolmaster and the minister of the white settlement is false and fictitious. The English words that now and again surface from his memory are inadequate to tell his story, that "unspeakable word" (64). Nevertheless, in these written documents, Gemmy finds the magic of the language, a language not read or spoken but synaesthetically smelled:

> he raised the sheets to his nose and sniffed them, and might have been preparing to lick and maybe swallow them [...] believing that the magic they had been practising here was not yet over [...] Magic, as Gemmy understood it, had been the essence of the occasion [...] the whole of what he was, *Gemmy*, might come back to him, and he began to plot, as he thought of his life out of sight there in the minister's pocket, how to steal it back. (20)

He thus becomes an outsider who is denied any part in his own story, the story that makes him a citizen of the Empire. Conversely, Ovid in *An Imaginary Life* is exiled for "putting his nose" into private affairs "perhaps most political just then" (25) – a theme, that of the nose (here, of course, alluding to the nickname "Ovidius Naso"), which reminds us of Rushdie's Saleem. Like Ovid, Gemmy has been deprived of his language and of his story. For this reason, he steals some papers from the schoolmaster's desk and runs into the forest, where the rain dissolves the ink and with it the story of his assimilation. He cannot give up his dual identity; he belongs to more than one space, to more than one *langue*-scape. He is part of a hybrid space where his twin natures coexist.

The settlers are obsessed with words, the only reality surrounding them. They suspect Gemmy's encounter with the Aborigines, perhaps because no words are exchanged between them. This episode represents one of the magical and lyrical moments of the novel:

> They had come to reclaim him; but lightly, bringing what would feed the spirit. They spread the land out for him, gave him its waters to drink. As he took huge draughts of it, saw it light his flesh [...] In the little space of dust between them as they sat, they danced, beat up clouds, threw rainbows over their heads. Then they rose, exchanged the formalities of parting, and went. (118)

In a desert of silence, Gemmy and the Aborigines exchange a magical silent speech in the form of visions, as if reality existed beyond the words that can name it – as a creation of the imagination. Appearing as if by magic from a demonic landscape, ostracized by the villagers, Gemmy has revealed something to the two children he first met: the epiphany of the coexistence of reality and magic, *naturalia* and *mirabilia*. The swarm of bees which seem to attack Janet, as in a symbolic initiation rite not dissimilar to an episode in Robert Kroetsch's *What the Crow Said,* is the vehicle of this epiphany:

> You are our bride, her new and separate mind told her as it drummed and swayed above the earth. Ah, so that is it! They have smelled the sticky blood-flow. They think it is honey. It is. [...] But it made no difference, now, the distance, three feet or a thousand years, no difference at all; or whether she was a girl (a woman), or a tree. She stood sleeping. Upright. A bride.[...] her mind had for a moment been their unbodied one and she had been drawn into the process of the mystery of things. [...] she saw it through Gemmy's eyes. (142–44)

Janet will become a nun and will dedicate herself to apiculture, to the cult of Nature. But Lachlan, too, the fiery soldier who reduced Gemmy to a "British object," finally admits his debt to this marvellous creature: "what they were dealing with, in Gemmy, might be closer to them, to *him*, than he knew" (179). For they had seen Gemmy in his transparent alterity: "I have never seen anyone clearer in all my life. All that he was. All" (194).

Like the Child, who exceeded imagination while concealing a mystery, in the same way Gemmy, the savage, the playful marionette, the carnivalesque character of this novel, is "an in-between creature" (28), guiding the two children towards that other world of Nature and towards a sense of "loving-kindness," as Patrick White would call it. Thrown to shore by the waves, half-phantom and half-fish for the Aborigines, a Caliban-like figure (the comparison is suggested by Roslyn Jolly's study on the subject),[31] half-white and half-black for the settlers, imprisoned by the words of the latter and set free by the visionary creativity of the former, Gemmy is an embodiment of Malouf's own language: his lyrical prose, made of constellations of images dancing on a tightrope suspended between reality and magic, but substantiated by both.

ଓ • ଉ

---

[31] "The sense of amphibian sympathies, intimate knowledge verging on the mutability of forms, also suggests links with the Ariel–like transformations which fascinate Malouf and Atwood. Caliban's relation to language is also typical of the colonial situation"; Roslyn Jolly, "Transformations of Caliban and Ariel: Imagination and Language in David Malouf, Margaret Atwood and Seamus Heaney," *World Literature Written in English* 26:2 (Autumn 1986): 296.

Salman Rushdie's Special Effects

─────────────── 🙰

Shaul Bassi

> We are ready to believe almost anything about what is far away
> from us. [1]

S ALMAN RUSHDIE'S MAJOR NOVELS (*Midnight's Children, Shame, The
Satanic Verses, The Moor's Last Sigh*) contain events that are bizarre but
plausible (babies exchanged in the cradle), and highly improbable but
not impossible (a child with three mothers, a man ageing at double speed),
or quite incredible (a woman with glass skin; two men surviving a fall from
the sky). Such events may together be taken to constitute what critics
customarily refer to as Rushdie's 'magical realism,' a quality that, with a few
exceptions, is usually taken for granted.

This essay addresses the question of whether it is useful to group all
these elements within a single, stable category. Although the term 'magical
realism' is no doubt convenient, its indiscriminate application to every piece
of literature produced east of the Caucasus and west of Gibraltar smacks of
a neo-exotic fascination with the originality of the style(s), and is at the same
time oblivious to geographic peculiarities and variants. Indeed, the definition is European in perspective and implies a novel 'magical' variation on
classic Western realism. In other words, magical realism is often treated as
though the child of a mixed marriage, the father being Western realism and
the mother autochthonous folklore. I want to challenge this view with
regard to Rushdie by claiming that his 'magical realism,' like some of his

───────────────

[1] Franco Moretti, *Modern Epic: The World System from Goethe to García Márquez*, tr.
Quintin Hoare (*Opere Mondo*, 1994; Turin: Einaudi, 1996): 249.

characters, has many mothers and fathers, all of whom have contributed their genes, even though their presence on the family tree often goes unrecorded.

To demonstrate this, I will not be using the term 'magical realism' (for the above reasons), resorting instead, as a tribute to Rushdie's declared love for the cinema, to the more neutral denomination 'special effects,' which I consider within six different contexts.

1 *Brahma and the Termites*

The termites say to Brahma: "To disturb one in sleep, to interrupt a story, to separate a husband and wife and also a mother and child – these things are tantamount to killing a brahmin."[2] That the interruption of a story is seen as a crime equivalent to murder is a good way to illustrate the importance of narrative form within Indian culture. Narrative design is more than a way of preserving and disseminating collective beliefs; it is a cognitive instrument that Indians employ to make sense of the world.

At the beginning of *Midnight's Children*, Rushdie describes the boatman Tai, whose toothless mouth is filled with a "chatter, which was fantastic, grandiloquent and ceaseless" and who speaks a "magic talk, words pouring from him like fools' money."[3] Tai, significantly, exercises a decisive influence over the westernized Aadam Aziz (the protagonist's grandfather), of whose Heidelberg friends he is the "living antithesis." These young German intellectuals may be seen as metonyms for Western philosophy, whereas Tai stands for Indian fabulistic thinking. Rushdie has elaborated this concept in a conversation with Günter Grass:

> What made me become a writer was the simple desire to tell stories [...] the context in which I began to think was governed by the principle that stories didn't have to be true. [...] Horses were expected to fly and so did carpets. And it was believed that by telling stories of this kind, marvellous stories, it was possible to tell a kind of truth that it was not possible to tell otherwise. So I grew up assuming that this was the normal way of telling stories and then, when I began writing seriously, I found I was writing within a literature that for a long time had shaped an opposite view [...] a novel had to be mimetic, to

---

[2] *Devi Bhagvata*, quoted in Sudhir Kakar, *Intimate Relations: Exploring Indian Sexuality* (New Delhi: Penguin, 1989): 2–3.

[3] Rushdie, *Midnight's Children* (1981; New York: Avon, 1982): 9, 10. Further references are in the text.

imitate the world, the rules of naturalism and realism. [...] It seemed to me that
in a certain sense realism was not realistic.[4]

Apropos story-telling, it should be noted that Rushdie's novels (with the
exception of the less successful *Grimus*) are all *told* stories. *Midnight's Children* and *The Moor's Last Sigh* have an autodiegetic narrator who is identical
with the protagonist, while *Shame* and *Satanic Verses* have a heterodiegetic
but very intrusive narrator.

What is still more important is that stories in India tell the truth without
imitating the world. Realism is not their degree zero of representation. This
is not because in India carpets actually fly, but because, in order to describe
and comment on reality, carpets may be made to fly. People experience and
construct the world through imaginary elements, too: this is *their* realism.
Rushdie has ironically observed that his works have often been read as
fantastic in the West and as wholly realistic in India and Pakistan.[5] In this
context 'magical realism' would be a misleading definition, in the absence of
a shared basic notion of realism.

Let us now consider the other side of the Indian coin. On his journey to
Nicaragua (which inspired the book *The Jaguar Smile*) Rushdie met a poet
who expressed his admiration for Tagore (or, in his pronunciation, Tagoré).

> "I admire him for his spiritual qualities, and also his realism."
> "Many people think of Latin America as the home of anti-realism."
> He looked disgusted. "Fantasy?" he cried. "No, sir. You must not write fan-
> tasy. It is the worst thing. Take a tip from your great Tagoré. Realism, realism,
> that is the only thing."[6]

---

[4] I am forced to translate back into English a passage that has only been available to
me in Italian. "La cosa che mi ha fatto diventare uno scrittore è stato [...] il desiderio
semplicemente di raccontare storie [...].Nel contesto in cui cominciai a pensare vigeva il
principio che le storie non dovessero essere vere. [...] Ci si aspettava che i cavalli
dovessero volare e così i tappeti. E si credeva che raccontando storie di questo tipo, storie
meravigliose, si potesse realmente dire un genere di verità che non era possibile dire in un
altro modo. Così crebbi presumendo che quella fosse la maniera normale di raccontare
storie e mi ritrovai, quando cominciai a scrivere seriamente, nel contesto di una
letteratura che si era per lungo tempo formata un'idea opposta [...] un romanzo doveva
essere mimetico, imitare il mondo, le regole insomma del naturalismo e del realismo.[...]
Mi sembrava [invece] in un certo senso che il realismo non fosse realistico." Günther
Grass, Salman Rushdie, "Scrivere per un futuro" in *Gli scrittori e la politica* (Milan: Linea
d'ombra, 1990; English ed. 1987): 79.

[5] A 1987 interview quoted in Sara Suleri, *The Rhetoric of English India* (Chicago/Lon-
don: U of Chicago P, 1992): 176.

[6] Rushdie, *The Jaguar Smile: A Nicaraguan Journey* (London: Picador, 1987): 56.

A Latin-American poet reproves an Indian author for not writing in a realist style, and thereby following *the Indian tradition*! But this anonymous poet was correct on one point at least: in spite of our notion of Indian fabulism, the novel in India has been traditionally realist in the European sense, and anglophone writers have been no exception, as the works of Mulk Raj Anand, Nirad Chaudhuri, R.K. Narayan, Anita Desai, and Vikram Seth show.

2   From Nicaragua to Brazil

From roots we pass to influences, and from Nicaragua we move to Brazil, intrigued by a curious statement of Rushdie's: "I am a Brazilian."

However, this Latin-American connection proves no less illusory, since what is alluded to is not the country of Jorge Amado but the dystopic film by Terry Gilliam, whose ambiguous atmosphere puzzled Rushdie and made him reach the following conclusion about its imaginary setting:

> I suggest that the true location of Brazil is the other great tradition in art, the one in which techniques of comedy, metaphor, heightened imagery, fantasy and so on are used to break down our conventional, habit-dulled certainties about what the world is and has to be.[7]

"The other great tradition": the history of literature is here read as the dialectic between realism and anti-realism, to which latter Rushdie ascribes a progressive and liberating function.

> *Play. Invent the world.* The power of the playful imagination to change for ever our perceptions of how things are has been demonstrated by everyone from Laurence Sterne, in *Tristram Shandy*, to a certain Monty Python in his *Flying Circus*. Our sense of the modern world is as much the creation of Kafka, with his unexplained trials and unapproachable castles and giant bugs, as it is of Freud, Marx or Einstein.[8]

Rushdie is fond of quoting (openly or not) authors whose representation of the world is unconventional, authors such as Sterne, Carroll, Kafka, Grass and García Márquez, to name but a few. More than intertextuality is at stake here. If we think of literary influence not as a passive phenomenon but as an active process of identification with formal strategies suited to one's cultural

---

[7] Rushdie, *Imaginary Homelands: Essays and Criticism 1981–1991* (London: Granta/Penguin, 1991): 122.

[8] *Imaginary Homelands*, 123.

identity,[9] we may conclude that Rushdie consciously subscribes to this "other great tradition," which he construes as an inherently corrective one.

After an instance of Indian filiation (section 1) and one of Western affiliation (section 2), I insist on familial metaphors and discuss a case of rebellion against the father: namely, the British Empire.

3 Imperial times, imperial genres

> without [a] hunger for the rich and strange, it is impossible for the West to assimilate India.[...] Its very name echoes the name, as it sugests the power, of Earth's Eternal City. We know it as Romance.[10]
>
> Rushdie's lies, if such they are, are the lies Indians and Pakistanis tell about themselves, rather than the lies British people tell about them.[11]

By "imperial times and genres," I mean to suggest those historiographical patterns and literary genres that Great Britain imposed on India with a view to justifying its colonial enterprise. Patterns and genres aimed to create an image of India as a country bound to receive the civilizing mission of the West, and of Great Britain as bound to perform it. They were articulated in a complex web of discourses – legal, journalistic, historiographical, artistic, cinematographic, and literary (high and low) – informed by what Sara Suleri termed "the rhetoric of English India."[12]

Post-colonial writers, especially when writing in English, have found themselves inevitably entangled in this rhetoric and have struggled to find a way out of it in order not to replicate stereotypical representations of their world. In this context, 'magical realism' has been a double-edged weapon. For, while it has served to demystify hegemonic discourses, its metonymic relation to the 'fantastic' involves a dangerous proximity to the code of the romance, which (as the first epigraph to this section demonstrates) was a key genre in the construction of an imaginary India prone to colonization. Post-colonial texts thus run the risk of being drawn into the same rhetoric they seek to oppose.

---

[9] Chana Kronfeld, *Modernisms on the Margin* (Berkeley/Los Angeles: U of California P, 1996).

[10] Robert Sencourt, *India in English Literature* (1923), quoted in Sara Suleri, *The Rhetoric of English India*, 11.

[11] Una Chaudhuri "Writing the Raj Away," *Turnstile* 2.1 (1990): 35.

[12] Suleri, *The Rhetoric of English India*, 11.

Rushdie's special effects successfully avoid this, by playing a crucial role in the anti-colonial discourse of his novels, and at the same time by resisting the myth of a supernatural India.

Let us consider this latter aspect first. For centuries, Western culture has projected its desires and anxieties onto India, a country it has imagined as peopled with fakirs, gurus, and snake-charmers.[13] This stereotype still prevails in mass culture, even more so in countries as yet impervious to postcolonial critiques. The recent TV film *Sandokan*, based on the Indian character created by the popular nineteenth-century Italian writer Emilio Salgari, is a case in point. Although it reproduces the fiercely anti-British propaganda of the original, the film presents a clear-cut division between good and bad Indians. The former are noble, courageous, loyal to good Europeans, and blessed with a reassuring Mediterranean complexion, while the latter are innately treacherous, devoured by ambition, and many shades darker.

In *Midnight's Children*, Amina Sinai goes to consult the seer Shri Ramram Seth and finds him "sitting cross-legged, six inches above the ground." She cannot help screaming with the shock of what she sees. Two pages later she (and the reader) discovers that "of course, Ramram the seer was not really floating in mid-air [...] She noticed the little shelf, protruding from the wall" (96). The episode raises questions about Amina's superstitious nature, but also, in my view, the Western reader's expectation of a 'magic' India. Something similar happens with the community of magicians who give shelter to Saleem toward the end of the novel. They turn out to be Communists, suggesting that the individuals who most typically embody exoticism were engaged both in hypnotism and in the class struggle. Rushdie has a talent for placing the unexplainable where we least expect it, and vice versa.

Sandokan easily lends itself to parody, but it is far more problematic to confront the long shadows of Kipling and Forster, whose potent and engrossing visions have had a profound influence on post-colonial literature in India. Suleri argues that both authors are obsessed with a magical realism that in their works takes the shape of romance. In *Kim*, the plot unfolds as "a contiguous chain of surprise effects,"[14] signifying an India resistant to rational categorization. In *Passage to India*, the Malabar caves represent the ultimate inaccessibility of the country to foreign minds.

---

[13] For a brilliant analysis of projective European visions of India, see Ashis Nandy's fundamental study *The Intimate Enemy: Loss and Recovery of Self Under Colonialism* (Delhi: Oxford UP, 1983).

[14] Suleri, *The Rhetoric of English India*, 113.

Rushdie carefully avoids the logic of romance. His 'marvellous' is never surprising or destabilizing. It is a 'natural' element of the fictive world and is not set up in opposition to more realistic events. In *Shame*, nobody wonders at Omar Khayam's being the child of three mothers. In *The Satanic Verses*, neither the policemen who capture Saladin nor the young girls who rescue him show any amazement at his metamorphosis into a beast.

In his revision of colonial rhetoric, Rushdie counters colonial historiography as well. In *Midnight's Children*, Aadam Aziz breaks with his German friends because, progressive as they are, they believe that "India – like radium – had been 'discovered' by the Europeans" and that "he was somehow the invention of their ancestors" (6).

Much has been written, with regard to Rushdie, on the relationship between history and the novel. Less attention has been paid to the relationship between historiography and the novel, in the light of the debate on the rhetorical quality of historical narratives triggered by Hayden White's *Metahistory* (1972).[15] Some of the issues raised by the American theorist are interestingly echoed in Rushdie: "I, too, face the problem of history: what to retain, what to dump, how to hold on to what memory insists on relinquishing, how to deal with change."[16] Paraphrasing a remark by Grass, Rushdie has said that, in a time when official sources lie, it is the writer's task to tell the truth.[17] Yet the truth is never simple and, once again echoing White, he leaves unresolved the debate as to which genre is the most suitable to emplot the political vicissitudes of India (in *Midnight's Children*) and Pakistan (in *Shame*). This hesitation may bespeak awareness of the powerful generic and chronological patterns imposed by Western history, given that even Marx, who denounced colonial cruelty and rapacity, credited England with bringing about the revolution needed to put an end to "Oriental despotism" in India.[18]

Perhaps the many temporal distortions that occur in Rushdie's novels are just another attempt to resist the chronological regime inaugurated by colonial culture, as if his characters refused to be subject to the direction and

---

[15] From the vast bibliography available on the subject, I would select Amos Funkestein's "History, Counterhistory, and Narrative," in *Probing the Limits of Representation*, ed. Saul Friedlander (Los Angeles: U of California P, 1992): 66–81.

[16] Rushdie, *Shame* (1983; London: Picador, 1984): 87–88.

[17] Grass, Rushdie, "Scrivere per un futuro."

[18] For an analysis of Marxian ambivalence, see Edward W. Said, *Orientalism* (1978; New York: Vintage, 1979): 153–57.

pace of time and desperately tried to escape from the vortex of history and politics.

4   Autobiographies for the end of the millennium

> Magical realism restores the link that Joyce's generation had severed – technique and anthropocentrism.[19]

I remarked above that Rushdie's novels are told stories. They may also be considered (auto)biographical narratives. In *Midnight's Children* and *The Moor's Last Sigh*, the protagonists tell the story of their lives and sometimes those of their ancestors. *Shame* and *Satanic Verses* also follow their characters from the cradle on, and their narrators, though external, insert frequent reflections on themselves, underlining the analogies between their creatures and themselves.

If every biography provides a specific answer to the crucial question regarding the relationship between individual and history,[20] autobiography is a "laboratory of subjectivity," for philosophy, psychoanalysis, and the neurosciences have demonstrated that our identity depends on (or coincides with) a narrative vision of our existence, on an endless making and re-making of personal stories. On the basis of such observations, the anthropologist Michael J. Fischer has analyzed the important sub-genres of "ethnic autobiography and autobiographical fiction," which he considers "key forms for explorations of pluralist, post-industrial, late twentieth century society."[21]

This form of autobiography tells of individuals with mixed ethnic and cultural roots searching for an identity, as also "a voice or style that does not violate one's several components of identity." The result may be the discovery/invention (for ethnicity is reinterpreted and revised in every generation) of a given historical perspective, founding myths, and an ethical vision for a 'new' ethnic community which demonstrate that such narratives look to the future, not to the past.[22]

---

[19] Moretti, *Modern Epic*, 235.

[20] Giovanni Levi, "Les Usages de la biographie," *Annales ESC* 6 (novembre–décembre 1989): 1325–36.

[21] Michael J. Fischer, "Ethnicity and the Post-Modern Arts of Memory," in *Writing Culture*, ed. James Clifford & George Marcus (Berkeley: U of California P, 1986): 195.

[22] Fischer, "Ethnicity," 196, 199.

According to Fischer, the specificity of these texts lies in the recurrent use of certain "writing tactics" such as transference, dream-work, alternative-selves, bifocality, inter-reference, and ironic humour. These devices account for the fact that

> ethnicity is a deeply rooted emotional component of identity, [and] it is often transmitted less through cognitive language or learning (to which sociology has almost entirely restricted itself) than through processes analogous to the dreaming and transference of psychoanalytic encounters.[23]

Clearly these processes do not entail a notion of realism, out, on the contrary, lend themselves to the creation of "special effects."

In Rushdie we could find many examples of bifocality, inter-reference, ironic humour, and also, as our brief examples will demonstrate, alternatives selves and dream-work.

In the third book of *Midnight's Children*, Saleem becomes buddha, a person with an exceptional sense of smell who has forgotten everything about his past. Paradoxically, as this alternative self the midnight's child who embodied India becomes a soldier in the Pakistani army.

As for dream-work, many of the events involving Gibreel Farishta in *The Satanic Verses* seem to take place in his head, but the borders between dream and reality are thoroughly blurred.

> In magic realism, dream maintains its psychological finality, whether individual or collective or metaphysical, nevertheless it has the tendency to free and to distance itself – totally or partially, definitely or provisionally – from a psychism which on that account does not cease to feed it. Dream will seem to root itself fraudulently within sensible reality surrounding the being which engenders it.[24]

This dreamscape blurs the distinction between subject and world, calling into question the structure of both.

As a footnote to this section, it may be noted that Rushdie's protagonists often possess abnormal biological rhythms: Moraes Zogoiby ages at double speed, while Omar Khayaam cuts down on his sleep. The anthropologist Paul Spencer describes the way in which the Masai make sense of their

---

[23] Fischer, "Ethnicity," 202, 196.

[24] Michel Dupuis & Albert Mingelgrün, "Pour une poétique du réalisme magique," in *Le réalisme magique: Roman, peinture et cinema*, ed. Jean Weisgerber (Lausanne: Editions de l'Âge d'Homme, 1987): 224 (my translation).

existence by creating "automythoiogies in which temporality is altered to the extent that they claim incredible ages."[25]

In conclusion, special effects may look like a flight from reality, but they turn out to be strategies for the representation of identity that are more appropriate than the traditional ones (such as those of the *Bildungsroman*), in that they are more sensitive to the unique cross-cultural existence of the post-colonial individual.

5   Recalcitrant bodies

Rushdie's special effects always involve human beings, never nature. This seems to be a crucial distinction in the discourse of magical realism. In his novels, men age at double speed, reduce their sleep, become invisible, change into monsters, develop telepathic powers, and beam themselves across seas. Nature, on the other hand, remains the one we are familiar with: in *The Satanic Verses*, the Arabian sea does not part before Ayesha and her pilgrims as they expect, but mercilessly swallows them.

Saleem's endlessly dripping nose, Moraes' ageing, Saladin's bestial appearance are all examples of how Rushdie's bodies are recalcitrant, refusing to act *normally*, as if they consciously needed to proclaim their irrevocable singularity: perhaps, Saleem suggests, if one wishes to remain an individual in the midst of the teeming multitudes, one must make oneself grotesque (*Midnight's Children*, 126). This desire is not narcissistic but first and foremost political, as three different narratives will now illustrate.

Let me introduce a personal anecdote. Some years ago a woman told me how she had passed several months in a country under foreign military occupation. Bravely defying danger, she established contact with the local guerrilla, guided by a legendary commander. At a certain point, in the midst of her meticulous ethnographic account, otherwise based on historical, political, and social data, she explained that fortunately the commander was endowed with the supernatural gifts of invisibility and invulnerability, which had allowed him to survive a great many mortal attacks. What struck me was the narrative continuity between the realistic political overview and the magical portrait of the resistance leader.

As a comment on this case of extra-literary magical realism I would like to quote a key passage in Alejo Carpentier's celebrated manifesto of the *real maravilloso*:

---

[25] Paul Spencer, "Automythologies and the reconstruction of ageing," in *Anthropology and Autobiography*, ed. Judith Okely & Helen Callaway (London: Routledge, 1992): 50–63.

I found myself in daily contact with something that could be defined as the
marvelous real. I was in a land where thousands of men, anxious for freedom,
believed in Mackandal's lycanthropic powers to the extent that their collective
faith produced a miracle on the day of his execution.[26]

Finally, in an episode in *Midnight's Children*, Saleem, now become Buddha, is
held prisoner by the Indian army. Another midnight's child, Parvati-the-
witch, comes to the rescue and makes him invisible and weightless, so that
he can escape hidden inside a basket.

In each case a sort of miracle takes place, whose function is one of
opposition and resistance in a situation of political emergency. The woman
in my personal anecdote was no doubt capable of a serious and rational
analysis of the situation and had ably eluded the rigid controls of the
colonial force. Yet she must have breathed the same air of the resistance
fighters, for whom it was *indispensable* (in accordance perhaps with some
local tradition) to think that their leader had supernatural powers. Fighting a
desperate struggle, and ill-equipped and politically isolated as they were,
they needed something to reassure them beyond everything. Sadly, the
leader not long afterwards fell into the hands of the colonial army. In the
Haitian instance, Carpentier explicitly says that what triggers the collective
faith in Mackandal is an intense desire for freedom. In Rushdie, finally, there
is no heroism, but the body of the protagonist grants him life and freedom.

The present century opened with a scientific attempt to classify bodies
which later degenerated into racist theories and genocide, and its end is
marked by the awareness that the body is also a public and political site
where different forces conflict.[27] Rushdie's special effects express the ambivalence of the body, vulnerable and unstable, yet resistant to the shaping
forces that transcend the individual. How could we be transformed into
monsters?, Saladin Chamcha asks the manticore, his fellow prisoner. "'They
describe us,' the other whispered solemnly. 'That's all. They have the power
of description, and we succumb to the pictures they construct'."[28] This
initially evokes a Foucauldian nightmare of total control of the body by the
institutions, but it ends with a note of hope: we change only if we succumb.

---

[26] Alejo Carpentier, preface to *El reino de este mundo* (1949), repr. in *Magical Realism:
Theory, History, Community*, ed. Lois Parkinson Zamora & Wendy B. Faris (Durham
NC/London: Duke UP, 1995): 86.

[27] See the illuminating reflections of Giorgio Agamben, *Mezzi senza fine* (Turin: Bollati
Boringhieri, 1996).

[28] Rushdie, *The Satanic Verses* (London: Viking, 1988): 168.

6   Chagall's cow

The terrible "power of description" that we have just encountered ushers us into the last section, where I briefly consider Rushdie's special effects as a metalinguistic game. An example from art history will be our starting-point. Everyone will recall the cows that hover in the sky in Chagall's paintings. This magical scene is merely the literal rendering of a Yiddish expression: "Meshuggener, arop fun dakh" (literally, "lunatic, get off the roof") which idiomatically means 'get back in touch with reality,' 'get a grip' on things.[29] Chagall has depicted a 'fact' of his language; and there are other literalizations of Yiddish in his works.

An analogous process of the literalization of figurative language is also present in Rushdie's novels, as noted by Anita Weston in one of the few essays that analyze magical realism *sub specie retorica*. She quotes the following passage from *The Satanic Verses*:

> to prove to himself the non-existence of God, he [the Muslim Archangel Gibreel] now stood in the dining-hall of the city's most famous hotel, with pigs falling out of his face. (30)

Weston's commentary is worth quoting at some length:

> The resulting image, Boschian and grotesque, performs a number of tasks: it expresses the character's horror at his ideological iconoclasm, takes a sly double-edged swipe at the doctrine of transubstantiation of which this seems to be the Muslim equivalent (bread into the body of Christ, pork into the body of pig), focusses our attention, through the minimal category gap between animate and abstract noun, on the delicate boundaries governing vast moral prohibitions, and in the unexpected animation of the vehicle produces an *effet de réel* which is the "effect of the magically real," one of the mismatchings of referent and metaphorical re-creation which is a constant of Rushdie's magic realism.[30]

Whether we subscribe entirely to this interpretation or not, it shows how an anti-realist effect can momentarily suspend the mimetic function of language and delve into deeper cultural realities. This device becomes particularly useful when the language is employed to express events that do not belong to its tradition (Muslim rules play no significant role in the history of English). The reader is estranged and his/her attention is thus drawn to the relativity of language, to its power of shaping concepts and constituting

---

[29]   I am grateful to Chana Kronfeld for this reference.

[30]   Anita Weston, "The Feasibility of the Chutnification of History: Rhetoric as Referent in the Magic-Realism of Salman Rushdie," in *La fortuna della retorica*, ed. Giuseppe G Castorina & Vittoriana Villa (Chieti: Métis, 1993): 498.

culture. Magical-realist effects can lay bare the political unconscious of a language and question its representational modes.

Conclusion

In this cultural–thematical reading of Salman Rushdie's novels, I have considered the writer's "special effects" within six contexts: 1) the fabulistic tradition of India; 2) the anti-realist tradition of the West; 3) the rhetoric of English colonial India; 4) the genre of ethnic (auto)biographies; 5) the discourse of the body in a state of political emergency; and 6) the performative function of language and the literalization of metaphor.

None of these heterogenous categories is in itself sufficient to explain all the effects, which can best be understood as a product of the interaction of all the contexts. An ideal continuation of this essay would proceed in the opposite direction, measuring each single effect against each separate context.

However, some conclusions may be drawn. Recent criticism has defined magical realism as "an assault on [the] basic structures of rationalism and realism."[31] Not only does this statement confuse interpretation and representation, it also makes unacceptable generalizations. Rushdie's style certainly implies a critique of Western realism, but under no circumstance can his narrative be said to be 'irrational' or to signal an alternative phenomenological world. His magic is linguistic, rhetorical, and thematic, but free of esoteric or paranormal temptations. Zamora and Faris's comment, while proposing the counter-hegemonic value of magical realism, implicitly iterates the stereotype of a 'rational,' and thus unimaginative, West versus an irrational, imaginative East.

What I propose is a mode of interpretation that always takes into account the historical and cultural specificities of the context in which a magical-realist text is written. This does not rule out the existence of parallels and similarities between cultures, but even formal strategies that are superficially identical can perform different functions in different situations. Rushdie's 'magical realism' answers the specific cultural condition of post-colonial India and of the Indian diaspora. It is not an echo of archaic myths re-emerging on the surface of Western narratives, but a spark produced by the collision of civilizations.

What I have called "special effects" may, finally, be considered as a basic ingredient of Rushdie's peculiar brand of 'irony,' which, in Richard Rorty's

---

31 Zamora & Faris, ed. *Magical Realism*, 6.

definition,[32] consists in rewriting and recontextualizing the vocabularies and the rhetoric in which the writer was born, as a means of struggling towards autonomy and doing justice to the complexity of that 'new' hybrid and translational individual generated by the post-colonial era.

ଔ • ଅ

---

[32] Richard Rorty, *Contingency, Irony and Solidarity* (Cambridge: Cambridge UP, 1989).

Worlds, Things, Words
Rushdie's Style from *Grimus* to *Midnight's Children*

─────────────────────────────── ဢ

Carmen Dell'Aversano

L ITERARY WORKS, AS EVERYONE KNOWS, are always about another
world. The subjects even of masterpieces of literary realism are universes that, though meticulously isomorphic, are never identical
with our own, if only because all objects that in the real world belong to
fiction, in the fiction belong to the real world, and the book containing them
does not exist. Raskolnikov will never be able to find an explanation for his
predicament in the pages of *Crime and Punishment*. Primary reality and
fiction may run parallel to one another, but like two parallel lines, they will
never meet. This simple nugget of hard fact is the starting-point of my
inquiry and motivates its basic question: What is the shape and makeup of
the fictive worlds of *Grimus* and of *Midnight's Children*?[1] The course of what
is to follow is actually implicit in the very term 'fictive world': if we liken the
world of a literary work to a planet and imagine looking at it through an
infinitely powerful telescope, increasing the magnification will allow us to
focus on increasingly smaller objects, not just the fictive world as such but
the things it is made of, and finally on the smallest units these things are
made up of, the atoms of literary cosmogony, elementary particles not of
matter but of meaning, not quarks or neutrinos but words.

I have chosen to concentrate on *Grimus* and *Midnight's Children* because I
am interested in discovering how Rushdie has shaped his narrative style,
initially marked by a high degree of conformity to the rules and conventions

───────────────

[1] Salman Rushdie, *Grimus* (1975; New York: Penguin, 1991); *Midnight's Children* (1981;
New York: Avon, 1982).

of the well-defined literary genre of science fiction, and later evolving into an unmistakably personal narrative technique, with a natural and necessary relationship to the individual peculiarities of his subject. Rushdie's course has evidently been non-linear, and was largely determined (as I will not attempt to show here) by his chance encounter with the English translation of Günter Grass's *The Tin Drum*.[2] This should be sufficient to do away once and for all with one of the most persistent myths of Western (not only post-Romantic) literary culture, that which joins style and personality in a kind of indissoluble and unanalyzable *unio mystica*. This theoretical point is not central to my inquiry, but it does widen its scope, which might at first sight appear to be limited to the painstaking analysis of the technical and stylistic idiosyncrasies of a single author.

Even a rapid survey of the fictional world of *Grimus* is sufficient to classify this first work of an undisputed master of magical realism unambiguously as one belonging to science fiction, a genre whose setting, ambitions and assumptions are quite different. The cover of the American paperback edition, which bears endorsements by Ursula Le Guin, only serves to confirm this hypothesis, which can be demonstrated on internal evidence. All the regions that make up this fictional world, including Calf Island, the Outer Dimensions explored by Grimus, Deggle and Virgil Jones and the Inner Dimensions crossed by Flapping Eagle on his initiatory pilgrimage, are completely imaginary, and owe their accessibility – indeed, their very existence – to supernatural actions that are made possible only by the powers of an alien object, the Stone Rose. Even the most realistic events in the novel, those that take place between Joe–Sue's birth on the Axona table-top and his arrival on Calf Island, display several supernatural features. Examples are the two magic drinks (both, as we learn later, of extraterrestrial origin; 263) which Grimus, disguised as the pedlar Sispy, presents to Bird-Dog and through her to Flapping Eagle, or Livia's inexplicably accurate reading of Flapping Eagle's hand, and his sea travels, which continue for about seven hundred years aboard the same vessel, and which eventually lead him back to his starting-point, where he again meets Deggle, who, like him, is one of the Immortals.

---

[2] "In the summer of 1967 [...] when I was twenty years old, I bought a paperback copy of Ralph Manheim's English translation of *The Tin Drum* from a bookshop in Cambridge, England [...] there are [...] books which give [readers] permission to become the sort of writers they have it in themselves to be"; "Salman Rushdie on Günter Grass," *Granta* 15 (1985): 187–93, repr. in Rushdie, *Imaginary Homelands: Essays and Criticism 1981–1991* (London: Granta/Penguin, 1991): 276.

But if we now apply our zoom lens and try looking at *Grimus* under a higher degree of magnification, the fictional world, which seemed original, turns out to be composed of entirely derivative elements. The hypothesis structuring the plot, that of the simultaneous existence of an infinite number of dimensions parallel to our own, is none other than the theory of parallel universes, of which science fiction has made much use, while the device of an object from an alien world which inexplicably appears in our own and permits the intersection of different dimensions has been exploited in the genre at least since H.G. Wells's "The Crystal Egg." The objects around which the narrative nuclei of the novel cluster – the life and death drinks which determine the main characters' extraordinary fates, the Stone Rose whose chance discovery triggers off the narrative, and the "pure, beautiful dance of life" which represents the deep structure of matter according to the scientist–poets of the Spiral Dancers (and which, in its opposite and specular forms, the Strongdance and the Weakdance, determines the direction and the outcome of the plot; 93, 319) – can just as easily be traced back to various symbolic and narrative traditions such as those of the fairy-tale or romance or, again, the occultist tradition which so influenced European literature of the Decadent era. All these elements, which were not original to begin with, undergo a kind of 'secondary encoding' whose purpose is to make them compatible with the constraints and formal principles of the quest-genre. Thus the Stone Rose, for all the mystical and symbolic connotations its name implies, is described according to the conventions of science fiction (304), and the "blinks" and the "Grimus effect" are ascribed, through an alienating use of symbolism, to "malfunctions of the mutilated Rose" (240).

These structural features of cosmogonic creativity in *Grimus* are even more evident in the second-degree cosmogony produced by Virgil Jones, thanks to his mastery of the secrets of the Stone Rose. The brief descriptions of the worlds he creates (or visits – the text is ambiguous here; 91), from the "instinct-logic of the plant-geniuses of Poli XI" to the "tonal sculpture of the Aurelions," are all based on the paradoxical combination of already existing elements. This compositional technique, which might be labelled 'creation by permutation,' is endemic to science fiction, and is the most dishonest device by which the genre eludes its institutional task of representing other-ness. It is no accident that Stanislaw Lem, the greatest-ever author of science fiction, the only one whose work wholly and systematically transcends generic constraints and can be classified without qualification as great litera-ture, employs this technique only for comic or satiric effect. The importance of creation by permutation in the construction of the fictional world of

Grimus is confirmed by the narrative and theoretical relevance which the text ascribes to anagrammatism. This structural device, however quaint, is particularly apposite as a symbolic equivalent of the compositional principle of permutation on the atomic plane of verbal expression. "Anagrammar," the "Divine Game of Order," is the defining activity of the Gorfs, "the most intelligent life-form in any galaxy" in *Grimus'* fictive universe (309). Its properties "extend [...] far beyond mere letter-puzzling; the vast mental powers of the Gorfs make it possible for them anagrammatically to alter their very environment and indeed their own physical make-up" (77). The analogy between Anagrammar and literary creation is made quite explicit by mention of a particular "branch of the Divine Game," conceptualism, whose basic tenet, "I think, therefore it is" (79), is also the cardinal principle of the poetic imagination. Indeed, in an increasingly transparent parallelism not so much with literature in general as with *Grimus* in particular, it leads to the creation of the other dimensions in which the actions of the book take place and the pivotal Stone Rose exerts its influence (79–80). This generalization of anagrammatism, which, from being a taxonomic device peculiar to the Gorfs, becomes the structural foundation of the whole fictive world of *Grimus*, is authorized by the narrator's observation that "Gorfs look like nothing so much as enormous sightless frogs." This reveals the operation of the anagrammatic principle beyond the construction of the fictive world in the very form of the narrative. Similarly, the riddle of the book's title, also the name of the character who created Calf Island, is explained anagrammatically by a reference to the Simurg, the bird of Sufi myth whose story is itself the most haunting embodiment of "creation by permutation': "thirty birds set out to find the Simurg on the mountain where he lives. When they reach the peak, they find that they themselves are, or have become, the Simurg. The name, you see, means Thirty Birds. Si, thirty. Murg, birds" (262).

Aside from the particularly striking example of the name Grimus, the symbolic plane is actualized in the novel by means of links operating on the plane of the signifiers, employing not only anagrammatism but also homophony and word-play. A case in point is the puzzling name of Calf Island, which is belatedly explained as a corruption, unavoidable in Western pronunciation, of the Arabic letter Kâf, the name of the mountain where the Simurg nests (262), and is thus revealed to be cryptically but wholly appropriate as the name of the mountain on whose peak Grimus has built his nest. The battle between Flapping Eagle and Grimus which ends the novel acquires equally mythic dignity from the fact that the fighters are named after the "prince of the earthly birds" and the "bird of paradise"

respectively (248). The trouble with all such links, which are far more pervasive than I can show here, and with the very principle of the manipulation
of signifiers as a structural and heuristic device, is that our culture, unlike
Eastern ones such as those of Arabia and Japan, whose poetic languages are
built on homophones and homographs, does not ascribe sufficient depth
and necessity to the plane of the signifier to motivate complex narrative and
conceptual constructions. This inescapable marginality, which Freud
accounted for in the distinction he drew between *calembour* and *Witz*, can
help give a more than merely subjective explanation of the impression of
arbitrariness caused by the extensive use of formal devices in the construction of the fictive world in *Grimus*.

ಀ • ಜ

Let us now try aiming our telescope at the fictive world of *Midnight's Children*. The difference between the two novels could not be more striking. In
Midnight's Children, places and events have exact parallels in the real world.
This correspondence is not limited to macroscopic facts like the geographical
makeup of the Indian subcontinent and its political history, but affects
ephemeral minutiae such as toothpaste ads or the city plan of Bombay. The
only evident discrepancy, which is enough to justify the inclusion of the
novel in the genre of magical realism rather than of simple realism, is the
description of the marvellous powers of Saleem and of his thousand contemporaries. Yet even these patently anti-realistic phenomena are described
according to the conceptual categories of classical realism. For, in *Midnight's
Children*, there are degrees of the marvellous (the children's' powers de-
crease as the hour of their birth gets further from midnight) and limits
(Saleem's telepathy does not inform him about the secret of his birth, which
he only learns from Mary Pereira's confession). The most intrinsically implausible elements are thus presented so as not to contradict verisimilitude
directly. The same is true of the "four modes of connection," the formal and
conceptual devices the narrator uses to demonstrate the centrality of his own
private story in the collective history of the subcontinent (238). For the last
two, the "active–metaphorical" and the "passive–metaphorical" are intrinsically irrational (hence by far the most productive in Saleem's idiosyncratic
rewriting of history), but their irrationality fades away under the apparent
logic of the symmetry and orderliness with which they are described. But
this constant verisimilarization and objectivizing of the supernatural is con-
current with an even more constant subjectivizing and mythicizing of the

real. As we increase our telescope's degree of magnification, the strictly realistic universe of *Midnight's Children* is shown to be an agglomerate of original objects selected according to quintessentially subjective and unashamedly arbitrary criteria, rather than for any cultural or aesthetic relevance they might possess in the real world, and then meticulously familiarized through repetition, until the mimetic world of realism is transfigured into the heartfelt and hallucinatory description of an inner landscape. Historical events, with their remote abstraction, are embodied in the concrete materiality of humble and familiar objects. Thus, the slow, unfathomable unwinding of the Great War, as it tears a far-away continent to pieces, is presented by the far more exciting advances and retreats of the "perforated sheet" on the body of the beauteous Naseem; the bloody repression of the Agra uprising has its inverse image in the Mercurochrome that Aadam Aaziz uses to dress the participants' wounds as best he can (35); the catastrophic end of the Free Islam Convocation and the murder of Mian Abdullah, "the Hummingbird," are linked to the "superb silver spittoon, inlaid with lapis lazuli," belonging to the Rani of Coch Naheen (45); lastly, the 1958 coup in Pakistan is anticipated and represented by the "movements performed by pepperpots" of the chapter with this title.

The metonymic links governing symbolic relationships in *Grimus* are here replaced by metaphoric ones. In the earlier novel, for instance, the past was contained in Dolores O'Toole's trunk (60, 67) or in the photograph album (123), while in *Midnight's Children* it is much more quaintly but much more memorably represented by the pickle jars Saleem lines up on the shelf as his literary and earthly adventure nears its end. The link between pickle and autobiographical writing is not culturally codified, nor even immediately evident, but is all the more apposite for this very reason. The relationship between the mysterious workings of memory and the delicate, uncanny alchemy that can alone ensure preservation of organic matter for a long but always unpredictable length of time, between the imperceptible alteration of the very fabric of reality in memory and the transubstantiation which familiar and all too well-known ingredients undergo in the pickling process, is far more powerful and suggestive than mere cultural habit or metonymic or synecdochic contiguity could ever hope to be.

The diverging attitudes of the two novels towards symbolism are paralleled by their attitudes towards another fundamental mode of literary signification: allusion. In *Grimus*, allusion works as it typically does in modern literature: intertextual links are never made explicit, and the search for allusive patterns (in order to give coherence to the apparent jumble of textual referents) makes up a statistically far from negligible part of the reader's work. The discrepancy between the cultural competence of the author and that of the empirical audience makes it necessary to explain some references – as in the case of the absolutely central, and particularly peregrine, allusion to the Simurg myth. Yet even this explanation comes late enough in the book to let the reader simmer in the search (as unfailingly instinctive as it is surely doomed to failure) for a solution to the riddle of the book's title. The other fundamental myth, which Rushdie probably thought more familiar to the majority of his Western–Christian audience, is unambigously hinted at in the shape and location of the island, as well as in Virgil Jones's name and narrative function; but it is nowhere made explicit, and its decoding is entrusted to the reader's knowledge of Dante.

This process of riddle-like encoding results in an increase in the text's perceived depth. The reader's appreciation is enhanced because the text is thus partly the result of his own work, because he has contributed to its creation by patiently decoding. This is undoubtedly an advantage, but the price to be paid is the epistemological subordination of the fictive world to other worlds, of which it becomes a kind of satellite, and the bold emphasizing of its literariness, which creates a marked and unmistakably anti-illusionistic effect. In *Midnight's Children* the attitude towards allusion, like that towards symbols, is reversed. All references, even those to historical events or figures of unquestionable prominence, or to mythical characters that cannot but be familiar even to someone whose only knowledge of Indian culture is derived from occasional visits to ethnic restaurants, are immediately and meticulously clarified. Allusion and explanation are so closely contiguous that the reader does not feel called upon to fill the gap between them with his own hypotheses or conjectures. The text contains and displays all the keys needed for its own decoding. It includes its own encyclopaedia, and its interpretation does not require any form of competence beyond what it itself makes available in its solid self-referentiality. This technique has the effect of replacing the real world with an alternative but equally complex and self-contained reality. The implied reader of *Midnight's Children* is a virgin: he knows nothing about India, its history, culture, mythology or geography. The empirical reader, on the other hand, is obliged to become a virgin, even if not one to begin with, because the ruthless propaganda of repetition has the effect of substituting the novel's own version of events for any other. An empirical but particularly telling proof of the extraordinary effectiveness of *Midnight's Children*'s propaganda is the boomerang effect it had on the author himself, who should theoretically have been in a position to preserve some shred of autonomy regarding his own fiction.[3] This is, in fact, the main task required of the reader of *Midnight's Children*, one both hard and sublime, like all tasks that may be mistaken for doing nothing: he must recognize the inadequacy of his own cultural coordinates, of his allusive compasses, of his hermeneutic anxieties. (Is this an unconscious *à la* Freud or *à la* Jung? a myth *à la* Frazer or *à la* Lévi-Strauss? What should I know, remember, have read, in order to be able to interpret this elusive passage? Answer: this book – and *nothing else*. Structuralism strikes back – late, but with a vengeance.) The reader must accept a new mythology, let himself be converted by a new sacred text, overcome his fear of the leap into the void entailed in the decision to give more credit to the words of an individual (and of a pretty cranky one, at that) than to the world's voices. In a word, he must have faith.

I am young (and ignorant) enough to be able to remember fairly well the sense of dismay that overcame me on first encountering a postmodernist novel: parallelisms and structural symmetries were so meticulously emphasized, intertextual links, whether mythical, historical or literary, so invariably made explicit, that I reacted with bewilderment and outrage. The author has no right to be doing this, I protested, this is my job as reader. How dare he make me redundant, or intellectually bankrupt! Now that I have read (and thought) a little more (though undoubtedly still far too little to presume to talk about such things with any competence or authority), I realize that my first impression that *Midnight's Children* might be attempting to relieve its reader of all interpretative duties is misleading and untenable. The reader's duties have simply evolved, because the process of literary encoding in Rushdie's second novel (and, more generally, in magical realism) assumes a different form from the one it had in his first. Literary discourse is always by definition opaque. We might even go so far as to say that we consider a given text to be literature when we decide to endow it with a certain degree of opacity, to deploy our intellectual and emotional powers in a potentially endless quest for a sense we assume it to possess above and beyond its literal and immediately perspicuous meaning. (Such a decision is self-evidently an act of faith, and as such cannot be objectively motivated, but derives its strength purely from each reader's inwardness. This is what makes paranoia such a useful and productive character-trait in

---

[3] A very interesting account of the process can be found in "'Errata': or, Unreliable Narration in *Midnight's Children*," *Imaginary Homelands*, 24: "*even after I found out that my memory was playing tricks*, my brain simply refused to unscramble itself."

a critic.) I am thinking of moral, figural and anagogic (not to mention halakhic, haggadic, khabbalistic, gematric and so on) interpretations of some biblical lists and precepts which may be taken to represent both the original paradigm and the *reductio ad absurdum* of Western literary criticism.

Yet no discourse can be entirely opaque, or the communicative link, however tenuous, joining it to at least a virtual audience and ensuring its survival will be severed. Thus, each and every text is faced with the necessity to choose when to be opaque and when to be transparent: in short, to elaborate an encoding algorhythm. In the case of *Midnight's Children*, it is worth noting as an example that the opposite and reciprocal themes of obsession and irrelevance, which were discussed openly and with a wealth of incidental detail in *Grimus* (like all works of science fiction, far from shy of direct confrontation with ultimate realities), undergo a process of double encoding in Rushdie's second novel: first through the filter of the first-person narrator, whose obsession is represented, but never stated, and secondly through the obstinately and ostentatiously referential drift of the narrative, which does not discuss ideas but only things, for the reflections that occasionally interrupt it are not authorial statements of purpose, but necessary, incoherent rationalizations of an individual destiny, and are as such themselves primary objects of interpretative attention. In *Midnight's Children* both things and words are opaque filters which the reader must penetrate, but which can never be completely overcome, because they make up the narrative. They are the cumbersome, odorous flesh which stands between symbol and allegory.

Rushdie employs specular forms in *Grimus* and *Midnight's Children*, making opaque in one novel what is transparently visible in the other. However basic this aspect may be to the characterization of an individual work, it cannot be assumed to be a purely individual trait, any more than the present-day reserve about feelings, which has replaced the mainly sexual sense of shame of our parents' generation, can be assumed to be an individual choice. The limits of what can be uttered, as Foucault prophetically saw, are never established by an individual, in either literary or cultural history. Rushdie's mode of writing, after *Grimus*, shares the features of exuberant inventiveness, encyclopaedic breadth and self-contained density which characterize the work of those post-colonial writers, from García Márquez to Harris, who have pushed back the boundaries of what can be uttered.

ೞ • ಜ

Representing the Worlds
Sanskrit Poetics and the Making of Reality

———————————————————————— ༀ

Alessandro Monti

ESPITE ALL ITS MERITS, the vast majority of critical attention
devoted to the notion of magical realism restricts itself by evoking
Western categories of textual analysis. I would prefer to bracket, as
it were, a few skeletal words from Sanskrit poetics and the Hindu religious
lexicon, each of them paralleling enhanced patterns of passage between a
'literal' sense and an 'intended' or 'added' sense. The taxonomic state held
by women in Hindu society can make a valuable test case, given their
relatively low position in the many traditional *sutras* (time-honoured
corpora of ethical and practical norms of behaviour) that serve to codify and
interpret distinctions of role and identity in Hindu society.

However, Hindu culture never seems to have known an absolute distinction between the factual (with its pitiless closures) and a meta-representa-
tional vision of reality. Consequently, the negative image of woman is
displaced into its correlative 'figuratived' (*laksana*) and 'inverted' (*viparita*)
identity as goddess. This continuous process of metaphysical hybridization
goes beyond a mere poetics of words and figures of speech, positing as it
does the existence of institutional passages across the border between the
human and the divine. These sites are specifically known in Hinduism as
tirtahs, their ontological dimension modifying *de facto* the illusory nature
(*maya*) of the material world. *Tirtah* places are fragmented islands belonging
to the dimension of *lila* (that is, the creative play of the gods) and connote a
state of 'magic reality,' although they are unnoticeably located inside the *lok*
('world') of men.

As agencies of spiritual liberation, such sites are endowed with dynamic
qualities, which their current designation as *tirtahs* ('fords') makes clearly

evident. However, a further and different place of 'sacred' and 'magic' geography deploys the scattered body of the Goddess as a mark of 'permanence' (*pitha*), sadly emphasizing the sacrificial role of women in Hinduism,
a 'redemptive' consequence of their ambiguous and 'unstable' nature.

౦ॐ • ౬౦

In *Gauri*, a novel by Mulk Raj Anand, the newlywed Panchi focalizes his
"golden" and fascinating spouse, Gauri, as a "black," destroying creature,
like the fierce goddess Kali.[1] This binary opposition, between the auspicious
('bright') side of her feminine nature and the inauspicious ('dark') quality
she is deeply imbued with, seems to be typically couched in terms of a
seductive appearance masking a violent, still untamed character.

It is held in Hindu lore that an act of seduction may involve a desire to
cheat and to trick, basically grounded as it is on such an ambiguous category
as *hava* – roughly speaking, a posture intended to attract and to fascinate.
(The Sanskrit root means 'call' in Hindi, *hav* standing for 'coquetry, bland-
ishment, airs'; the adjective *havi* translates the English word 'dominant').

In order to supply a speedy index for my agenda, I would posit a basic
scheme enabling the reader to understand how the pattern of seduction
operates in Hindu texts. Given the assumption that dissonant identities are
co-substantial within the feminine self, inversion or falsity of attitude
(*viparita*) foregrounds the issue. A *viparita* strategy to attain *hava* needs the
help of several agencies to inducing the requisite erotic sentiment (*srngara*),
lila being the foremost among them. *Lila* (literally, 'play') is a crucial Hindu
term, suggesting at its outermost semantic extension the basic nature of the
world as the pastime of the divinity and expressing in the quotidian the
relation between the divinity and his or her devotees:

> *lila*: play, sport; suggests the basic nature of the world as the pastime of the
> supreme, and expresses the relation between the supreme and his or her
> devotees; also provides the most profound 'explanation' for the incarnations of
> the supreme; in the *Devi–Bhagavata*, it is the play of a mother with her children,
> that ultimately characterizes the Devi's interaction with all created beings.[2]

In the erotic *rasa* ('mood'), however, *lila* manifests itself in the imitation of
the loved by the lover, particularly when no other form of intercourse is

---

[1] Mulk Raj Anand, *Gauri* (1960; New Delhi: Arnold–Heinemann, 1981). First published
as *The Old Woman and the Cow*. Further page references are in the text.
[2] C. Mackenzie Brown, *The Triumph of the Goddess* (1990; Delhi: Sri Satguru, 1992): 228–
29.

possible at that moment. A case of erotic *lila* is found in a story collected in the book *Dasakumaracarita*, by Dandin, recounting how a *rsi* (an ascetic living in complete seclusion) yields to a *devadasi* (here, a courtesan), who imitates his way of life (*dharma*). Acting as an agent of seduction, the *devadasi* finally induces the hermit to discard his *tapas* ('meditation') in favour of *artha* ('prosperity, well-being') and *kama* ('pleasure'), these two being the most mundane among the four goals of human endeavour.[3]

On a more complex level, the *viparita* strategy of seduction deployed by the courtesan evokes the so-called 'envy of the gods,' aroused by the state of holy perfection the *rsi* is achieving. In *Gauri* a similar emotional component restricts the underlying significance of Panchi's bitter reaction to his wife. The key to his confused and angry mood is contained in a typical Punjabi folk-song which the character quotes, "The Marriage of Hir and Ranjha," whose full version is collected in Temple's *Legends of the Panjab* (1884).[4] The character recites: "Your love, oh my Hire, has dragged me / through the murk of the world" (32). Once again, the love of a man for a woman entails a loss of male identity and status, in the wake of a paradoxical tension which splits away the submissive and reassuring image of Gauri, the conventional spouse, into the terrifying Kali. This metamorphosis ranges from fictionalized scenes of rustic life to the learned debate on the cosmogonic context in which the Goddess manifests the gendered fullness of her *sakti* powers, responsible for all the activity and energy in the universe.[5] The devotional renderings of the myth narrate how the Goddess restores peace to the *lok* ('world') of men, and safety to the threatened gods, by defeating an *asura*, or demon-like figure. The paradoxical appearance of the Goddess highlights her *viparita* ('contrary,' but also 'inauspicious') identity. She presents herself as a young and beautiful woman and yet she is not passionate, being endowed with the masculine *rasas* of heroism (*virya*) and wrath (*raudra*).[6]

ﾠﾠﾠﾠﾠﾠﾠﾠﾠﾠﾠﾠﾠﾠﾠﾠﾠﾠﾠﾠﾠﾠﾠﾠﾠﾠﾠﾠﾠﾠﾠﾠ୦ • ଚ

To highlight the issue, I will have to deal briefly with some points of Sanskrit textual criticism. The rhetorical figure termed *laksana* (meaning 'the word

---

[3] For a more comprehensive reading of the story, see Charles Malamoud, *Cooking the World: Ritual and Thought in Ancient India*, tr. David White (*Cuire le monde: Rite et pensée dans l'Inde ancienne*, 1989; Delhi: Oxford UP: 1996).

[4] Richard C. Temple, *The Legends of the Panjab* (1884; repr. Lahore: Allied, nd).

[5] Mackenzie Brown, *The Triumph of the Goddess*, 230.

[6] Mackenzie Brown, "The Two Devi–Mahatmyas: Revisions within the Tradition," part 2: 81–154.

power of figuration,' from the root *laksya*, 'indicated') comes into operation here because of the incompatibility of the literal sense with the 'indicated' contextual sense. It would then be possible to posit a further category of analysis, *vyajastuti* (from *stuti*, 'praise'), meaning 'the non-contextual sense,' which some branches of Sanskrit criticism focalize as being on a par with the notion of *viparita laksana*, or 'figuration by opposition.'[7] It ensues that a *viparita* identity structurally operates the movement from the straight representation to the intended or 'figured' sense.[8] Consequently, Kali is the *viparita* figuration of Gauri: ie, the contextual and implied extension of her nature and behaviour as a woman (*stri svabhava*).

The mood (*rasa*) of seduction by 'inversion' (*viparita*) bespeaks the relentless Hindu mapping out of identities and its epistemological relevance to the definition of a metacontextual sense to be added to the literal sense. A typical case of *viparita* strategy, implying the agency of 'figuration' (*laksana*), is given in the myth of the Goddess, she assuming a male and war-like identity so as to defeat the *asuras*, who misinterpret her appearance and discourse in terms of false suggestion (*vyanjana*). In fact, the council held by the enemies of the Goddess argues that, given her feminine nature, she cannot mean war or acts of violence, but only signify sexual passion. This false assumption (grounded on a radical inversion of meaning, or *viparita*) loads the figurative sense against the literal sense, thus replacing an attitude of censure (*ninda*) towards women and their dangerous nature with praise (*stuti*) for the powers of the Goddess.

The oppositive structure embodied by *viparita* overlaps with the cognate notions of *maya* ('illusion') and *moha* ('delusion'), both referring to the powers of fascination and enchantment the Goddess is endowed with. As a transformative force, *maya* creates through illusion and spreads delusion (*moha-kari*). It is worth observing that the root of the word *moh* designates either passion or confusion, and that the courtesan Mohini is an avatar of Vishnu assuming a seductive feminine identity, in order to trick the *asuras* out of the *amrta*, a kind of celestial ambrosia. *Maya* has its somewhat debased counterpart in *jadu*, or magic powers intended as mere jugglery.

ಣ • ಐ

---

[7] V.T. Zambare, "Aprastuta prasamsa and Vyajastuti: Is the 'prastuta,' relevant, conveyed by 'Vyanjana, word-power of suggestion,' or by 'Laksana, word–power of figuration'?," in *Glimpses of Ancient Indian Poetics*, ed. Sudhakar Pandey & V.N. Jha (Delhi: Sri Satguru, 1983): 100.

[8] Zambare, "Aprastuta prasamsa and Vyajastuti," 99–100.

A likely Indian rendering of such a notion as 'magical realism' should resort, then, to an operative chain of sanskritized critical terms, including at least *laksana*, *vyajastuti* and *viparita*, each of them setting up areas of semantic definition in the perception of reality.

Laksana (or 'word-power of figuration') refocalizes the discourse from the literal to the 'intended' sense. In *Gauri*, Mulk Raj Anand adopts a similar mode of expression, when Panchi the husband vents his sour concern for the drought which is searing his crops. He puts the blame on the destructive power of the Goddess (Gauri being turned into Kali), whose unsubdued *prakrti* a reader must infer from a sharp textual structure of inversion, since a Hindu wife named Gauri ought to be a mirror of domestic virtue, given the benign identity of the Goddess as Gauri, the tamed spouse of Shiva.[9]

The transition from Gauri the terrestrial wife to Gauri the golden heavenly bride, and finally to Kali the black destroyer, requires the agency of a further stylistic device, *samadhi*, this being grounded on the super-imposition of a secondary meaning, understood as a quality belonging by tradition to the word in question.[10] I would venture to observe that the ontological movement from Gauri (the name meaning 'luminous as a cow or bright as a lotus flower') to Kali (meaning 'the black one') reverses a time-honoured Puranic myth in which, after a long penance, Kali becomes Gauri to please her divine husband Siva. According to a modern version of the myth, Shiva calls Parvati "Kali" in a spirit of "sport," the Goddess being "as black as sapphire" – actually a metaphor indicating a colour known in India as *kalika*, or 'the dark-blue lotus.' Parvati misunderstands Shiva addressing her thus and thinks that the God does not like her black body. Consequently, she practises severe austerities, till the god Brahma, taking pity, changes her black complexion into *gaura*, or the 'colour of the bright lotus.' However, it is worth noticing that in the *Skanda Purana*, one of the holy books devoted to the Goddess, the identity of Parvati is split into a dual personality, com-prehending the golden Gauri and the black Kausiki, the latter being a sort of 'external body or frame' containing the goddess.

Such a structure of duality deploys *ninda* ('censure') and *stuti* ('praise'), these being two *gunas* (or 'qualities') roughly corresponding in Western

---

9 "*Prakrti*: nature; in Samkhya philosophy, active but insentient material cause of the universe, contrasted with spirit (purusa); in the *Devi–Bhagavata*, as a form or aspect of the Goddess, who is identified with both nature and the spirit" (Mackenzie Brown, *The Triumph of the Goddess*, 229).

10 G.H. Tarlekar, "The Merits and Demerits of Kavya, According to Bhamaha and Dandin," in *Glimpses of Ancient Indian Poetics*, 112.

theory to the denotative and connotative levels of language. The original myth entailing Parvati–Gauri and Kali–Kausiki connotes the former couple as *stuti* and denotes the latter as *ninda*, whereas Anand's character inverts the paradigmatic order, connoting Kali as *ninda* and denoting Gauri as *stuti*. Consequently, the passage from the mythic text to the fictive text suggests *ninda* rather than *stuti*. (Salman Rushdie, incidentally, follows a similar procedure in *The Satanic Verses* when dealing with the Qur'an.)

In Anand's novel, Gauri the woman is made compatible with Gauri the goddess through the agency of the traditional Hindu marriage, which connects, as it were, heaven and earth, the Hindu couple, or *jori*, partaking of a sacred and godlike nature. The discursive field of Hinduism focalizes the hybrid status (both divine and human) of the married couple in terms of appropriation and resistance. In the former case, the switching by means of *laksana* from the 'literal' sense of wife to the 'intended' sense of goddess 'adds merit' (*samadhi*) to Gauri the woman. However, the 'intended' identity of Gauri as the namesake of the goddess requires a strategy of disavowal, retaining the mark of difference despite the process of metabolization effected by *laksana*.

If the notion of magical realism deploys features of modified vision, blurring as it were the usual perception of reality into an ontologically hybridized image, *viparita* (as in the case of the hybridized identity of the Goddess, fighting the *asuras*, externally a woman to all appearances, but internally endowed with all the qualities of a man) re-signifies *laksana*, by emphasizing *ninda* as the necessary correlative of *stuti*. Then *laksana viparita* might be the *deshi* ('indigenous') version of magical realism, in both instances the juxtaposition of terms being the key to operating the transition from the real world to the imagined world.

In all of the examples given so far, the shift in identity implies an ambiguous *viparita* structure of inversion. A more positive side to the issue may be grasped with the aid of the term *tirtah* (also spelt *tirath*), meaning literally a place where one fords a river and, by extension, any place consecrated by a God and where one can encounter the divine. At such sites one may cross over from the *lok* ('world') of men to the sacred *lok* of the gods. This entails a privileged dimension of existence which in Hinduism takes the name of *satya* ('truth'), seen as a consequence of *salokya*, the act of dwelling in the same world as the deity, and one of the forms of liberation from the process of birth and rebirth (*samsara*).

ⓒ8 • ℬↄ

The holy city of Benares ("Kasi" in Sanskrit) is a major *tirtah* site in the whole domain of Hinduism, since it is the fruit of Siva's *lila*. However, more relevant to my perspective is the fact that it is the local identity of the spouse of Shiva, worshipped in Benares as the auspicious and bountiful Anna-purna, 'one who bestows food to the fullest.' Her maternal care (quite different from the passive attitude of the *pativrata*, the faithful Hindu wife devoted to her husband and suffering *vratas* or 'penances' on his behalf) qualifies the popular belief that nobody in Benares can starve. The sequence of Benares stories by Raja Rao[11] adapts the dictum to his more sophisticated vision of life, one in which the folk-dream of a sober Hindu Land of Cockaigne gives way to a more exalted myth of cosmogonic creation, through the accumulation of unblemished and sanctified lives. Consequently, the current notion of the city as a huge storehouse granting everybody unlimited abundance should be viewed in terms of cosmogonic growth, whose final integration with the world of the gods is specifically inscribed into a surplus leading to *kama* ('desire') as a necessary prelude to the act of moving across the two worlds.

The becalmed and docile nature of the Goddess considered in her association with Siva and his divine *lila* goes beyond a mere feminine role as a purveyor of unlimited abundance (Sri–Lakshmi, the Goddess typifying household order, would take care of that), deploying, rather, a more sophisticated emphasis on the unity of the Hindu cosmos. This unity can be attained through an accumulation of energy, metaphorized by abundance of food. Consequently, the sequence of stories in *On the Ganga Ghat* highlights the *advaita* (or 'undivided') vision of the world, in which men and gods coexist after achieving consubstantiality. In Hinduism, the crossing-over from the human to the divine requires the agency of a figure of mediation, embodying the redemptive qualities usually connected with a *tirtah* site. Mohini (or 'enchantress through seduction,' from the Sanskrit root *moh* mentioned above) is the name of the heavenly feminine presence meeting, in "Story III," Chota Munna Lal, the young Benares wrestler and seller of wood for the funeral pyre. More of a shadow than a real woman, she enters the world of men through a mirror, being one of a host of celestial creatures of the same kin.

Her seductive nature displays *prakrti* as an undiluted power or, in simpler terms, a tendency the Goddess has to overflow herself, suffusing the

---

[11] Raja Rao, *On the Ganga Ghat* (New Delhi: Vision, 1989). Page references are in the text.

world with her power of nurturing energy. If *maya* prevents one from seing things as they really are, *prakrti* is an endowment bringing phenomenal existence to its overall completion. However, the relationship of the Mohini with Munna Lal entails a paradigm of cosmogonic wholeness, rather than the possibility of encountering the Goddess and approaching her as if one were her lover, although she is often described by epithets that stress her power to arouse sexual desire. In this connection, to see the Mohini is a redemptive event in itself, her presence releasing the vision of imagined worlds, so far concealed to the human eye:

> But now he has the Mohini. One day some three years or so ago, when Madhobha was sitting in his attic, he heard the sound of anklets and bangles, and he knew a woman was near. And before he could know who, a melody arose more gracious than of any human tongue, and a lit loveliness danced before him as never man hath seen. He sat in rapt devotion to this feminine presence as if more than a goddess were there – a woman too was there. And she threw flowers at him and real flowers too they were, for he gathered them and stuck some behind his ears, for every time there was a visitation she clapped her hands and danced. (36–37)

> One day when I [Mohini] sat at dusk on the parapet of a terrace, and there was absolute noiselessness, I heard a strange sound as if Sri Rama was going back to Ayodhya, such the pleasant splendid noise of horses and elephants. I looked down and it was.you. I followed you to the temple. I saw Ramji himself standing behind Hanuman to bless you. I have lived so long looking for someone who could take me to Ram. For we're of such stuff made, we cannot approach a god directly. We have to go through a man. And a man who has never touched a woman is our man. (37)

I would posit a correlation between the brahmanic myths dealing with the creation of the world and the power the Mohini has to release new visions of the surrounding reality, in both instances the agencies at work drawing their basic materials from reserves of stored-up energy. Consequently, her meeting with Munna Lal should be viewed as a reduced version of Prajapati, the mythical being whose force becomes the underlying substance of the world. This process of creation, however, entails a sort of self-sacrifice, since Prajapati 'falls apart' after giving life to the whole cosmos.[12] As a result, he asks Agni (the god of fire) to restore him to his original state of integrity by performing the *agnicayana*, a symbolic ritual of rebirth based on the building of a sacrificial altar and the kindling of a sacred fire. In this connection, the role of Munna Lal, the Benares vendor of

---

[12] Herman W. Tull, *The Vedic Origins of Karma* (1989; Delhi: Sri Satguru, 1990): 95–102.

wood for the pyre of death and rebirth, might easily be equated with the ritual identity of the devotee performing the third and final stage of the *agnicayana*, in order to make himself ready for the journey to the world of the gods. Both the sacrificer and Munna Lal can shed their embryonic states of life, having attained (through the mediation either of the officiant or of the Mohini) their 'shares' in the upper *lok*.

ଓଃ • ଅଃ

Similar notions leading to sequences of fragmentation and reconstitution of the female body as a process necessary for the sacralization of the Hindu world also inform the rituals of *sati*, the Hindu custom in which a widow sacrifices herself by being burned alive on her dead husband's funeral pyre. It is possible to interpret *sati* as a source of inexhaustible energy, since the eponymous first wife of Shiva destroys herself out of devotion for her divine spouse:

> Sati's death is thus transformative. Through her death she provokes Siva into a direct conflict with the sacrificial cult and then an accomodation with it. In this way Siva is brought within the circle of dharma, within the order of established religion. Similarly, Sati's corpse, or pieces of her corpse, sacralize the earth. In dying she gives herself up to be accessible on earth to those who need her power or blessing. In transplanting or transforming herself into the earth, she also brings into the sphere of human society the invigorating power of Siva in the form of the linga.[13]

The parts of Sati's scattered body define the geography of India as a correlated chain of sacred places, each of them being associated with the Goddess and taking the name of *pitha*, or 'seat':

> According to this myth, then, the Indian subcontinent has been sacralized by the remains of Sati. India is in effect her burial ground. The subcontinent is sown with the pieces of Sati's body, which make the land especially sacred. The myth also stresses that the numerous and varied *pithas* and goddesses worshipped at them are part of a larger, unified whole. Each *pitha* represents a part of Sati's body or one of her ornaments; taken together, the *pithas* found throughout India constitute or point towards a transcendent (or, perhaps better, a universally immanent) goddess whose being encompasses, underlies, and unifies the Indian subcontinent as a whole. In short, the Indian subcontinent *is* the goddess Sati.[14]

---

13   David Kinsley, *Hindu Goddess* (1986; Delhi: Motilal Banarsidass, 1987): 40.

14   Kinsley, *Hindu Goddess*, 187.

Whereas *tirtah* places connote passage, *pitha* locations must be seen as points of permanence, or as a network of shrines encompassing the whole country, whose extended mapping coincides with the restored body of the goddess.

The Bengali writer Bankim Chandra Chatterjee elaborates on this notion in his novel *Anandamath* (1882), in which a fighting band of Hindu ascetics devote themselves to the service and liberation of their oppressed motherland, which they worship as the goddess Bharat Mata: ie, Mother India. Her cult emphasizes the maternal role of the goddess, although she requires the sacrifice of her children, as does the dangerous and liminal Kali. In the context of the novel the dishevelled appearance of Kali becomes a metaphor for the sad and desecrated condition of India, suffering bitterly under the colonial rule of the English. The shift in the interpretation of Kali operated by Chatterjee defuses the binary opposition between the dark aspect of the goddess and her beneficent and maternal nature, highlighting in its stead the self-sacrificial role she is exacting from her devotees.

The novel *Saguna* (published as a book in 1895 by the Christian convert Krupabai Satthianadhan) figures an inverted *pitha*, through the evil and haunting presence in an Indian forest of a widow who has refused burning: The modified geography laid down by the writer construes the whole Indian map as a darkened sequence of *sthalas* ('spots') devoted to the practices of heathen superstition:

> It needed very little imagination on our part to people this weird-looking spot with ghosts. There were countless dark haunts with grim-looking red figured gods looking out upon us, and the noise of the wind as it came moaning through the trees filled us with awe.[15]

However, this negative space crowded with twilight presences and half-perceived images of the gods percolates slowly into a quietened string of suggestive mythical tales, each of them constituting the kernel of a possible *sthala purana*, or 'local chronicle':

> Our Radha completed her journey in a strangely bewildered dreamy way. For the journey was full of religious associations, and her mind was elated and refreshed by the sight of many a sacred temple, tank and river of which she had heard so much. That pure crystal gurgling spring was caused by mighty Rama's arrow. That rugged hill was a stone that fell from Ravan's hand, when chased by Rama, and that cave in the midst of hills, overgrown with creepers, was Seetabai's arbour during her exile; and Radha's grief was somewhat relieved by the medley of thoughts suggested by such scenes. (40)

---

[15] Krupabai Satthianandhan, *Saguna* (1895; Delhi: Oxford UP, 1998): 25. Further page references are in the text.

Krupabai Satthianandhan evokes a landscape whose soothing properties are toned down to a subdued sensibility, innocent of any numinous presence. As the context goes, the primary meaning (*mukhyartha*) usually associated with the representation of *sthala* locations percolates from *laksana* to *vyanjana*, or 'word power of suggestion.' A further case in point is marked by the event of the Mohini viewing Munna Lal as the *laksana* figuration of the god Rama. In this instance the image figured is *prastuta* ('relevant') to the identity of the character, whereas the too-crowded Indian landscape suggested by Krupabai Satthianandhan achieves an inferior stylistic effect, known as *gunibhutavyangya*, in which "the literal or expressed sense is not relevant to the context and hence needs to be rationalized by the suggested sense."[16]

In his preface to *Kanthapura*, Raja Rao reasserts the immanence of *sthalas* to the area of rhetorical figuration, connecting them to the traditional puranic procedures of narrative language:

> There is no village in India, however mean, that has not a rich sthala–purana, or legendary history, of its own. Some god or god-like hero has passed by the village – Rama might have rested under this pipal-tree, Sita might have dried her clothes, after her bath, on this yellow stone, or the Mahatma himself, on one of his many pilgrimages through the country, might have slept in this hut, the low one, by the village gate. In this way the past mingles with the present, and the gods mingle with men to make the repertory of your grandmother always bright. One such story from the contemporary annals of my village I have tried to tell.[17]

In this passage, the literal and non-contextual sense is connected with the indicated sense by an 'effect–cause' relation (*karyakaranabhava*), which loads the narrative issue, the effect of the event being related to its cause: the dynamic quality which animates the terrestrial *lok* of Hinduism.

All such examples enhance a strategy of Hindu rhetoric which uses theological figuration as a key to focusing a double layer of meaning, both literal and 'intended.' Given that the literal sense parallels the world of men, and that the world of men is mere appearance (or *maya*), it is necessary, in order to attain ontologicallly reliable meaning, to superimpose a second semantic layer (*laksana*). The outcome is that the world of gods, which is both transcendent and immanent, stands to the world of men as the signified stands to the signifier. As a consequence, any Hindu notion not entailing at least suggestions or hints of 'magical realism' should be efficaciously grounded on the possibility of 'moving across' the human border. To mis-

---

16 Zambare, "Aprastuta prasamsa and Vyajastuti," 98.
17 Raja Rao, *Kanthapura* (1936; New Delhi: Orient, 1971), "Foreword."

quote well-known Hindu paradigms, I would attribute the label 'twice-born' to the *deshi* idea of realism, without discounting, however, the cognate term 'magical,' which should connote (as *lila* does) the creative work of the gods. Magical realism might then be translated into something like 'the divine play in the world,' provided the world be the text and the god be the writer.

⠣ • ⠮

The Ragged Edge of Miracles
or: A word or two on those Jack Hodgins novels

————————————————————————— &ᴐ

Lucia Boldrini

Sheer Edge

Here at the sheer edge
of a continent dry weed
clutches, grey gulls turn
from the sea and gather
here, precariously
building their nest.

And here too at the edge
of darkness where all floors
sink to abyss, the lighted
bar is of light
the furthest promontory
and exit sheer fall,

though words slide off, and hands
catching fail to hold,
here also may flower,
precarious as weed
or grey gull's nest, the moment
of touching, the poem.[1]

E DGES ARE PRECARIOUS, like a grey gull's nest on a windswept shore.
Yet the nest is home, the place of breeding. At the edge between the
land and the sea, words are precarious and can slide off, yet it is

---

[1] David Malouf, *Selected Poems 1959–1989* (London: Chatto & Windus, 1994): 3.

here that they blossom into life. All poems are, in some way, at the edge of language, though the poem quoted in the epigraph of Jack Hodgins's novel *The Resurrection of Joseph Bourne*, Amelia Barnstone's "The Last Days of Port Annie," aspires to the status of that most central of Western genres, the epic,[2] and deals with the most universal of themes, life and death:

> Of life and death, oh Muse, these lines will sing:
> Ambition, love, the souls and other things. (241)

> But oh, what fuss these earthbound mortals make
> When asked to pull up roots, or new life take... [epigraph]

Yet, like Malouf's poem, Mrs Barnstone's epic of the town on the Ragged Green Edge of the World deals with that unstable strip between the land and the sea, where "other things" of various substance and provenance meet:

> Of street still strewn with seaweed, all a mess;
> Port Annie people living under stress. (241)

Port Annie may be a place where people live on edge, but in the twenty years of its existence it has certainly become a nest for more than just a grey seagull. Indeed, though Raimey the seabird girl has flown away – rather: has been washed in and out – others (from whales to simple men and women) have found it good soil to nourish their nomadic roots.[3] Edges are fertile places, where creation thrives, where worlds can be invented and miracles are the norm. Jack Hodgins has set all his novels at the western edge of the American continent. What follows is simply a series of reflections written on the margins of Jack Hodgins's *The Resurrection of Joseph Bourne, Or a Word or Two on Those Port Annie Miracles*, with some additional glosses on the earlier novel *The Invention of the World*.

ଓ • ଓ

---

[2] Mrs Barnstone plans "a grand epic in the tradition of Homer and Milton [...] all in heroic couplets too"; *The Resurrection of Joseph Bourne, Or A Word or Two on Those Port Annie Miracles* (Toronto: Macmillan, 1979): 223. Further page references are in the text.

[3] And this despite Joseph Bourne's disapproval of people who anchor their lives to a place or wrap their roots around things (228). For Angela Turner, Port Annie is nothing more than a few "buildings perched on the edge of nothing" (34), a "dead-end place so far from the rest of the world." Nevertheless, she cannot bring herself to leave this "beautiful spot" (41) and is thankful that she lives "in this town where such a thing could take place" (61). Jenny Chambers, who comes to Port Annie on a tour as a stripper, also decides to stay, and indeed stays on till after the end, when the town disappears in a landslide.

First of all, however, a word or two on the question of the *real maravilloso* and 'magical realism.' The former term places an emphasis on the real, which appears marvellous to the viewer because of the startling associations of its unfamiliar colours and forms. In one of his seminal essays on 'marvellous realism,' Alejo Carpentier writes of the first European explorers' wonder at the extraordinary colours, shapes, and size of things in South America, which they thought must be the land of Amadís of Gaul.[4] 'Magic,' or 'magical realism,' on the other hand, seems to place an emphasis less on things themselves than on conventions of writing and representation (as is also the case in such expressions as 'the realist novel' or 'social realism').[5] Carpentier has himself argued very eloquently against a conflation of the two definitions.[6] Implicit in the very terminology, then, is a series of alternatives: 'real' or 'realism' (truth or convention)? Effect on the reader or spectator (marvellous), actual transformation of the object (by miracle, as in Port Annie, or as in the various events of which the mysterious Mr Horseman is a protagonist in the earlier novel), or illusory effect (as in the magic of such illusionists as Donald Keneally, also in *The Invention of the World*)? These ambiguities and oscillations are central to both novels. In the sharp opposition between, for instance, the Irishman Keneally (or Wade's fake history) and Horseman, *The Invention of the World* seems to propose a version of the clear-cut distinction drawn by Carpentier between the 'real' marvels of (South American) reality and the contrivances of (European) artificial 'magical realism.'[7] The central issue of this novel, Hodgins has said, is the

---

[4] "The Baroque and the Marvelous Real," in *Magical Realism: Theory, History, Community*, ed. Lois Parkinson Zamora & Wendy B. Faris (Durham NC/London: Duke UP, 1995): 104.

[5] See also Amaryll Chanady, "The Origins and Development of Magic Realism in Latin American Fiction," in *Magic Realism and Canadian Literature: Essays and Stories; Proceedings of the Conference on Magic Realist Writing in Canada, University of Waterloo / Wilfrid Laurier University (May, 1985)*, ed. Peter Hinchcliffe & Ed Jewinski (Waterloo, Ontario: U of Waterloo P, 1986): 52–53.

[6] See Alejo Carpentier, "The Baroque and the Marvelous Real" and ˙ On the Marvelous Real in America" (an expanded version of his introduction to *El reino de este mundo*), *Magical Realism*, 76–88.

[7] Carpentier rails against what he sees as the "the marvelous, manufactured by tricks of prestidigitation, by juxtaposing objects unlikely ever to be found together" of French Surrealism, English Gothic, etc. "The result of willing the marvelous," he comments, "is that the dream technicians become bureaucrats" ("On the Marvelous Real in America," 85). But this opposition, so clear–cut for Carpentier, is rejected by other critics, who refuse to condemn the authenticity of such European movements as Surrealism or, in painting, Post-Expressionism (for which the term "magical realism" was first used, by Franz Roh, in 1924). On this, and on the formative role that Surrealism may in fact have had on Latin

opposition between invention – which is artificial and can lead to falsehood – and creation, which pertains to a higher level of reality:[8] two types of 'magic,' radically different, are thus evoked. In *The Resurrection of Joseph Bourne*, published two years later, the opposition is to some extent still present in the contrast between the ludicrous advertising tricks of Mayor Weins, whose only dream is to be in the newspaper and "put Port Annie on the [tourist] map" (eg, 75–76), and the fabulous, miraculous events that really take place – the whale's "translation" (66) into a woman, Raimey's arrival, Joseph Bourne's resurrection and miracles. However, the opposition between different kinds of 'magic' is in actual fact sidelined, as no one (probably not even the Mayor himself) believes in Wein's ploys, whereas everyone first doubts, but finally has no difficulty in accepting, the truly miraculous or marvellous. Indeed, the tension between these two types of 'magic' disappears, and the dichotomy is relocated at the level of more or less explicit literary/generic discussions (I shall come back to this later). Indeed, as I shall also show presently, the novel seems to be in part an allegory of the arrival in Canada, by a northbound sea route along the west American coast, of the South American *real maravilloso*. The truly 'magical,' on the other hand, remains peripheral and is largely replaced by the miraculous, or simply 'strange.' This is why, for the rest of this essay, I shall place the fabulous events of Port Annie under the heading of 'miraculous realism.'

Like magic, miracles affect objects as well as persons by changing their essential nature and, often, their visible traits. Of course, miracles and magic can also influence the natural course of events and thus modify history by introducing the eternal, or timeless, into the temporal. As I have already mentioned, 'marvellous realism' has been explicitly associated with the immense spaces of the American continent, its wealth of colours and unusual shapes and dimensions. Thus, time, space and the real, both in their visible and in their invisible features, are the three areas on which I wish to concentrate. However, of these it is space that interests me most. For, if in traditional realist narrative it is chronology that organizes the life of the

---

American theorizing and development of 'marvellous realism,' see Chanady, "The Origins and Development of Magic Realism in Latin American Fiction," 49–60, and Geoff Hancock, "Magic or Realism: The Marvellous in Canadian Fiction," *Magic Realism and Canadian Literature*, 30–48.

[8] Quoted in Cecelia Coulas–Fink, "'If Words Won't Do, and Symbols Fail': Hodgins's Magic Reality," *Journal of Canadian Studies – Revue d'études canadiennes* 20.2 (1985): 118–19. I shall come back to this interview, and the opposition between invention and creation, at the end of this essay.

characters and their development or decline, in these novels the story/ history often appears to be subordinated to location, so that writing may take the form of a 'topography' (in Hodgins's fiction there are many references to geographical and topographical maps, many descriptions of places, whether panoramic, as if from a plane or as in a bird's-eye view, or in slow motion, focusing on details taken in as a character moves slowly down the streets of the town).[9] I would like to pick a few discrete items out of these magical or miraculous spaces and try to show how their relationships are articulated, and how the novels re-design, or blot out, their fluid, uncertain, ragged edges and boundaries. The items I wish to focus on are: Joseph Bourne himself; the waves; shells; the chronotope, or unit of space–time; maps; literary genre; and, underlying all of these, the metaphoric function of 'miraculous real(ism).'

I shall start with Joseph Bourne, a sour old man dressed in rags – as ragged and frayed as the "green edge of the world" where Port Annie is situated – who dies on the spot when he learns that the beautiful Raimey, just landed from a Peruvian freighter that has been left stranded in the town by a tidal wave, has come to Port Annie expressly to look for him. But, thanks to the "walking miracle" herself (1), Joseph Bourne is resurrected as a happy and rejuvenated sweet old man.

Names in Hodgins's work are often significant, and Bourne carries several meanings; *borne*, for example, past participle of 'to bear,' to transport (into and across *Port* Annie). Many things are indeed transported in this novel, especially by the two tidal waves: the freighter from which Raimey descends; and, twenty years earlier, on the crest of another tidal wave, the blue whale that cries like a human and, by the next day, has become the beautiful fat woman from whom the town takes its name (65). The waves signify the intrusion of the extraordinary into the ordinary (a common alternative definition of 'magical realism')[10] and of nature into culture

---

[9] See, for example, *The Invention of the World*, vii–x and 318–24, and *The Resurrection of Joseph Bourne*, 2, where Raimey's moving body traces the topography of Port Annie as she walks along every street, past every door, from one end of town to the other.

[10] Patrick White talks about the "extraordinary behind the ordinary" in "The Prodigal Son" (*Patrick White Speaks*, London: Jonathan Cape, 1990: 15), and Carpentier regards the "extraordinary" as one of the identifying features of marvellous realism: "The extraordinary is not necessarily lovely or beautiful. It is neither beautiful nor ugly; rather, it is amazing because it is strange. Everything strange, everything amazing, everything that eludes established norms is marvelous" ("The Baroque and the Marvelous Real," 101). From these words we can glimpse one reason for Carpentier's aversion to the term

(though, as we know, the culture of Port Annie is already extraordinary). The waves bear people and things, and mark the historical confines of the life of the community – from Fat Annie, who founds the town, to Raimey, who renews it but also triggers a chain of events ending with the landslide that blots out the settlement. As George Beeton, the service-station man, says:

> She's been in town for less than a day and already the world is beginning to change [...] My clock even stopped. No connection of course but what a co-incidence when it's kept perfect time for twenty years. (8)

One miracle delivered by a wave starts time, another ends it. "No connection of course"; but the reader will naturally make the connection, of course. The waves also bear handsome, miraculous men, like the sailor who lands on Angela Turner's bed and leaves her with child. This may very well be the first baby to be born to the new community forming at the end of the novel, among the shacks at the edge of Port Annie – those shacks that the Mayor and the respectable citizens of the town regard as an eyesore inhabited by the refuse of society, such as Joseph Bourne, and wish to destroy. In a sense, then, the new community's first-born is also delivered by a wave. It may be relevant to recall here that Strabo Becker, the 'historian' who reconstructs the identity of the community in *The Invention of the World* by 'transporting' the past into the present, is by profession a ferryman who bears souls and bodies across the waters, crossing the boundaries between different worlds. However, Becker is not just a historian but, like his Greek namesake, is also a geographer, because the history of a community is the history of its places.

Yet Joseph Bourne is also borne across the boundaries of life and death, and can travel in the 'wrong' direction. Indeed, he is reborn, resurrected through the wave: he resurfaces. And if we think at first that this is an unusual event, we have to revise our judgement, because Joseph Bourne has already disappeared and reappeared (like a *bourn*, or stream that disappears under the earth and then resurfaces later in its course),[11] has already died and been resurrected by his Jamaican wife. Indeed, as Larry Bowman the town librarian remarks, "the man may be easier to bring back to life than another person might be; he was used to it, it was always happening to him"

'magical realism': if 'realism' suggests conventions of writing, then marvellous realism is its exact opposite – that which evades all established conventions and norms.

[11] At the end of the novel Joseph disappears from the town – but the reader somehow knows that he will reappear in another place, perhaps in another life: "somehow it seems impossible that such a life could end," reads the novel's first epigraph, "quoted" from a "magazine article at the time of Joseph Bourne's disappearance."

(60). It is certainly no coincidence that his wife lives in Port Royal – another port on the edge, but one which, as it were, slid off the edge into the sea following the earthquake of 1692. However, like Joseph Bourne, Port Royal refused to die and can still be seen today under the clear water of the Caribbean, while, according to local lore, the tolling of its church bells is heard by fishermen when the sea is rough.

Again, Joseph Bourne is bourne, or bourn, in the sense of boundary stone; he is the very edge that he breaches. Even before he 'resurfaces,' he can hardly be distinguished from the town invaded by the sea creatures,[12] and after his resurrection his power is like the earthquake which caused the wave, a power, according to Larry Bowman, that can "slip the world out from everyone's feet any minute" (198).[13]

Joseph Bourne is resurrected as a "new man" – this is the title of the third part of the novel. In *The Invention of the World*, Maggie and Wade are, at the end, the "new man" and the "new woman," thanks to the interventions of Horseman, that strange personage who travels in a car so silvery that it is almost transparent and who can walk through the walls of a locked dungeon; a creature who, like the centaurs, half man and half horse, can cross the boundary between the world of the dead and that of the living.

The route followed by Raimey to reach Port Annie is significant. The miraculous girl comes from Barbados, the easternmost isle of the West Indies. She meets Joseph Bourne's wife in Jamaica, then boards a ship bound south, crosses South America from east to west, boards a northbound freighter, and rides into Port Annie on the crest of the wave caused by an Alaskan earthquake. The earth itself has moved to rush her here. Her journey reproduces the metaphoric journey of 'marvellous realism.'[14] First

---

[12] "His rags settled heavily around him, as if he too were draped with sodden strips of kelp like the roadside trees" (8).

[13] In a sense, this power, in the form of the waves, engulfs people and only those who know how to swim can stay on the surface and survive. Everyone is amazed at Angela Turner's strength as a swimmer, and it is she who gives birth to the new community's first child. Larry bathes with Raimey, and he is there at the end too, at Angela's side. This may also be the deeper significance of Mr Manku's determination to acquire his rightful "citizenship" of the town through the courageous act of overcoming his fear of water and learning to float. Despite the humiliations to which he is subjected, he keeps his dignity and will remain on the surface as one of the citizens of the new community.

[14] The suggestion has been also made by Geoff Hancock. "It is tempting to regard this 'marvellous' invasion coming in from the sea as the introduction of the South American 'real maravilloso' in Canadian Literature"; thus Jeanne Delbaere in her "Magic Realism: The Energy of the Margins," in *Postmodern Fiction in Canada*, ed. Theo D'haen & Hans

experienced by European explorers, it then travels across South America, acquiring different versions of itself as it goes. It subsequently moves north towards Canada (picking up echoes of the American myth of the frontier on the way). The journey is literally metaphoric: it bears across borders that are thus annulled in a cultural *trans-latio* and metamorphosis. Indeed, even when Raimey leaves, or simply disappears, her presence is still felt and *trans-forms* the town and its inhabitants. In a sense she does not leave at all, but disperses: Rita Rentalla inherits her walk (150); Angela Turner, her laughter (172); Kamalijit, Mr Manku's grandson, the light in her eyes (195); Jenny, in her final, regenerating erotic dance, her grace (268). I shall come back to metaphors and metamorphoses. First I wish to consider the frontier, and then the wave, this literally metaphoric wave that crosses natural boundaries and transforms the very spaces it traverses.

Jeremy Fell, who has recurrent nightmares of having to appear before Judge Joseph Bourne, berates the citizens of the town, who "just couldn't seem to get it into their heads that this was the frontier they lived in, and what they were trying to beat down was the frontier spirit of progress" (107). And, later on, Damon West, the devilishly "goodlooking stranger" (147) from the land development agency, exhorts the same citizens to vote in favour of the development of the land around Port Annie: "The spirit we are here to celebrate tonight is the spirit of the frontier," he claims (240). It seems clear that the meaning of the "frontier" is quite different from that of the precarious and fertile "edge" on which Port Annie is perched: it is a com-modified myth imported – like Damon West and the desired American Tourists – from "below the border" (165). The myth is as perverted as West's name: the marvellous Port Annie is on the western edge of an island off the western coast of Canada, and the land developer who wants to destroy its natural environment should have no right to this surname (his first name, evocative of demons, is certainly more appropriate). In an essay entitled "Landscape and Literature," Kenneth Mitchell has described how the myth of the frontier which has shaped the literature and the literary history of the United States cannot be applied in the same way to Canadian literature. In Canada, Mitchell claims, the frontier is still unconquered, hostile, and that is why there is no consistent myth of the conquering individual. Mitchell quotes Margaret Atwood's words: "Nature seen as dead, or alive but indif-ferent, or alive and actively hostile towards man is a common image of

Bertens (Postmodern Studies 6; Amsterdam & Atlanta GA: Rodopi/Antwerp: Restant, 1992): 90.

Canadian literature." This, Mitchell rejoins, is because "Canadians have never been able to dominate their environment, historically or culturally."[15] Yet the landscape in Hodgins's novels does not necessarily annihilate: mudslides may consume whole towns, but the harmony between man and the environment is not broken, as I shall argue in more detail later (this is probably one of the features of most magical-realist, or marvellous-realist, fiction). The opposition dramatized in Hodgins's novel is therefore between the idea of 'frontier' (with its associations of division between man and his environment), aggressiveness (as in the myth of the 'conquest'), or commodification (as in the perverted "spirit of the frontier" advocated by West, the Mayor and their supporters) and the idea of 'the edge,' the place to be lived in and on, the unstable but rich strip of dreamland (see below), where invasions are natural and where people decide to settle. The edge cannot be 'conquered' because there is no conquerable land beyond it, only an absolute 'beyond.'

But, if edges cannot be conquered, they can still be crossed; by waves, for instance. Port Annie's final wave brings about the invasion of a space by its opposite, a literal displacement. Thus the town is invaded by the creatures of the sea:

> Just the tail end of a gigantic wave that had nearly worn itself out, but still it had swept in with enough force to leave salt water and sand, stunned fish and shreds of tortured driftwood on the streets and front yards of houses for two rows up the hill. Long strips of kelp and seedy knots of seaweed lay in doorways, starfish and blue mussels bloomed like brilliant flowers in the spongy grass, and periwinkles spilled themselves like tiny jewels across the roads. When that seabird [Raimey] walked across the streets she might just as well have been walking on the bottom of the ocean; it was only natural that every eye should follow her. (3)

Like Port Royal, Port Annie has metaphorically slid off the edge of normality and mixed with the ocean. Here a bird can walk on the bottom of the sea; here the extraordinary has become "only natural," and a resurrected man who keeps eating in order to avoid "slipping off" the edge of humanity and disappearing into pure spirit (233) can perform miracles as a matter of course.[16] Throughout the novel, the town remains full of seaweed, boats on

---

[15] Kenneth Mitchell, "Landscape and Literature," in *Geography and Literature: A Meeting of the Disciplines*, ed. William E. Mallory & Paul Simpson–Housley (Syracuse NY: Syracuse UP, 1987): 26–29.

[16] This normality of the marvellous can be contrasted with Damon West's arrival in town, when the day has an "unnatural" look (149).

the tops of trees, fish, and shells. The shells are especially interesting creatures, with such beautiful, perfect shapes, borne by the sea onto the land. It is like an invasion by aliens of a space not theirs, which they then transform; metaphorized across space, they metamorphose it. Port Annie is transformed into marvellous dreamland: "The tidal wave of sea-gifts had left the lower town decorated with the underwater brilliance of a dream and filled the rainy air with the unfamiliar scent of a stirred-up sea" (7). How many places are there, Angela Turner wonders,

> where the grass and the sidewalk were studded with beautiful shells and glittering stones from the ocean even after a hundred people had spent hours trying to get rid of them – as if they multiplied by themselves, or as if someone was scattering them around in the night while no one was looking? (62)

Shells, with their regular and yet fantastic geometries, as Gaston Bachelard writes in *The Poetics of Space*, are a source of marvel, magic, and miracles:

> And these forms are so numerous, often so original, that after a positive examination of the shell world, the imagination is defeated by reality. Here it is nature that imagines, and nature is very clever.[17]

Is this not a possible translation of the *real maravilloso* – reality that defeats imagination?[18] A nature both imaginative and very clever? Bachelard continues:

> One has only to look at pictures of ammonites to realise that, as early as the Mesozoic Age, mollusks constructed their shells according to the teachings of a transcendental geometry.

---

[17] Gaston Bachelard, *The Poetics of Space*, tr. Maria Jolas (*La Poétique de l'espace*, 1958; tr. 1965; Boston MA: Beacon, 1994): 105.

[18] The shells are, as I said, aliens that invade familiar space. As Chanady has pointed out, in order to see the real as marvellous, it is necessary to be an outsider – like the Spanish *conquistadores* Carpentier writes about, but, by the same token, like Carpentier himself, a descendant of those colonizers ("The Origins and Development of Magic Realism in Latin American Fiction," 52–53). However, Carpentier points out that his sense of the marvellous has been heightened by his experience of returning to Latin America after travelling in Europe and in the East: "The Latin American returns to his own world and begins to understand many things" ("On the Marvelous Real in America," 83). In Port Annie, everyone is a stranger, an "alien." As Raimey says: "A strange town [...] where everyone treated her like some kind of foreign creature, not even human, when as far as she could see there was not a person in the place who wasn't as foreign as she was, everyone of them came from somewhere else" (128). The shells are as alien as the people: they come from somewhere which is "elsewhere" by definition, and thus it is "only natural" that sea creatures should exist alongside birds and humans, as well as whales, in such a place.

Geometry transcends reality. So this is not just a magical or marvellous reality, but a miraculous one too. "Ammonites built their homes around the axis of a logarithmic spiral."[19] Fossil ammonites buried in the ground might have inspired Donal Keneally's fantastical spiralling descent into the earth, but this is an inverted miracle that does not produce marvels and, instead, destroys.

Shells are indeed containers from which, in medieval grotesque representations and in illuminated manuscripts, almost anything could come out, as though from the hat of a magician: hares, birds (like Raimey the seabird girl), deer, dogs. Indeed, shells contain marvels and miracles, and goddesses like Venus may be born from them.[20]

The waves bring things to the surface: twigs, driftwood – such as the piece used by Fat Annie to make herself a husband – seaweed, shells, fish, and of course whales that become women, and ships from which beautiful girls and sailors/gods emerge. An upward movement is counterbalanced by the downward course of the mudslide that threatens and finally engulfs the town. Down and then up; up and then down. When Fat Annie organizes her own and her husband's funeral (the husband's body is found under the roots of a tree 934 years old, and she wants their funerals to be celebrated together), the garbage trucks hired to carry the coffins (the town does not have proper hearses) race each other up the winding mountain road, and, on a sharp bend, Annie's coffin shoots off the truck, over the precipice and into the sea. After this episode, Annie decides "to ascend" (70), and so climbs up to the first floor of the town's hotel, built where the centenary tree had been, not to be seen again for the next twenty years. However, the Mayor, who wants to celebrate the twentieth anniversary of Port Annie in grand style, decides to go up to her room and bring her down. Thus he finds that Annie is no longer the fat and beautiful woman of twenty years past, the legendary "tub of love" that everyone remembers, but a shrunken, wrinkled, little thing sitting in a rocking-chair, her feet not even reaching the floor. He nonetheless wants to take her down, and picks up chair and all. However, on the stairs his foot slips over the edge of a step, and Annie once more goes shooting down as she did when stuck in her coffin twenty years earlier; only, this time she dies. As Annie shoots down, the landslide descends, carrying tons of mud that bury the town.

---

[19] Bachelard, *The Poetics of Space*, 105.

[20] Bachelard, *The Poetics of Space*, 107–108. Bachelard adds: "The surest sign of wonder is exaggeration. And since the inhabitant of a shell can amaze us, the imagination will soon make amazing creatures, more amazing than reality, issue from the shell" (107).

The vertical axis also unites various episodes of *The Invention of the World*. Donal Keneally, son of a woman and a bull, is born on top of a mountain, and his life is a constant descent, until he buries himself in the spiralling tunnel under the house in the Revelation Colony of Truth on Vancouver Island. Again, ever since her childhood, when she had to hide under the floorboards of her parents' house, Maggie Kyle's desire has been to go up, higher and higher. Finally she climbs the mountain where Keneally was born and then, from the aeroplane, sees the ragged coast of Vancouver Island and finally gives up her obsession with maps, aware at last that their representation of the land never corresponds to reality.

The question of conformity between the topography of a place and the history of its community or, conversely, the non-conformity of the reality of a place and its printed representations calls to mind a number of disparate, but not unconnected, ideas – Jean Baudrillard's reflections on the decline of the geographical map; Benoît Mandelbrot's fractal geometry; and Mikhail Bakhtin's 'chronotope.'

According to Baudrillard, when there is nothing more to add to the geographical map, the mysteries of the earth subside and the fantastic abandons this planet and goes off, beyond terrestrial space, to discover interstellar reality.[21] I would argue, however, that this need not be the case. In Hodgins's fiction, maps cease to conform to reality. Maggie gives up their use, not in order to penetrate to the other side of planetary space – as if the map were a frontier – but in order to stay on *this* side, in the minute spaces of the territory that maps cannot represent. What we see is the search for a new way of representing the earth *as human space*, one that can account for the "ragged green edge of the world" where Port Annie is situated and where people are under stress, the sheer edge where poetic language is born. What is needed is a means of representation that can measure the relation between a place and the subjects that inhabit it. We may thus turn to Mandelbrot's fractal geometry, which looks at the spaces between integral numbers in order to discover fractional dimensions and thus represent what

---

[21] "When there is no longer any virgin territory, and thus one available to the imaginary, *when the map covers the whole territory, something like the principle of reality disappears*. In this way, the conquest of space constitutes an irreversible crossing toward the the loss of the terrestrial referential. There is a hemorrhaging of reality as an internal coherence of a limited universe, once the limits of this universe recede into infinity. The conquest of space that follows that of the planet is equal to derealizing (dematerializing) human space, or to transferring it into a hyperreal of simulation"; Jean Baudrillard, *Simulacra and Simulation*, tr Sheila Faria Glaser (*Simulacres et simulations*, 1981; Ann Arbor: of Michigan P, 1994): 123–24 (emphasis in the original).

no geographical map that follows Euclidean geometry or any of its adaptations can actually find. For Mandelbrot's geometry reveals the geography of the interstices and ragged edges of space, capable of containing infinite lines within limited spaces. In almost miraculous fashion, it allows the transcendent to intervene in the finite human and terrestrial spaces and demonstrates that by increasing geographical approximation we come no nearer to a true and accurate representation of space than does any large-scale map. In other words, the real is ultimately unrepresentable.[22]

But the question of maps and of the representation of territory is still more complex. Maps try to keep pace with reality, but are always at least a step behind. They are implicated in the question of frontiers and discovery/ conquest: as explorers and conquistadores have 'discovered' new worlds and lands, so the maps have changed shape and size and countries have been moved from one place to another. When America was 'discovered,' it took some time for geographers to know where to put it. Apparently, a globe manufactured in Spain in the early sixteenth century and owned by the university of Cracow around 1520 placed the newly discovered continent in the Indian Ocean, south-east of Madagascar. One would have expected Spaniards to have known, but America evidently wandered the seas before it settled where it is now. Indeed, it has barely settled yet, as earthquakes that deliver various types of god-like creatures show. Maps somehow fail to catch up with the land they attempt to pin down in a precise place.

If waves are transcendental forces that transport objects and people and transform shapes and maps, then the primordial wave that delivers Fat Annie – the first woman, who creates the first man from twigs and rushes – may be seen as a marvellous inverted metaphor for the myth of the

---

[22] It is uncannily resonant in this context to read the work of the artist/cartogapher Tim Robinson on the landscapes of the western edge of Ireland: "'Interdigitation' is the fine term I overhear the scientists using for the way in which one natural zone meets another along a complex boundary of salients and re–entrants; [...] but etymologically it is a little inadequate to such cases as this Connemara coastline where land and sea not only entwine their crooked fingers but each element abandons particles of itself temporarily or permanently to the clutch of the other. [...] To the bays that ramify into inlets and creeks correspond the peninsulas with their subsidiary headlands and spits; the lakes of the boglands are sometimes linked into archipelago–like sequences, as the major islands are joined by causeways; there are matching ambiguities too, lakes that become inlets at high tide, and islands that can be reached on foot when the tide is out"; Robinson, "Setting Foot on the Shores of Connemara," in *Setting Foot on the Shores of Connemara & Other Writings* (Dublin: Lilliput, 1996): 21–22. See also Robinson's later reflections, both on the landscape and on the essay I have just quoted from, in "A Connemara Fractal," 78–102.

creation.[23] It may also evoke the miraculous transformations of humankind into the increasingly more perfect, semi-divine forms of life described by David Malouf in *An Imaginary Life*.[24] Hodgins uses some lines from Malouf's lyrical novel in one of the epigraphs of *The Resurrection of Joseph Bourne*:

> What else should our lives be but a continual series of beginnings, of painful settings out into the unknown, pushing off from the edges of consciousness into the mystery of what we have not yet become, except in dreams....

Life is but a ragged, unstable edge to be pushed off from in order to go forth into new, uncharted mysteries. Joseph Bourne himself, after his resurrection, is still a human being, but one "impatient with human evolution" (248), who needs to push off from its edges.[25] Central in the quotation above is the emphasis on a "series of beginnings." There may be related to Bourne's resurrection and the rebirth of the community after the landslide. The idea of renewal is, indeed, implicit in the new men and women of both *The Resurrection of Joseph Bourne* and *The Invention of the World*. The wedding of Maggie and Wade, which Hodgins calls a "second growth" (the immediate reference is to the second growth of trees cut for timber), associates the regeneration of the earth and the trees with the regeneration of the community of loggers on the island. This is the context in which one thinks of Bakhtin's 'chronotope,' originally a term used by Einstein to designate the unity of time and space.

According to Bakhtin, the original chronotope denotes a close, harmonious relation between man and the environment, between natural and human rhythms, and between time and space. This harmony has been lost

---

[23] Indeed, the story of Fat Annie is in a way the revised story of humanity – after the creation, her fall down the stairs is indeed the Fall of Port Annie, and the mayor, who causes it, is, like Adam, "preparing himself to accept the blame for everything that happened next. The future, whatever it may include, was already all his fault" (247). But another myth, another form of creation, is also evoked: in the boat stuck at the top of the tree and finally freed again by the mudslide, one discovers a whole marine world, a "colorful living stew" (260) that cannot but recall the primordial soup from which life first developed.

[24] "I speak to you, reader, as one who lives in another century [...] to you, unknown friend, who do not exist at this time of my writing and whose face, whose form even, I cannot imagine. Can one imagine the face of a god? For that surely is what you must be at your great distance from us – the god who has begun to stir in our depths, to gather his being out of us"; David Malouf, *An Imaginary Life* (New York: George Braziller, 1978): 18.

[25] In fact, as soon as Raimey reveals that she has come for him, he feels that "his head was about to split, he felt the screaming sound of his whole body being torn open, pieces of him pushing to be born" (34). In Malouf's novel, Ovid dreams that he is a pool of water whose surface is fractured: "I break in circles. [...] I am broken again. The disturbance is fearful, a noisy crashing of waves against the edges of me" (*An Imaginary Life*, 61–62).

in modern literature owing to the advent of literary symbolization, which grew together with the division of society into classes.[26] But Hodgins's novels, like much magical-realist narrative, restores the lost harmony with natural space and time,[27] even if the scale here is not that of the seasons and of the rising and setting of the sun, but the longer cycles of the growth of the trees or of the telluric movements along the Pacific rim.[28]

The history of a place and of a community, resurrection, renewal – these are clearly epic topics. Indeed, like any epic, both *The Resurrection of Joseph Bourne* and *The Invention of the World* draw from myth, history, legend, folklore, and exaggerate, mythify, compile infinite lists. However, *The Resurrection of Joseph Bourne* – like *The Invention of the World* – also mocks the epic genre, most explicitly in Mrs Barnstone's poem "The Last Days of Port Annie." If an epic tradition is in any way positively invoked, it is the Rabelaisian one, as in Fat Annie's exaggerated proportions and "gargantuan mouth" (67), in the battles of *The Invention of the World*, its banquets and mock-epic list of wedding gifts. However, Mrs Barnstone's poem, just like any inadequate map, has a major fault: it fails to connect with or grasp reality, or even to come anywhere near it. She blames the inhabitants of the town for lacking a clear vision, when in fact it is her vision that is inadequate: "maybe because they lived in real life and not in a poem they were too uncertain about the issues to see things in terms of black and white" (236). Mrs Barnstone's poem draws a clear line between black and white, life and death, missing the uncertainties of the edge on which they live. She knows she is missing something, but just what this is escapes her:

> Why couldn't she see it? She had the uncomfortable feeling that, though her masterpiece was recording all the action she could find, the real story was going on behind it somewhere, perhaps invisibly, or just out of the range of her vision. (236)[29]

---

[26] See Mikhail M. Bakhtin, "Forms of Time and of the Chronotope in the Novel," *The Dialogic Imagination. Four Essays*, ed. Michael Holquist, tr. Caryl Emerson (Austin: U of Texas P, 1981): 84–258: esp. 205–40.

[27] It is on these grounds that one therefore needs to reject the idea of a straightforwardly hostile environment (and, if the "frontier" comes with it, of this myth too).

[28] From the start, *The Resurrection of Joseph Bourne* replaces official dates with a temporality measured on natural events: "When the girl from the Peruvian freighter walked for the first time through Port Annie, on the twenty-second day of constant rain" (1).

[29] When the mudslide comes down, even the stiff Mrs Barnstone begins "get a glimpse of what her epic poem had entirely missed," but her reaction is typical: "and the faster she put it all behind her the better. 'Just keep on going,' she told her husband" (254), as they abandon the town.

In *The Resurrection of Joseph Bourne*, there is an abundance of literary discussion relating to genre and explicit questions about the relationship between literature and reality.[30] This may be taken as evidence of further reflection on the failure of established, rigid literary conventions, such as realism, to account for reality. No established literary form will do; any convention will fail, because it loses touch with reality as soon as it becomes convention. So that literary form, like everything else, must be put 'under stress,' on edge, and be constantly transformed. Only thus can it keep up with the incessant metamorphoses of the real.

According to Bakhtin, Rabelais' carnivalesque epics succeed in reintegrating chronos and topos, and in finding a new harmony between the body and the rhythms of nature, life and death, thus interrupting, at least momentarily, the process of symbolization that distances man from natural times and spaces. Indeed, in both *The Invention of the World* and *The Resurrection of Joseph Bourne*, there is an explicit lack of trust in symbols: "Words only nibble at reality," says Becker the ferryman/historian/geographer in the former novel; "symbols not much better." Then, "if words won't do and symbols fail," what can one do but listen to instinct to "translate the fake material world we seem to experience back into pre-Eden truth"?[31] And what can one do, asks Joseph Bourne, "if old metaphors won't work [...]?" "Eternity," is the reply, "can only be expressed by implication" (226).

What can one do? If language is not enough and symbols fail, if old metaphors no longer work, then perhaps the answer is not necessarily to abandon language, but to try to renew its metaphoric force – place language at the edge, put words under stress, push off from their edges into uncharted territories, perhaps push them over the edge; make language perform its metaphors and turn it into a continuous metamorphosis (as in Malouf's novel, where Ovid translates, metaphorizes, metamorphoses him-

---

[30] For Honorelle Skinner, Joseph's resurrection may make a good topic for an *episode* but not as a story, "because of course the narrative was dead, a useless dated form of literature as everybody knew" (63). Larry Bowman prefers romances to novels because in the former "hoping was not considered a crime" (143) and he can fantasise about himself as a hero. Marvellous real fiction allows the commonplace to coexist with the extraordinary, the pusillanimous with the heroic, hope to survive, and stories to be told; but the literature that Larry reads has no more contact with the real than Mrs Barnstone's poem – it does not leave any space for the "small and foolish and scared" like himself (199), and becomes a mere form of escapism.

[31] Jack Hodgins, *The Invention of the World* (Scarborough, Ontario: Macmillan, 1977): 321.

self and the Child on the *tabula rasa* of the physical and mental landscape of the steppe).[32]

This is one of the strengths of magic/miraculous real/ism – the capacity of the work actively to transform space, time, existence and its categories, whether literary genre, biological genus, life and death, by travelling across, redefining or cancelling any type of border, by translating across cultures. "Actively transform" should thus not be read as synonymous with the artificial transformations and juxtapositions denounced by Alejo Carpentier, but as an invitation to draw on the different cultures that have contributed, and still contribute, to the nature of (in this case) the American continent and its inhabitants, to its *human geography*. It means uncovering the coexistence in the real of the ordinary and the extraordinary, the normal and the marvellous or miraculous, the rational and the mysterious. As Jenny Chambers says, not everything in this world may easily be understood: "there were still some mysteries left, thank goodness, and lots of room for new ways of looking at things" (205). Thank goodness. This is also the way Joseph Bourne looks at his lines of poetry, "taking his time, looking over every line from a dozen different angles before recording it, and even questioning the value of his work while he was at it" (226).

In the interview mentioned earlier, Hodgins clearly distinguishes between invention and creation. In *The Invention of the World*, the main issue is the reality "that exists beyond the imitation reality that we are too often contented with. The created rather than the invented world." The novel is "a story about counterfeits."[33] Maggie's maps are as much a counterfeit as Wade's fake historical fort and Keneally's illusionist magic. In *The Resurrection of Joseph Bourne*, the Mayor's attempt to "put Port Annie on the map" through advertising ploys and tourist traps fails – indeed, leads to the town's disappearing under a mountain of mud. At the top of Keneally's mountain in Ireland, Wade stamps Maggie's map into the mud.[34] Mayor

---

[32] For a study of the meaning and transformations of space in Malouf's novel, see Carmen Concilio's fine essay "Topology vs Geometry: The Relational Geography of Self and Other in David Malouf's *An Imaginary Life* and *Remembering Babylon*," in *Routes of the Roots: Geography and Literature in the English Speaking Countries*, ed. Isabella M. Zoppi (Rome: Bulzoni, 1998): 736–50. On the representation of territory in Canadian and Australian literature, see Graham Huggan, *Territorial Disputes: Maps and Mapping Strategies in Contemporary Canadian and Australian Fiction* (Toronto: U of Toronto P, 1994).

[33] Coulas–Fink, "'If Words Won't Do, and Symbols Fail': Hodgins's Magic Reality," 118.

[34] Jeanne Delbaere has described this moment as one of the examples of magical ʳealism as hyper-realism in Hodgins's novel: "we have here an example of the way in

Weins' fake magic is nothing more than a "monkeying with metaphysics" (78) – but a monkeying which forgets that here metaphysics and physics may coincide. The land is already marvellous; it does not need "improving" as Mayor and Damon West the land developer from "below the border" suggest. Creation is miraculous, but mere invention opens the door to false-hood, or to counterfeits that do not actively change but just pretend to do so. Yet literature, as we know from the classics, is also, and above all, *inventio*. Where does this leave us? Perhaps with just another sterile literary discus-sion, like the one among the women of the Port Annie Creative Writing Club, chaired by Amelia Barnstone (63). Or perhaps with Joseph Bourne's poetry, which undergoes transformation under the very eyes and in the minds of its readers, and whose meaning constantly changes, offering to each a personal vision.[35] Or with the erotic dance of the stripper Jenny Chambers, whose final creative act (epic, insofar as it regenerates the com-munity) transports the survivors of Port Annie into a new existence, giving them new life and making them "new men" and "new women" (Joseph Bourne, that regenerate prophet, had told her, when she was in despair, that one day she would dance for them):

> their own contribution to the music's beat, the body movements, the frenzy of her need to free herself from the thing, all of it united them somehow. This old earth could throw you off its back like a bronco any time it wanted, but it couldn't break that link which ran from soul to soul [...] In Jenny's dance they all saw something different, something the same. (270)

First of all, *inventio* means to find. The poet and novelist must thus look for their subject-matter and inspiration in the human and physical landscape of their everyday, ordinary and extraordinary reality. Like Strabo Becker, who 'finds' the history of this community and of the place in the memory of the island's people, they must write a mnemotopography. Their 'magic' literature, despite its current label of 'realism,' needs to find the as-yet-undiscovered real, rather than reproduce the visible, and will thus re-metaphorize language as well as the real. It must seek to breach boundaries,

---

which such a magic realist juxtaposition – Wades shoe in the middle of Maggie's map – subtly shifts into hyper–realism owing to Maggie's new clarity of vision" (*Postmodern Fiction in Canada*, 78).

[35] For Larry the poems are pornography, for Angela they are love poems; for Jenny they are about looking for a place, for Charlie Reynolds the journalist they are about communication (cf 91–95). After all, this is just a reflection of Joseph's protean nature itself: "inside all those layers he was an undefinable shape – perhaps as lumpy as a potato, perhaps as thin as a wire, perhaps a shape as changing as his changing moods" (7).

place itself on "the ragged edge" and accept – indeed, seek – the risk of going 'over the edge' (which of course also means to go mad: and madmen, as we know, create, do not simply invent). For it is necessary to go 'over' and 'beyond' "the ragged edge of this world" in order to become the subjects of metaphors endowed with magical, miraculous powers; because it is only in the interstices of the ragged edge of miracles that everyone is always alien and the extraordinary is "only natural."

 og • ຂ

Bees, Bodies, and Magical Miscegenations
Robert Kroetsch's *What The Crow Said*

———————————————————————— ℈

Luca Biagiotti

W HAT THE CROW SAID was published in 1978, a year before Jack Hodgins's *The Invention of the World* and three years after *World of Wonders*, the third novel in Robertson Davies' *Deptford Trilogy*. A fictional westward journey of literary exploration, from Davies' Ontario to Hodgins's Vancouver, which seems to take place in the second half of the Seventies, examines and scans new approaches both to reality and to narrative conventions. Their coast-to-coast journey takes these novelists from the circus where Magnus Eisengrim, Davies' Ontario magician in *World of Wonders*, performs his tricks, through Kroetsch's blurred borders between Alberta and Saskatchewan, to Hodgins's island of 'resurrections' and postmodern mythical colonies. Each carries with him his own epistemological and conceptual tools. However, a common feature of their literary pilgrimage is that magical investigation of the real, or rather, their thorough investigation of the magic *beyond/in* the real, whether the 'real' be understood as the external world or as the self, whenever the subject's channels of perception are other than those imposed by acquired epistemological (and narrative) models.

In the course of this hypothetical pilgrimage through Canada, Jungian psychology seems gradually to lose its function as a mediatory hermeneutic grid (as in Davies) and to become an identifiable inter-discourse.

Davies' novels are permeated by the Jungian process of discovery and acceptance of the marvellous in the real, a position explicitly held by Dunstan Ramsay, the narrator of two of the three volumes of the *Deptford*

Trilogy. Dunstan undergoes a process of self-knowledge, spiritual crisis, and rebirth. He ends his fictional career in the awareness that the marvellous, irrational and instinctive are an integral part of the self, which, if it is to achieve psychological wholeness, must acknowledge spiritual domains repressed by Western *ratio*-centred culture, which is radically dualistic and has separated matter from spirit, body from soul, male from female, repressing and splitting psychological experience. This entails a painful journey within the innermost self, in order to become more open and permeable to what has been, or is, unconscious. The aim of this journey is to reassemble libidos connected to fragments of the self that are at work, unacknowledged, in the shadows.

Dunstan Ramsay's book on the psychology of myth and legend, his final legacy to future generations, is an attempt to give systematic structure to his ideas on the authentic understanding (in a Heideggerian sense) of the human condition, ideas on which he finally builds the architecture of his interior life as narrated in the *Trilogy*. Ramsay's rebirth is exclusively spiritual or metaphorical. And all the *Trilogy*'s main characters have to face their Jungian 'dark side' if they want to survive. Those who are unwilling to do so live a life devoted to the suppression of instinct and the exaltation of rationality. Yet these, too, have to come to terms with their dark side, as happens grotesquely to the tycoon Boy Staunton in *World of Wonders*. They all face mystery, irrationality; but most of them end up on the Jungian analyst's couch. Jungian psychology provides the *Trilogy* with a specific and coherent frame of reference.

Davies' fictional world is inhabited by relatives of Lawrence's Kate or Hesse's Harry Haller, and the world which constitutes the framework for the spiritual dis/adventures of his heroes imitates the one we ourselves more or less comfortably inhabit, and which we can recognize and identify. The marvellous, in turn, is explained by analytical psychology and by the circus (Magnus's magic is merely a set of tricks), and the only really mysterious, unexplained accident remains Boy Staunton's death.

One trait that unites all of the novels mentioned above is the frequent presence of antinomies and dualities. The clashing and intermixing of two different areas, thus producing a new reality, which in Davies may be spiritual (matter versus spirit), epistemological (Cartesian knowledge versus faith) or psychological (unconscious versus conscious, *ratio* versus instinct), is also a prime constituent of Kroetsch's *What the Crow Said*, and of Hodgins's *The Resurrection of Joseph Bourne* and *The Invention of the World*.

If Kroetsch's work echoes any particular philosophy, it is the philosophy of nature of the Romantic period, which had revived the myth of the androgyne (a profound influence, incidentally, on Jung's theories). This philosophy argued the essential unity of man and nature, and saw each individual being as a specific form engendered by the eternal struggle of contrasting powers: the male–female polarity issuing from the split of the primordial androgyne. However, these antinomies are discussed in Kroetsch in a different narrative form, quite distinct from that adopted by Davies. If they are finally resolved, it is not through the attainment of a new psychological status: Kroetsch deals with the same issues but shifts the main focus of investigation from the mind to the body, from the written to the oral word, and from an analytical process to one of 'semiotic miscegenation,' a 'beyond-the-ordinary' encounter with signs.[1] This paper concentrates on the significance of these miscegenations in *What the Crow Said*.

Geographical miscegenation

Big Indian (Municipality of Bigknife) is a small town that Kroetsch places on the indeterminate border between Alberta and Saskatchewan: "The Municipality of Bigknife lay ambiguously on the border between the provinces of Alberta and Saskatchewan."[2] Kroetsch very carefully locates his fictitious town between two "conflicting" toponyms, one imperial (Alberta), the other indigenous (Saskatchewan), and explicitly declares his difficulty in giving its exact place on the map:

> no one, due to a surveyor's error, had ever been able to locate conclusively where the boundaries were supposed to be. The south end of the municipality, beyond the poplar bluffs and the fields of grain, faded into bald prairie and a Hutterite colony; the north end vanished into the bush country and an Indian reserve. (36)

---

[1] The encounter, in a fictional frame, of characters with a different ontological status is employed by a branch of contemporary fiction that deals with the investigation of an 'other' reality: history. Much of the historiographic metafiction in the English language shocks the reader by making famous historical people coexist with fictional characters invented by the author (Nigel Williams's *Star Turn*, Salman Rushdie's *Midnight's Children*, Simon Schama's *Dead Certainties*, Chris Scott's *The Heretic*), or with characters derived from literary tradition (Timothy Findley's *Famous Last Words*).

[2] Robert Kroetsch, *What the Crow Said* (Don Mills, Ontario: General, 1978): 36. Further page references are in the text.

If the municipality itself lies between two provinces that evoke a conflict between different cultures and languages, the borders of Big Indian, located within the municipality, are equally blurred. Big Indian is a small town that has grown up in the middle of a landscape with the characteristically Canadian morphological features of prairie and wilderness, upon which the attempt to impose borders and delimitations has been in vain. The space around Big Indian significantly tends to "fade" (south) or "vanish" (north). In the encounter between two different cultures, encoded in the names of the neighbouring provinces, an (according to rational criteria) undefined and undefinable geographical area is situated. This land has no precise borders. Kroetsch's focus is not so much on separateness or division as on the questioning of limits and borders imposed on any kind of 'body,' whether human, textual or, in this case, geographical. The only recognizable points of delimitation are the Hutterite colony and the Indian reserve, with their clear political implications.

The small town has no margins and no centre, and the only attempt at finding its centre, where suddenly summer never comes, is unsuccessful. John Skandl tries to fulfil his dream of erecting a huge tower of ice:

> A center. A beacon. A guide. A warning sign. On the ice on the river, a high flame in the closing night. (41)

He actually succeeds in building this tower, but someone lights a fire in it and this causes it to melt. Skandl's furious desire for verticality (common to many male characters in the novel) and a centre signifies power and control; but his ambition is frustrated.

The 'ambiguity' of the geographical collocation is significant, insofar as the town becomes not so much a *trait-d'union* or a 'link' (a synthesis) between the two colonial cultures as a morphological point of contact and fusion between two different cultural 'tectonic plates.' It is a moment of spatial and cultural 'folding,'[3] where different languages decide to listen to, rather than silence, each other.

∾ • ∾

---

[3] For the use of this term I am indebted to Rawdon Wilson's essay "The Metamorphoses of Fictional Space: Magical Realism," in *Magical Realism: Theory, History, Community*, ed. Lois Parkinson Zamora & Wendy B. Faris (Durham NC/London: Duke UP, 1995): 209–34.

Other miscegenations

What the Crow Said opens with a magical miscegenation, a 'seduction' scene
in which a woman is impregnated by a swarm of bees. Vera Lang changes
into something new: "The drones, bigger, slower, moving with a hot deli-
beration, seeking always the queen bee. Vera herself, swarmed into a new
being" (10). Her body does not belong to her any longer; it has fused with
nature. The body becomes the privileged means of a kind of communication
with the world that is inevitably forbidden to other, more intellectual, codes.
With Vera, the body becomes the vehicle of a wider knowledge, which
releases all its power through the ecstasy of the senses. Like the queen bee
that has been impregnated and is hiding inside her, Vera becomes pregnant
and will have a baby that the wolves will bring up. The very moment Vera is
about to reach the climax of her sexual encounter, her body absorbs the
surrounding space: "The hum of wings melded earth and sky into the thick-
ness of her skin" (11). For the first of many times in the novel, up and above,
sky and earth become one. Vera has "no mind left for thinking, no fear, no
dream, no memory" (11). Instinct and the unconscious have caused this first
miscegenation. How is the event narrated? A brief look at the narrative situation may help define how, and where, the reader is placed in relation to
Vera's magical adventure.

The erotic encounter, the act of the bees' entering into Vera's body and
the enraptured movements of her body in response to them, is narrated in a
sensuous and simple manner:

> Without quite opening her eyes she knew they had touched down onto her
> arms, onto her belly, her legs. For how long she lay transfixed there was never
> a way to tell. Somewhere, long ago, the queen had been impregnated, her body
> never more to need that mating. Why the drones followed her, why they
> mistook a swarming into a new nest for a mating flight, was simply a mystery.
> Vera, the bees in her blond hair now, touching onto her cheeks, could only lie
> still. (10)

Vera Lang's "motives" are unknown both to the narrator and to the citizens
of Big Indian. All they are aware of is the almost "human cry" coming down
to them from the patch of flowers where Vera is living her erotic experience.
The citizens are waiting for the train-whistle, a sound that symbolizes the

progress and the technological colonization of their land, but what they actually hear is a sound they are not able to decode.[4]

Narrator and citizen equally accept the event; they do not question its reality. Like so many historians, they wonder if the event could be the cause of "everything": years of plenty and disaster, the summer that never comes, biblical plagues, a flood. The narrator neither offers a rational explanation for the encounter nor encourages a sense of doubt in the reader. He/she simply accepts it. What the narrator and the citizens wonder at has to do with the natural course of mating between drones and queen bee: how do the drones mistake a simple search for a new nest for a mating flight? In this sense, it is not the sexual encounter between Vera and the bees that is questioned, but why the drones, in a certain sense, altered the laws of nature.

The narrator's neutral tone, together with the marvellous character of the events established from the very opening of *What the Crow Said* (echoing another famous opening by García Márquez), positions the reader within the narrative.

> People, years later, blamed everything on the bees; it was the bees, they said, seducing Vera Lang, that started everything. How the town came to prosper, and then to decline, and how the road never got built, the highway that would have joined the town and the municipality to the world beyond, and how the sky itself, finally, took umbrage: it was all because one afternoon in April the swarming bees found Vera Lang asleep, there in a patch of wild flowers on the edge of the valley. (7)

The narrator knows no more than the reader or the citizens of Big Indian. The neutrality of the narrator's tone fills the gap between the magical events and the reader's possible questioning of them. The act of wondering or questioning itself becomes utterly meaningless in the interval of space/time as configured by Kroetsch. The reader is invited to join in, according to narrative modalities which are also exploited by Jack Hodgins in *The Resurrection of Joseph Bourne*. The reader must, from the very beginning, accept the fictive familiarity of Vera Lang, the existence of Big Indian as indicated by the definite article in "the town" (implying mutual knowledge), the erotic event that is about to be narrated, and the offended sky. In addition to this, the place where the encounter occurs is shown to the reader through the use of the deictic "there," which, once again, joins reader (or, rather, 'hearer')

---

[4] Stephen Slemon has analyzed the novel as the embodiment of an encounter/conflict between two different languages, autochthonous and colonial, in a post–colonial context: "Magic Realism as Post-Colonial Discourse," *Canadian Literature* 116 (Spring 1988): 9–24.

and speaker in a situation as though of oral telling. The mainly oral narrative mode is also signalled by a repeated reference to the voice of the community, which, chorus-like, both authenticates and comments on the events that take place in *What the Crow Said*. As happens with Hodgins, and with many magical-realist writers, the narrator's psychological dimension is reduced to the absolute minimum. In *What the Crow Said*, the narrator becomes the voice of the community and is part of the flow and interweaving of voices and discourses within it.

The correspondence between human and natural world is so extensive that it becomes the conceptual framework of the novel. If Vera is partly transformed into a nest and into a queen bee, the bees' social system and their 'treatment' of gender (division of tasks between the two sexes) also become the metaphor upon which the whole architecture of the novel rests.

Kroetsch uses the image of the bees' world every time he wants to create meaningful similes and metaphors. Gus Liebhaber, for example, editor of the *Big Indian Signal*, is rescued from frostbite by Tiddy Lang, his lifelong erotic dream, and years later his only memory of the episode is the feeling of "the bee-like swarming of the flakes of snow, out of her hand, down onto his parted legs" (28) as she rubbed his body with snow. The snow-flakes falling down ceaselessly on Big Indian resemble "myriads of white bees," a simile that becomes reality at the end of the novel, when the citizens of Big Indian fight a war against the sky, as rain and rivers flood the town. In a desperate attempt to conquer the sky, Liebhaber shoots Vera's bees at the sky, and later the town is literally covered by myriads of bees.

The microcosm of Big Indian mirrors the complex social system of the bees, allowing Kroetsch to debate some fundamental issues. All the main events in the novel take place in the Langs' farmhouse, a female reserve, in that the only male in the family, Martin Lang (Tiddy's first husband and Vera's father), spends most of his time in the beer parlour and soon dies a sudden, grotesque death, frozen on a plough. Langs' house/hive includes grandmother Gertrude, Tiddy, and her six sisters, each of them, like perfect worker bees, with her specific task to carry out. The farm is frequently visited by men, whom Kroetsch's narrator significantly calls "drones," a word meaning both male bee and idler. These drones[5] hum and buzz around the Langs' house, most of the time with the intention of 'mating.'

This hybrid world, in which nature and human beings find extraordinary ways of communicating, is the framework within which significant

---

[5] Anna Marie Lang's husband is Nick Droniuk.

issues are dealt with, all of them undergoing the same process of miscegena-
tion/hybridization rather than analytical resolution. Raymond Wilson has
already demonstrated the 'folding' of space in the novel, but other categories
also undergo a magical process of decomposition, such as history, which is
deprived of its causal chain, and whose transmission of events and knowledge through the written word is questioned: Liebhaber remembers the
future and publishes the death of Martin Lang before it actually takes place.
Time itself goes through the same process: "Time was something of a
mystery to Liebhaber" (15). All the activities connected with the normal
passing of time are revolutionized: "everyone was losing track of time" (38).
Legitimated hierarchies are tested and annulled through exposure to
different modes of perceiving, approaching and dealing with the 'other'
(whether the world, the other sex, or the word).

In this context, the body becomes the privileged organ of perception and
knowledge, the means whereby man can recognize nature (as happens to
Vera) and overcome the traditional Cartesian antinomy between man and
the world or reality. It is not a matter of setting up a specific icon of bodily
perfection, as every great culture has always done.[6] The body is not the
identity-card of a given culture here, one with its distinctive intellectual,
artistic and moral productions. The body, rather, becomes a key to open up a
new system of communication with the Other. The body becomes another
language and, perhaps more importantly still, another 'ear' or gateway to
the Other. This is why *What the Crow Said* is full of images of bodies and of
whatever is closely connected with the physical and physiological activities
of bodies.

Representation of the body, and communication between and via bodies,
allows Kroetsch not only to annul antinomies such as man–nature but also
to deal with one of the fundamental dichotomies of the novel, that between
male and female.

Men's bodies are either crippled or have parts missing: Bill Morgan is
blind in one eye; Alphonse Martz is deaf; Mr Aardt, the undertaker, suffers
from a painful hernia and is bald; O'Holleran has "lost his right leg and his
private parts" (66), though he admits "he not only felt the presence of his
missing leg and private parts, but could actually use them" (66–67). Andy
Wolbeck has lost his toes and had them replaced with small ivory balls that

---

[6] Examples range from the samurai, who were trained in the martial arts in feudal
Japan, to the anorexic models preferred by the worlds of fashion and advertising in our
time.

ache every time the weather changes. Loss of limbs or physical disability is common to almost all the 'drones' in the microcosm of Big Indian, and is a sign of their failure as human beings. There are several crippled men in other novels by Kroetsch, and these often embark on a journey into the landscape to redeem themselves from failure. In *What the Crow Said*, it is men's obstinate self-affirmation through isolation that sentences them to mutilation. On the other hand, when the wish for affirmation and complete-ness is pursued by means of real contact with the Other, this becomes an expression of a life force that reveals deep magical possibilities, as the unmediated encounter between Vera and the bees shows.

Almost all the principal male characters, Liebhaber included, are ready to give up their daily occupations to spend all their time in a carnivalesque game of cards, called *schmier*. The game starts during a break from work before dinner at the Langs' farm and is carried on for 151 days anywhere – on carts, in a crypt during a wedding, in the fetid hut owned by the sceptical Heck, who claims "to believe in nothing." When he breaks a big toe by dropping a post maul on it, he heals himself by "disallowing the theory of gravity" (76). For the men, this game of *schmier* becomes a private war against the women, who carry on their jobs and repeatedly invite the men to stop their carnivalesque game. This state of isolation corresponds to increas-ing degrees of degeneration: they play their game in surroundings full of excrement, urine, bad smells, and vomit.[7] Like Rushdie's narrator in *Midnight's Children*, these men are physically disintegrating, and often coexist with liquids emitted from their own bodies. Liebhaber is the leader of these players, who see the game of cards as a desperate act of resistance against female power:

> "We're surrendering, aren't we?" Eddie Brausen said. He was in pain at the thought of Cathy's wedding. He was too young to know when to lie.
> "Surrender?" Liebhaber said. "To what?"
> "To the women."
> "Never." (101)

The war against women ends, predictably enough, in the annihilation of the men's physical and moral dignity.[8]

---

[7] As elsewhere in the novel, increasingly squalid settings in which the game is played are described with extreme straightforwardness and with no kind of censorship or moral judgement whatsoever on the part of the narrator.

[8] This is how the narrator presents the vision of the men at the end of their mock–epic game of cards: "The eleven remaining players were more corpses than men. They hardly stirred, hardly looked up from their cards, when the door squeaked open on its frosted

If men's bodies belong to a 'low' form of mimesis, those of women (and their representation of bodies) belong to the world of romance. They are able to reach complete union with nature (Vera), or else they are the mouthpieces of Eros: Rita Lang, Vera's sister, writes erotic letters to men imprisoned "for any crime whatsoever" (88), without ever responding to their replies. Her attitude to writing entails total identification of word with deed, and differs from Liebhaber's frustrated attempts to record the past, in that, for Rita, what is important is the moment, in which *le temps du discours* and *le temps de l'histoire* coincide with the physical act of writing, engendered, once again, by the body:

> She gave the promise of her words. [...] She imagined them all. Her faithful men, ripping open the scented envelopes that she so carefully slipped into the mail: Rita, bent at the table, slowly unbuttoning her blouse, furtive and wanton, lifting a nipple to her mouth. The quick flesh of her tongue against the rising nipple, the motion of her pen. (192–93)

Jerry Lapanne, a criminal sentenced to death, desperately tries to force an entrance into the interstices of this living language and to make it real. After thirty-eight attempts to escape from the penitentiary at Prince Albert, Jerry invents a flying machine and flies to Rita. However, "in his passion and haste" he forgets to invent a mechanism to get back to earth. After two and a half days' circling over the Bigknife valley, he dies, leaving unfulfilled his erotic desire to join her. Rita's words stem from her body; her words "caressed their thighs" and "kissed the hairs of their bellies." Nonetheless, men are excluded from this act of communication: it is an act of love which leaves both men and herself inexorably separated.

Writing and the written word form another dichotomy, closely related to the gender issue. Unlike Rita, Gus Liebhaber is obsessed by Gutenberg, who he thinks should be blamed for our loss of memory. In this community, where memory is essentially preserved through the oral transmission of history, the introduction of printing has started a process of loss, or detachment: the past becomes a monument, a trace, and the obsession with words frustrates the printer Liebhaber, who repeatedly and desperately tries to cast off the chains of printed words. Liebhaber cannot bear for his letters to be alphabetically arranged:

---

hinges. Tiddy beheld the spectres of men she had once fed. even fattened. They'd suffered from frostbite, in the earlier days of the winter, one of the coldest on record: the feet of some of the men smelled of rotting skin and gangrene. They'd tried cooking an old set of harness and the smell of boiled leather and sweat and horse shit mingled with that of dead flesh and dirty socks" (126).

In terror at the domestication of those free, beautiful letters – no, it was the
absurdity of their recited order that afflicted him: ABCDEFGHIJKLMNOPQR
STUVWXYZ – he opened a twenty-six of rye and, with immense effort, tried to
disentangle himself from the tyranny of rote. (69)

His heroic attempt to substitute his own anarchic vocabulary for the one he
feels is oppressing him leads to a sequence of meaningless signifiers,
"sounds for which he had no signs at all" (69).

On the other hand, the woman he loves, Tiddy Lang, is quite free from
the constraints of language and memory. She is incapable of writing. She
tries once or twice to make some notes, but fails, and the consequence of her
failure is that she cannot remember.

At the end of the novel, the main dichotomies are reconciled. Again, the
process is not one of synthesis, but the last stage in a dialectical process, a
hybridization or miscegenation, always changing, always in progress, a
partial fusion in which both elements change into something different.

The novel ends with the citizens of Big Indian embarking on their heroic
struggle against the elements, or war on the sky. The town is struck by a
series of pseudo-biblical plagues: salamanders, houseflies, vees of geese
("one man counted fifty-nine vees of geese in the clamouring air"; 153), and
a flood. During the first plague, sky and earth seem to join "into the one
androgynous moment of heaven and earth." "Androgynous" becomes a key
notion for Kroetsch: the water falling from the sky and flowing out of the
river's banks invades the whole town, annulling the two borders. The whole
microcosm of Big Indian (a geographical synecdoche for the whole universe)
becomes a single entity, where differences and dichotomies are drowned.

Kroetsch evokes the double significance of water as the primeval element
of death and fertility. Water annuls and joins. All the futile remnants of
men's attempts at establishing a centre and a point of control are attacked:
John Skandl's tower of ice tumbles down. His rational wish for a hegemonic
centre, signalled by this enormous pinnacle of ice, again marking differences
and establishing dichotomies, is philosophically and physically frustrated.

In order to stop the rain, Liebhaber shoots Vera's bees at the sky from a
circus cannon. As the bees drop down, Vera undresses, as at the beginning,
and calls the bees to join her. This time a man, Marvin Straw (the hangman)
takes off his "ragged clothes" and joins her, "her final lover." At the same
time, Gus fulfils his lifelong wish and marries Tiddy.

In describing the love-making between Gus and Tiddy, the narrator
suddenly shifts from past to present tense, thus including the reader in the
'here-and-now' of the event and allowing him or her to spy on Gus and

Tiddy, whose intercourse is described with tenderness, irony, and lyricism. While outside nature is apocalyptically annulling differences, here, before the readers' eyes, in Tiddy Lang's bedroom, new human beings or 'hybrids' emerge transformed. Liebhaber is at last happy, as "he cannot remember anything." He has finally lost his obsession with memory through words, and is now able to use his body as an instrument of perception and communication; he "smells" and "sniffs" Tiddy's body. Tiddy is also different. She can remember now, at least in part, and is able to recollect her child, JG, who died when he fell from a tree in an irrational attempt to conquer the sky. Kroetsch sustains the bee metaphor until the very end: after the ritual of the mating is over, Liebhaber dies like a drone:

> Liebhaber is happy. He cannot remember anything. He rests one side of his head on the towel. He tastes his own semen on Tiddy's belly. He tries to remember the future. Perhaps the crow is telling him that morning has come. He doesn't call out, for fear of waking Tiddy. Liebhaber is happy. After all, he is only dying. (218)

What the Crow Said resonates with voices from myths, both Christian (the biblical plagues; Noah's Ark) and classical (Tiddy's epic courting by the pretenders; the tower of ice; Vera's child brought up by the wolves). It also creates its own myths, like Vera's encounter with the bees, which "started everything." However, myth in *What the Crow Said* is not a narrative around which a given culture has structured its own forms of power and control, but an experienced reality, something that really happened in the past and has since then exerted an influence over the world and men's actions. In *What the Crow Said*, the magical element is experienced, via the body, as a moment of integration and transformation of the self (of miscegenation and metamorphosis), in which language, though inevitably a prey to its own antinomies, can encompass their representation and dissolution. Kroetsch's literary exploration of a 'real' that enlarges its boundaries to include what is extraordinary and magical is a spiritual act that translates into seemingly surprising and wonder-engendering narrative strategies.

☙ • ❧

Myth, Magic, and the Real
in Gwendolyn MacEwen's *Noman*

⟶ ༄

Biancamaria Rizzardi Perutelli

> God is alive. Magic is afoot. God is alive.
> Magic is afoot. Magic is alive.
> Alive is afoot. Magic never died [...]
> Magic never weakened. Magic never hid.
> Magic always ruled.
> (Leonard Cohen)

BOUT HER WORK, Gwendolyn MacEwen writes: "In my writing I am concerned with finding the relationships between what we call the 'real' world and that other world which consists of magic and myth. I've never felt that these 'two worlds' are as separate as one might think."[1] *Noman*, more than all her other works, shows MacEwan's capacity for blending the "two worlds' of the real and the imaginary; a fascinating compromise between a collection of short stories and a serial poem, this work is the fruit of an extraordinary linguistic experiment, resulting in prose whose essential qualities are passionate intensity, suppleness and malleability in dealing with clusters of colourful images and unpredictable metaphors, and with multiple levels of meaning. The poet, in the Greek sense of *poietés*, at last has the upper hand, and the personality of the artist as poet is once again celebrated in this work. It is no wonder that since her untimely death Gwendolyn MacEwen has been recognized as one of the outstanding poets of her generation by fellow writers such as Margaret Atwood and Joe Rosenblatt. *Telle qu'en lui-même l'éternité la change.*[2]

---

[1] Gwendolyn MacEwen, *Rhymes and Reasons*, ed. John Robert Colombo & Roy Bentley (Toronto: Holt, Rinehart & Winston, 1971): 64.

[2] Stéphane Mallarmé, from "Le tombeau d'Edgar Poe."

Behind *Noman's* apparently fragmentary façade lies a delicately structured or, rather, orchestrated unity based on a network of correspondences
and symmetries. Meaning is generated by the play of echoes and resonances
across a complex architectonic structure, in which the figures dissolve, as in
a kind of grotesque dance, and are transformed one into another. In *Noman*,
MacEwen combines the magical landscapes of Egypt, the Orient and Greece
with settings typical of Canada – or, rather, "Kanada." Kanada is, in
Margaret Atwood's words, a no-man's-land, a land of "bacon and eggs and
nonrevelation,"[3] while the result of MacEwen's combination is the possibility of individual or even national identity, and in addition the possibility,
to put it in the words of Robertson Davies, of understanding "that the
marvellous is indeed an aspect of the real."[4]

The structure of *Noman* is fundamental to the collection: it implicitly
reflects the circular movement associated with the alchemical process of
creation and destruction which so intrigues the writer, as well as the structure of reality, in which ending and beginning are parallel to one another.

The final section, which provides the title for the whole collection, is
composed of two stories featuring the same characters, but with a different
narrator. This section reintroduces themes found in the previous stories:
characters reappear and images recur, thus creating a marked sense of unity.
In the final part, the reflection of events that have already been described
takes the reader back to the beginning of the work, with the result that the
ending is at the same time a beginning: this "beginning–ending paradox" is
a characteristic of MacEwen's writing, both in verse and in prose. As a form
of structural organization, it allows her to reach complex levels of meaning,
and to discover the mythic in the mundane, or to show, in her own words,
"that the ordinary is extraordinary."[5]

Thus the book also narrates a complex metamorphosis, whose first stage
is the story of Lucas George, and whose last is that of Noman, whose name
is the one Ulysses gives himself in the *Odyssey*.

Lucas George is a young Haida Indian poised between the world of his
origins and the modern Western world, between the "wilderness" and the
city. After losing his identity and drifting in a kind of no-man's-land be-

---

[3] Margaret Atwood, *Survival* (Toronto: Anansi, 1972): 177.

[4] Robertson Davies, *Fifth Business* (1970; Harmondsworth: Penguin, 1977): 254.

[5] As Elsa Linguanti remarks of Patrick White's language: "worlds that are totally
separate seem to be in search of forms of osmosis." See also Carmen Concilio's essay in
this volume.

tween the world he no longer belongs to and the other world to which he
cannot yet belong, Lucas George ends up inside a prison – a cage for the
biggest bird of all, himself. As he tells us, the eagle is his totem and the cage
is thus the limited totemic kingdom of his soul. What is left of his identity is
also his prison. We thus discover the story underlying all the stories in the
collection, that of the yearning for freedom and that of the search for what
the alchemist requires to create its essence.

As he writes to his friend Aaron from his prison, Lucas George has given
up his totemic, magical, "myth-drenched" world in order to enter the world
of the white man, civilization, and "moneyed" cities. To use his own words,
he passes from the world of the eagle, soaring on high, to the world of
abysses, the world or house of the whale, Toronto (the title of the first story
is "The House of the Whale"). "Of course," he says, "I was never a whale, I
was an eagle." In this first line of the book, he defines an opposition between
the two worlds which is not just that between the "wilderness" and the city,
nature and civilization. It also problematically coincides with the "fine line
between what is living and what is dead."[6] What is living belongs to the
world of the eagle, and what is dead to the abysses of the whale. The house
of the whale, Toronto, is thus presented as the place of the dead, an all-
devouring *porta inferorum*.

The passage from the world of the eagle to the netherworld of the whale
also implies an act of negation and destruction, symbolized by Lucas's first
job, that of a woodcutter. He chops down trees to permit the construction of
civilization, but he well understands the harm he is doing to nature:

> In one year I don't know how many trees I killed, too many, and I found
> myself whispering "Sorry, tree" every time I felled another one.
>
> For *that* I should be in prison. (10)

The destruction of the magical world is counterbalanced by the construction
of history, and of civilization: Lucas subsequently finds a job at Toronto with
a firm that builds skyscrapers, which he perceives as blasphemous substi-
tutes for his ancient totems, the trees. His friend Aaron, who, like Lucas
himself, is destined to live on the edge, works in the sewers. All this establishes a powerful, albeit obvious, symmetry of high and low: eagle/whale,
skyscrapers/sewers, destruction of the totemic world/construction of civilization. Not only does Aaron tell Lucas that they are both fated to live on

---

6 Gwendolyn MacEwen, *Noman* (1972, Toronto: General, 1985): 7. Further page references are in the text.

the edge of society: like a hero of Indian or Orphic myth, Lucas will find his Psyche here in Toronto, the house of the whale – he will find what he is looking for. However, he will not be able to do this if he remains on the edge, high above things like an eagle, at the top of skyscrapers, or in the bowels of the city. He will only succeed if he enters the still centre of things (on their arrival in Toronto, Aaron says to Lucas, "You'll live on the sweet circumference of things, looking into the centre; you'll be less than a shadow or a ghost").[7]

What Lucas is looking for, even if he is not aware of it, is the re-assembling of his lost magical world, as may be seen from his final question: "What did you say I would find in the House of the Whale, Aaron? Aaron? Aaron?" The house of the whale would appear to have won, and together with it, history, the city, civilization; but Lucas's journey is only beginning.

This first story includes a reference that might appear to be accidental, but which subsequently becomes an important thematic nucleus of the book – the Indian use of potlatch, the fire into which possessions are thrown in order to demonstrate one's contempt for property and wealth. Potlatch teaches one how to defeat the whale and escape from its house. It is no co-incidence that the second story, "Fire," tells of a couple who one night throw everything in their house into the fire, in an apparently senseless frenzy, and, so we are told, in order to keep the fire burning. The Indian custom of potlatch can be traced back both to the destructive process of alchemy, in which objects are melted down before coalescing, and to the idea of the destructive potential of fire, a theory, elaborated by Jacob Boehme, which fascinates Gwendolyn MacEwen.

At first, the sacrifices that the young couple offer to the fire may not seem particularly important, though they are quite meaningful: a cheap edition of Webster's Dictionary, a few branches, and a copy of *The Golden Bough*, which burns with an "intense heat." The magical power which the fire possesses has the effect of hypnotizing the woman with its flames, taking her back to the early inhabitants of Canada, whose daily activities were closely linked with fire. From here, the step to the essence of life is extremely short: "But

---

7 This question of 'marginal position' relates to Jeanne Delbaere's contention that magical-realist texts occupy a 'marginal' space not only in the geographical sense, but also insofar as they are kept on the periphery by the central forces of the cultural system, though they are destined, through the dynamic at work in every system, to come together at the centre, just as Aaron tells Lucas. See Delbaere, "Magic Realism: The Energy of the Margins," in *Postmodern Fiction in Canada*, ed. Theo D'haen & Hans Bertens (Postmodern Studies 6; Amsterdam & Atlanta GA: Rodopi/ Antwerp: Restant, 1992): 75–104.

then who are we? What is the we that's being consumed?" Finally, it is
affirmed that "We are the fire!" (22). The following morning, the spell is still
not broken, and the shadows of myth, in the form of smoke and ashes, linger
in the apartment, like witnesses defending their primitive identity.

Perhaps there is a double lesson here: on the one hand, renunciation of
objects in the house of the whale; on the other, an entirely ironic description
of the system of consumerism. Yet this absurd fire, which is also sacral,
stands for the work, the energy, that the fire unleashes and consumes and
which devours life itself.

The same elements also underpin the structure of "The Day of the
Twelve Princes." Like Lucas George, the boy Samuel, the main character of
this story, loses the magical world of nature in which he grew up when he
comes into contact with the violence of the city: "The city had no winged
sphinx at its entrance, no riddle and no reward." The city is "dark" and
"metallic," and Samuel (whose name in Hebrew means 'heard by God')
"hated the city." The story ends with the surrender of Samuel's magic
spirits, whom he fantastically imagines as twelve warriors, like the biblical
Samuel, surrounded by the twelve tribes of Israel: "They lay their golden
bows on the ground before them, and held twelve white flags of surrender
to the sun" (46). This is clearly an image of the circularity of time, or the
cyclical time of nature, whose magic is defeated by the linear time of history.
However, these twelve princes also represent the night-world of dreams,
which disappears at sunrise. Samuel, an outsider and, like all the characters
in the book, both foreigner and "Kanadian," also lives in a kind of no-man's-
land, and prepares the way for the stories of Julian and Noman in the second
part of the book, where, after a temporary victory which is strategically
functional for the purposes of the book's message, the world of history, the
time of history, and the house of the whale are finally defeated.

With "The Day of the Twelve Princes," we are still in the early part of
this work, concerned with the affirmation of reality, or, rather, of history,
even if reality is gradually consumed by a sort of dream-fever. The power of
dream and nightmare is seen in "The Oarsman and the Seamstress." Here
the narrative voice is that of a woman watching over the sleep of her man,
Constantine, one of whose recurring dreams she is acquainted with: he
dreams he is an oarsman in a Byzantine galley. At the end of the story, the
woman wants to penetrate "into his otherness" by entering her man's
dream. However, this is a movement in which dreams are, so to speak, invaded by the 'real' world, whereas the journey is leading in precisely the

opposite direction, towards a place where dreams invade reality, either giving it form or destroying it. But on closer examination, perhaps it is not so much dreams that are invaded by reality: the woman's desire to enter her man's dream or nightmare betrays the already perceptible corrosion of the 'real' world.

"Kingsmere" represents the central stage in the process. This is a very short story, only three pages long, which provides the key to the whole work and is its real turning-point, introducing reader and writer into the land of the dead, and conducting them to the origins of poetry and creation. Kingsmere is a historic place of the imagination. Here William Layon Mackenzie King (1874–1950), the famous Canadian statesman and minister, lived in a world of neurosis and magic, talking to the portrait of his dead mother, and to the dog he believed to be her reincarnation. The place stands in the imagination as a sort of "time-travel place, a doorway between the past and the future," as Margaret Atwood writes in her essay "Canadian Monsters."[8]

Kingsmere exists against the background of the historical ruins that Mackenzie King had transferred there from all parts of Europe, in order to situate them in the Canadian 'wilderness,' creating truly outstanding effects of dislocation and alienation: ruins, scattered remains, relics of history at the edge of the Canadian forest or (from the point of view of human history) of nothing. At the centre of Kingsmere, where history and imagination pursue each other and intertwine, is an "archway" or "naked ancient door" (54). The enigma represented by the ancient door is thus given prominence:

> You only have to pass under the arch to be free, to be away from this place, but you watch the arch and you grow afraid, for the arch is watching you. The little King and the fairy Queen are watching you.
>
> And all the trees are silently screaming. (54)

This paradox, the silent cry, is the fixed point accounting for correspondences and symmetries. It is no coincidence that this archway is actually found at the physical centre of the book, dividing the first four stories, which speak of the destruction of the world of magic, from the last four, which deal with the magical destruction of reality and of the city.

In "The Second Coming of Julian the Magician," the protagonist has many things in common with the main character of the eponymous novel by

---

[8] Margaret Atwood, "Canadian Monsters: Some Aspects of the Supernatural in Canadian Fiction," in *The Canadian Imagination: Dimension of a Literary Culture*, ed. David Staines (Cambrige MA/London: Harvard UP, 1977): 116.

Gwendolyn MacEwen. In both works, Julian aims at "The Imitation of Christ as the Artist," as George Bowering points out in discussing Margaret Avison's poetry and MacEwen's poetry of magic: in both writers' works, "Christ appears as the meta-human artist, the *maker* who can observe or perhaps perform the creation of life, the model for the human artist."[9]

In the short story, Julian pursues this aim by calling up a "black inverted fire," a demonic, apocalyptic, negative conflagration, symmetrical with the potlatch of the first two stories. Noman is seen for the first time at work in a demolition company not surprisingly called "Apocalyptic Demolition & Co." (104). Though Julian and Noman also live on the edge, "looking towards the centre," they follow a route towards the centre and towards Kingsmere and the Archway, towards the dark, shining, magical world. They symmetrically destroy what Lucas George has constructed, and they give new life to what was destroyed for him, thus indicating the way of escape through a destructive potlatch. After working for a lifetime as a magician, Julian finds a job in the city, defined by him as a "power house":

> from midnight to dawn in the humming guts of machine, myself a huge beating heart in the Power House, my pulse beating with a different rhythm than the pulse of the machine.

Julian "wanders like Theseus through the throbbing maze of pipes and coils." Julian is inside the whale: "Why do I endure it? I begin to understand the anatomy of my enemy. I study the telepathy of wires, its serpentine transforming coils" (68). Julian dreams of the city as a white spider whose expanded body becomes one with the body of Julian himself (65). At the end, Julian, who is one, no-one, and everyone, the man of the beginning and the dead man reborn, seizes a thunderbolt and hurls it at the "power house," source of the city's energy and power. The centre explodes in the night, amid a dance of colours. Julian sails off towards nothingness on board his "ferris wheel" (78), towards another dawn. The structural function of the "ferris wheel" in this story may remind the reader of the "ferris / fiery wheel" with which Malcolm Lowry's *Under the Volcano* opens and closes, and which dominates the central (seventh) chapter. "For MacEwen," as Margaret Atwood says, "the magician is a poet, concerned with the transforming power of the Word."[10]

---

9 George Bowering, "Avison's Imitation of Christ the Artist," *Canadian Literature* 54 (1972): 63.

10 Margaret Atwood, "MacEwen's Muse," *Canadian Literature* 45 (Summer 1970): 31.

Magicians, dancers, artists, "shadow-makers," and yet also men of fire, of the fire of the spirit, or of a "black inverted fire": for these the theme of meta-art is developed in their magic which destroys and renews, in the magic of art, of fire, and of the spirit, which traces the pathway towards the motionless centre, beyond time, beyond the threshold, as far as eternity.

Similarly, the story of Grigori contained in the tale "Snow," with its icy inversion resembling that of the paradox of Julian's "black inverted fire," is opposed to, and symmetrically overturns, the theme of the fire of art in the first part. Grigori is also an artist – not an artist in fire, but in ice. Together with his companion, Grigori uses the mantle of freshly fallen snow, which is something completely new for him (he comes from a Mediterranean country), as a backcloth for his fantastic creations, to evoke battles of pre-historic monsters whose traces the two friends draw in the snow. The snow has artificial designs traced in it, in order to commemorate something that has never been there, except by virtue of this play of illusion and fantastic marks, which always lead to the *limen*, or, here, "archway." Thus Grigori goes to the park one night during a "blizzard," undresses, and consigns himself to the ice, so that his body may become the perfect work, a frozen, smiling angel. He is thus finally possessed by the ice that represents the genesis, field and substance of his art, whose icy, mortal inspiration obsesses him. Art or magic are here seen as fatal, mortal forces: in art, the dream freezes and takes its true form, the illusion becoming corporeal at the moment when Grigori pays the price and crosses the threshold, smiling and "naked," like Noman at the end of the book (120). To put it in the words of Richard Cavell, "According to the national idiom in art, madness and magic in art portray an ambiguous attitude toward the land revealing, one may say, the Canadian artist's innermost experience."[11]

The book comes to a close with the story "Noman," which is divided into two parts: "Part 1, The Book of Jubelas" and "Part 2, The Book of Kali." Through the orchestration of its figures and episodes, the story brings together all the threads. The narrators of these stories, whose names have been given them by Noman, enjoy a strange relationship with the hero. In the first, Jubelas throws light on the inexplicable death of Noman, which had occurred during a re-evocation of the ancient feast of the Saturnalia, cele-brated as a magic rite rich in gestures. He remembers when his wife, Omphale, after meeting him, dreams that "she has given miraculous birth to

---

[11] Richard Cavell, "Pazzi e maghi: versioni dell'artista nella narrativa canadese," *Can-ada: testi e contesti*, ed. Alfredo Rizzardi (Abano Terme: Piovan, 1983): 13–30.

Noman in the middle of Bay Street after stars and planets had rolled around in her belly." The woman's name, taken from Greek mythology, has a meaning connected with *omphalos,* the navel. In her umbilical function, she represents the centre towards which both Jubelas and Noman tend, and, at the same time, she unites with them in a relationship which defines each with respect to the other. In the second part, we discover that Samuel, the protagonist of "The Day of the Twelve Princes," is the adolescent Noman who has worked in a circus as clown, escapologist and dancer. When Kali takes up with the protagonist, the references and mythological allusions become more significant. The name chosen for her by Noman is that of the wife of the dancer Shiva in Hindu mythology. The sexual union of Noman and Kali is analogous to, or part of, the alchemical process: it begins with destruction and ends with the creation of new elements of harmony.

One night, Noman and Kali return to the ruins of Kingsmere, at an hour when the columns and statues belonging to a borrowed history appear distorted by moonlight and mist. Noman, "naked," heads towards the "archway," inviting the other characters to follow him, but he does not reveal what is hidden behind it, because it is in this void that the deepest meaning of the whole story is hidden.

There is still the story of Lucas George, who, after sinking into the house of the whale or the city of the dead, must return home. A destiny of *nóstos* or heroic return is thus shared by Lucas, Samuel, Julian, Noman and Grigori, through the "archway," the fixed point or hub of a wheel whose overall function, as Mario Domenichelli has written, "lies in its movement, as we read in the ancient Tao, yet paradoxically lies solely in that motionless void at the centre."[12]

Noman also has its intertextual reference to the *Odyssey.* As already indicated, "No-one" is the fictitious name that Ulysses gives himself when questioned by the Cyclops, with the result that, when the giant is injured, he invokes the aid of his companions against "no-one." The protagonist is Noman because on several occasions he reveals himself to have no identity (no past, no language and no nation). Like Ulysses, he is a foreigner. Yet above all, Noman possesses the Greek's principal quality, that of being *polytropos,* capable of changing appearance and identity as circumstances require. Like some magician, this hero pursues the game of metamorphosis,

---

[12] Mario Domenichelli, "Il mozzo della ruota: *Noman* e *Noman's Land* di Gwendolyn MacEwen," in *Moderni e Post-Moderni: Studi sul romanzo canadese del Novecento,* ed. Alfredo Rizzardi (Abano Terme: Piovan, 1994): 162 (my translation).

a magical game which is a continuous search for one's own being, a game which only at the supreme moment of death finally reaches its goal, as so exemplarily occurs at the end of David Malouf's *An Imaginary Life*. Of all the relationships between myth, magic and the 'real,' it is metamorphosis that is foregrounded. Transformation is deemed necessary for the characters to enter into contact with different levels of reality, thus allowing other possibilities to emerge.

ଔ • ଚ

Bewildered With Nature
The Magical-Realist in Joe Rosenblatt

---- ∞

Alfredo Rizzardi

A S IS GENERALLY RECOGNIZED, except where a movement develops as a school or as a group closely linked with a particular project, critical labels are useful signposts on a map which is exclusively the property of, at the service of, and of interest to, cartographically-minded critics. At worst, such labels are formulated in a casual, superficial manner, often with a derogatory meaning, by ironically uncomprehending modern-day and bygone contemporaries, as in the case of the Metaphysical poets of the seventeenth century, the Impressionists of the nineteenth, and the Hermetics and Beatniks of the twentieth. At best, they serve to mark off the new from continuations of the old.

The consistent and persuasive aspect of the grouping of writers under a single formula is a theoretical hypothesis of an ideal convergence of widely differing experiences, even if it often remains an abstraction formulated in accordance with the imaginative requirements of the period. We know very well, for example, what Impressionism is, but no two great Impressionist painters will be found to be the same. We know full well what Romanticism is, but we are forced to the conclusion that there are no two Romantic poets whose language, technique, and themes coincide.

Magical realism would appear to be a perfect example of this phenomenon: rather than a school or a movement led by a specific group of writers – among those best-known internationally, Günter Grass, Gabriel García Márquez, and Salman Rushdie – it is based on the common denominator of the appearance of the *maravilloso* in a historical context, thus giving rise to a wholly new situation uniting above all the literatures (as well as the other arts, including cinema) of a number of countries that have undergone profound political, social and cultural transformations. Magical realism could also be correctly defined as an epistemological theory based on literary texts, whose aim is to account for planetary changes now underway, of which the literary phenomenon is a limited, albeit significant, manifestation. This is a theory that has been debated for years, and continues to receive support, because this literature, like the process of innovation that underlies it, is developing and growing before our very eyes. It is thus a situation in which creation and theoretical reflection proceed side by side, one which ought to bring excellent results. But it is clear that if the writers were to find inspiration in the critics, the result would be extremely negative, and magical realism would be guilty of the same ingenuousness which disqualified and made impracticable its opposite, socialist realism. In actual fact, all post-colonial literatures seem pervaded by magical realism, even if each writer may be seen to offer his or her version of it. Nor could this be otherwise; the underlying factors determining a creative period cannot be summed up, except approximately, under a single label. If this label is not understood in its broadest sense and acknowledged as problematic, the complexities of a possible semantic synthesis will be sacrificed to the vulgarized appeal of its literal meaning.

ಆ • ಬ

I have chosen the poetry of Joe Rosenblatt for this study of magical realism because I believe it contains some highly significant elements which allow us to understand certain aspects of this topic in depth. Some of his poems may only be understood through an oral approach. This is especially true for his visual poems, although the remark may be extended to all his poetry. His own reading of his poems is particularly important, as we shall see, because, as almost always happens, the poet's voice throws light on his conscious and semi-conscious intentions (and the latter are highly significant) in a far more authoritative manner than any external attempt to rationalize his writing. How can one forget, for instance, Rosenblatt's exhilarating rendering of "Extraterrestrial Bumblebee,"[1] the *pièce de résistance* of his poetry-reading? Composed of short words and fragments of words, insistently repeated and arranged on the page in accordance with the visual logic of a geometric design, in its oral presentation it follows a mysterious score which is thoroughly personal. I have had occasion to hear Rosenblatt read it (live,

---

[1] *Bumblebee Dithyramb* (Erin, Ontario: Press Porcepic, 1972): 44–46.

not a recording) several times over a period of at least fifteen years, at seminars and other public appearances both in Canada and in Italy. Two things have always struck me about his reading of this poem. First, its utter individuality: Rosenblatt's reading has the peculiar sureness of a song. Second, it is curious that he always reads it in exactly the same way, with the same cadences, the same variations, and the same basic tune. Ultimately, the meaning is concentrated in the musicality that he impresses on the glossemes. After a while the amusing, humorous surface discloses a visual/ musical structure which, at first apparently meaningless, gradually acquires the form of a dirge, hymn, or litany. You listen to it and follow it *seriously* as a hymn of praise, a giving of thanks for natural existence that rises up with the airy, musical buzzing of this "extraterrestrial bumblebee."

Reading as a form of interpretation is common to all poets, the voice restoring the word to the body that gave birth to it. It becomes particularly useful with a *difficult* poet like Rosenblatt. What is it that is difficult about Rosenblatt? If we consider his non-visual poems, it is certainly not his language, which is almost always direct, clear, and classical in its form, with a vein of humour and a sharp sense of contemporary idiom. What is difficult is the semantic route followed by the word, which at a certain point stops, like a mountain track amid a myriad paths that are more or less imaginable, but never fixed or certain. The form becomes multimedial, so to speak, linked to the vivid quality of the iconic representation, the unpredictable nature of sound, and the apparent unintelligibility of verbal meaning. But then, our dreams, too, are often multimedial, and even more often unintelligible (the loveliest ones); and if nothing else can be said of it, Rosenblatt's poetry is undoubtedly of the stuff that dreams are made on.

Rosenblatt unites two worlds, the real world and the magical world of nature rediscovered, or redeemed, proclaiming himself to be "a voluptuous gardener." And he certainly goes in and out of his green doors as if coming in from his garden – the Garden of Eden. It is not surprising that his recent collection of poems, pen-sketches and drawings in colour, which together sum up his attempts to give visible form to the creatures of his imagination, should take the expression *The Voluptuous Gardener* as its title.[2] However, the garden in question has not been transformed into a work of art by European culture. It is, rather, the garden of nature as the Douanier Rousseau might have interpreted it, where phosphorescent eyes stare out from luxuriant

---

2 *The Voluptuous Gardner: The Collected Art and Writing by Joe Rosenblatt 1973–1996* (Erin, Ontario: Press Porcepic, 1996).

foliage – or, better, as the Canadian painter Emily Carr might have represented it, in canvases springing from her experiences at Nanaimo, at the heart of Vancouver Island, where Rosenblatt lives, and where, fifty years ago, Carr succeeded in giving form to a perception of the world that was astonishing for its modernity, in which the connection with the cypresses of van Gogh and the starry nights of Arles is immediate.

If we look at the poems, we find that the juxtaposition of 'realist' and 'magical' which characterizes Rosenblatt's vision is already present in the use that he makes of the language. The poet is perfectly well aware of this when he announces, "into the glow of an atom / I place the moth of language." The following lines from "I want to hijack a bumblebee"[3] offer a clear example:

> I want to hijack a bumblebee
> & fly over th'marygold
> home where the fires begin
>
> in the orange moonlight
> I'll reset the buzz machine's speedometer,
> start from zero in the centre
> & when Death signals from his control tower
> I'll take my flight out in the morning.

The sources of Rosenblatt's linguistic realism, if we analyze it *in vitro*, are easily recognized: current affairs (hijack), the machine (the buzz machine's speedometer), and the functional form of the term (control tower). These motifs no longer derive from Futurism, via modernism, but from the dominance of daily language by the lingua franca of the global village. This technological idiom is grafted onto another, magical blend of language. For the poet's obsessive, hallucinatory vision of nature renders it fabulous and fantastic. In an article in the *Weekend Sun*[4] on *The Joe Rosenblatt Reader*, the poet Susan Musgrave expresses regret that children in Canadian kindergartens and primary schools are compelled to learn dull nursery rhymes made up for them by adults, adding that if these were replaced by the simpler poems of Joe Rosenblatt, in which the imagination has a solid basis in intense visionary and emotional quality, "all of them would grow up continuing to love poetry." The marvellous may be seen in the bumblebee,

---

[3] *Poetry Hotel*, 50. See also the Italian edition, with the original text, in *Gridi nel buio: Poesie di Joe Rosenblatt*, ed. Alfredo Rizzardi (Abano: Piovan Editore, 1990): 52.

[4] Susan Musgrave, "Joe Rosenblatt's Writing Caresses the Language," *Weekend Sun Saturday Review* (29 June 1996).

which turns quite spontaneously into an aeroplane that can be hijacked and can buzz its way over the marigold, on a return journey home through the natural microcosm – to the heart of nature, zero, a new starting-point. This journey home accepts both the immense freedom and the infinite possibilities of the natural condition and also its iron laws and the conclusive signal of Death, pronounced, in a mixture of the fabulous and the humorous, from the control tower, which parodies the airport and its mechanical function, and opens up, with child-like wonder, the possibility of flight, up and away for ever.

I doubt that Susan Musgrave (a highly refined poet who has dressed up as a witch so often that it is rare to see her appear in any other guise in print) would include among the poems that might be read by children others of the same kind, more closely linked than "I want to hijack a bumblebee" with the cycle of *experience* than with that of *innocence*. For Rosenblatt, the real can take on the quality of the marvellous only if it is inserted into a natural context. This is the case with that "half an egg on the lawn" which has caused readers some difficulty, but the meaning of which seems to me to be quite clear:

> The topless zero is a miniature of my mind
> without the bird, the sick enigma
> fed on light –
>
> Half an egg on the lawn, haunted
> loveless like a vacant motel room.
>
> My nerves want to lie down inside, & sleep.[5]

The object casually caught sight of, brought into focus and rendered almost as an object of hallucination, somewhat like what happens with van Gogh's chair or William Carlos Williams' red wheelbarrow, is a broken eggshell, left on the lawn. The eye perceives the contrast of colours, while the mind is assailed by analogies which are rather more than analogies, in that this most insignificant object, a piece of refuse, is reconstructed as it was: an egg, which, for all its everyday banality, is the beginning of life and identifiable with the first shell of existence. The jerky language, devoid of all sweetness, is hard, elliptical, and realistic: the sentences, which are forced out rather than spoken, are fragments of an interior monologue in which allusions abound. Does the zero go topless, or do we, rather, detect Swift re-read by Pound ("dead at the top") in that "topless zero" which the poet sees as an

---

5 *Poetry Hotel*, 60, and *Gridi nel buio*, 54.

image of *his own* mind? Again, in that "sick enigma," the living being fed on light, isn't there a mandatory reference to Sartre's *Nausée*? There is a continual oscillation between the aseptic realism with which the object is drawn and the emotional intensity that increases the allusive quality of the vision, making it a dramatic and desperate 'experience of life.' For the devastating squalor of that half eggshell (haunted perhaps by insects or by human glances) is loveless (but the egg is the fruit of love), like a vacant motel room. These associations reach their climax in a line that is little more than a sigh, a prayer, an imprecation (note the ampersand), expressing in broken, realistic language (hence incomprehensible for many) the desire for annihilation through return to a period before birth and to the pure delight of floating in nothingness within the maternal egg.

Between these two poles, one positive and the other negative, stretches Rosenblatt's magical-realist vision. In *Tentacled Mother*, the poet takes his stand on an unlimited stage: the sea, with its stretches of light and inlets of shadow, its obscure depths, inhabited by thousands of creature. There is ceaseless movement in this element, which has no knowledge of stagnation (which is death): the motion of the waves parallels the unceasing movement of beings pervaded by the endless hunger for food and sex. The author does not actually say so, but we might imagine that, in the noonday sleepiness, the dreamy fisherman, waiting motionlessly on board his colourful boat with his rod in his hands, penetrates ever further into the depths of nature by surrendering himself to transformation and dream. Real fact is thus always encircled by an oneiric light: everything that comes to the perceiving eye, the marine reality represented with the precision and graphic vividness of the great naturalistic tradition, is at the same time the reality of unconscious memory, reality of desire, and reality of dream.

My close, and now longstanding, contact with the work of Rosenblatt culminated in the real-time reading of the poems in *Tentacled Mother/Madre Tentacolare*.[6] This was the result of firm friendship with the poet, and involved numerous meetings and faxes, in which we explored his newly written poems (especially the *lignes données*) and animatedly (electronically) discussed the ones he had to write in order to complete the sonnet, *pour s'ajouter* (as Paul Valéry would say). This privileged participation in the progress of composition, followed immediately by the translation of the

---

6 *Tentacled Mother/Madre Tentacolare*, Italian edition, with the original text, ed. Alfredo Rizzardi (Abano: Piovan Editore, 1995), published a year before the Canadian edition of *Tentacled Mother* (Toronto: Exile Editions, 1996).

texts (and for me, translation is always and only an attempt at interpretation), convinced me that his poetry is made up of two intertwining
elements, which can be described, for the purposes of discussion, as a male
element and a female element. These are bound together organically, like the
common organs of Siamese twins, which can only be separated by means of
a drastic operation, fatally destined to fail. However, these elements may be
isolated theoretically and analyzed separately *in vitro*.

In his very first poem (and in his memorable autobiography), Rosenblatt
gives an unequivocal description of the meeting of the self with nature in
terms of falling in love and marriage: a complex, traumatic form of initiation
into 'the Other.' These are some of the most intense passages in contemporary literature, combining ancient myths with motifs of a subtle modernity. Today we can re-read the poem in Michael Ondaatje's fine anthology,
From Inklake,[7] which takes its title from the prose of Rosenblatt. However,
the encounter between the self and nature is found above all in his poetry, in
an even more explicit and essential form, if that is possible: see, for example,
"The whole academy explodes":

> My body surrenders to female green
> to female sleep; I'm plugged into an emerald.
> Zebra fish divide ... divide ...
> The whole academy explodes, Neptunites
> flutter into calmness, into curious tigers
>
> who invite me to a cookout in blasphemous coral
> bathe deeper, follow the adhering eggfish
> the white spines, the water ghosts.
>
> The solids dissolve. The narcissist is free,
> weightless on the belly of a breathing woman.
> I plunge my hands through her flimsy gown
> at the laughing school mobs scattering
> through phosphorescent corridors, toward
> the pulverized sand, the white millionaire, basking.[8]

Each of these elements of opposite, complementary sex possesses a fullness
and an expressive urgency not only in his poetry's themes, but also in its
technique and language. If these elements were not so closely bound together, they might easily fit into creative experiences that are already well-

---

[7] From *Inklake: Canadian Stories*, sel. Michael Ondaatje (Toronto: Lester & Orpen
Dennis, 1990).

[8] *Poetry Hotel*, 32 and *Gridi nel buio*, 44.

known: logical, rational order, and emotional, fantastic adventure; recourse
to literary and poetic tradition and vitalistic, surrealistic explosion; the
opaque, scientific term and the transparent, polysemic word born, as Emily
Dickinson would say, of "a quicker blood." It seems to me appropriate to
speak of distinction/opposition and the forced reunion of the two elements
that make up Rosenblatt's poetry: the male element, which always accompanies the perspective of the virtual subject, the monologue of the self
spilling over into poetry, and the female element, which wholly characterizes the real protagonist of the marine adventure, whom the poet sometimes
calls Mother Nature, at other times Mother Sleep, and, lastly and iconically,
Tentacled Mother.

The poet–fisherman, the poet–dreamer, has a passion not only for *le mot
juste*, the word that dances harmoniously with the others, as Eliot might
have put it, but also for the precision of the term used, especially if referring
to forms, animals, or objects of the natural world, as well as for scientific or
everyday elements. The word *fish* rarely appears, and when it does, it is not
in descriptive contexts. Most often it is a particular species of fish – a certain
type of salmon, the octopus, the eel, the parrot-fish, the starfish, the rockfish,
a certain type of mollusc, each with its peculiar name and properties – which
appears in his vision. And he intends this as a realist vision, even if it is set in
the depths of the ocean, and even if, instead of airy skies and terrestrial landscapes, it takes place in an upside-down world. For the common element
here is the marine world, and our world, the everyday one, suddenly turns
out to be a dystopic landing-place, where marine creatures suffer mortal
dislocation: "we're frightened children without our fins."[9]

This is one of many interpretative clues to be borne in mind once it has
been intuitively perceived. The narrator tells a *mythos* including fragments of
ancient myths – starting from that of Narcissus – which, however, are
distorted and repositioned within the chaotic structure of an obsessive,
stratified, pervasive, prevaricating vision. This vision aims at the discovery
of our true nature, the one revealed in our dreams, which extract it from the
collective fund of our unconscious. The figures that appear in the poems,
wondrous in their beauty or extraordinary monstrosity, and the I itself
(which is never a well-defined I, but a potential entity continually transformed into each of them, in the bestiary of its mind) are often called
"dreamers." Narcissus falls in love, not with his pale reflection, but with the
watery mirror, and dives voluptuously into the enigmatic, silent 'other' life

---

[9] *Tentacled Mother/Madre Tentacolare*, 92.

where his narcissism melts away and he at last feels free (the water – this amniotic element – is, of course, another metaphor for the happy life of origins in nature's bosom).

Furthermore, this marine fiction is a way of subjecting the real to revelation and recognition – that is to say, to wholesale transformation: the ocean to which the poet refers in moments of great visionary breadth (such as in "My soul and I are now obese")[10] really is "our ocean," and this *reality of ours*, which the language of poetry transforms into a magical ghost, shows the same laws as govern all the forms of nature at every instant of their existence: "our ocean is both frenzied paramour and stomach." It seems to me that the monologizing voice wishes us to understand that the mechanism of the dream, whose dynamic quality is identified with the energy of *natura naturans*, is simply the marvellous reverse, the revealed, authentic, or, perhaps more correctly, magical form of the real.

Thus the forms of nature are at the same time fish and human. The "minnows" that the poet follows are the manifold creatures that are desired and loved and which he chases and desires to possess. Yet at the same time they are the thoughts of the present and the memories of the past, in an eddy of associations which becomes a part of the irresistible dynamism of nature. The mud of the depths is made up of fragments (sensations and memories) that are expelled by movement and accumulate on the sea floor – which is to say, at the bottom of memory. The I has no respite in the course of these associations, or in the ceaseless hunt for food and sex imposed by the iron laws of nature. It may be useful to give an example of this central aspect of Rosenblatt's poetry, although it is difficult to extract a single tessera in order to show the entire figure in its complexity. Poems like "Our wishes are eaten entirely raw," "My soul and I are now obese," "Edible fantasies," or "The sacred caviar" are wholly based on this theme. But the voracious dynamism of this marine universe finds its culmination in "A gustable journey":

> An inverted sky – the ocean is spitting raindrops
> as crowds of minnows undulate in a silvery storm.
> Their flesh is being served in a cabin of the sea
> but I've not been invited in to taste those tears:
> fragments of my life flash before me and dissolve
> in kissing mouths of salmon on a gustable journey;
> these are the final sentences of a grim biography.
> Mother Sleep, indomitable, scribbles out my dream.

---

10 *Tentacled Mother*, 44.

Everything is eaten: I see grisly jaws everywhere.
Even caviar precepts are devoured in their nursery;
so it goes with minnow stars in the sky of my skin
mobbed by ghostly fish along a reef of immortality.

Evening, in envy I gaze into your twinkling mouth:
there are no horizons to the nibbly joys of eternity.[11]

Surrounded by this pervasive greed for food, the monologizing I arrives at a paroxysmic conclusion. The final couplet uses a lucid, liberating image to express the universal hunger that is impressed on the vault of heaven itself, at night, in the form of a wide-open mouth with its rows of twinkling stars. A magic spell is afoot: it is reaching its culmination now.

Another sonnet, "Mother Sleep," clearly reveals the second element informing the world of nature with a dynamic impulse, the hunger for sex, which is the reverse side of the same obsession.

I know you're not alone under the hard gray sand,
bivalve beauty, I'm digging into your gritty world.
On a bright late April afternoon you hide your muse
with all its tubule urges inside of a diving mausoleum.
How futile, your descent to elude the machinery of my fingers
for even before the tide recedes exposing your closed house,
my crooked shadow falls across your tiny elliptical door.
Listen, lover clam, you can't keep playing chameleon with the sand
not when love finds me crawling along your residential boulevard;
yes, I'm moving toward that joyful geyser spitting mollusc memory.
No one escapes this happy digger tunnelling giddily until his eyes
perceive an open bedroom: 'Hello in there ... darling, are you home?'
Slowly I follow the dark snail of your mind into its blessed chamber
where, in her bathysphere, Mother Nature has prepared our bed.[12]

I might have quoted "Heavy Sex," where the erotic fury of the octopus is transformed into a grotesque, tormenting vision, emblematic of the inexhaustible sexual impulse, or "Incendiary Arms," or again "Shameless Pressures." But here the subject is treated more straightforwardly and tellingly by the juxtaposition of heterogeneous elements, like the grotesque monologue of the I, concerned this time with the love-hunt. The object of the hunt is a mollusc: the effect of alienation is not only the result of the absurd attribution of passion to the bivalve creature, but above all of the realistic

---

[11] *Tentacled Mother*, 42.
[12] *Tentacled Mother*, 68.

and colloquial language, whose aim is to offer a representation of eroticism in nature as an incessant digging in the sand.

The truly magical can be found in its purest form when this hunger for love is represented in an elegiac manner, without grotesque, ironic or humorous ingredients, which are magically dissolved in the emotional intensity of the affections. It is no longer surprising that the most human of natural conditions is that of the starfish. The fact that starfish reproduce by parthenogenesis is not taken into consideration. The reader is wholly involved in an oneiric vision in which reality and dream are inseparable and indistinguishable.

THE CRYSTALS IN THEIR DREAMS

Have I come upon a starfish mortuary at low tide?
There's the stillness here of an underwater cave
where troubled couples in the moistened darkness
longitudinally adhere for a passionate farewell.
A purply desire blooms from every phosphorescent rock –
and like parrotfish attacking the coral of a reef
these dreamers relish the crystals in their dreams.
They feed upon reminiscences through digestive fire
certain that memories will retain their sparkle
beneath a moving kelp bed heavier than nostalgia.
I'm sure it's like this with other hungry lovers
resting in the shadows after reflective coitus.

And each time a tide abandons her incandescent children
I find myself alone with them along some deserted beach.[13]

The sonnet possesses a metaphysical quality similar to that of John Donne's "A Valediction: Forbidding Mourning." It is no coincidence that both compositions build upon a highly realistic, macabre *incipit* (in Donne the death of the wise man, here the evocation of a mortuary) to present a series of fabulous, complex images that are intended to alleviate the despair of farewell, but at the same time attempt to dispel the anguish of separation. The sense of the last two lines of Rosenblatt's sonnet is connected with the awareness of solitude in the immensity of space that hovers over all his poetry and which is undoubtedly one aspect of the Canadianness of the poet. Indeed, Margaret Atwood describes this anguish, in an effort to define her local and existential identity, by means of the metaphor of the Canadian 'pioneer':

---

[13] *Tentacled Mother*, 62.

He stood, a point
on a sheet of green paper
proclaiming himself the centre,
with no walls, no borders
anywhere; the sky no height
above him; totally un-
enclosed
and shouted:

Let me out![14]

ଓ • ଛ

The intrusion of the act of writing into the body of fiction, which is a common element of his poetry, makes Rosenblatt a typically postmodern writer. It occurs quite naturally in his works, showing that the barriers that once protected the 'suspension of disbelief' have been thrown down and that everything has become potential and virtual. The monologizing I in its continual transformations shows that it is searching for an identity that it fails to find. The I brings with it not an existential agony but, rather, something new and silently devastating; an epistemological bewilderment which is universal. But here, it finds an immediate form of representation, being connected with dislocation (Frye's "where is here") and a history still to be invented – with the difficulty of recognizing oneself in a world that has new coordinates, new mythologies.

This epistemological bewilderment may be the cement that unites, deep down, the antithetical elements present in Rosenblatt's writing, with the result that his poetry may be brought under the heading of magical realism.

'Realism' is a markedly male term, 'magical' an intensely female one (especially in the age of feminist 'witches'). Together they form an andro-gyne, a hircocervus, or, linguistically speaking, an oxymoron. For realism, in what is perhaps its principal meaning, makes us realize that we inhabit a particular world, a period of time and a society, and demands fidelity of representation. The magical, on the other hand, is what the poet creates, and he can do this more clearly and effectively in one of these "borderline countries," as McLuhan called Canada, because they are immune from the excessively burdensome conditioning of the past. So realism can also make

---

[14] Margaret Atwood, *The Animals in that Country* (Toronto: Oxford UP, 1968): 36.

us realize the dream, the interior vortex, the backward path, and the unconscious collective forest.[15]

An *in vitro* reading has led me to this conclusion. One step further on, the androgyne, hircocervus, or oxymoron that is magical realism is perhaps still, in every form that it takes, what has always been called, and what we continue to call, poetry.

ဢ   •   ဢ

---

[15] Marshall McLuhan, "Canada: The Borderline Case," in *The Canadian Imagination: Dimensions of a Literary Culture*, ed. David Staines (Cambridge MA: Harvard UP, 1977): 248.

Coterminous Worlds

-- &

Robert Bringhurst
(A Selection by Elsa Linguanti and Carmen Concilio)

I N CANADA, IN BRITISH COLUMBIA, on the edge of the Pacific Ocean, at
the end of and between periods of roaming around the world, lives a
poet, hermit, linguist, typographer, translator, and anthropologist,
whose production includes various collections of poems and essays.

His poetry represents the most mature achievement of the movement
which started in Vancouver, in the early Sixties, in the pages of the magazine
Tish. His prose writing consists of introductions to his own poems and to art
exhibitions of Haida sculptors and painters. He has also edited the catalogue
of an exhibition of literary publishing in British Columbia (from the arrival
of the first printing press in 1856 to the date of the exhibition in 1984) and
has given occasional lectures and talks on poetry. His essays are on various
subjects, ranging from a comment on a fragment of Gorgias of Lentini to an
analysis of Arabic terms in Joyce's *Finnegans Wake*. He has also translated
from Greek, Arabic, Haida, etc, and is the author of *The Elements of Typographic Style*.[1]

If Robert Bringhurst's poetry "has to do with crossing borders," as he
maintains is always the case with poetry – adding: "bearing precious loads"
– his prose speaks explicitly about the refusal of a negative, exhausted
cultural outlook and the recovery of cultural roots which have apparently
been lost, and of myths of the origin. It advocates a renewed connection with
the world around us, the non-human world and the world of the dead, the
connection of poetry with science, the other arts and thought; and the
necessity "to salvage and preserve."

---

[1] Robert Bringhurst, *The Elements of Typographic Style* (Vancouver: Hartley & Marks,
1996).

Bringhurst, then, adopts an intellectual position that is also at the basis of the poetics of most writers to whose work we have felt the definition of 'magical realism' could reasonably be applied.

ଔ • ଅ

From: "Thinking and Talking: A Prose Caboose," in *Pieces of Map, Pieces of Music*[2]

"Breathing Through the Feet: An Autobiographical Meditation"
Poetry has to do with *crossing borders* and with bearing precious loads. That is what *metaphor* seems to mean – to carry things across – and that is what the loons and the goldeneyes do as they dive and rise, feeding in the bay [...]. In myth, form and content are not identical, nor is one an extension of the other, though there is living tension between them, just as there is in our bodies and in the annual migrations of those birds. (By the form of a myth or a poem, I mean more than its acoustic or typographic form; I mean its narrative or meditative shape, plot, structure, the higher grammar of image and event. And by content I mean, among other things, what José Ortega y Gasset had the wisdom to call the higher algebra of metaphor. (99–100)

The north end of Watts, where my parents were living in the mid-Forties; the Heart Mountain compound; Red Lodge, Montana; Calgary; Butte; the wild valleys I hiked as a child – those of the San Juan River and the Green, which are now underwater, while the huge reservoirs they contain are filling with speedboats and marinas [...]. A litany of places, to conjure the long spaces between them. *The earth itself is a living body*, and a kind of brain. It is living information, like the cortex and the genes. We flood it with water and asphalt and concrete and standardized grass, and with signs that say Fried Chicken or Mountain Estates or Colour TV in Every Room or Jesus Saves, and we think *that* is information. I was born in the home of the celluloid vision and the armour-plated American dream, but I cannot remember a time when I was not horrified by that face of America: by its superficial brilliance, its arrogant self-assurance, its love of itself, its insentience, its greed. (102)

---

[2] Robert Bringhurst, *Pieces of Map, Pieces of Music* (Toronto: McClelland & Stewart, 1987). Author's emphases.

Those of us raised in Colonial North America have been taught a vision of endless progress [...] in the presumption that the world of endless development is a universal world, one that has room within it for everything. But *a world with room for nothing outside itself*, room for nothing beyond its control, is a world in which liberty and prosperity are hollow, and one in which justice is severed from both its origins and its ends.

I and the audience I try to write for live not in but on the edges of that world, in order always to remember that it does have an outside. As a *creature of the edges* instead of the collapsing centre, I have made it my business not to parody or portray the central insanities of that world – which is what much current writing is about – nor even to praise the still functioning graces – which are many after all, and which again much current writing is about. I have made it my business simply to find what I thought I could *salvage and preserve*, and to pack it out into another, *coterminous world*. There, with no hope of enduring success – and with no need of a new physical structure, so numerous are the ruins – I have been trying to live on closer, less arrogant terms with *the real – which is [...] for the most part nonhuman*. (103)

I've brooded here on the distinction between the colonial and native American cultures. But in the tangled roots of the European tradition lay cultures which must, in significant ways, have resembled the ones that, for three hundred years, we have worked to extinguish throughout North America. The remains of those old, now voiceless, cultures of Europe – from the paintings of Lascaux to the fragments of Empedokles and Herakleitos – though they come to us in pieces, speak of a *wholeness* which, in our rapacious industrial society, is almost unknown.

I have lived and worked with the discontinuous ghosts of the old philosopher–poets of Greece for a long time, and I admire about those poets in particular their *refusal to be compartmentalized*. I admire their assumption that poetry, philosophy, physics, biology, ethics and even theology are all one pursuit. I admire, in other words, their moral and spiritual and intellectual integrity. [...]

In the midst of an empire as arrogant, ethnocentric, greedy and corrupt as the North American empire at present, the sages of Tang Dynasty China practiced and preached a tradition of freedom both from the pride of imperial service and from the anesthesis of complicity. Like the pre-Socratics, they reached toward the joints and roots of poetry and thinking.

Most of them were wanderers, and most of them resettled, taking new names from the neighbouring mountains. They are not just people who were places; they are people who *became* places – when everything encouraged them instead to become consumers and provisioners; bureaucrats or managers; trapped, coopted labourers or lords. (10)

I find that same integrity in many of the philosopher–poets of the Orient.[..] It is there to be read in the *salvaged* scraps of oral literature (the native American), and it is still there to be heard in the mouths of a steadily shrinking number of native gardeners, hunters, and herders who live in the steadily shrinking real world – the lean tracts not yet consumed by an insatiable white society with the stupidest goals in the world: money and jobs. Not piety, grace, understanding, wisdom, intelligence, truth, beauty, virtue, compassion. None of these. (109)

ᛦ   •   ᛤ

From "Vietnamese New Year. In the Polish Friendship Centre," in *Pieces of Map, Pieces of Music*

Biology, physics, mathematics, the painting of paintings, the telling of myths, metaphysical reasoning – all of these are ways of listening to and speaking with the world. They are aspects of intelligence. [...]

That which is too exclusively human is not human *enough*. Our deepest passions push us way *outside ourselves*. They lead us to talk about mountains and stars and to know our deep kinship with birds and shellfish and flowers. Geology and astronomy and biology are, or can be, ways of attending that wholeness and allowing it to be whole instead of turning it into a deadly totality. Knowing the *wholeness of the world* is not the same, after all, as building a great dictatorship of self-consistent theory – something science and religion both seem to become if we let them.

Science, like art, is founded on *wonder* [...].

Art is not a house. Art is an opening made in the air. It is seeing and saying and being what is in the world. Homer's naming of the gods is a discovery, not an invention, and it is an achievement of perception on a par with Dmitri Mendeléyév's mapping of the periodic table – that chart of the elements which hangs now in chemistry labs all over the world. [...] Homer and Mendeléyév both knew themselves to be parts of a *collaborative venture*, building on the findings of their predecessors, drawing from their colleagues and making something which they and their successors would revise.

The Lithuanian philosopher Emmanuel Levinas spent some of the second world war in a prison camp, where he wrote a little book called *De l'existence à l'existent*. He makes some interesting remarks there on the arts. 'Painting,' he says, 'is a struggle with sight.' Many poets nowadays hold the lazy, ethnocentric view that literature is merely a struggle with *speaking*. But follow the analogy of Levinas's statement and you will come to a very different proposition: that literature is a struggle with *hearing* and *listening*. The writer needs a *stethoscopic ear*, and he can – I prefer that he should – lay it against the stones and wild grasses as well against his own chest. And the chests, of course, of other human beings. (111–12)

Reworking the gifts and givens of other thinkers feels to me like an essential part of the task. That is a use of poetry: To sing thought back into being, to personify it, state it, locate it, to clear the haze. [...] And I see no virtue in being original in the cant sense of the word, but only in the obvious sense: I want the work to be authentic; I want it deeply *in touch with origins*. (113, 114)

Poetry seems to me to be a name for something in the very texture of being, so I don't see that any of us can genuinely escape it, though many of us these days do relentlessly try. [...] I mean it when I say poetry is in the very texture of being. I hear it from the rocks and trees and the sea I live with and the widgeons who are here all winter every year. (117)

Levinas and Heidegger and George Grant and other western thinkers of the last few generations have rekindled this preindustrial, anti-imperial tradition, which is as long and rich in the west as it is in the east, though for centuries it has lain deep underground. But it doesn't seem enough to me to speak of these things in the Euroamerican tradition. Imperialism is age-old and worldwide. So is demagoguery. In every nation on the planet, the world is being sterilized by greed. But *the alternatives are also worldwide. They are plural*, and we need to know that. [...] Those voices are also necessarily *multilingual*, and if we are going to hear them, we have to hear them that way.

E pluribus unum, it says on your coins: one from many; and that is the rule of empire. The rule of the longer term is many from many, *e pluribus plus*. (119–20)

ﾂ • ဆ

From "Foreword" to *The Calling*[3]

In [my] poems, the voices of the dead are also quoted or evoked. The dead, in my experience, are indispensable too, especially when they are silent, watching and listening as they do in the land, the air, and us. I don't suppose the dead are reading books, yet they seem present far more palpably in books, where we read them, than they do in magazine racks or in stadiums, gymnasiums and classrooms, where the living crowd them out. Some books, at any rate, seem able to *desegregate the living and the dead* – and that is the only kind of book I have ever wanted to read or write. (13)

ଓ • ଅ

From "The persistence of poetry and the destruction of the world": Tenerife lecture

What it pleases us to call the New World is in fact a very old world – just as old, at any rate, as Asia, Europe and Africa. It is part of the ancient continent of Pangaea, born from the same geological matrix as Europe. Its rivers and forests, and its ecology and geology, were thoroughly developed long before Columbus. And it has been inhabited by thinking, speaking, knowing human beings for several thousand years.

But an inhabited world, with its own philosophical, artistic, scientific and literary traditions, is not what the European conquerors and colonists wanted to find. It is therefore not what they saw. They saw instead an empty world, free and ripe for the taking. They saw a gift of God meant for no one but themselves.

This deliberate hallucination is still with us, like the star of a Christmas without end.

The European colonists' arrival in the New World marks the escalation of a war that had been fought in Europe and Asia for more than two millennia and continues even now. It is the war between *those who think they belong to the world* and those who think that the world belongs to them. It is the war between the pagans, who know they are surrounded and out-numbered by the gods, and all the devotees of the number one – one empire, one history, one market or one God – and who nowadays insist on the preeminence of everyone for himself: the smallest number one of all.

---

3   *The Calling: Selected Poems 1970–1995* (Toronto: McClelland & Stewart, 1995).

It is no accident that prophets of monotheism, such as Plato and Mohammed, have often banished the poets. These prophets understand that the poet is a pagan and polytheist by nature. In a certain sense, even Dante, Milton, San Juan de la Cruz, Teresa of Ávila, Gerard Manley Hopkins and T.S. Eliot are pagans. Without admitting it, they seem to understand, like the peoples of the Altipiano of Bolivia and Peru, and like many Native Canadians, that it is best to interpret Christianity as one more form of paganism.

The great danger is single-mindedness: reducing things to one perspective, one idea, a single point of view.

A polytheistic understanding of the world survived in Europe even in the time of the conquistadors, though it was then forced to take a wordless form. Music gave it refuge. It is found in polyphonic music, which is the music of multiple, simultaneous and independent voices. The churches of Europe overflowed with music of this kind in the fifteenth, sixteenth and seventeenth centuries. It did not change the course of history, but it preserved an essential perception of the *plurality of being*. It preserved the true heresy that reality is not of just one mind.

European music of more recent centuries is, for the most part, homophonic. It is the music of one voice that speaks in the name of all and of many voices that answer as one voice.

The conquest continues – in South America, North America, Asia, Australia, and in Europe too. It continues in Bosnia and Hercegovina, where a tradition of oral epic poetry survived from Homer's time until even a few months ago. Now, at this moment, the villages in which those poets lived are rubble and mass graves.

From Alaska to Tierra del Fuego and from Ireland to Japan, the forests fall and subdivisions replace them. The homes of the gods are supplanted by the houses and garages of human beings. It is hard work, this eviction of the gods and of all the cultures that acknowledge their existence. We keep at it even so.

One of my geographic grandfathers, the poet Skaay of the Qquuna Qiighwaay of the village of Ttanuu – an oral poet who dictated his long and complex poems a century ago, in the Haida language, to an anthropologist – says that we human beings are *xhaaydla xitiit ghidaay*: ordinary surface birds. Creatures with more power – killer whales, loons, grebes, sea lions, seals – dive. They *pierce the surface*, the *xhaaydla*. When we go with them – when we are invited to go with them – we enter the world of the myths. We come back speaking poetry.

There are other views of the proper nature of relations between humans and other beings. For example, 2,000 km south of the country of the poet Skaay, in the Ruby Mountains, the country of the Paiute people, in what is now the state of Nevada, there are pines of the species *Pinus aristata*, bristle-cone pines. These trees live longer than any other creatures on the earth. The oldest individuals – not much taller than I am – are 6,000 years of age. A few years ago, a so-called scientist found in these mountains a pine that he thought might be the oldest of all. He cut it down to count its rings. He killed what may have been the oldest being in the world, to convert it into a statistic. Then he published his report, without the least apology, in a scientific journal.

This is not science. It is one more manifestation of the ongoing conquest, and of the reduction of the world to human terms.

The American novelist William Faulkner, when he received the Nobel Prize, concluded his address by saying, "Mankind will not only survive, he will prevail." This prediction seems to me logically impossible. If humanity survives, it will be because it does not prevail. If it insists, like Ozymandias, on prevailing, it will surely not survive.

I have been listening to the world for no more than fifty years. I do not have the wisdom even of a young tree of an ordinary kind. Nevertheless, I have been listening – with eyes, ears, mind, feet, fingertips – and what I hear is poetry.

Being mute doesn't really trouble me. Being deaf would trouble me far more. There is a lot to see and hear. There is, for instance, the intelligence of all the other creatures of the world. There are the pines and the strelitzias, for example, performing their dance all around us, fast and slow, unfolding their intricate structures and the cunning strategies they have for staying alive. This too is poetry, speaking very rich, complex and subtle languages. We can learn to hear and read and in some measure understand these languages, even though we never learn to speak them.

What does this poetry say? It says that what – is is, and that it is alive. It speaks the grammar of being. It sings the polyphonic structure of meaning itself.

In the great ceiling of the Sistine Chapel there are readers rather than writers. The prophets and sibyls scrutinize their folios and scrolls. Nothing is written there. The great pages reflect what happens as if they were mirrors, and in front of these blank mirrors the blind prophets are listening.

There is only one writer, in the corner: the little scribe with his scrap of paper, listening to those who really listen.

The theme of the ceiling is the poetry of the world, not the glory of the poet.

It is true that the face of Michelangelo is there in the midst of the Chapel's big back wall. It is rendered, this self-portrait, as a face still attached to a human hide freshly peeled from someone else's living body. The sculptor is subsumed in his own tale. The listener listens to himself. In the midst of his own vision, the visionary can be seen.

When I was a youngster in school, someone asked me, "If a tree falls in the forest with no one there to hear it, does it make a sound or not?" The question is demented. If a tree falls in the forest, all the other trees are there to hear it. But if a man cuts down the forest and then cries that he has no food or firewood or shade, who is going to hear *him*?

Poetry is the language of being. The breath, the voice, the song of being. It does not need us. We are the ones in need of it. If we haven't learned to hear it, we will also never speak it.

Beings eat one another. This is the fundamental business of the world. It is the whole, not any of its parts, that must prevail, and the whole is changing all the time. There is no indispensable species, and no indispensable culture. Especially not a culture that dreams of eating without being eaten, and that offers the gods not even the entrails or the crumbs.

These lines of Sophocles are nearly 2,500 years old – less than half the age of the assassinated tree:

> πολλὰ τα δεινὰ κοὐδεν ἀν-
> θρώπου δεινότερον πέλει·
> τοῦτο καὶ πολιοῦ πέραν
> πόντου χειμερίῳ νότῳ
> χωρεῖ, περιβρυχίοισιν
> περῶν ὑπ᾽οἴδμασιν, θεῶν
> τε τὰν ὑπερτάταν, Γᾶν
> ἄφθιτον, ἀκαμάταν ἀποτρύεται,
> ἰλλομένων ἀρότρων ἔτοσ εἰσ ἔτοσ,
> ἱππείῳ γένει πολεύων.

> *Strangeness is frequent enough, but nothing*
> *is ever as strange as a man is.*
> *For instance,*
> *out there,*
> *riding the great-maned water,*

heavy weather on the southwest quarter,
jarred by the sea's thunder,
tacking through the bruise-blue waves.
Or he paws at the eldest of goddesses,
earth, as though she were made
out of gifts and forgiveness,

Years ago I tried to make an English version:

Strangeness is frequent enough, but nothing
is ever as strange as a man is.
For instance,
out there,
riding the great-maned water,
heavy weather on the southwest quarter,
jarred by the sea's thunder,
tacking through the bruise-blue waves.
Or he paws at the eldest of goddesses,
earth, as though she were made
out of gifts and forgiveness,
driving the plough in its circle year after year
with what used to be horses.

When he sees his own people destroying the world, what is the poet to say?
Stop? Or more politely, *Please stop, please*?

All the poets of all times can only say one thing. They can say that what –
is is. When he sees his people destroying the world, the poet can say, "we're
destroying the world." He can say it in narrative or metaphoric form, tragic
or ironic form, short form or long form, in verse or in prose. But he cannot
lie, as a poet, and offer himself as the savior. He can believe or not believe
that salvation is possible. He can believe in one God or in many gods or in
none. He can believe or not believe in belief. But he cannot finally say
anything more than the world has told him.

When he sees that we human beings are, in absolute terms, too
numerous in addition to the fact that we seem too powerful as a species –
what is the poet going to do? Pull the trigger? Sing a song of praise to Herod
or to Hitler?

In the words of the American poet John Knoepfle,

when one is guided by conscience only,
there is no other side
to which one can cross.

There is no other earth to cross to either. There are no new worlds. Paradise will not be our asylum. And our hell will not be anywhere other than here. The world is one, at the same time that it is plural, inherently plural, like the mind. The proof of this plurality is the persistence of poetry in our time. It persists – it survives – in the voices of human beings just as it does in the voices of all the other species in the world.

 os • ဆ

The Magical Reality of Memory
Janet Frame's *The Carpathians*

———————————————————— ℬ

Isabella Maria Zoppi

L ANGUAGE AND POWER. The Power of Language. The power language loses when it confronts the natural laws of that ordered chaos we call Nature. Or when it confronts the magic rules and events of that parallel, disordered world we do not name, because the act of naming it would make it come into existence, but which we are so often ready to swear exists. This dialectic of dual realities may be the unifying thread on which the narrative of Janet Frame's *The Carpathians* (1989) is artfully constructed. In fact, a close reading of this novel has to be filtered through the lenses of what has been defined as 'magical realism,' an oxymoron which represents a binary opposition between reality and imagination, a permanently contradictory relation between two worlds, or apparently incompatible systems of signifiers and signifieds. These find a meeting-point in magical-realist writing, thus giving voice to the unthinkable, and unspoken, or to those "living on the margins,"[1] in a perspective which is implicitly "ex-centric."[2]

The position of Mattina Brecon, the protagonist or, better, the main character in this polyphonic narrative is explicitly ex-centric. A well-off New Yorker, driven by an unquenchable intellectual curiosity, both puzzled and fascinated by the concept of distance – and by its power of changing views

---

[1] Linda Kenyon, "A Conversation with Robert Kroetsch," *New Quarterly* 1 (Spring 1988): 15.

[2] Stanley McMullin, "Adam Mad in Eden: Magic Realism as Hinterland Experience," in *Magic Realism and Literature: Essays and Stories; Proceedings of the Conference on Magic Realist Writing in Canada, University of Waterloo / Wilfrid Laurier University (May, 1985)*, ed. Peter Hinchcliffe & Ed Jewinski (Waterloo: Waterloo UP, 1986): 13–22. See also Stephen Slemon, "Magic Realism as Post-Colonial Discourse," *Canadian Literature* 116 (Spring 1988): 9–24.

and things – Mattina has long toyed with the balance between reality and imagination, buying real estate all over the world, in the urgent need to know different people and own remote objects (generated perhaps by a lack of exchange and communication with her husband, a novelist suffering from a distressing writer's block). It is in order to collect facts and material that will help her husband get out of the blind alley in which he is losing his self-esteem that Mattina leaves New York, the centre, to move to the margins. In a tourist leaflet about New Zealand – a totally different world – she reads of the legend of the Memory Flower, which tells how a girl, chosen by the gods to retrieve the memory of the land from oblivion, eats a fruit at the end of her journey and thus tastes the yesterday and the tomorrow of the town of Puamahara, where she spends the rest of her days recounting the memory. At her death, as an antipodal Daphne, she metamorphoses into a tree on which it is said that the Memory Flower continues to blossom.[3] Intrigued by this legend and by the lure of distance and hungry for the treasure of knowledge and for the roots of memory, in search of a remedy she does not yet know she needs, Mattina settles in one of the detached houses on Kowhai Street:

> I do feel that having the memory at hand, even if it is buried in legend, is having access to a rare treasure. Such memories are being lost rapidly and everywhere we are trying to find them, to revive them. Puamahara in the Maharawhenua could be the place for pilgrims (I guess I'm a pilgrim) to be healed of their separation from the Memory Flower [...].[4]

In a desperate bid to record the 'true' reality of Kowhai Street – a metonym for all strange places,[5] because what is normal to the residents is strange to Mattina – the New Yorker investigates the lives of her neighbours. She observes them, pays them visits, asks them questions, exchanges flowers, food, and information with them, and keeps a diary where she notes their actions, thoughts, dreams and memories. As time passes, this record almost turns into an obsession, one which leaves no space for certainty, not even about human relationships, language or memory. Lost in her dream of pure

---

[3] On this subject, see also Jeanne Delbaere, "Daphne's Metamorphoses in Janet Frame's Early Novels," *ARIEL: A Review of International English Literature* 6 (April 1975): 23–37.

[4] Janet Frame, *The Carpathians* (London: Bloomsbury, 1988): 61. Further references in the text are to this edition.

[5] See Alison Lambert, "The Memory Flower, the Gravity Star, and the Real World: Janet Frame's *The Carpathians,*" *New Zealand Literature Today* (New Delhi: Indian Society for Commonwealth Studies, 1993): 102–20.

call-and-response, sought-and-found truth, Mattina wonders "if her questioning might destroy the answer. 'Who are you really? What do you think and feel and remember in this town of the Memory Flower? Tell me, tell me!'" (70). Meanwhile, she reveals very little of herself, since her own real life is not at the core of her reflections. She takes pictures of the landscape, sketches, and uses a tape recorder to register the soundscape. In her diary she records the ordinary and the absurd, what she can describe and what she cannot explain, thus rendering her picture of the real world she is so concerned with, elusive and contradictory, "unless of course the 'real world' is simply defined as one's personal interpretation of reality."[6]

ଓ • ℬ

As a group, the inhabitants of Kowhai Street offer a specimen of the marginalized side of the New Zealand population, each of them symbolizing and displaying a peculiar disadvantage or want. As Lambert points out, in *The Carpathians* "several new characters, representing facets of construction of New Zealand identity, join the family of the aged, the insane, the artists, and other social misfits that Frame has brought out of the cold."[7]

The Shannons run a computer shop and have adopted a consumer-based way of life. At home, the idol venerated by Ed and by his son Peter is the computer they spend most of their spare time playing and conversing with, while Ed's wife Renée keeps dreaming of moving to Auckland, which she believes is the centre of everything, and therefore the opposite of the provincial town of Puamahara: "She said, 'We're so far away here,' without entering the everlasting argument of far away from what, from whom, which distant people and places?" (59). Ed Shannon plays murder games on his computer, which he takes very seriously, as Peter points out, and which have recently and unusually been echoed in Kowhai Street by the murder of The Penultimate Madge. Both father and son play war games and flying games. Their main interest seems to be the border between Reality Mode and reality, if there is any border at all. "'I fly *only* in Reality Mode, now' [...] 'It's more real than real, isn't it, Peter?'" (110). At the Shannons, Mattina starts losing her confidence in the solid 'earthiness' of the earth and in the inevitability of three dimensions, thus preparing the ground for a conception

---

6 Amaryll Chanady, "The Origins and Development of Magic Realism in Latin American Fiction," also in *Magical Realism and Literature*, 49.

7 Lambert, "The Memory Flower," 102.

of the world utterly new to her, in which fractal geometry allows more than one possibility at a given crossing between Time and Space:

> The idea 'more real than real' captured Mattina's fancy. She could not place 'more real than real' within its dimension of comparison; [...] Yet if 'real' were the flat surface, was 'more real' below or above the surface? And where, then, was 'unreal' – airspace, earthspace, outer space, inner space? Or were the three compressed into one rich slab of cognition? And how then might they be separated? (110)

From Mattina's point of view, this dialectical relationship with the computer is an extended metaphor of difficulties, encountered in the modern world, in communicating between generations or across social classes. It could also be a way of expressing the complex geography of communication extending between the central Western point of view and that of the Outer Provinces. Every conversation at the Shannons is a microcosm which is offered as a metonym of a magical-realist text or context. Considered a "dreamer" by his father, Peter is the one who seems most clearly to see the objective physical aspects of the recent murder and the necessity of keeping alive those legends, traditions and traditional tools that have served to define humanity for a long time. Peter's computer game is programmed for "earth-weapons," and he is the one who bothers to answer Mattina's inquiry into the meaning of the Memory Flower, reminding her of the old roots of his country. Nevertheless, he does not manage to pass on to her his perception of reality: "'Of course the flying's real,' he said fiercely. 'Pilots use the simulator to learn to fly.' 'Then how can you tell which game's real and which isn't?'" (62).

In Kowhai Street, all the residents seem to cherish a personal perception of reality, their particular idea of space and time. Though all of them apparently came there of their own free will, they keep thinking of themselves as uprooted or displaced persons, whose lives should have been spent somewhere else. Every time she makes a new encounter or visit, Mattina has to reconsider her own sense of place and distance. Very soon she notices that "the residents she had met had spoken of themselves as strangers. [...] Perhaps strangers never became at home in Kowhai Street?" (39). Indeed, Mattina sees Kowhai Street as a succession of arrivals and departures, some of them actual, some of them desired, foreseen, imagined, recorded, remembered. The Shannons want to move to Auckland, the economic navel of their world. The Townsends ask the grandmother from abroad to move in with them where she is needed to look after the children and the house. When she finally comes, they tell her there are neither room nor tasks for her to do, and they even forget to talk to her. George Coker, who is coming to the end of his life, uses his time to look after his roses and make of his garden his true home, while the interior of his house looks as though it had been abandoned, and is kept like a museum. At his death, his things are sold at auction, and Mattina, after having explored his store of memories while he was alive, decides to share some of his earthly belongings and buys (or 'rescues') some of his bedspreads, "never used," as the sound of his voice reminds her in her mind. These could represent George's personal memory flower, "for Mattina's afternoon at the auction had convinced her that the memory tree might be hung not with flowers but with the items of household furnishing" (99).

Among the residents, the Hanueres are more evidently displaced, as they live so far from their Maori origins that they have even forgotten their tribal language; this is a loss they are aware of, and with which they are trying to come to terms, because "You know, it's been lonely without our language" (26). Less visible is the mental displacement of Hercus Millow, whose life is spent in a two-dimensional, borderline territory balanced between past and present, with not even a thought addressed to the future. In his timeless old age, he contemplates the remote mountains through haze and clear air. At dawn and sunset, he sits "changing unattainable distance to palpable closeness, and back again to distance" (64). Her conversations with the veteran offer Mattina new insights into the power of distance and the illusions of closeness: "Last week – now last week's gone forever. But the war – for me it's still here. [...] It's still here, but distant" (41). In a useless effort to cross the generational gap between her and her niece and before being killed in bed by a young robber, The Penultimate Madge hands the girl her ring, thus trying to link her to the old tradition and to her own memory, filling the distance with the language of symbols. When Mattina arrives in Kowhai Street, Madge is already distant, already gone, "spoken of as a stranger" (39), reduced to a sentence in the residents' conversations. The Jameses, both piano tuners, have a tragic story about distance and communication to be recorded, too. Their adolescent daughter Decima is autistic, and they have had to place her in the Manuka Home because it has become dangerous for them to keep her at home. Unable to cope with her condition, they "had shifted the burden of their daughter and their daughter's burden to a place where words no longer mattered; and even beyond the notes of music, to the rest on the other side of music" (73). Maybe it is no coincidence that both the manuka and the kowhai are local trees, and that Maori toponyms link the

voluntary "strangers" in town and the insane just out of town to one another
and the roots of the earth, whether they are conscious of the fact or not.
Finally, Dinny Wheatstone's account is both similar to, while also opposed
to, the autistic child's. Decima's refusal of language, her total lack of words,
is countered by the imposter-novelist's excess of words, which in reality is
less her own than a trait of the characters she is writing about: "'The human
race is an elsewhere race and I am an imposter in a street of imposters. I am
nothing and no-one: I was never born. I am a graduate imposter'" (51).[8]

In her notes on the Puamaharians she meets, Mattina stresses their
difficulty in communicating. To her New Yorker eye, their life at the margin
is a life on the outskirts of verbal exchange. As in one of Janet Frame's early
novels, in the provincial colonial society of Kowhai Street, people balance on
the edge of the alphabet, "where words like plants [...] grow poisonous tall
and hollow about the rusted knives and empty drums of meaning, or, like
people exposed to a deadly weather, shed their fleshy confusion and show
luminous, knitted with force and permanence."[9] The "deadly weather" in
The Edge of the Alphabet could be read as an anticipation or a forecast of the
"midnight rain" which falls on Kowhai Street and its residents, whose
words and meaning, place and placelessness, generates a widespread but
subterranean feeling of confusion and insecurity. All the same, they all seem
to share a general sense of inadequacy, as if they had failed to accomplish
something expected of them, or else had failed to do it properly or completely. Mattina's language, throughout her diary, shows how she looks at
her neighbours. These are part of her experiment; she examines them under
the lenses of her microscope. Yet they are caged in a sort of invisible zoo
where they observe the observer, like

> those yellow birds that are kept apart from their kind – you see their cages
> hanging in windows, in the sun – because otherwise they would never learn
> the language of their captors...[10]

People in Kowhai Street are caged in by the fences they themselves have
built around their homes. Intent on keeping due distance from one another,
Mattina's neighbours consume their lives in their private cages. They
cultivate a sense of their own extraneousness, dedicating their energies to
learning new languages or new ways of communication, the Shannons with
their computers, the Jameses with their keys, the Hanuere with their Maori.

---

[8] The spelling is the author's.
[9] Frame, *The Edge of the Alphabet* (Christchurch: Pegasus, 1962): 13.
[10] Frame, *The Edge of the Alphabet*, 302.

Yet they all seem to forget that the simple secret for a successful conversation is to listen carefully to one's interlocutor.

ଔ • ৩০

Mattina herself is made to face and listen to (and read about) a very singular interlocutor, when she meets Dinny Wheatstone the imposter novelist. This encounter between Mattina and Dinny – the former in search of material for the novel someone else would have to write, and the latter materially offering a novel she should not have written – signals the first fracture in the realist texture of the narrative,[11] leaving room for a new, fractal dimension which threatens to uproot Mattina's cardinal beliefs. Ill at ease, Mattina recognizes herself (as she was both before and after settling down in Kowahi Street) in the thoughts and actions of a character in the typescript Dinny has put in her letterbox. At this point, as if in a Chinese-box sequence or 'speaking mirror' plot, one is easily reminded of the village of Macondo, and of Melquíades' Sanskrit manuscript in *One Hundred Years of Solitude*, a manuscript which writes itself and which, in the end, the reader discovers, tells the story of the person who has finally managed to decipher it, who is at the same time reader and character. Thus, in reading Dinny's typescript, Mattina finds herself at the same time actor and spectator, reader and character of her own life. Previously, her disorientation and confusion were self-indulgently justified by her jet-lag and by her literal/literary way of decoding the signs and contents of the 'real life' surrounding her. From now on, they start to affect the whole of her perceptions, while she is forced to observe herself and her world through the imposter-novelist's two-dimensional vision, founded on the coordinates of Dinny's personal view of time and space. Thus, the logical and hyper-rational New Yorker is now obliged – and allowed by her Self – to admit the irrational and magic into the solid box where she has shut up her consciousness. Reality, as depicted by Arturo Uslar Pietri, is generally mysterious. Man himself is a mystery, and a magical-realist piece of writing can be neither more nor less than "a poetic divination or a poetic negation of reality."[12] For the first time in her life, in

---

[11] Jeanne Delbaere, "Psychic Realism, Mythic Realism, Grotesque Realism: Variations on Magic Realism in Contemporary Literature in English," in *Magical Realism: Theory, History, Community*, ed. Lois Parkinson Zamora & Wendy B. Faris (Durham NC/London: Duke UP, 1995): 249–66.

[12] Arturo Uslar Pietri, *Letras y hombres de Venezuela* (Mexico: Fondo de cultura económica, 1948; repr. Madrid: E.M. Edition, 1978): 161–62.

Kowhai Street, Puamahara, North Island, New Zealand, Mattina the explorer encounters the mystery. And for the first time a crevice in the narrative is opened up, through which magic seeps into the text. At night, Mattina starts to feel an inexplicable presence in her room:

> an animal of long ago breathing near her in the dark [...]. (79)

> She felt that the presence, contained within two dimensions like a flat shape upon a map, might indicate not a breaking of the fabric of space and time but a levelling of the present, the beginning of the reduction of the room, Mattina, the house, the street and its people [...] to a two-dimensional existence, people-shapes and house-shapes [...]. (100–101)

> [...] an ancient and distant presence that was new and close by, affirming the world of the Gravity Star. (115)

This penetration of magic into the New Yorker's bedroom introduces into the novel what Wilson Harris has called the "occult dimension of the past."[13] Mattina's Self encounters the Other. Beyond all convention, beyond all laws of logical thought or of the exact sciences, the woman's consciousness attains a different level of perception, where she can cross the limits of substance and of reality and make contact with true essence. The "animal of long ago" represents some primordial element linked to the magic of the earth, or to that ancient knowledge which has been awakened by Mattina's investigations. In the dark cave of her bedroom, she dives deep into the dreamtime of the aboriginal peoples,[14] where she meets the spokesmen of the land she is trying to examine, classify, cut up and take away in her diary – in other words, to colonize once again. In the meanwhile, since she is the unconscious writer of a narrative in the notes she believes she is taking for someone else, Mattina experiences the gift of the poet, the great observer *par excellence*, the story-teller, the gift that provides a key to the overcoming of distance, in time and space, in order to be able to perceive "*realism* and *fantasy* as a threshold into *evolution* and *alchemy*." It is at this point that Mattina crosses that threshold which is "a component of the 'mental bridge' within and across cultures [...]."[15]

os • so

---

[13] Wilson Harris, "The Fabric of Imagination," in *The Radical Imagination*, ed. Alan Riach & Mark Williams (1973; Liège: L³ – Language and Literature, 1992): 87.

[14] Delbaere, "Psychic Realism, Mythic Realism, Grotesque Realism," *Magical Realism*, 258.

[15] Harris, *The Womb of Space* (Westport CT: Greenwood, 1983): 69–70.

The second fracture in this realist discourse occurs the night Mattina is woken by a disturbing sense of uneasiness and by certain inexplicable sounds to find that she has been chosen to witness the effect of the Gravity Star on the inhabitants of Kowhai Street. Gravity Star is Frame's name for a quasar which had been recently discovered at the time she was writing *The Carpathians*. In an interview with Marion McLeod, the author herself explained that she had entirely invented the legend of the Memory Flower – a hint of magic – but that she had read something about the new galaxy – the realism of sciences and technology.[16] The concept of the quasar has great appeal for Janet Frame: a quasi-radio stellar object bearing within itself the notion of being so full of power, *so far* (really) and *so* (apparently) *close*. The quasar is called a 'galaxy' but is an extragalactic agglomerate of energy still to be observed, studied and understood, yet fascinating and figuratively intelligible even for the non-initiated. The quasar is described as

> a star that annihilates the concept of near as near and far as far, for the distant star is close by, puncturing the filled vessel of impossibility, overturning the language of concept, easing into our lives the formerly unknowable, spilling unreason into reason. (52)

The Gravity Star shivers over Kowhai Street and then, suddenly, one night the residents lose their language, their capacity for verbalizing, their words and their meaning. They run, screaming, out of their houses or cages, but the sounds they utter are desperate, primitive animal wails. Not only have they lost all human speech, their appearance is non-human, too: their clothes are in shreds as if they had been attacked, their eyes are void of hope, petrified. "It was not entirely the cries that brought a renewed feeling of horror: it was the faces, the bodies, the clothes [...] Mattina, feeling she had *known, invested* in each family, observed [...] all changed beyond belief" (126).

Mattina's point of view is privileged, because neither she nor Dinny Wheatstone has been affected by the phenomenon; Mattina is a real foreigner and the imposter is foreign to this world, being mentally displaced in her imposture. This may be the reason why they are "spared transformation within Puamahara, this night as the Gravity Star shines besides the Memory Flower" (127). It starts raining, but every raindrop is

---

[16]   Marion McLeod, "Janet Frame in Reality Mode," interview, *New Zealand Listener* (24 September 1988): 25. About the Gravity Star, in the "Introductory Note," Frame quotes directly from her source, the *Dominion*, as she says in a radio interview with Elizabeth Alley (Radio New Zealand, November 1988).

in shapes of the 'old' punctuation and language – apostrophes, notes of music, letters of the alphabets of all languages. The rain was at once alive in its falling and flowing; and dead, for it was voiceless, completely without sound. (127)

At this point, the plague of amnesia in the village of Macondo naturally comes to mind. There the inhabitants lose their capacity for verbalization less suddenly, but in an equally tragic way. The difference is that, after the plague, Macondo returns to 'normality,' whereas Kowhai Street, after its overwhelming loss, remains empty, the residents disappearing without a trace: "everyone in Kowhai Street had died or been killed and removed" (149). Through losing their language, they have lost their identity. Therefore their humanity is changed into a non-entity, which is why they have to be erased from the 'real' world to enter a different dimension where they can become part of that Other Mattina has recently experienced in her room:

> The people of Kowhai Street had experienced the disaster of unbeing, unknowing, that accompanies death [...] still alive, [they] were now unintelligible creatures with all the spoken and written language of the world fallen as rain about them. [...] They were alive, yet on the other side of the barrier of knowing and being. (129)

For the nocturnal event which occurred in Kowhai Street there is "no frame of reference in reality,"[17] but, as often happens in magical-realist writing, no explanation is offered: "Having found their new voice, they accepted it and soon began to control it. They no longer screamed" (128). The reader is guided through the implausible plot by a distant, neutral narrative voice, which affirms that Mattina and her neighbours "had entered the time of the coexistence of dream and reality, had absorbed and explored the principles of the Gravity Star" (131). Later, Mattina tries to account to herself for the fact that she had been ignored by the Gravity Star. This may be due to her concern with time and distance, and especially with the power of distance to change and save things and memories. In a crucial moment immediately following her realization of the tragic nature of the events, Mattina secludes herself within her Self and returns in memory to her past life in New York, where she finds secure shelter:

> she had given her thoughts most entirely to memories of her past life [...] when the other residents of Kowhai Street were being destroyed by the experience of the night, she had removed her self, her real being, to New York City, that is,

---

17 Delbaere, "*The Carpathians*: Memory and Survival in the Global Village," in *The Ring of Fire: Essays on Janet Frame*, ed. Delbaere (Mundelstrup/Sydney: Dangaroo, 1992): 199–208.

to Memory, and while races and worlds may die, if they are to change, to resurrect as new, they must remain within the Memory Flower. (151)

Embracing her past reality as a creed, Mattina finds resurrection through her imagination, perhaps strengthened by the closeness of the Memory Flower. Nevertheless, her inexplicable survival does not make her life last any longer than those of the lost Puamaharians. Shortly after the alphabetical rain, that midnight rain which "would fertilize and feed nothing" (168), she goes back to New York, after having bought the empty houses – the empty cages – in Kowhai Street, as a sort of immense tombstone or a memorial for those who have been wiped away and promptly forgotten. Mattina dies a few months later, of a cancer she had long suspected and whose reality she had almost been ready to admit when she settled in Kowahi Street. In Puamahara, she notices that at ground level, as opposed to in New York skyscrapers, it is no longer possible to avoid the secret pain which sometimes asks to be heard: "There's no escape now, Mattina thought. I'm at earth level" (36). At earth level it is easier to catch the signals of that Other world, and contact with the realm of magic is more likely. During her long agony, Mattina tells her husband the real story of her visit to New Zealand, including every aspect of her experience of ordinary normality and extraordinary alienation. She wants him to remember all the details, urging him to take up her burden, the burden of being the living memory of the missing ones.

> she repeated solemnly the familiar words spoken at ceremonies, memorials to the dead in battles, to the brave for their self-sacrifice. 'I will remember them.' She knew she would carry each life the near distance to New York, and like the witches and story-tellers of old tales, pour her memories, like a potion, in Jake's ear. (156)

Partly incredulous but intent on honouring his late wife's last wish, Jake tells Mattina's story to their son, before making his own pilgrimage to Kowhai Street. Here he meets the estate agent who is in charge, to show him his inherited property, but he cannot believe the agent when he says that everyone moved away at once, without warning. He turns to Connie Townsend, the desired and soon forgotten grandmother, who seems to be the only survivor of the secret holocaust precisely because she had been rejected by her family some time before. Connie treasures her memories, which sum up her connection with humanity: "I'm the only one now to remember, the only one left. And it's real memory" (184). Unaware that Mattina is dead, with tragic irony the old woman tells of her story there, of its purpose, and of the stories she saved for Jake's sake, as well as for that of the Puamaharians and for herself:

> And there was a woman here, an American like you, who escaped, she'll have the memory too, she took it with her; in her notebooks, in her bag, in her head, she won't lose it. She wrote it down on paper to be made into book. (184)

Mattina's diaries and recordings, the facts and the material she has collected, will not be wasted: the book will be written by her son John Henry. In the end, what the reader is dealing with no longer seems Mattina's story as told by herself, or in her notes, but Mattina's story as told by her son, just as before Mattina's story was told by the imposter-novelist Dinny Wheatstone. "Mattina died in February, surrendering at last her point of view" (170).

ଓ • ಬ

Mattina's path is a journey of initiation, in search of the true or the 'real' essence of beings and things; but, most of all, it is a journey in search of the core of language and of its deepest meanings and values. Her obsession with the term 'real' and its valencies is the pivot of her quest: until the borderline of reality is defined, analyzed and assimilated, it is not possible to tune into that Outer world which might pivot on what we label 'magical' (we have no words to name the unfamiliar). Mattina's concern with language as a medium through which she can get closer to people has always been relevant. Long before her visit to New Zealand, standing in the nursery in front of her only child, she feels like a spectator, "needing to have him translated by someone who knew his language, trying to read him as if he were a small comma or a question mark" (136). Mattina senses that the presence of the Gravity Star over this antipodal world is not fortuitous, and she fears the changes the Star will provoke. She understands they are going to affect the domain of logic and language, which are at the root of every human relationship:

> the demolishing of logical thought, its replacement by new concepts starting at the root of thought, would cause the natural destruction of known language. A new language, a new people, a new world: and perhaps the end of known civilization as human cognition, no longer supporting and supported by the words of the former languages [...]. (119)

Mattina's perception of language moulds it as if it were a living being, of which she can observe the winding growth, "the slow development of a language that shifts at the pace of geological time, a new vowel each thousand years" (102). In order to erect fences around her sense of reality, Mattina searches for information about her neighbours and surroundings, about the 'real' world around her. This information, which "comes with voice, body, mind, clothes, the capacity to argue, agree, to make love" (57), is expressed everywhere through language. This is why she makes "a career of being there and talking to *them* in all parts of the world" (59). Mattina settles in Puamahara, attracted by the idea of finding the blossom of the Memory Flower, and so discovering the memory of the land. She is convinced, however, that she will not exploit it, but, on the contrary, preserve it, sure as she is she will meet "everyone certain as could be of the knowledge of the programme of time learning the language of the memory, like the computer language, [...] creating the future" (60). Words will be her tools, unspoken words or words that are the "unassailable answer to all arguments" (70); words the Maori used to name the unfamiliar and the ordinary, giving everything a sense of identity which is not "mere lighthearted metaphor," but "a tale of search, capture, imprisonment: the everlasting hunt" (96). Words spoken with "a lingering tone like a falling musical note" (105); small words spoken too much, "tired by use" (119); unusual words held back, waiting for a better moment, because "some may live a lifetime before they used a cherished word or phrase with special meaning to them" (66).

All of the Kowhai Street residents have a special symbolic relationship with language, but this is especially true of one who does not strictly belong to the community any more. Decima James has been placed in a rest home, for her sake and for that of her parents, but not even this radical change in her life has made her speak or given her the slightest desire to communicate with the rest of the world. When Gloria James speaks to Mattina of her daughter, she once more introduces the concept of distance, and the power distance has on beings and things, which anticipates the events caused by the so-far, so-close Gravity Star:

> she hears everything, she sees everything, [...] but she's lost to us, she could be
> thousands of miles away, in the Andes or in the Carpathians, or she could be in
> your home town. (106)   .

"She has no words" (106). This is Gloria's complaint, expressed in plain words, from the distance of an incurable pain, while she depicts her daughter as if she were "a distant correspondent who never replied to mail" (106). Even after the disaster in Kowhai Street, Decima's dumb and dead existence goes on as ever. The girl continues to inhabit her single-inhabitant planet, like a bitter parody of the Petit Prince, where she can be subject and

Queen, make laws and undo them, take and give from herself to herself, in that desperate freedom represented by the total absence of desire. Mattina is singularly struck by the idea of an existence spent in a complete lack of communication, knowledge, or exchange: "That's the pity. Unknown by herself or anyone. I never realised how important it is to be *known* and to *know*" (73).

The climax of Mattina's initiation journey focuses precisely on the concept of knowledge and exchange. It occurs at the Maori village, where Mattina has an enlightening conversation with the matriarch. The old woman explains to the New Yorker the necessity of talking the language of nature in order to plait flax and to give voice to that secret exchange which is fundamental between the craftsman and the subject/object of his craft. "'First,' she said, 'you must *know* flax. I know flax and flax knows me. You understand the sort of knowing I mean?' " (86). Mattina is thrilled

> at the recognition that here was *her* kind of knowing; and that of the James family; and Hercus Millow; and of the others in Kowhai Street; the knowing that included but was not dependent on the Memory Flower or the Gravity Star; that by itself could banish distance, nearness, weight, lightness, up, down, today, yesterday, tomorrow. (86)

If the voice of Nature is the only language that it is still possible to speak, the only sheet anchor left after the irruption of magic into the realist world, then the old Maori's flax might be the true Memory Flower tree, the origin of which has long been forgotten.

In a certain way, this initiation into the language of the earth counterbalances Mattina's shock in coming face to face with herself throughout Dinny's typescript. The imposter-novelist, in whose language, fiction and 'real' life are so strictly interwoven that it is impossible to reconstruct the truth, remains trapped in a cage she well recognizes but cannot avoid, in an eternal/alternative dialectical game, itself another direct consequence of the Gravity Star. Significantly, Dinny herself chooses to enclose her avowal within brackets:

> (I, Dinny Wheatstone, author of this imposter record, divine the activities of Kowhai Street, the street of the Gravity Star among the ordinary extraordinary people, while I study the primer possible impossibility, the meaning of the meaningless, as if the Gravity Star irons all displayed meaning into nothingness, obliterates the significant signs and prints of the alphabets of all languages, leaves a smooth language of nothingness and also of possible impossibility for a new world to walk on, making new footprints or talk of making new tongue-prints.) (57)

In her typescript, Dinny does not say explicitly that she is 'writing' anything, but she uses the verb "divine," thus giving a hint of the true identity of the narrative voice, since, by the end of the book Mattina's son John Henry is said to have published a novel entitled, remarkably, *The Diviner*. This cross reference to divination is in some ways typical of Frame's writing, as the author has always been aware

> that the world owes its conditions of existence to a realm of being far beyond the immediately visible. Many of her protagonists engage in a relentless quest for these far-away roots of reality. Consequently, Frame's questers are often borderline figures, loosely anchored in the world of accepted rationality, poised on the edge of vision and prophetic utterance.[18]

Indeed, all the questers that wander through *The Carpathians* – such as Mattina, Jake and John Henry, Dinny, the Hanueres and Hercus Millow – balance their search between the established patterns of behaviour in their caged houses, whether they belong to the New York intelligentsia or to the provincial middle class, and the magical suggestions of an elusive, parallel world, located somewhere in that remote distance which they do not manage to describe but which they desperately try to circumscribe. Throughout the narrative, the importance of language as a vehicle of memory, which allows and guarantees its existence, is variously stressed. And language, in *The Carpathians*, is strictly linked to narrator, narrative voice and points of view. In the Note that precedes the four sections into which the book is divided, the reader is not only given the 'scientific' coordinates of the phenomenon called the Gravity Star, but also a key to the interpretation of the whole work. The note is signed by John Henry Brecon:

> Writing this, my second novel, I became absorbed not in my power of choice but in the urgency with which each character equated survival with maintaining point of view, indeed with *being* as a point of view. The coincidence of the rediscovery of the legend of the Memory Flower, and the discovery of what I have called the Gravity Star, tended to make both memory and point of view (removed, overturned by the Gravity Star) the character and the scene now of celebration, now of battle.

Having a point of view, therefore, is equivalent to *being* a point of view. This paradox, so similar to the so-far, so-close essence of the Gravity Star, is at the very heart of the novel.

---

18 Marc Delrez, "'Boundaries and Beyond': Memory as Quest in *The Carpathians*," in *The Ring of Fire*, ed. Delbaere, 209.

The fundamental concept on which quantum theory is based might be summed up in one single sentence: the observer influences reality through his act of observation. Heisenberg's Uncertainty Principle states that, when one is measuring certain pairs of quantities, such as position and speed, or energy and time, it is not possible to measure one of them with infinite precision – for instance, position – without fundamentally mistaking the other – speed. The paradox in the narration of *The Carpathians* can be inscribed within the canonical formulation of the principle of uncertainty or indeterminacy. Analyzing the Kowhai Street people's lives and even memories more closely, Mattina acts as the microscope which, by increasingly magnifying the enlargement, makes the system unpredictable and unobservable. The act of observation or of analyzing is an act of measurement. In the case of Frame's novel, the writing is itself the act of measurement and thus carries out the analysis. In measuring, the means or agent of analysis and measurement – here the writing itself – is first applied. Then, once the system has been fixed, it is possible to determine the number or measurement that is the result of the operation of measuring. Yet the act of measurement itself modifies the system, because the observer influences reality through his act of observation. For the observer has in a sense interfered with the system observed; by fixing it, he has stopped it, infinitesimally, in search of an even more precise measurement, thus introducing mistakes relating to the second pole of the system.

In conformity with the principle of indeterminacy, the writing of a novel, or the writing of Mattina's notes, can be interpreted as an act of measurement or observation, meant to fix a system, to pin Kowhai Street people down on a page or in Mattina's memory, as well as in that of her husband and her son. However, the act of observation, Mattina's presence/ interference in Kowhai Street, changes the system observed. Reiterated and better-focused acts of observation make the system unobservable, according to Heisenberg's principle. This is why, when the Kowhai Street people and their memory, which is what gives them their identity as human beings, are observed too closely, they dissolve, melting into an alphabetical rain containing all the languages of the world. Memory – the system – has become unobservable, so that, in the end, it has to be represented with a metaphor which is the apotheosis of unpredictability: the scattered alphabets are the omega of the expression of a system deprived of any possibility of being measured – which is to say, of being grasped and understood. Mattina's hand and eye are the instruments of observation; significantly she notices traces of the midnight event on her left hand, traditionally the 'sinister' hand of unpredictable emotions:

> She noticed a small cluster like a healed sore on the back of her left hand. She picked at it. The scab crumbled between her fingers and fell on the table into a heap the size of a twenty-cent coin. Examining it, she discovered it to be a pile of minute letters of the alphabet [...]. (129)

Ironically, the explorer who goes on a pilgrimage to Puamahara in the hope of being "healed of [her] separation from the Memory Flower" (61), is given by the Gravity Star the illusion of healing through a fake "healed sore" induced by the Gravity Star.

Yet, if the observer is part of the observed system, he or she is changed by the act of observation. For every time Mattina leaves New York to set out on another journey in search of 'real' people and real estate, she is conscious that, once back home, she will be changed by the search itself, and the changes will affect her thoughts and way of life:

> Mattina had changed following each visit she made in what Jake thought of as her 'peculiar exercise' to 'get to know the people'; yet returning, she had been full of new love and delight and in the midst of their loving, their most private world, she seemed to bring her new knowledge [...]. (175)

After the New Zealand experience, Mattina goes back to New York not only changed in her mind and perceptions, but in her body, too, conscious as she finally is of the cancer which will put a stop to all her journeying. Curiously, she shares this knowledge with Dinny, along with the point of view of the narrator. Dinny makes Mattina aware of her condition twice, through an 'ordinary' conversation, and through her typescript.

According to the dual theory of magical-realist writing put forward by Stephen Slemon and Suzanne Baker,[19] all the features in *The Carpathians* belong to two different and opposite fields. On the one hand, there is the language of nature, intuition and divination, the language of the poet, of memory and of the land, unheard words, words spoken by the few, because the majority have forgotten them, words from the margins. On the other hand, there is the language of the global village, of the village of technology, of the world of information, words heard too often, words spoken by the majority and understood by the few, words from the centre. With its myriad

---

[19] See Stephen Slemon, "Magic Realism as Post-Colonial Discourse," 12, and Suzanne Baker, "Binarism and Duality, Magic Realism and Postcolonialism," *SPAN* 36.1 (1992): 82–87.

simultaneous observers and observed and observable systems, with its teeming acts of observation, the global village reveals itself as an act of observation totally out of focus. The global village is an easily distracted eye which concentrates on everything at the same time, whereas Mattina's is a very careful eye focused on a tiny portion of reality. The structure of the novel is built on a dialectical vision, a dual system providing on the one hand a complete, planetary, widespread de-focusing of the system of observation, and, on the other, an excess of observation focused on one single point. The balance of this dual system collapses through Mattina's confusion of space and time and her excess of observation. The New Yorker's confusion between being a point of view, a character in someone else's narrative, and having a point of view, thus being the narrator or the chronicler, makes her the catalyst which acts as the second focus of the gravitational lens situated in front of the quasar. It is thus the unconscious and unwilling Mattina who catalyzes the revolutionary effects of the Gravity Star on her adopted Kowhai Street:

> because her flight's destruction of time and distance brought her here in a shredded state of mind where hours equalled years and the time became a spiral ribbon striped with the past, present and future, she became unknowingly a focus of the Gravity Star. (95)

ൠ • ℬ

Imagination in Frame's writing often carries a sense of secret knowledge or privileged access to the treasures of language. Many of her characters exhibit a need to narrate, in order to exert their control over the world, to find coherence and to clarify identity. Yet, most of them – mainly women, speaking from a marginalized point of view – are not able to exploit the magic connection with language to which they are entitled, and end by locking words into their private selves, thus severing their primordial links with the world. This is the experience of Daphne, whose vision is left unspoken (*Owls Do Cry*, 1961), of Vera Glace, who refuses to speak (*Scented Gardens for the Blind*, 1963), of Istina Mavet, who imaginatively foresees her healing and resurrection (*Faces in the Water*, 1961), of Zoe Bryce, whose refusal is the most definitive, when she ends her artistic career by committing suicide (*The Edge of the Alphabet*, 1962), and finally, as a sort of anticipatory clue, of the autistic child in *Intensive Care*. All of these characters have to cope with the failure of their privileged position in respect to the mystery of language.

These mistresses of the word, these sybils with their insights and their sharply satirical depictions of 'the plodding rituals and confusions that composed the mass living of the human race,' are incapable, within the fictions they inhabit, of conveying what they know.[20]

As narrators are said to be all facets of the same character,[21] Mattina can hardly escape this destiny of failure and wordlessness, of missed relationships and loss of memory. Nevertheless, she rescues her wanderings and her wonderings through her final act of narration. Mattina's story is saved when it is told in the ancient pre-alphabetical way from mouth to mouth, and her memory (including the treasures of her language) and *knowledge* are equally saved. If "magical realism is the name that one currently gives to the fictional space created by the dual inscription of incompatible geometries,"[22] then the four 'spaces' into which Frame divides her novel turn on that same alchemy: "The Gravity Star," "Wheatstone Imposter," "The Memory Flower," "Housekeepers of Ancient Springtime." This last phrase, which recalls a line in Rilke,[23] should have been the title of the novel: the housekeepers are the poets, who are charged with offering humanity its survival, handing down to posterity the characteristics of 'humanity,' those qualities which make a human being unique. This is what Mattina achieves despite her confusion and her sense of failure and inadequacy – and, indeed, her death. For, in repeatedly recounting her experience to her husband, she manages to transmit to him her feelings and memories as a whole, thus providing the Kowhai Street people with the only lasting memorial they will ever have. The unifying thread running through the narrative is to be found neither in the Carpathians, metonym for remoteness and alienation, nor in the blossom of the Memory Flower, an emblem for the uncertainties of language and identity: in other words, neither in distance nor in time. The main theme developed in the novel is humanity's urge for survival, notwithstanding differences in point of view, mixed identities, exchanges between incom-

---

[20] Vincent O'Sullivan, "Exiles of the Mind: The Fictions of Janet Frame," *The Ring of Fire*, ed. Delbaere, 26.

[21] Delbaere, "*The Carpathians*: Memory and Survival in the Global Village," 206.

[22] Robert Wilson, "The Metamorphoses of Space: Magic Realism," *Magic Realism and Literature*, 72.

[23] Rainer Maria Rilke, *Sämtliche Werke*, Zweiter Band (Frankfurt am Main: Insel, 1956): 532. In a poem – written in French, because the word "Verger" sounded more appealing in French than the correspondent for "Orchard" in German – Rilke wrote about ancient springtime: "Nom clair qui cache le printemps antique / tout aussi plein que transparent...."

patible geometries, imposter narrations of the ordinary and of the magic which rule this 'real' world.

Mattina's pilgrimage is motivated by the need to rediscover the memory of the land, in order to come into closer contact with her primal Self. It offers her a chance to face the Other. She says she is inspired by the legend of the Memory Flower, the pretext for her search. Thus, the legend is also at the origin of the writing of the novel, Jake's would-be next novel, Mattina's diaries, Dinny Wheatstone's typescript, Janet Frame's novel. Nevertheless, if it is true, as Frame herself has declared, that the legend of the Memory Flower is an invention of her own, in this magical-realist realm of metamorphoses where everything has been uprooted and all things are possible, perhaps the imposter-novelist is not the person he/she claims to be, but the person whose name is on the cover of the book we are reading, and we are all characters in her fiction, ready to follow her on her own pilgrimages, willing to cross with her the threshold into other dimensions – be their reality understandable or ungraspable. The joy in the journeying remains.

ଓ   •   ဢ

Re-Dreaming the World
Ben Okri's Shamanic Realism

———————————————— ∞ ————————————————

Renato Oliva

I N HIS SEMINAL DISCUSSION of marvellous realism (*lo real maravilloso*), Alejo Carpentier rejects the marvellous pursued by Surrealism as an artificial and premeditated literary fabrication:

> If Surrealism pursued the marvellous, one would have to say that it very rarely looked for it in reality. [...] The painter who stood before a canvas would say, 'I'm going to make a painting with strange elements that create a marvellous vision.' [...] I would cite as a typical example the soft clocks by Salvador Dali [...] or that other canvas by a Surrealist painter that shows a perfectly banal staircase with doors opening onto a hallway. On those stairs there is only one strange element. There is a *visitor*. It is a snake meandering up the steps. Where is it going? What is its purpose? No one knows. A mystery. A *manufactured* mystery.[1]

Too many artists manufacture the marvellous by sleight of hand:

> The result of willing the marvellous or any other trance is that dream technicians become bureaucrats. [...] The problem is that many of them disguise themselves cheaply as magicians, forgetting that the marvellous begins to be unmistakably marvellous when it arises from an unexpected alteration of reality (the miracle), from a privileged revalation of reality, an unaccustomed insight that is singularly favoured by the unexpected richness of reality or an amplification of the scales and categories of reality, perceived with particular intensity by virtue of an exaltation of the spirit that leads it to a kind of extreme state [*estado límite*]. To begin with, the phenomenon of the marvellous presupposes faith.[2]

---

[1] Alejo Carpentier, "The Baroque and the Marvelous Real," in *Magical Realism: Theory, History, Community*, ed. Lois Parkinson Zamora & Wendy B. Faris (Durham NC/London: Duke UP, 1955): 103–104.

[2] Carpentier, "On the Marvelous Real in America," 85–86.

If poets and artists must "bet their souls on the terrifying card of faith,"[3] they may find the courage to put so much at stake with the help of the culture they belong to. Carpentier's Latin America or Ben Okri's Africa are cultures not dominated by rationalism and still open to a magic–mythic world view, cultures where one can still find oneself "in daily contact with something that could be defined as the marvellous real," and where "an entire mythology is preserved by an entire people."[4] A culture whose definition of reality is less rigid than that of the Western world, and where magic is part of the traditions and faith of the community, will prompt the writer to embrace that faith without which realism is neither a profound experience, nor an exploration of the mystery of things and of human life, nor again an attempt to go beyond the dualism of natural and supernatural, or explicable and inexplicable, but merely the monotonous display of literary tricks.

This is not to say that magical realism may be given a geographical collocation, much less that it is the exclusive prerogative of certain cultures. Carpentier's argument, according to which Latin America is inherently marvellous – indeed, permeated by the marvellous real in its raw state – runs the risk of leading to a too "virulent territorialization of the imaginary."[5]

While magical realism certainly affords Caliban the opportunity to "write back" and reject some of the cultural paradigms of his colonial heritage, it is no less true that Caliban is our Shadow,[6] and that magical realism is founded in our unconscious. Archaic man, with his primitive mentality and tendency to magical thinking, survives in each of us. Each of us will certainly, though often unconsciously, have come into contact with that archaic psychic realm in which our faith in the marvellous and in the supernatural is rooted, a faith without which, as Carpentier argues, magical realism is nothing more than sleight of hand.

We all dream, and in our dreams we speak the language of magical realism. Dreams, the product of the mythologizing activity of the psyche, are

---

3 Carpentier, "On the Marvelous Real in America," 86.

4 Carpentier, "On the Marvelous Real in America," 86–88.

5 Amaryll Chanady, "The Territorialization of the Imaginary in Latin America: Self-Affirmation and Resistance to Metropolitan Paradigms," in *Magical Realism*, 131.

6 According to Jung, the Shadow is the negative or dark underside of the personality, the primitive side of man's nature. For the definition of Jungian concepts such as Shadow, *anima* (a word used by Jung to indicate the passive, feminine side of a man's psyche), complex, archetype, see Andrew Samuels, Bani Shorter & Fred Plaut, *A Critical Dictionary of Jungian Analysis* (London/New York: Routledge, 1986).

for us a habitual source of mythological representations. They transform the course of the individual life into *mythos* and, drawing on the collective unconscious, revive the great mythical themes of humanity. In dreams, images of demons and gods are brought back to life in various disguises, not only as *representation* but as *presence*, because the archetypes of demons and gods alike are alive and active in the psyche. In this sense, dream-images are real, since according to Jung every psychic event is an image and an imagining; and every image has a psychic reality. Images are of the essence of the psyche. Images are real in the same sense that our psyche is real. Our psychic energy, or libido, takes shape in these images and our instincts are made manifest as archetypal images. Thus dream-images put the dreamer in touch with his instinctive nature, with the archaic zone of his psyche.

The language of dreams – in which we talk to ourselves in an altered state of consciousness, one below the level of waking consciousness – is an emotionally charged symbolic and metaphoric language which has much in common with magical-realist writing. Dreams have a tendency to dramatize, often to overdramatize. Dreams, like magical realists, love hyperbole and use it extensively. Dreams are a magical literalization of metaphors. Like magical-realist writing, they materialize metaphors. In dreams, our emotional sufferings become bleeding wounds and heart diseases, our breakdowns ruins and earthquakes, and the unconscious worries that gnaw at us rats. If we do not keep our feet on the ground and we get lost in abstract thought and planning, we levitate and fly, while if our feelings grow cold we find ourselves surrounded by snow and ice.[7]

In dreams, the ordinary logic of cause and effect is disrupted, metamorphoses are a common event, and inner and outer are not separated. In the dream-world, magical unidimensionality prevails. A dream never

---

[7] An amusing example of literalization or materialization of a metaphor is cited by Carl Gustav Jung in "Symbols and the Interpretation of Dreams": "I recall a dream of my own that baffled me for a while. In this dream, a certain Mr. X was desperately trying to get behind me and jump on my back. I knew nothing of this gentleman except that he had succeeded in twisting something I had said into a rather grotesque travesty of my meaning. This kind of thing had frequently happened to me [...]. The dream pointedly brought up the incident again in the apparent disguise of a colloquialism. This saying, common enough in ordinary speech, is 'Du kannst mir auf den Buckel steigen' (you can climb on my back), which means 'I don't give a damn what you say.' One could say that this dream–image was symbolic, for it did not state the situation directly but in a roundabout way, through a concretised colloquial metaphor"; Jung, *Collected Works of C.G. Jung*, ed. Sir Herbert Read, Michael Fordham, Gerhard Adler & William McGuire (Bollingen Series; Princeton NJ: Princeton UP, 1980), vol. 18: 204,

expresses itself in a logical or abstract way, but, rather, in figurative language that is a survival of an archaic mode of thought. This imaginal form of communication is primary and comparable to that of the child, of primitive cultures, and of the poet.

If magical realism presupposes a certain faith on the part of both author and audience, we all possess that faith, inasmuch as we are the authors and audience of our dream. For, according to one of Jung's definitions, dreams are a theatre in which the dreamer is himself the scene, the player, the prompter, the producer, the public, and the critic.

The magical continent exists, but cannot be given a geographical collocation. It is within us, in the unconscious, where we think according to the categories of magical thought and speak the magical language of dreams. The experience of magical realism is a marginal experience, that of someone standing on the border between two nearly merging realms:

> The magic realist vision exists at the intersection of two worlds, at an imaginary point inside a double-sided mirror that reflects in both directions. Fluid boundaries between the worlds of the living and the dead are traced only to be crossed.[8]

A literature that "weaves a web of connections between the lands of the living and the dead,"[9] that crosses, blurs or dissolves the boundaries between these two lands, may perhaps be termed a shamanic literature, caught, like Okri's *abiku*, "in the middle space between the living and the dead."[10]

The shaman stands on the border between the human realm and the spirit-realm, and can cross it in either direction. For the shaman, there is no break between this world and the next. The spirit-realm is continuous with ordinary reality:

> According to a Siberian shaman, 'As I looked round, I noticed a hole in the earth... The hole became larger and larger. We [shaman and spirit ally] descended through it and arrived at a river with two streams flowing in opposite directions.' The two directions of the journey, one pointing to the temporal and the other to the atemporal, meet at cosmic centre. The 'opening' between realms is frequently represented as a hole, like the birthgate, that is the threshold between womb and consciousness.[11]

---

8 Wendy B. Faris, "Sheherazade's Children," in *Magical Realism*, 172.

9 Faris, "Sheherazade's Children," 172–73.

10 Ben Okri, *Songs of Enchantment* (London: Vintage, 1994): 258.

11 John Halifax, *Shaman: The Wounded Healer* (New York: Crossroad, 1982): 70.

The World Tree – a symbol of regeneration – is one of the points of contact and intersection between earth and the heavenly realm; in certain ceremonies, the shaman climbs a pole representing this Tree. The shaman knows the invisible paths leading to (and through) the underworld. Here he establishes relationships with good spirits – helper-guides in either human or animal form – and evil spirits. He finds allies and enemies, and he is dismembered by ravenous devouring spirits. Through this ordeal he finally acquires special magic powers and mastery over physical and mental forms of energy.

Mircea Eliade sums up the steps of the shamanic initiation, based on death–rebirth symbolism, as follows:

> First, torture at the hands of the demons or spirits, who play the role of masters of initiation; second, ritual death, experienced by the patient as a descent to hell, or ascent to heaven; third, resurrection to a new mode of being – the mode of 'consecrated man,' that is, a man who could personally communicate with gods, demons or spirits."[12]

When the shaman has demonstrated his ability to suffer death and be reborn, he can begin his career as wounded healer, setting out, in a state of trance, on the journey to the next world in search of suitable cures for the patient, or accompanying the patient on a symbolic journey into the other dimension, with the help of images, symbols, myths and prayers.

There is a grain of truth in the idea that shamanism is a form of mental illness, though the shamanic experience cannot be reduced to the status of a psychopathological phenomenon. It is true that the shamanic vocation is revealed through mental illness, a schizophrenic crisis, or an attack of epilepsy, and some shamanic experiences do seem psychotic.[13] However,

---

12 Mircea Eliade, *Rites and Symbols of Initiation: The Mysteries of Birth and Rebirth* (New York: Harper & Row, 1960): 91. For a comprehensive discussion of the problems of shamanism, see Eliade, *Shamanism: Archaic Techniques of Ecstasy*, tr. Willard R. Trask (Bollingen Series 76; Princeton NJ: Princeton UP, 1964).

13 For a striking parallel between the inner journey of the shaman and psychotic experience, interpreted as a process of renewal of the self by John Weir Perry in *The Far Side of Madness*, see Halifax, *Shaman: The Wounded Healer*: "The insights of psychiatrist John Weir Perry into the psychosymbolic processes of individuals diagnosed as schizophrenic give us important clues about the archetypal nature of the shamanic complex. Dr. Perry elaborates ten features that characterise the reorganisation of the Self. 1) Psychic, cosmic, and personal geography are focused on a *centre*. 2) Death occurs in the process of dismemberment and sacrifice; the person is tortured, chopped up, and his or her bones are rearranged; one can also be dead and talk with presences of the spirit world. 3) There is a *return* to an earlier time, to paradise, or to the womb; the theme of regression can also be reflected in the individual manifesting the behaviour of an infant.

the shaman is not just a sick man, but a healed one, a man who has been able to cure himself of his own sickness. The shaman has succeeded in traversing the realm of chaos without being overwhelmed, and has come back to tell the tale. While someone who is mentally ill is possessed by his sickness, the shaman dominates and controls his 'spirits,' in the sense that he, a human being, is able to communicate with demons and the dead, or with the spirits of nature, without becoming their passive instrument:

> The key factor in the shaman's activity is his capacity to retain control of his vision. In contrast to a medium he directs his role to encountering the spirits and gods of his mythological pantheon and learning from them. His trance is essentially a dream of knowledge which leads in turn to enhanced prospects for the hunt, a cure for the sick or the return of a stolen soul. The trance technique in the shamanic context is thus undoubtedly integrative and not self-destructive.[14]

The shaman is able to control his state of trance and to use his altered state of consciousness to explore the unconscious. Unlike the medium, moreover, who remembers nothing of his trance on emerging from it, the shaman preserves a conscious memory of his descent into the underworld or of his magical flight through the air, and on returning from his journey into the unconscious brings back scenes from his people's mythology, religion, and past or future history, visions which he then passes on to the community. Nor does the shaman only cure individual members of the community; he also has an important social role, being concerned with the community and its well-being:

> The ability of the shaman to be in a special and particular relationship with the elements, the creatures of nature, and the spirits from the unseen world, makes the shaman an invaluable member of his or her social network. Through the wisdom and work of the shaman, social and environmental crises can be mitigated and the possibility of survival increased.[15]

---

4) There arises a *cosmic conflict* between forces of Good and Evil, or other pairs of opposites. 5) There is a feeling of being overwhelmed by the opposite sex; the *threat of the opposite* can also manifest in terms of a positive identification with one's opposite. 6) The transformation of the individual results in a mystical *apotheosis* where the experiencer becomes identified with a cosmic or royal personage. 7) The person enters into a *sacred marriage*, a coming together of the pairs of opposites. 8) A *new birth* is part of rebirth phantasies and experiences. 9) A new age or the beginning of a *new society* is anticipated. 10) The balance of all elements results in the *quadrated world*, a four-fold structure of equilibrium and depth" (7).

[14] Nevill Drury, *The Shaman and the Magician: Journeys between the Worlds* (London: Routledge, 1982): 17.

[15] Halifax, *Shaman: The Wounded Healer*, 15.

It must not, however, be forgotten that though the shaman transforms madness into visionary knowledge and wisdom, he is always dangerously close to the edge of madness. His continual to-ing and fro-ing across the threshold places the stability and cohesion of his ego at risk.

If, as we have already noted, one of the characteristics of the shaman is his ability to shift his level of consciousness, thus moving between conscious and unconscious, reality and dream, natural and supernatural, this is equally true of magical realism. One of the typical elements of magical realism is, in fact, the constant crossing of thresholds and frontiers: from the conscious to the unconscious, from wakefulness to dream, from the familiar to the *unheimlich*, from the explicable to the inexplicable, from the natural to the miraculous, from the rational to the irrational, and from normality to madness.

The predilection for metaphor and symbol itself highlights magical realism's interest in crossing thresholds (at the level of language, too), since metaphor brings together remote, non-contiguous semantic fields, abolishing the distance that separates them, while symbolism mediates between known and unknown, consciousness and unconsciousness, light and darkness, rational and irrational. In Jungian terms, the symbol is a bridge between opposites, the *tertium* by means of which they may be reconciled and transcended in psychic experience, though in terms of logic (*tertium non datur*) this is inadmissible. Magical realism often makes use of materialized metaphors, the literary equivalent of oneiric language and of the *Konkretismus*[16] of psychosis. The process of literalization cancels the border between metaphorical and real: "The reader may experience a particular kind of verbal magic – a closing of the gap between words and the world [...]. This magic happens when a metaphor is made real."[17]

ઈ • ജ

If we now go on to examine *The Famished Road* and *Songs of Enchantment*, we will note that the dynamic of both books is generated by the repetition of one basic experience: crossing the threshold. Okri has stated that *The*

---

16 *Konkretismus* (concretism) is typical of infantile and primitive thinking; it is a form of archaism. According to Jung, the concretist way of thinking is always in relation to the impressions given by the senses, and is based on exclusively concrete conceptions and concepts. In concretism, the thinking function and the feeling function are not differentiated from sensation.

17 Faris, "Sheherazade's Children," *Magical Realism*, 176.

Famished Road illustrates "the possibility of a life being lived simultaneously at different levels of consciousness and in different territories."[18] In another interview, he describes the co-presence of these levels of consciousness in the following terms:

> In *The Famished Road* you have this spirit-child: one half of him is in the spirit world, the other is in the world of the real. Whenever he looks at reality, he does it through the eyes of a spirit as well as through those of a human being, so everything is both ordinary and transfigured, simultaneously. I'm not saying reality is fantastic as [García] Márquez did, Azaro is not blown off to the skies by the wind. Because of the fact that this boy is half spirit and half human, with the doors of death perpetually open inside him [...], even time is different, what we perceive as future consequence for this child is present. [...] I needed this poetic point of view, half here and half there [...]. It's all one at the same time, seen through the turbulent consciousness of this child who has chosen to live in this reality. It is a terrifically difficult point of view to write from, you have to inhabit it as well as be out of it. I nearly went mad trying to keep that perspective all the time.[19]

Azaro, too, almost goes mad with the strain of living in a double perspective, straddling the threshold between the human and spirit worlds, and continually to-ing and fro-ing between the two realms: "We [*abiku*, spirit-children] were the ones who kept coming and going, unwilling to come to terms with life."[20] Like the fairies of Irish folklore –

> Come away, O human child!
> To the waters and the wild
> With a faery, hand in hand,
> For the world's more full of weeping than you can understand[21]

– Azaro's spirit companions tempt him to return to the "world of pure dreams, where all things are made of enchantment, and where there is no suffering" (4). His refusal to return to the lands of origin is punished by repeated hallucinations, which, however, are not only a chastisement for breaking his pact with his spirit companions. The hallucinations that invade the mind of the *abiku* are also "images of the future" and give him the shamanic gift of prophecy: "Our mouths utter obscure prophecies" (4).

---

18 Jane Wilkinson, ed., *Talking with African Writers* (London: James Currey, 1992): 83.

19 Pietro Deandrea, "An Interview with Ben Okri," *Africa, America, Asia, Australia* 16 (Rome: Bulzoni, 1994): 80.

20 *The Famished Road* (London: Vintage, 1992): 4. Further page references in brackets are in the text.

21 W.B. Yeats, "The Stolen Child," in *The Collected Poems of W.B. Yeats* (London: Macmillan, 1955): 20.

At times Azaro is assailed by hallucinations and unable to resist them. At other times he himself chooses to plunge into himself and finds "other worlds waiting" (325). But the journey to the other world is always much harder than expected (327). From the moment when, won to human life by the love of Dad and Mum, Azaro overcomes the sickness that has all but killed him and chooses to go on living, his hallucinations cease for a time, and when they resume, they have partly changed character. Now they are concerned with the African past and with his ancestors (456), or with African history ("The white ones, ghost forms on deep nights, stepped on our shores [...] I witnessed the destruction of great shrines [...] I saw the forests die"; 457); they contain information about the nature of the unconscious, of which the forest is one of the symbols ("I ran through the night forests, where all the forms are mutable, where all things exchange their identities"; 457). Or again, they testify to the presence, behind individual reality, of another, archetypal reality. Men may be "disguised spirits" (137). Inside men are animal drives:

> In the terrible heat of the dance I saw that, among the erotic dancers, the politicians and chiefs, the power merchants, the cultists, paid supporters, thugs and prostitutes [...] there were strangers to the world of the living. I saw that some of the prostitutes [...] had legs of goats. Some of the women [...] had legs of spiders and birds. Some of the politicians and power merchants [...] had the cloven hoofs of bulls. [...] Everything around me seemed to be changing and yielding its form. (459–60)

The dancers look like men and women, but are in fact dead people, spirits and animals in disguise. They are "part-time human beings" (460), spirits who have "borrowed bits of human beings to partake of human reality" (136). In Jungian terms, these men, possessed by spirit powers, are governed by their archetypal complexes.

Carried in flight by a spirit over an abyss full of lurking terrors, led along roads flanked by corpses and skeletons,[22] to swamps full of snakes and crocodiles, Azaro reaches the border of Hades, marked by the river where the ferryman of the dead awaits him. This is the point at which he decides to turn back from his shamanic journey: symbolically dead, he may be reborn. Azaro's shamanic experiences, his "vision of another world hidden behind ours" (*Songs of Enchantment*, 161), are parallel to and contemporaneous with

---

[22] For a detailed discussion of the symbolic value of death and skeletonization, see Halifax, *Shaman: The Wounded Healer*, 46, 76–77.

Dad's. However, while for Azaro's ability to cross the threshold is part of his being an *abiku*, for Dad it can only be won with a struggle.

Dad has decided to become a champion boxer; and since this is a challenge of cosmic proportions, he must train not just physically but spiritually, punching at flies, jabbing at mosquitoes, fighting his own shadow, and sparring with the air (352). Dad is like a hero of the night, fighting "imaginary foes, as if the whole world were against him"(353). But the superhuman strength that assures him victory is above all drawn from his initiation bout with the ghost of a dead boxer. This clash occurs by night – which is to say, in the darkness of the unconscious, further symbolized by the swampy terrain from which the huge form and shining yellow eyes of Yellow Jaguar emerge.

In this pre-individual and pre-conscious darkness, the two fighters are less individuals than elemental powers, drives, ferocious energies, forces of nature, whirlwinds, storms (356). Dad's experience is obviously regressive. As he watches his father, Azaro realizes that he is being transformed and is "going back to simple things" (357). Dad's regression puts him in touch with the flow of primordial forces and unconscious energies: he assimilates the elemental forces which from this point on will be at his disposal. Dad is turned into a vessel of boiling manic energy, on the point of overflowing. Like the shaman, he has magically appropriated animal energies to himself and is "like a great animal startled by its own ferocity" (364). Not only is he called Black Tyger, he *is* Black Tyger.

The blows he receives reduce Dad to a "state of shock between agony and amnesia" (359) which lasts six days. On the seventh day, he is symbolically reborn ("How many times is a man reborn in one life?"; 362), and looks like "the biggest newborn baby in the world" (359). Like a shaman, after his healing Dad develops "interesting powers and a kind of madness" (364), and acquires a new vision of the world:

> "I am beginning to see things for the first time. This world is not what it seems.
> There are mysterious forces everywhere. We are living in a world of riddles."
> (388)

Thanks to the primordial energies that he is able to evoke, he can defend himself against the violent supporters, bodyguards and thugs of the Party of the Rich, knock out Green Leopard, the chief thug, and defeat the ideology which the thug represents: "I will beat you and disgrace your philosophy" (396).

The fight with Green Leopard exhausts Dad, who, overcome by extreme tiredness, sleeps for three days. His life is once more in danger. In his delirious dreams, he goes back to the forest, where he has to face seven spirits that want to kill him, and thus wins another shamanic battle against death. Reborn a second time and bustling with energy, his mind full of "grand schemes" (408), he talks of building houses for all the large families who live in one room, of opening stores that would sell food cheaply to the poor people, of clearing away all the rubbish that has accumulated in people's minds.

The shaman accepts the turning against him of the forces of the universe because he knows that if he heroically accepts the risk of being destroyed, he will be able to rebuild his personality on a higher plane, renew himself, and receive instruction. His is a quest for power and a quest for knowledge. His experience of death and rebirth gives him a breadth of vision that also has a social function, permitting him, as it does, to heal society and to restore its lost equilibrium.

There is widespread suspicion that Green Leopard's blows have dislodged something in Dad's brain, for he now announces that he wants to become a politician, a Head of State, and to act for the good of the suffering people of the world. Formerly passive, he has become active. No longer a porter or treated like a slave and forced to sweat under enormous loads if he is to survive, he has become a boxer, a fighter, and above all, a thinker who conjures up the image of the ideal city, a sort of African Utopia.

Under the influence of drink he sets himself up as a Christ-figure and promises miracles – not the multiplication, as in the Gospels, of loaves and fishes, but the division of a single chicken (419). He praises liberty and exhorts his listeners in tones of pathos to change the world. He is still regarded as crazy, but "the new lights that Green Leopard has knocked into his head" (410) are, as *Songs of Enchantment* confirms, the lights of the ecstatic madness of the shaman in search of a solution to the problems of a community that has plunged into utter social and political chaos, a community crushed by oppression, exploitation and violence.

Dad's artless visionary enthusiasm is moving and is certainly positive in meaning, even though he is dominated by the archetypes of the Magician and the Wise Old Man,[23] and runs the risk of living in a state of psychic

---

[23] See the entry for "Mana personalities" in Samuels, Shorter & Plaut, *Critical Dictionary of Jungian Analysis*, 89–90.

inflation,[24] as is shown by the fact that, in *Songs of Enchantment*, he feels like a prince in his own kingdom, speaking of the obscure royal origins of his family (220) and fighting against the destroyers of his kingdom (248–49). His condition corresponds to Perry's description of the phase of psychotic experience in which the individual identifies himself with a cosmic or royal personage.[25] In the shamanic experience,[26] this phase of mystical apotheosis manifests itself in a mystical identification with the sun, with fire, and with the mastery of fire.

Dad, then, is transformed. The theme of transformation may be singled out as one of the most representative in Ben Okri's work. Okri has said:

> I am interested in affecting consciousness. I do not have time for idle exercises on colonisers and so on. It seems to me defeatist. I am much more interested in transforming consciousness, which goes beyond colonialism.[27]

Transformation comes about through suffering, which is another of Okri's central themes. Here is another clear parallel with the shamanic experience. The tortures he endures transform the shaman and enable him in turn to transform his patients, nature and society.

Towards the end of *The Famished Road*, Dad dies and is symbolically reborn for a third time. Challenged by a tall man in a white suit (467), he fights him in a kind of "magic boxing" match (471) and wins. Overcome

---

[24] *Inflation* is a regression into unconsciousness. One is assimilated by a numinous archetypal image and identifies with the powers of the unconscious. The consequences of falling under the power of an archetype are a puffed-up attitude and a feeling of immense power and uniqueness. See the entry for "Inflation" in Samuels, Shorter & Plaut, *Critical Dictionary of Jungian Analysis*, 81–82.

[25] See John Weir Perry, *Roots of Renewal in Myth and Madness* (San Francisco: Jossey-Bass, 1976), especially ch. 5.

[26] See Halifax, *Shaman: The Wounded Healer*, 88–91.

[27] Deandrea, "An Interview with Ben Okri," 66. Ben Okri answers a rather provocative question about the necessity of rethinking the colonizers' language ("Do you think you're trying to do it, to reshape the language that your people were imposed on?") in equally provocative terms ("That seems to me like an exercise; I'm not interested in exercises"). Of course, though it is true that Okri does not generally think in terms of colonialism, there is no lack of anticolonialist polemic in his work (as in *Songs of Enchantment*, 281). A sentence has been added to *Dangerous Love* which was not in *The Landscapes Within*: "Beyond the ghetto, in the distance, shone the lights of multinationals, the lights of the rich, the flares of oil terminals burning precious unused gases away into the night air" (312). But the most significant addition is the episode of the "house of shame" (297–99), a ruined house where the chains of slaves are kept. The responsibility for slavery is not, after all, attributed solely to the whites ("Perhaps his ancestors had helped sell slaves"). There is a similar suggestion of shared responsibility: "'Those bloody white people. They interfered too much.' 'It's us. We're too greedy'" (210).

with emotion, and with the strain and "horror of his victory" (474), he sinks to the ground and, taken for dead, is carried home. There he has visions and "cyclical dreams" (493) in which he escapes into the worlds before birth, roams the spheres that restore earth's balance, and is reunited "with his own primeval spirit and totem" (493), just like a shaman, whose ancestral initiation master or guardian spirit may be an animal. Now Dad is able to re-dream the world as he sleeps and to see the scheme of things (492). Finally he sits up in bed "like Lazarus" (484) and rises from the bed "as from death" (497).

In *Songs of Enchantment* Dad perfects his shamanic vocation. He is a "tempest of energies" (275). He gathers the secrets spoken to him by the forest of the unconscious (287) and goes around shouting that he remembers fragments of his dreams and the messages given to him while he was asleep, "with the peculiar madness of those who survived a perilous dream" (163). He sits up far into the night, "re-dreaming the world" (221), fights multiplying ghosts, imaginary dragons, gigantic spirits, chaotic nightmares, and wins all the battles (250–51). He spins blindly "like a heroic dervish" (248), and in his divine madness he recognizes the folly of history ("I saw history as a madman with a machine gun, eating up the twisting flesh of the innocent and the silent"; 89). He creates new laws for his country (122–23). What Dad and Azaro discover in their visionary pilgrimage may be summarized as follows:

a) There is a constant struggle in the unconscious between opposites, between conflicting archetypal powers: "For every blast of wind from evil wings, and for every power on the sides of those that feed on the earth's blood, a fabulous angel is born" (*Famished Road*, 496).

This dualism ("Between extremities / Man runs his course"),[28] whose history can be traced from Empedocles and Heraclitus to Yeats, to say nothing of Oriental and, more generally, non-European civilizations, is one of the elements by which Jung distinguishes his own view of the psyche from those of Freud and Adler. For he places these polarities at the very basis of the psyche's dynamics. Every psychological extreme has hidden within it its opposite. It is from the tension between opposites that psychic energy derives.

b) The opposed archetypal forces live within us, and the ego must reckon with them: "Angels and demons are amongst us; they take many forms. They can enter us and dwell there for one second or half a lifetime.

---

28 W.B. Yeats, "Vacillation," in *Collected Poems*, 282.

Sometimes both of them dwell in us together"; what at first glance seems no more than the substance of Dad's psychotic delirium ("I entered a space ship and found myself on another planet. People who look like human beings are not human beings") is at the same time a discourse on the archetypal forces which may partially or wholly dominate man (*Famished Road*, 498–99). For example, when Madame Koto gives way to her longing for power and wealth, she loses her positive qualities and is possessed by the archetype of the Witch, thus finally embodying the dark side of the archetype of the Great Mother (the 'dark' side of Mother Africa). The unity of the ego is merely apparent: "Many people reside in us, [...] many past lives, many future lives" (*Famished Road*, 499). In Dad, for instance, resides a demon girl who could be interpreted in Jungian terms as an inner *anima*-figure. Certainly this double demon has the typical ambivalence of the archetype of the *anima*. The positive side of the Janus-faced archetype of the *anima* is Helen, the beggar girl, whom Dad sees as a princess from a strange kingdom and whom he wants to marry: thus Helen also corresponds to the mystic bride of the shaman.[29]

c) The movement of history is not defined solely by external causes, whether social, political or economic, but also by internal, psychic, archetypal causes: "Wars are not fought on battlegrounds but in a space smaller than the head of a needle" – "A single thought of ours could change the universe," says Dad (*Famished Road*, 497, 498). And, in *Astonishing the Gods*, Okri says that there are people who "enrich the dreams of the world, and it is dreams that create history" (115). This may be compared with what Yeats writes in *Magic*:

> We should rewrite our histories, for all men, certainly all imaginative men, must be for ever casting forth enchantments, glamours, illusions [...]. Our most elaborate thoughts, elaborate purposes, precise emotions, are often, as I think, not really ours, but have on a sudden come up, as it were, out of Hell or down out of Heaven. The historian should remember, should he not?, angels and devils not less than kings and soldiers, and plotters and thinkers. What does it matter if the angel or devil, as indeed certain old writers believed, first wrapped itself with an organised shape in some man's imagination? [...] We must none the less admit that invisible beings, far – wandering influences, shapes that may have floated from a hermit of the wilderness, brood over council – chambers and studies and battlefields. We should never be certain [...] that the passion, because of which so many countries were given to the

---

[29] *Songs of Enchantment*, 13–17.

sword, did not begin in the mind of some shepherd boy, lighting up his eyes
for a moment before it ran upon its way.[30]

From Okri's point of view,

> The greatest inspiration, the most sublime ideas of living that have come down
> to humanity come from a higher realm, a happier realm, a place of pure
> dreams, a heaven of blessed notions. Ideas and infinite possibilities dwell there
> in absolute tranquillity. [...] We should sit still in our deep selves and dream
> good new things for humanity. We should try and make those dreams real.[31]

The same neo-Platonic, Romantic, Yeatsian and Jungian note is sounded
in Okri's celebration of the imagination and of myth.[32] The battle against
those human beings who "are dreaming of wiping out their fellow human
beings from this earth" is a political battle; "We must take an interest in
politics" (*Famished Road*, 498), a daily battle fought in this world with the
persistence, physical strength and elemental animal rage of Dad, as well as
the tenderness, practicality and faith of Mum; but it is a battle fought
simultaneously in the beyond (in the psyche), in that other world hidden
behind ours.

The unconscious is also a political battleground: "They are holding
elections in heaven and under the sea" (*Famished Road*, 497–98). This is why
Dad works on two levels: he triumphs shamanically over the ghosts and the
nightmarish forms visible to him in his temporary blindness, and at the
same time he uses his fists to drive away the thugs who rule the compound
in a reign of terror (*Songs of Enchantment*, 250–51).

Just as the shaman and the magician fight other shamans and magicians
(the shaman and his spirit allies are capable of healing or destruction), so
Dad, in *The Famished Road*, engages in spiritual battle with Madame Koto,
who uses her power maliciously. An ambiguous Great-Mother figure,
Madame Koto has a generous, charitable side, but, given that she opts for
the Party of the Rich and with her bar and whores is concerned only to
increase her own influence and wealth, she has an evil effect on the psyche
of those around her:

> She wore clothes that made the beggars ill [...] At night, when she slept, she
> stole the people's energies. [...] Madame Koto sucked in the powers of our area.

---

[30] "Magic," in W.B. Yeats, *Essays and Introductions* (London: Macmillan, 1961). All
other quotations will be from this edition.

[31] *Birds of Heaven* (London: Phoenix, 1996): 12–14.

[32] "The imagination is one of the highest gifts we have"; "To find life in myth, and
myth in life" (*Birds of Heaven*, 42).

> Her dreams gave the children nightmares. [...] She expanded over the air of our existence. (495)

Dad challenges the dark powers of this demonic queen of the night, who manipulates men and women by commanding their psychic centres (*Songs*, 140) and sucks up their vitality and will like a vampire. If the cosmic battle between the powers of good and evil is fought in the psyche, the political battle, which is part of that more universal struggle, is also a psychological battle, fought both by day (consciously) and by night (unconsciously):

> I understood that conflicting forces were fighting for the future of our country in the air, at night, in our dreams [...] The political parties waged their battles in the spirit spaces, beyond the realm of our earthly worries. They fought and hurled counter – mythologies at one another. (*Famished Road*, 495)

Thus the war between the Party of the Rich and the Party of the Poor in *Songs of Enchantment* is a "war of mythologies" (247), a war between "political magicians" (144–48) in which it is difficult to separate the actual devastations from the strange effects they have on the mind (151). Violence generates terror, terror madness. Terror and fear materialize in concrete bestial forms (144). People are brain-shocked: "Everywhere we looked our stunned brains conjured further devastations. The chaos made us hallucinate" (151). Here is one of the most significant social and political points made by Okri: violence is enacted and suffered not only physically but also psychically.

"I've come to realise," Okri has said "you can't write about Nigeria truthfully without a sense of violence."[33] Scenes of physical violence – quarrels, brawls, punch-ups and fist-fights – recur throughout *The Famished Road* and *Songs of Enchantment*, with the typical repetitive rythm of oral narrative, as also of the cyclic conception of history (and of story-telling) common to African cultures. Then there is social violence, too, as in the degrading toil of porters like Dad and of the nightsoil men: "Our society is a battlefield. Poverty, corruption and hunger are the bullets. Bad governments are the bombs. And we still have soldiers ruling us."[34]

A story like "Worlds that Flourish," in *Songs of Enchantment*, is the Kafkaesque epitome of the theme of violence undergone. But the most insidious form of violence is psychological, that exercised by those in power who rule through fear. Dark and magic powers are used to oppress, starve and kill people, devouring their dreams and draining their will to rebel (121).

---

[33] Wilkinson, *Talking with African Writers*, 81.
[34] *Dangerous Love* (London: Phoenix, 1996): 109, 216–18.

Politicians make use of *jujus*, masks and masquerades[35] – and, generally, of African traditions – to provoke terror. The terror of the masquerades, whose political use is denounced by Dad (123), invades the mind. The people stand defenceless against the "curfew-making of political thugs" (112), hired by the "political sorcerers" who spread "terror and curfew" (138). The masquerades wake the terrible ghost of the remote African past and, when they are used as a political tool, generate a terror that is introjected into and penetrates the psychic structure of those experiencing it (178).

The African soul has a luminous and a dark, unconscious side. Africa is an earth-goddess who nourishes and gives life, but she is also a mother who kills – "See how Africa kills her young ones"; she has killed the girl found dead in the park by Omovo and Keme, for instance: "Poor mutilated girl, why did they do this to you? Sacrifice to African night?"[36] Africa is also "a dark stream of terrible ancient legends" (*Songs*, 67).

To enter the world of dream and vision is also to draw near to the ancestral world of tradition, a world which must be rediscovered, revisited, and re-dreamed. Yet there is a danger that those in power may weave a pernicious web of ritual and belief in order to stun the minds of the people and make them prisoners: "The rituals confused our minds with too many manifestations, too many gods, too many dreams, confusing us in order to rule us" (*Songs*, 146).

It is clear that for Okri history is psychohistory. The course of history is in part the fruit of irrational factors and of the operation of unconscious archetypal factors which he (like Soyinka) calls spirits or gods. The influx of these spirits or gods is like an underground river flowing beneath the surface of visible events. At this deep level, events are connected by links that are not causal but synchronic. Often to be found in magic realists such as Gabriel García Márquez, Salman Rushdie and Wilson Harris, "synchronicity"[37] relates both to archaic, magical thought and to analytical psychology, according to which certain conditions of psychic tension and of intense activity of the unconscious may prove to be synchronic phenomena.

In Okri's view, the movement of history is to be both linear and circular: linear, because he believes that society may be transformed, and this entails

---

[35] Rich descriptions of rituals and Masquerades can be found in Margaret Thompson Drewal, *Yoruba Ritual: Performers, Play, Agency* (Bloomington: Indiana UP, 1992).

[36] *Dangerous Love*, 47, 49.

[37] *Synchronicity* is an "acausal connecting principle." See the entry for "Synchronicity" in Samuels, Shorter & Plaut, *Critical Dictionary of Jungian Analysis*, 146–47.

individual processes of psychological transformation; circular, because he revives the African conception of time as Eternal Return, as an infinitely repeated cycle of death and rebirth in which the worlds of the unborn, the living and the dead revolve in everlasting rotation. This cyclic conception has its correspondingly cyclic mode of narration in the *griot*, who tends to make extensive use of repetition. There are repeated situations and gestures, such as Dad washing himself, smoking, drinking *ogogoro*, and knocking Azaro on the head, and these are marked by an almost ritual cadence, producing an effect of cyclical recurrence and immutability, and suggesting the Eternal return of the identical. The wandering *griot* in *The Famished Road* warns Azaro that no story can ever be finished (481).

d) Dreams are a source of teaching and contain the past and the future. According to magical modes of thoughts, as Yeats writes in *Magic*, "there is a memory of nature that reveals events and symbols of distant centuries." The unconscious (the forest, one of the most important of the symbolic places described in *The Famished Road* and *Songs of Enchantment*) reveals its secrets to Dad. When Azaro and Dad venture into the forest of the unconscious in the latter book, they move in a labyrinth of secrets and dreams which contain within them the seed of an infinite number of possible worlds: "We ran into a quivering universe. [...] We broke into another level of time [...] New worlds were bursting out of the egg – shells of a million mutinous dreams" (25–26).

In his shamanic dreams, Dad discovers "worlds behind our world, parallel worlds, simultaneous realities, inverted universes" (*Songs*, 290; a good capsule-definition of magical realism), and he sees how we create our lives in thought and how thought – including that which takes form in dreams – creates reality.

The road to redemption for the African peoples, and the restoration of all oppressed peoples, must be sought in dreams and visions. Like the shaman, we try to restore the lost "balances of the earth" and fight the growth of chaos (*Famished Road*, 93–94, 493). In this battle, the shaman is assaulted by "gusts of emptiness and fear."[38] He must overcome the temptation to let himself be swallowed up by Nothingness, and must not listen to the "choruses of the abyss calling him into the happy home of the world-effacing white wind."[39]

---

[38] *Dangerous Love*, 203.
[39] *Astonishing the Gods* (London: Phoenix, 1996): 20.

Azaro's mind is invaded by a great darkness peopled with spirits who represent the forgotten African gods and 'transformative' African ancestors. It is in the course of a vision – whose purpose is to transform the dreamer and his image of the world – that the secrets and mysteries of the African Way (*Songs of Enchantment*, 159–60), the Way of imaginative life and transformation, are revealed to him.

e) The imagination is a means to knowledge and to the transformation of ourselves and of the world. The imagination and dreaming are at one and the same time forms of symbolic thought and active forces which make it possible to foresee and programme the future and to modify the world. The sympathetic, anticipatory and utopic nature of the imagination help us create a new reality. To dream and imagine the future is to begin to build it, to bring into being a "new unblinded mythology" (*Songs of Enchantment*, 279). It is to make the transition from blindness to vision which is the dominant theme of Books Three and Four of *Songs of Enchantment*.

"A dream can be the highest point of a life" is the concluding sentence of *The Famished Road*. It is repeated in *Songs of Enchantment*, with the addition: "Action can be its purest manifestation" (275). Dream precedes action, but is itself action. Dreams can activate hidden energies, or can actualize frightening phenomena (148, 167). The first step in transforming the world is to re-dream it: nothing is ever finished, and "we have to re-dream our lives" (3). We "have to re-dream the world anew," and "with more light" (280–81). For centuries the earth has cried out for more vision and more transformation (295). Men and women have to transmute their own chaos, wake up, and renew their dreams (279).

This process of interior awakening and transformation is first individual and then collective: the freeing of one person's vision is the freeing of all others' (283–84). The collective dimension is of great importance in Okri's work: the visionary madness of Azaro and Dad becomes a communal insanity (155). Dad's blindness corresponds to the plague of blindness that strikes the community, and the miraculous restoration of his sight at the same time heals all the people who had been blinded. While Dad dreams, everyone else does so too (283). Like Dad, everyone has acquired a form of second sight and feels that "there could be more astonishing lives beyond the mirror" (288). Dad and Mum are all African men and women who suffer; Dad is any porter who collapses under the weight of inhuman loads and Mum is any market woman. Azaro is an *abiku*, but "isn't it just possible that we are all *abikus*?"[40] If Nigeria is an *abiku* country, many nations, civilizations, ideas, art forms and historical events are recognizable as *abiku* (*Famished Road*, 478, 487).

f) Everything is connected, everything is alive (*Songs of Enchantment*, 147, 222). "All that exists lives," says a Chukchee shaman.[41] The idea that All is One is equally magical–shamanic: "Inside a cat there are many histories, many books. When you look into the eyes of dogs strange fishes swim in your mind," and: "There are dolphins, plants that dream, magic birds inside us. The sky is inside us. The earth is in us" (*Famished Road*, 498). We contain the whole universe (*Songs*, 133). There is no distinction between within and without, nor any break between external and internal worlds.

In the world of magic everything is permeable. You can enter the spirit of things and they can enter you (*Songs*, 123). The ego's outer limits shift and may easily be transgressed, for the conscious ego is constantly invaded by unconscious content, the individual unconscious of each one of us being in constant communication with the individual unconscious of others, and is lost in the vast sea of the collective unconscious. Others can enter us and our dreams, just as we can enter them and their dreams.

Azaro penetrates the dreams dreamed by Mum and follows Dad in his (*Famished Road*, 478, 494), flying in and out of the dreams of the living and the dead (*Songs*, 275). In Dad's dreams, Mum fights him and tries to get him back into his body; Madame Koto's dreams give the children nightmares, and she asks Azaro: "What were you doing in my dreams?" (*Famished Road*, 480, 495, 350). All dream together simultaneously, and dreams are transferred from one person to another (*Songs*, 151, 255).

It is clear that what we are dealing with is a magical conception of the world, such as Yeats sums up at the beginning of *Magic*:

> I believe in the practice and philosophy of what we have agreed to call magic [...]; and I believe in three doctrines, which have, as I think, been handed down from early times, and been the foundations of nearly all magic practices. These doctrines are:
>
> 1) That the borders of our mind are ever shifting, and that many minds can flow into one another, as it were, and create or reveal a single mind, a single energy.
>
> 2) That the borders of our memories are as shifting, and that our memories are a part of one great memory, the memory of Nature herself.
>
> 3) That this great mind and great memory can be evoked by symbols.

---

[40] Wilkinson, *Talking with African Writers*, 84.
[41] Quoted by Halifax, *Shaman: The Wounded Healer*, 9.

Imaginative writers, particularly magical realists, are enchanters, continuers of magical practices whose songs carry art back to its magical origins. As Yeats, further, writes in his essay on magic: "Have not poetry and music arisen out of the sounds of enchanters made to help their imagination to enchant, to charm, to bind with a spell themselves and the passers-by?"

Magical thinking[42] is pre-logical and knows nothing of the principle of contradiction. It mystically unites and fuses what the eye of reason sees as separate and distinct. It hypothesizes the essential homogeneity of all beings, making no distinction between animate and inanimate objects and allowing for all kinds of metamorphoses. According to magical thinking, stones, rocks and trees are endowed with *mana*, a universal energy or soul inherent in all things, which has different names in different cultures and which constitutes a single essential reality (one and many, material and spiritual) that inhabits all creatures and is in constant movement.

According to archaic psychology all over the world, animals are in part divine and the divine is in part animal. Thus the human and animal worlds are intimately linked and metamorphose into one another. We need only think of the women–antelopes of *Songs of Enchantment* and of the transformation of Mum (43), who changes into a creature that is half-woman and half-antelope. Man and nature speak the same language: the people understand the language of trees and animals (76). In a magical perspective, the contours of individuality are fragmented and the ego's hegemony is overturned. This permits doubling ("Dad's other form"; 48), dual location (Mum is in two places at the same time; 70), and the mutual permeability of the worlds of the dead and the living (a dead man speaks through Azaro; 260).

---

[42] Jung's view of magic is summarized in Samuels, Shorter & Plaut, *Critical Dictionary of Jungian Analysis*: magic is "an attempt to intercept or to become one with unconscious forces in order to use, propitiate or destroy them; thereby to counteract their remarkable potency or to ally with their competitive purposes [...] Often psychic contents will be met as quasi-external apparitions, either in the form of spirits or as magic powers projected upon living people, animals, or inanimate objects" (88). Freud links magic to the omnipotence of thought typical of children who are not yet able to recognize the data of reality, and to obsessional neuroses: in fact, the rituals of obsessive neurotics are an attempt to control the unconscious internal forces which they fear may overwhelm them. Piaget studied magical thinking in children, who, like primitives, believe that everything is animate and gifted with intentionality. It is characteristic of magical thinking to believe in a "universal sympathy," a "vital fluid that unites all animate beings – humans, animals, plants – with the elements, the planets and the stars"; Octavio Paz's formulation of this universal sympathy is quoted in Zamora & Faris, ed. *Magical Realism*, 549.

Magical thinking is not only characteristic of, say, the mentality of 'primitives,' of psychotic delirium, pathological delusions or the delusory systems of paranoia. The *participation mystique* (or the archaic identification of subject and object) prevalent in children and primitives, who "live immersed in a stream of events in which the inner and the outer world are not different, or very indistinctly so,"[43] is an extreme case of total projec‾ tion.[44] Yet all of us project continually. We all transfer subjective psychic elements onto outer objects. Projection is a psychological fact that can be observed everywhere in the everyday life of human beings.

In the language of analytical psychology, demons are autonomous complexes. Jung noticed that in dreams and visions the archetype seems to act independently of the beholder: the archetype manifests itself as a personal being (spirit or demon) which possesses a life of its own. There are still gods and demons, but (as Jung[45] and, later, Hillman have explained), they have become psychic pathologies. Gods and demons continue to roam through our dreams. For, every dreamer knows, in the nocturnal theatre of dreams, where psychic dynamics are presented mainly as dramatic interactions between diverse characters, the unconscious tends to personify. It is not we or our egos that personify autonomous complexes: according to Jung, they have a personal nature from the very beginning. The shaman has the power to cure those who are possessed by demons or evil spirits because during his intiation he has overcome and controlled his own state of possession.

---

[43] Carl Gustav Jung, *Letters*, ed. Gerhard Adler & Aniela Jaffé (Princeton NJ/London: Princeton UP, 2 vols., 1973-75), vol. 1: 549.

[44] In "General Aspects of Dream Psychology," Jung writes that we assume that the world is as we see it and that people are as we imagine them to be. Therefore "we go on naïvely projecting our own psychology into our fellow human beings. In this way everyone creates for himself a series of more or less imaginary relationships based essentially on projection"; Jung, *Collected Works of C.G. Jung*, ed. Sir Herbert Read, Michael Fordham, Gerhard Adler & William McGuire (Bollingen Series; Princeton NJ: Princeton UP, 1972), vol. 8: 237-80. The mind in its natural state presupposes the existence of such projections. Our ideas or feelings or impulses are attributed to the external world. In a primitive person this creates that characteristic relationship to the object which the anthropologist Lévi-Bruhl called *"participation mystique"* (mystic identity, unconscious identity, projective identification).

[45] For a psychological interpretation of the problem of spirits, demons, ghosts, apparitions, souls, daimones, states of possession, etc., see Jung, "The Psychological Foundation of Belief in Spirits," in *Collected Works*, vol. 8; Aniela Jaffé, *Apparitions* (Le Mail: Mercure de France, 1983); and Marie-Louise von Franz, *Projection and Re-Collection of Jungian Psychology: Reflections of the Soul* (La Salle/London: Open Court, 1980).

The course of magical–shamanic experience can also be traced in *Dangerous Love*, a rewriting of *The Landscapes Within*, which offers a portrait of the artist as a young man and as an apprentice shaman. Omovo, who lives too much inside his head (96), moves in and out of strange mental territories (257) and often feels as if he had strayed into a dream (275). He makes a constant effort to understand what his deeper mind is trying to tell him (77), and like Ifeyiwa pays close attention to dreams.

At the age of thirteen he makes a drawing which seems to represent confused archetypal forms:

> It was composed of jagged lines that suggested the obscure shapes of pyramids, rock-faces with the eyes of birds, mountain ranges inseparable from sea and sky. The ends of the lines were lost in the maze of entanglements. (76)

An old painter, Dr Okocha, teaches him that to paint a dream will mean a long descent into himself ("We cast our nets out into darkness and draw in ourselves"; 101), and that we all have a duty – one demonstrated by the shaman–artist – to make manifest the good dreams and visions we are given: "An Indian poet once wrote that 'In dreams begin responsibilities.' I prefer the word 'vision' to 'dreams' in this context" (101).

Omovo's is a shamanic vocation. In the "landscapes within" he looks for a secret knowledge and new energies:

> He felt himself submerge, felt himself journeying at a strange speed through primeval caves accompanied by shadows. And as he sank into the new darkness he prayed that he could reach greater powers, greater visions and the intimations of a greater life that flowed somewhere in the landscapes within the new darkness. (170)

Only an esoteric "secret way" can lead him out of the mazes of daily life and the maze of history (156), out of the hell-hole of Lagos (81) and miasmic landscapes around him (68), out of a chaotic society (150), out of the widespread violence and corruption and out of a world he cannot understand (102). The desire to flee from a world "tougher than fire or steel" (*FR* 71) is not escapism, but a consequence of the awareness that, since historical reality cannot readily be modified with sociopolitical instruments, it is necessary to undertake a longer journey, to use the strange new energies ready to burst inside him (288), to enter the dimension of vision, plunging into the "ancient streams" and "deep currents" of love and of physical eros (213, 214). It is only in this way that those who are "handcuffed to history" – as Salman Rushdie puts it – can fight for their freedom.

As a shamanic artist, Omovo goes through the "blue door" which opens
magically onto the unconscious, and onto the ancestral African past (286), in
the attempt to reach "the flood of origins, the birth of gods" (202). Yet he
must also face "the terrifying shapes, the evil-fighting forms, the ritual
powers" of African art, powers that are part of the order of things and that
are within him (201). Omovo is aware of the great risk he is running. He
knows that he takes a terrifying path and that many have died on it. Yet he
must nevertheless undergo a profound change. His identity will be
"scrambled up" (285). And so he courageously takes on the task of finding
"a mystic understanding" (290–91). He thus has his illumination and comes
to understand that "in dreams begins responsibility," "in vision begins
responsibility," "in vision begins action," that "we can utter psychic
decisions and set forces into motion that could change our lives forever,"
that we must "re-dream the world" and "restructure self" (293–95).

If chaos is the beginning of creation, there is nevertheless a danger that it
may overwhelm the shamanic artist. A new man is emerging and a secret
self is forming, but the danger of madness is always lying in wait. At the end
of the novel (297), a madman emblematically lurking in the bushes jumps on
Omovo and blocks his passage. The madman symbolizes both shamanic
madness and those who went insane because they could not bear their hard
lives (108). Omovo's feeling towards this madman is of "a vague and
tangential affinity" (298).

Dangerous Love, like the two preceding novels, focuses on the process of
becoming aware and taking on responsibility ("It seems that the moment
you see something is wrong you have a responsibility"; 321), an internal
transformation which should, ideally, trigger a transformation of the world,
though it may take a long time and be a labour of Sisyphus:

> He saw a naked child running in the field. It stumbled, fell, and went on run-
> ning. The earth was its treadmill, for hard as the child was running it did so on
> the same spot, getting neither closer nor farther away. But it went on running,
> the spirit of unconquerable being. (312)

Okri is a utopian who has faith in the resilience of the African spirit and
in the great dreaming capacity of African art. He believes in the transforming power of suffering,[46] which eventually may become "the bedrock of
[a] great new civilization,"[47] and he looks forward to a reversal of history:

---

[46] See Wilkinson, *Talking with African Writers*: "Suffering is one of the great characters
of *The Famished Road*, the different ways people suffer. It defines the boundaries of self but
also breaks down the boundaries of individual identifications. [...] There are hundreds of

We are in a very, very interesting age: we could go either way. We could go towards the greatest stage of creativity yet, world creativity. But unless we change the way we perceive history, we're not going to be able to do this. [...] It is consciousness, it is the way we perceive the world, it is our mythic frame that shapes the way we affect the world and the way the world affects us. It's these invisible things that shape the visible things. [...] One has to know about the very hard facts of the world and one has to look at them and know how deadly and powerful they are before one can begin to think or dream oneself into positions out of which hope and then possibilities can come.[48]

In accordance with these premisses, Okri's writing aspires to the visionary and often takes on the tones of prayer[49] and prophecy. The shamanic writer takes flight towards the invisible realms in *Astonishing the Gods* where the masters of the art of transcendence live (9), the enchanted islands where the elements are in perpetual alchemical transformation and where a whole people – one that trades in philosophies, inspirations, intuitions, prophecies, paradoxes, riddles, enigmas, visions and dreams (74) – is approaching the condition of divinity (72). Yet he will very soon be obliged, in *Dangerous Love*, to leave the ethereal and weightless substance of his utopia to go back down to the "miasma of Lagos life" (41) and its anonymous crowd of

---

variations, but there is just one god there, and that god is suffering, pain. But he's not the supreme deity. The higher deity is joy. Again, that's just part of the paradox. Paradoxes keep running through the book, about what it is that redeems the sufferings of that continent and what all the people go through. What is it that redeems it? [...] The 'famishment' has its shadow side in the book, which is joy, which is myth, which is spirit" (85). An echo of this paradoxical balance between extremes, between the monstrousness of the present and an inextinguishable hope in a better future, can be detected in the article (*The Guardian*, November 1, 1995). Okri wrote to denounce the Nigerian military regime, responsible for condemning Ken Saro-Wiwa to death. Okri here denounces the death of democracy, rigged elections, courts subjugated to the regime, the spread and flood of injustice, the damage done to the environment by oil companies. But at the same time, in passionate, almost prophetic tones, he praises love for the poor – one thinks inevitably of the beggars in *The Famished Road* and *Songs of Enchantment* who symbolise the sufferings of the earth and of the people – and for the humblest of workers, for the women who bear the burden of pain and work – like Mum, for the disinherited, children robbed of their future – like the youngsters in *Dangerous Love* – by corrupt governors. Okri clearly shows that his hopes rest in a greater justice which one day may inhabit the earth. If a writer has been condemned to death because he wanted a better life for his people, there are still things in this world which are stronger than death: love, the search for justice. Note that this article also contains the idea that archetypal powers, demons of war and black angels of disruption and fragmentation operate in history.

[47] *Astonishing the Gods*, 28.
[48] Wilkinson, *Talking with African Writers*, 87–88.
[49] "Creativity is a form of prayer" (*Birds of Heaven*, 43).

ghetto-dwellers moving around like sleepwalkers (175), through the night-mare of history. After this mystic, utopian flight, he must come back to earth, to a reality worse than nightmare, to the raw world of the ghetto where the poor are confined in *Songs of Enchantment* (296–97). This is indeed what happens to Dad at the end of that book:

> He sat in his three-legged chair with the look of a man who had been cheated of his most precious possessions. He had re-entered the kingdom of sight, but had lost the other enchanted kingdom of which he was sole ruler and defender. He had lost his magic servants, his invisible wives, and the splendid lights of that world. He had lost them all, and had found us, lean, famished, and patiently awaiting his return from his forest of dreams. While he dreamt, while he was blind, we suffered. I had never seen him look so defenceless or so ashamed. (291–92)

The return of the shaman to this hard world and to the true wretched-ness of the human condition entails the loss of that marvellous place of fables and magical lights whither the wings of imagination had carried him. Yet it is only through the arduous dialectic of reality–dream, only by being both realist and magician, and only by being at one and the same time chronicler of the everyday and seer or prophet, that the magical-realist writer can avoid the danger of psychic inflation, or indeed of literary inflation. This might otherwise lead to his floating away, lost in an excessively disembodied aura – a too-luminous abstraction and passionate, high-flying rhetoric; an aphoristic and prophetic language, finally, that may be chanted in the temple of world-dreams[50] but is unfitted to the chronicling of the daily suffering of humanity.

ଏ • ଞ

---

[50] *Astonishing the Gods*, 17.

Reality and Magic
in Syl Cheney–Coker's
The Last Harmattan of Alusine Dunbar

————————————————————— ℰꙨ

Paolo Bertinetti

I N CONCEPTION AND NARRATIVE FORM, the novel *The Last Harmattan of Alusine Dunbar* falls within the category of magical realism. This may be confidently stated, since the author himself admits the decisive – though not exclusive – influence on his book of García Márquez's *One Hundred Years of Solitude*, one of the leading examples of magical realism.[1]

It may be worth emphasizing, by way of a premise, that this critical classification cannot be used in the same way as we speak of, say, Romanticism or Naturalism, which were ideological and cultural movements expressive of their *Zeitgeist*. This is what makes it possible to attribute Romantic or naturalistic characteristics to the work of an artist who may not be a card-carrying member of these movements.

Magical realism is not like that. It is a narrative form, or a kind of writing which, in aiming to communicate experience through the medium of literature, chooses to present the ordinary as extraordinary and the extraordinary as ordinary, or as part of everyday reality. For a writer to be a magical realist presupposes an earlier choice affecting the whole of the text (from its narrative structure to its individual aspects), according to which reality can only be communicated in depth, not just superficially, through a mingling of the real and the imaginary.

---

[1] Aside from the largely unconnected European use of this expression in the Twenties, we know that the concept of magical realism originated and to a substantial degree developed in Latin America, with one of its chief starting-points being the formulation in 1949 of the concept of the *real maravilloso* by the Cuban Alejo Carpentier.

This is a choice which finds its place within the broader strategy, common since the Twenties at least, of representing reality by means of techniques that are not, in fact, realist.[2] For magical realism is one of the various narrative forms adopted by twentieth-century writers in order to set down their vision of human beings and of the world in a form that shows the inadequacy of realism. The fact that it has been used above all by South American novelists – by writers in European languages from countries which at one time were colonies – has led some critics, especially Australians and Canadians, to say that magical realism may be regarded as a form of post-colonial discourse or strategy. Yet, in doing so, they often risk twisting the term to suit their own argument. They take no account of the fact that magical realism, as I have said, is simply one of the possible alternatives to realism in twentieth-century writing. More importantly, it is almost wholly absent from the novel in literatures in English, where the preference has generally been for decidedly realistic kinds of narrative solutions.

In certain cases, the pressure of the marvellous in a novel simply places it within the wider context of non-realist narrative. In others, the same element derives directly from a cultural hinterland – Yoruba in the case of Tutuola, or Aborigine in the case of Mudrooroo – where what we call the marvellous is seen as an integral part of reality. In such cases, there is no question of adopting a kind of writing in which the factual and the counterfactual are co-present, as in South American novels. Rather, there is a literary imagination that reflects a vision of the world in which the two dimensions coexist. Tutuola's novels simply 'absorb' the cultural context into which he was born and of which he is part. In the novels of, say, Manuel Scorza, on the other hand, there is a literary inventiveness which, in representing the world of Peru and of the Andes, accepts and draws on the intellectual traditions of the world of the Indios.[3]

ೞ • ೞ

---

[2] A striking example is Günter Grass, whom Salman Rushdie has openly acknowledged as an influence on his own work; there are also other major figures, such as Italo Calvino, Samuel Beckett, Max Frisch, Thomas Bernhard and, considerably earlier, Kafka and Mikhail Bulgakov.

[3] As for certain unacceptable attributions of various post-colonial novels to the classification of 'magical realism,' an observation may be apposite: a particular episode, a scene, an aspect of a character – even, perhaps, part of the plot – may very well be presented in a narrative form which links, or coincides with, that of magical realism. But this in no sense allows us to consider the whole work as an example of magical realism. The parts are not the whole: in the context of literary evaluation, synecdoche has no part.

Interviewed at his home shortly after the publication of his novel, Syl Cheney–Coker openly stated that, when he was writing *The Last Harmattan of Alusine Dunbar*, he had Gabriel García Márquez's masterpiece in mind. More recently, in a 1994 interview, Cheney–Coker specified the limits of that influence. "Were you influenced by Márquez? – The answer is yes and no. If we are discussing form, yes."[4] If magical realism is considered first and foremost as a narrative form, Cheney–Coker's "yes" is, as we have already suggested, sufficient to place his novel in the context of magical realism, not because it is an imitation of García Márquez (a suggestion to which Cheney–Coker reacted with justifiable irritation), but because it is an independent example of that kind of writing and literary communication.

This becomes still clearer when we turn our attention to another part of the interview, where Cheney–Coker, who is well-known and highly regarded as a poet in Sierra Leone, explains why he decided to write his first novel: "I think the decision was made because I realized that the novel has never really been developed in Sierra Leone" (10). In his collections of poetry he had already explored the contradictory history of his country, mingling the story of native Africans with the history of the slaves in America (starting from his own position as a Sierra Leonean Creole, a descendant of the liberated slaves who had populated Freetown at the end of the eighteenth and the beginning of the nineteenth century). He then transformed himself into a novelist in order to celebrate the achievements and sacrifices of those remarkable people, who "did so much not just for Sierra Leone but for West Africa" (12).

The main difficulty, for this poet-turned-novelist, lay in the feeling that "the novel in Africa had been as it were cloistered within very precise forms. It was either you had a sociological view of the novel within the Achebean definition, or you were a political novelist within the Ngugian concept of it" (10). Cheney–Coker felt the need for new directions outside of the rigidly prescribed forms, outside the "perceived notions of what the African novel should be like" (10).

It is interesting that, though what he had in mind was a story that would cover two hundred years of history, he did not think in terms of the historical novel, a well-established genre in literatures in English. He thought, rather, of the fictional form adopted by García Márquez, where history is transfigured by myth and where character and incident, with the

---

4 Brenda Cooper, "Syl Cheney–Coker: *The Last Harmattan of Alusine Dunbar*," and an "Interview," *ALA Bulletin* 20.3 (Summer 1994): 10. Further page references are in the text.

complete liberty of the literary imagination, contain the ultimate meaning of the history that is taking place alongside them. The story of the Buendías and of Macondo is a metaphor for the history of Latin America.

The Last Harmattan tells the story of the Cromantines, who reach the Kasila coast from England with their fellow freed slaves, some of whom, like Sebastian Cromantine, had fought on the side of the English in the American War of Independence. Years later, another ex-combatant, Thomas Booker-man, who lost an eye in the colonial war, arrives, leading 1200 men and women. These too are former slaves, who had been permitted to scrape a threadbare existence in the marshlands of Canada after the war ended. Just as the first of the Buendías founded Macondo, so Sebastian founds Mala-gueta; and after the disastrous sweet-potato blight, which scatters the inhabitants, Sebastian and his wife Jeanette are among the leading figures in the renaissance of Malagueta, under the energetic leadership of Thomas Bookerman.

Taking her place alongside these former slaves is the striking figure of Isatu Dambolla, a local girl who marries Gustavius Martins and thereby embodies the rediscovered link with the African land where the "Black Americans" have chosen to live. Jeanette and Isatu are destined to live to be over one hundred years old; and, as in García Márquez, this extraordinary longevity has an important narrative function, giving continuity and unity to the story through the presence of these two women in each successive phase of the life and destiny of Malagueta. Indeed, there is a sense in which the women's presence brings those events closer together, for it encloses them within the confines of their lifetime and at the same time blurs chrono-logical time, in which one event succeeds another, thus placing them in a temporal dimension that is epic, not historical.

In the course of the novel, sporadic reference is made to historical circumstances – in the mention of the American War of Independence, steamships, or the First World War, for instance. Yet the story of Malagueta – the clash with the natives after the first phase of peaceful coexistence, the arrival of the English soldiers, the revolt, the retreat into the forest, the second fight against the English, the slaying of the governor, the new political regime with Alphonso Garrison as Mayor of Malagueta – clearly alludes to the history of Sierra Leone, though it is presented in a dimension in which historical accuracy is irrelevant and the atmosphere is that of epic.

There is also an echo of America in the novel (that "place of horror and damnation," as Sebastian Cromantine says to his son),[5] the plantations in Virginia, Carolina and Mississippi, where the former slaves lived before they retraced the Middle Passage across the Atlantic to Africa. Moreover, there are echoes of the African past, in references to the legendary King of the Mali, Sundiata Keita, the Moors, the Tuareg, the Arabs of Zanzibar, the Watusi, the Fulani and the Yoruba; to say nothing of Sulaiman the Nubian, who foresees it all, including the destinies of all the characters in the novel.

It is through this double echo (the experience of slavery on the one hand and the link with the heritage of African civilization on the other) that the cultural and spiritual destiny of the central characters of *The Last Harmattan* is reconstructed. At the same time, their present grows out of their encounter with the coastal Africans, one characterized both by temporal conflict and by union, symbolized (and in part idealized) in the marriage of Gustavius and Isatu. After the natives' attack on Malagueta and the flight from the city, it is Isatu who teaches the women "how to cook new foods [...] how to preserve meat" and how to identify "herbs with which they were able to survive during the languid torment of their flight" (107).

The tone of the narrative is of particular importance here. The memory of the 'American' past and reference to the African past exist in an epic dimension which transfigures people and events, placing them in a legendary space beyond history. There is hardly an episode or a character that does not give the narrator the opportunity to evoke ancient warriors, sovereigns, heroes, or memorable undertakings, extraordinary facts and fascinating tales belonging to fabulous African civilizations of the more or less distant past. Yet this is also true of the present. It is not just the Malaguetans' exploits in battle, but also their peacetime projects, their love affairs, the birth of their children, and their deaths, that assume epic proportions.

To obtain this effect, Cheney–Coker does not generally turn to hyperbole, which, by contrast, is of fundamental importance in the narrative strategy of *One Hundred Years of Solitude*. Where the two writers resemble each other is in the way their characters' stories are seen as titanic achievements, prodigious happenings, the deeds of figures who are always larger than life. This effect is rarely achieved by means of the first of the two fundamental strategies of magical realism: namely, the presentation of the ordinary as extraordinary. In most cases it is the second mechanism that vivifies the

---

[5] Syl Cheney–Coker, *The Last Harmattan of Alusine Dunbar* (Oxford: Heinemann, 1990): 138. Further page references are given in the text.

narrative: the extraordinary is seen as ordinary. The magical component invades reality and is presented on the same level as the real, or as a part of reality itself.

This, of course, is precisely what writers like José María Arguedas, or García Márquez, or Manuel Scorza have done with unsurpassed mastery. Yet, if it is true that this is one of the basic components of magical realism (allowing *The Last Harmattan* to be placed without a shadow of a doubt in that category), it is also true that use of the 'magical' element may be prompted by very different cultural factors. Thus Syl Cheney–Coker is right to claim that the roots of the imaginative universe of his novel are clearly African, and so attributing its conception, on the one hand, to a "fictional method" which is García Márquez's and, on the other, to a vision of the world and of the relationship between the factual and the counterfactual which is typical of the African imagination.

Cheney–Coker makes explicit reference to Tutuola, stressing the inability of African, especially Nigerian, criticism to appreciate his literary work. It has already been mentioned that Tutuola should not be considered a magical-realist writer. Yet, in committing the Yoruba vision of a vital force to paper, he clearly indicates one of the "several different directions" in which Cheney–Coker maintains the West African novel might go. The supernatural element is present in *The Last Harmattan* in a way that often recalls Tutuola, and certainly reveals how deeply it is rooted in African culture. It may thus legitimately be stated that Cheney–Coker, with his own African version of magical realism, is also offering a "different direction" for the novel to go in – a direction, by the way, which has so far rarely been followed. "This is utterly ironic," Chimalun Nwanko has rightly remarked, "because the African imagination powered with a unique cosmology and a dynamic eschatology appears more fertile for this kind of expression than that of any other culture."[6]

Perhaps the most interesting instance of the extraordinary being seen as part of reality in African culture is the case of the two dwarfs who teach Isatu how to bring her pregnancy to full term. Explaining the nature of their existence, one of them says that each of them "represents several lives in the intrepid kingdom of children forced to live without mothers, but once in every twelve years [they] recognise a woman who has suffered, and in whom one [of them] chooses to be reborn" (205). This immediately brings to

---

[6] Chimalun Nwanko, review of *The Last Harmattan of Alusine Dunbar*, *African Studies Review* 35.1 (1992): 134–35.

mind the *abiku*, the spirit children of Yoruba folklore and the focus of Ben Okri's *The Famished Road*. Aside from the obvious differences, dwarfs and *abiku* are equally supernatural creatures who are in tune with the reality of human beings. This is explained a little later by Isatu's mother (a native) to her son-in-law Gustavius (who as an ex-slave has partly lost touch with his African origins). She tells him to follow the dwarfs' instructions: "This is as it was before your time, because we are all segments of the dirt of the world, and an inescapable part of living is recognising our relationship to spirits, to nature and to these creatures of the underworld" (206).

A crucial aspect of this novel is the non-separation of the worlds of the living and the dead. While still in America, Sebastian Cromantine has a terrifying vision, later shown to be "friendly and reassuring": he is touched by the hand of a dead man, a hand he subsequently recognizes to be that of his father, ten years dead, who wakes him from "an intolerable burden" (10) and thus prepares the crucial turning-point of his life. Years later, after the founding of Malagueta, Sebastian's father once more appears to him in a dream, gently urging him to shake off the torpor that has taken hold of him. Once again the effect is comforting and beneficial, and Sebastian confronts life with renewed vigour. These are dreams, or visions, which on the face of it have nothing to do with the supernatural. But the father who appears to Sebastian on African soil is different from the other vision: he is a spirit who is living a sort of second life, "cured of wandering, spending his days as a fisherman," and listening in the evenings "to the poetic birds settling down for the day" (88).

In Africa, the dead are really present and 'naturally' cross the path of the living. Thus, when Gustavius and Isatu reach her father's home, "the dead were beginning to come out for their walk" (196). And when the old man dies, he goes on living in his old home, sitting in his wicker chair on the porch in the suffocating afternoons, drinking his coffee alongside his wife. "Gustavius Martins was the only one who did not see the dead man moving about the house. Years of being in the wasteland of America had stripped him of the power to make contact with the dead" (202). On the other hand, though Thomas Bookerman has also lived in America, he has preserved that power. At the celebration organized by the Cromantines for the end of the dry season, the dead are peaceful guests along with the living, and Thomas speaks to them, "pouring out libations of welcome" and, at the end of his speech, putting "morsels of meat and bean cakes into the holes where he hoped the wandering living–dead would come to feast" (146).

The dead are the ancestors who look down on the lives of their descendants, protecting and furthering their work in the fields (see 203). They are the loved ones who are still present in the lives of those they have left behind. They belong to another country which is still in touch with our world. "Come any time you feel like it," says Isatu to her dead husband, "from de other country, where ah know you will be going for a while; come because you know ah shall be there always, with de doors open, wid my heart waiting for you" (252). From this point of view the magic element may be seen as having anthropological roots, so to speak. However, what is entirely the fruit of the literary imagination is the invented character who recurs throughout the novel, Sulaiman the Nubian, later known as Alusine Dunbar.

In the prologue to the novel, General Tamba Masimiara reflects, as he languishes in his cell, on his past and on the future of his country. In Book One, Chapter One, Jeanette Cromantine is on the bridge of the *Belmont* as it lies at anchor in the English harbour, about to set out on the journey which will lead to the foundation of Malagueta. This is the beginning of a story that is to lead, after almost two hundred years, to the attempted *coup d'état* by General Masimiara and to his execution.

All this is foreseen in Sulaiman the Nubian's looking-glass a hundred years before the *Belmont* starts its journey. The narrator takes us back in time to the arrival of Sulaiman at Kasila, announced by N'jai the gold merchant, back to his prophecies and back to his meeting with Mariamu, the merchant's wife, who asks him "to give her a child" (27). Sulaiman comes back years later, as a very old man, and disappears, dragged away by a herd of baboons, only to reappear some time later, coming "through the door of the mirror from another country" (41). "Another country," perhaps the very country Isatu spoke of. Here again, literary inventiveness is freed by a vision of the universe which does not recognize separation between the world of the living and the world of the dead.

Sulaiman comes back yet again, not only through the frequent echoes of his prophecies, but as a physical presence with the name of Alusine Dunbar. He leaves "the high plateau of the dead" from which he had seen the ruin threatening Malagueta, and arrives in the city, unconquerable because he "had conquered the last mystery of how to be alive in the same place where he had died over a hundred years before" (289). He is present when Emmanuel Cromantine kills the first British Governor of Malagueta, as he had predicted. In the epilogue, Alusine Dunbar appears on a flying carpet, carried by the raging wind that accompanies the death of General Masimi-ara. On the last page, Alusine Dunbar avenges the killing of the General by wiping out the culprits: the corrupt politician Sanka Maru is raised from the ground and thrown to his death in the middle of the road, while Colonel Akonmgo, entwined between the legs of his svelte mistress, is flung into the air, condemned to an "eternal public disgrace in *The Last Harmattan of Alusine Dunbar*" (398) – that is, in the novel itself, which thus becomes part of the reality it has narrated. It is as though, paradoxically, it were not that the novel is meta-literary, but that reality is meta-fictional.

The narrative devices used in the last chapter of Book Four and in the epilogue, in order to bring the novel into explicitly political terrain, are far removed from realism. The characters of the General and of Sanka Maru, and their situations, clearly allude to what really happened in the period following Sierra Leone's independence, when a greedy, corrupt class of politicians arose to sack the country and thus condemned it to extreme poverty. This concern with politics is present throughout the novel as an undertone, and is found not only in the opposition between Malaguetans and English, but also in the description of the rapid formation of a sort of local aristocracy (191, 213, 263) and, in Book Four, in the 'Márquesan' affairs of the Garrison family and in the figure of Garbage, the committed poet and almost magical son of Isatu. Importantly, however, this comes about through narrative choices that belong to the epic, metaphoric, or magical dimension. Again, in the fifteenth chapter, where we reach incidents that take place during the two World Wars, there is a figure who assumes special significance in this context, the enormous Hediza Farouka, doll-faced but the size of a baby elephant, who keeps her decuplet daughters under her skirt. The development of trade with the Arabs and the discovery of diamonds, which have such dramatic consequences for life in Malagueta, are told as though they were part of a fable.

In addition to Sulaiman, there is another dominant figure in the first part of *The Last Harmattan*: this is Fatmatta, whom we meet at the beginning of the novel, when she dies on board ship with the Kasila coast already in sight. Cheney-Coker here adopts a strategy found throughout the novel: a character appears and acts in the present, but only after s/he has been intro-duced are we told, retrospectively, of his/her often fabulous past. Thus Fatmatta's story emerges later: she is the daughter of Mariamu and Sulai-man, and is gifted with a mysterious power: any man who desires her and approaches her against her will is struck down by the "scorpion in her eyes." When Fatmatta falls in love, it is at first sight, with the handsome Camara, whom she marries, only to discover on her wedding night that he is an albino of mysterious origin, and that his physical beauty is the temporary effect of a magic lotion, without which he begins to disintegrate, crashing "with a thud on the floor, foaming at the mouth, beside his wife" (58). Fatmatta goes to pieces. She dully agrees to marry Ahmed and, after his death, is captured by a bandit, then sold and taken off to Virginia. The "scorpion in her eyes" and the magic glass beans prepared by her father Sulaiman protect her there from her owner's lust and from the "voracity of other slave breeders" (67). She will not give birth to mulattoes fated to become slaves, but chooses to remain forever in communion with her ancestors, regarding her life in the New World merely as a period of transition. Ultimately she returns to her own land, though only to be buried there.

It is clear that Fatmatta is a richly symbolic character. She is the incarnation of the survival of the African spirit in that "place of horror and damnation," the American colonies, and of the dream of returning to Mother Africa. This is why her spirit is present when Jeanette Cromantine gives birth to her first son, a child of dreamers who have crossed the ocean to come home. She also appears to the English Captain and prevents him from shooting Thomas Bookerman as he leads the crowd of Malaguetans to the garrison. Fatmatta is a protective presence throughout the novel and is finally commemorated in the name given to Emmanuel Cromantine's daughter (the lovely Fatmatta – Emilia, with whose daughter Sadatu General Masimiara falls in love). Fatmatta inherits the extraordinary powers of her father Sulaiman. Garbage, the most important character in Book Four, is in a sense 'illuminated' by Sulaiman while still a child: Sulaiman guides him into the "labyrinth of the past" of Malagueta, which Garbage later re-creates in his poems.[7]

Garbage is *the* poet. Not only do his lines on the founders of Malagueta inflame Arabella Garrison; they are a shock for the whole city. In a novel which mingles the ordinary and the extraordinary, which has the dead inhabiting the world of the living, which shows magic working 'naturally' in reality, and which demands of its readers total suspension of disbelief, this is

---

[7] "He searched for Malagueta in the tempestuous seas of former times where the conches of its birth stones had been trapped by the planktons of oblivion since the time of the first war. He brought back from the unfathomable bottom of the sea the coelacanth that had guided Sebastian and Jeanette Cromantine, clumsily navigating the route to the promised land" (329). This is, in fact, what Syl Cheney–Coker does in his novel.

perhaps the greatest challenge Cheney–Coker faces us with. For the most extraordinary aspect of the whole story is surely the idea that poetry can meet a whole society head-on, and that – apart from the personal sacrifice of the poet who sets himself up in opposition to the powers that be, as recent events have dramatically reminded us – it can excite so urgent and vital a response in a world which seems to listen no more than half-heartedly to the motives and voice of the poet.

ଓଷ • ୨୦

"History never walks here, it runs in any direction"

Carnival and Magic in the Fiction of Kojo Laing and Mia Couto

———————————————— ℬ

Pietro Deandrea

O NE OF THE VERY FEW ATTEMPTS to give a theoretical account of magical realism in anglophone African literature is represented by the Nigerian critic–novelist Kole Omotoso's *The Form of the African Novel* (1979), where the definition 'marvellous realism' is employed. The concept in question is interpreted in its ontological and historical implications as "the juxtaposition of the belief system of one archaic economic and social system side by side with the belief system of another economic and social system, this time capitalism."[1]

Omotoso thus brings into focus the 'marvellous' as an approach to reality – originally pre-colonial – experienced collectively on a daily basis. It is not a marginal clarification, but one that has links with some influential Latin American theorists. In the well-known Introduction to his novel *El reino de este mundo* (1949), for instance, Alejo Carpentier also claimed his *real maravilloso* to be a mythical ontology, rather than a literary ruse.[2] Again, a few years later, Jacques–Stéphen Alexis rejected the cold explorations of Western Surrealism in favour of a Haitian "marvellous realism" founded on

---

[1] Kole Omotoso, *The Form of the African Novel* (Akure & Ibadan: Fagbamigbe, 1979): 26. See Fredric Jameson's similar analysis in "On Magic Realism in Film," *Critical Inquiry* 12.2 (1986): 311.

[2] Alejo Carpentier, *El reino de este mundo* (Mexico City: E.D.I.A.P.S.A., 1949).

human existence and its struggles.[3] Omotoso's choice of the term 'marvellous' is clearly influenced by these illustrious artists, but the transcontinental bond works both ways, if one considers the influence of African cultures on the novels of Carpentier, Alexis and other magical-realist authors. To mention a more recent example, the 'magical' dimension of Gabriel García Márquez's *Of Love and Other Demons* (1994) has explicit Yoruba origins.

Omotoso's assumptions, of course, imply the rejection of any form of escapism. The life of the characters is accurately portrayed as a necessary requisite for a radical employment of marvellous realism.[4] The works by Syl Cheney–Coker and Ben Okri analyzed in this volume by Paolo Bertinetti and Renato Oliva certainly meet such a condition, being centred respectively on the struggles of a settlement of former slaves and on the degradation of an urban ghetto.

The same may be asserted about *Search Sweet Country*, Kojo Laing's first novel. Set in Accra in the Seventies, it develops a series of characters, each of whom is striving to carry out his/her social and personal project.[5] The book's language is extremely lyrical and imaginative, while its dialogue re-creates the peculiar rhythms and polyglot nature of Ghanaian English, thanks also to the insertion of terms from various local languages and of neologisms by the author.[6] In other words, the novel is a trenchant linguistic tour de force that has received great acclaim by demanding critics such as Robert Fraser and Adewale Maja–Pearce.[7]

The beggar Beni Baidoo seems to represent a concentration of the features outlined above, while also constituting a link between the rest of the characters. His jokes, vulgar exploits, cryptic sentences and ability to guess people's thoughts make him resemble a Shakespearean fool, or West African trickster.

---

[3] "Du réalisme merveilleux chez les Haïtiens," *Présence Africaine* 8–10 (June–November 1956): 264.

[4] Omotoso, *The Form of the African Novel*, 57.

[5] Kojo Laing, *Search Sweet Country* (London: Heinemann, 1986). I have already discussed Laing's works in "'New Worlds, New Wholes': Kojo Laing's Narrative Quest for Social Renewal," *African Literature Today* 20 (1996): 158–78. A number of points from that essay are repeated, developed or mentioned in passing in this essay.

[6] See Mary Esther Kropp Dakubu, "*Search Sweet Country* and the Language of Authentic Being," *Research in African Literatures* 24.1 (Spring 1993), passim.

[7] See Robert Fraser, "Kojo Laing: Profile and Extract," *Wasafiri* 3 (Autumn 1995): 9; Adewale Maja–Pearce, *A Mask Dancing: Nigerian Novelists of the Eighties* (London: Hans Zell, 1992): 102–103, and Maja–Pearce, "At Last, the Real Thing!," *New African* (January 1991): 43.

Not satisfied with the coexistence of the two 'belief systems,' the characters face an *impasse*, exemplified by the autobiographical sociologist, Professor Sackey, who complains that "the weight of our past seems to be crushing the present [...] and the future will not be born!" The "new worlds, new wholes" (241) still waiting to be created in post-colonial Ghana require closer interrogation of supernatural and factual spheres, "a fairly easy flow between abstract, symbol, action and thing" (234). A more dynamic magical–symbolic realm is needed, one more likely to affect the daily speed of life and less trapped within its own force-field.

As Ato Quayson has noticed, the dichotomy is resolved only at a linguistic level; the characters themselves cannot negotiate the conflict between traditional and modern worlds.[8] From a collective and political point of view, the pessimistic ending of *Search* is related to the works by Cheney–Coker and Okri mentioned earlier.

After the novel's publication, Laing declared that

> It's almost a paradox but the more self-sufficient literature is the more effect it will have on other sectors, including the political [...] I am fundamentally committed to literature and I consider it an end in itself.[9]

This may help interpret his later novels, which go beyond the conception of magical realism quoted earlier, and in which the dead-end is apparently solved by moving the action to other worlds and dimensions, which, because they are linguistically based, offer the dynamism that the setting of *Search* could not provide.

Laing's second novel, *Woman of the Aeroplanes*,[10] is set in the Ghanaian town of Tukwan and Scotland's Levensvale, each peopled with immortals and not to be found on the map of either country. A "far-flung vision" which "has no parallel I can think of," is Chris Dunton's comment.[11] The temporal dimension is also completely disrupted. Tukwan is called a "happy renegade of history" (17), living as it does in every year and none at the same time, because "History never walks here, it runs in any direction."[12]

---

8 See "Esoteric Webwork As Nervous System: Reading the Fantastic in Ben Okri's Writing," in *Essays on African Writing 2: Contemporary Literature*, ed. Abdulrazak Gurnah (Oxford: Heinemann, 1995): 147–48.

9 Adewale Maja–Pearce, "Interview with Kojo Laing," *Wasafiri* 5–6 (1987): 28.

10 Kojo Laing, *Woman of the Aeroplanes* (1988; London: Picador, 1989).

11 Chris Dunton, "Far-Flung Vision," *West Africa* 3782 (26 February–4 March 1990): 317.

12 1; see also: 26, 49, 78, 104–107, 166.

Every day realities and relationships between characters are continuous-
ly dismembered by Laing's English. On the first page, Kwame Atta is so
agitated

> that when he inadvertently picked up a piece of rubbish on the clean streets of
> Tukwan, he threw himself in the bin instead, with the rubbish motionless in his
> left footprint.

After six pages, the reader discovers that Pokuaa, the woman of the title, is

> the mistress of two small aeroplanes which both stood at the level of her lips:
> one at her upper lip, and the other at her lower lip. She perfumed her aero-
> planes every morning with frangipani lavender.

These same planes, however, will be employed to carry a delegation of
Tukwanians to their Scottish twin town. The book is full of similar inventions: a movable lake (18), pens writing on their own (25, 73), photograph-
able dreams (159–60), rain falling upwards (138), aeroplanes with sentient
noses (140), to cite only a few. These instances should not be taken as mere
metaphoric constructions, whether symbol or hyperbole, because they really
denote things and events occurring in the novel. As T.S. Eliot wrote in
"Prufrock," "I have measured out my life in coffee spoons." In Levensvale,
Margaret Mackie goes "round the sitting room at exactly the same speed as
her husband was stirring his tea [...] he gave his wife a rest by reducing the
speed of his controlling teaspoon" (64). This is how Laing describes marital
harmony.

Tukwan's sage, Kofi Senya, is found "perched on his own pipe with his
vulture, while he was still smoking it" (185). Sometimes he blows

> words out of his pipe, as others blew smoke rings. This was when he did not
> want to talk. The words would rise up blue in elegant short sentences, and
> then disappear when the vulture flapped his wings. (13)

The latter image is significant within the economy of the book as a whole,
for *Woman* could be said to depict a cartoon world, the bizarre humour
reaching its apex when the characters start exchanging parts of their bodies
(22, 86–87, 193).

An interpretative key to the novel is provided in the character of the
trickster. In the first chapter of his *The Trickster in West Africa* (1980), Robert
Pelton delves into the folktales of the Ashanti area of Ghana, where Tukwan
is located. Their protagonist is the spider Ananse, a figure that survived the
Middle-Passage experience and appears in Caribbean folktales. In the Akan
language, all folktales are called *anasesem* or 'Ananse's stories,' even when

this trickster is not present in the narrative.[13] One of his principal features is the violation of biological rules, including the modification and removal of his own and others' bodily parts.[14]

If, in *Search*, the trickster role is performed by a single character, in *Woman* it is played out in the language and in the incidents narrated, thanks to a cumulatively ingenious style studded with neologisms and employing novel graphic layouts. Tukwan's writer and historian Kwaku de Babo even accuses native-speakers of English of becoming "too soft and self-indulgent" with their own language (62) – a momentous assertion in the context of post-colonial literatures.

Nevertheless, one character is unmatched in trickster-like transgression: Kwame Atta, the historian's twin brother, whose impudence, dishonesty and vulgarity are balanced by a creative spirit. He is capable of taking off propelled by his own flatulence (42–43), but also of saving the town through his inventions (155), to the point where he threatens to "stop thinking" so as to leave his fellow townspeople to rot (21). This dual aspect suggests a further analogy with Ananse. In Pelton's opinion, the spider's coarseness, sexual exuberance and selfishness, as well as the laughter he provokes, are a means of highlighting the social and moral workings of Ashanti society. Ananse's insolence in the face of any law, taboo or even divinity is not inspired by a Promethean instinct or a drive towards chaos, but is to be seen as a way of disclosing Ashanti religious and ethical mechanisms, with a view to regenerating them in new forms.[15] Kwawisi Tekpetey stresses the cathartic function of *anansesem* as

> tension-relieving aesthetic devices. The members of the audience purge them-
> selves of tensions built up by social restrictions and thus of their latent desires
> to become involved in Ananse-like adventures.[16]

On both sides of the Atlantic, Ananse's relevance is unabated. In his collection of stories *Anancy's Score*, the Jamaican writer Andrew Salkey shows the spider's connections with contemporary issues.[17] Karin Barber explores cultural syncretism through the example of some Ghanaian mimeo-

---

[13] See Robert D. Pelton, *The Trickster in West Africa: A Study in Mythic Irony and Sacred Delight* (1989; Berkeley: U of California P, 1980): 49.

[14] Pelton, *The Trickster in West Africa*, 35.

[15] Pelton, *The Trickster in West Africa*, 35, 60.

[16] "The Trickster in Akan–Asante Oral Literature," *Asemka: A Bilingual Literary Journal of the University of Cape Coast* 5 (September 1979): 81.

[17] Andrew Salkey, *Anancy's Score* (London: Bogle–L'Ouverture, 1973), passim.

graphed comics from the mid-Seventies in which Spiderman and Ananse
join forces to combat military and political corruption, each making use of
his superhuman powers and organizing popular uprisings.[18]

Ananse's disruptions are constructive, then, and the same is true of
Laing's writing, where the extraordinary setting is not severed from social
issues belonging to post-colonial Ghana: "History is there and its brutality
acknowledged," as Dunton has remarked.[19] Recurrent references to political
power, for instance, remind us of the age-old controversy over the failures of
democracy in post-colonial Africa. Laing does not invoke a return to a
purely ancestral ruling, but tries to deconstruct the most rigid aspects of
tradition, especially through Nana Bontox's display of wealth and power
(10, 113). Ben Okri's *The Famished Road* adopts a similar stance: Azaro, the
spirit-child *abiku* who chooses to live, clearly goes against the Yoruba belief
that "no *Abiku* ever pledges to stay put in life, which explains why the *Abiku*
is indifferent to the plight of its mother and her grief at leading a childless
life."[20] Tukwan was banned from the real Ashanti town of Kumasi precisely
on account of its "subversive activity, for refusing to listen to *all* the songs of
the ancestors" (1–2), and because it entrusted Kwaku de Babo with "the task
of modernizing all proverbs from all tribes" (36). The new Tukwanian
society is necessarily a hybrid product, where Western and Ashanti cultures
meet and where both must be supple enough to adjust to contemporary
needs: "it was generally agreed that new things were as wise as the old at
Tukwan, and that the opposition between the two was welcome and con-
trollable" (36). Laing's detachment from realism focuses on a communal
project. The Tukwanians' efforts to regain mortality clearly manifest the
author's awareness of the difficulty involved in pursuing such a project in
real life.

Laing's third novel, *Major Gentl and the Achimota Wars* (1992),[21] is set in
the (actually existent) Ghanaian town of Achimota in the year 2020, and
follows along the same stylistic lines as *Woman*. The soldier of the title is the
military leader of the town, engaged in the second War of Existence against
the Western forces led by Torro the Terrible, who speaks spaghetti English
and grew up under the Italian Mafia and South African apartheid. In the

    18 Karin Barber, "Popular Arts in Africa," *African Studies Review* 30.3 (September 1987):
40.
    19 Chris Dunton, "Far-Flung Vision."
    20 Timothy Mobolade, "The Concept of Abiku," *African Arts* 7.1 (Autumn 1973): 62.
    21 Kojo Laing, *Major Gentl and the Achimota Wars* (Oxford: Heinemann, 1992).

novel, war is a representation of the ideological and economic hold imposed on contemporary Africa by the neo-colonial world-order.

Once again, an issue of extreme importance is approached through a general infringement of expected logic, in a combination of breathtaking language, imagery and plot that Odia Ofeimun describes as doing "self-conscious violence to time, space and the English language."[22] In one of his several intrusions as storyteller, Laing writes: "*If the life had to be backwards before you won it, then so be it, so be the language*" (124, italics in the text). In Achimota, the brakes of Torro's Fiat echo his extramarital love-making (35), parts of the sky destroyed by missiles get sown up (101), and so on. Here is another world, narrated as though it were a cartoon, as may be seen in the following passage: "Pogo had solved simultaneous speed and stillness [...] the horses galloped on the same spot, thus fooling the beefy beef-eating Torro" (162). The three elders who rule the city in wartime (political posts are normally filled by means of a referendum system involving the whole population) decree that "all established relationships" be treated as "un-sacred," invoking the principle of "disestablishmentarianism" (128).

Distinctions between categories such as symbols and their objects, or the tenors and vehicles of metaphors, fall apart. The golden cockroach that is the emblem of the city, for instance, becomes a real character at the very start of the novel. Among other distinctive marks of magical realism, Wendy B. Faris singles out

> images that take on lives of their own [...] a closing of the gap between words and the world, or a demonstration of what we might call the linguistic nature of experience. This magic happens when a metaphor is made real.[23]

Even Achimota city reflects a new relationship between metaphorical and concrete realms, because it has

> devoured Accra almost completely while at the same time most of the rest of the country had inexplicably vanished, land and all. Thus, by the year 2020 Achimota was a truncated city bursting to survive and to find the rest of its country soon. (3)

The vanished land is a metaphor for the Western ideological and economic assault that has led many people to leave their land. In the novel, they have literally taken their land away with them, and the War of Existence is a

---

22 "Surrealistic Power–Play," *West Africa* 3918 (19–25 October 1992): 1794.

23 Wendy B. Faris, "Scheherazade's Children: Magical Realism and Postmodern Fiction," in *Magical Realism: Theory, History, Community*, ed. Lois Parkinson Zamora & Wendy B. Faris (Durham NC/London: Duke UP, 1995): 164, 176.

means of reconquering it. One of the first signs of success in the conflict is the return of fragments of the lost land: "There, miles off beyond Achimota City, a rectangular piece of land slowly crawled through the void, and joined the land of the city!" (104).

The book includes an explicit attack on Western technology. One of the aims of Torro's army is to help virtual reality swallow up all sensory and physical activities: "The most advanced thing they want to do is turn thought into a sense, diiirectly!" he says (41). Torro, in his turn, has become so suspicious

> that he used a computer to map the route of food from his fork or his hands to his mouth: he couldn't trust what could happen in that tiny interval of oral travel. (116)

The critic Derek Wright rightly remarks that "Laing's satiric point is, of course, that Africa for Europe has always existed in a state of virtual reality."[24] The author's accusation reminds one of Guy Debord's view of postmodern culture as a "society of spectacle," where lived experience has become a representation, or of Jean Baudrillard's "desert of the real," an image borrowed from Borges.[25] The disconcerting sense of having lost touch with reality – palpable in Western societies – is not limited to intellectual theories and virtual fantasies. A case in point might be Mike Leigh's prize-winning film *Naked* (1993), where the picaresque protagonist Johnny wanders through a dreary and cynical London speculating on the doom of mankind. In an ultra-modern but empty building he has a long conversation with the nightwatchman:

> JOHNNY: By the very definition of Apocalypse, Mankind must cease to exist, at least in a material form.
>
> *(Brian stops in another doorway)*
>
> BRIAN: What d'you mean, in a material form?
>
> JOHNNY: Well, 'e'll evolve.
>
> BRIAN: What into?
>
> JOHNNY: Into something that transcends matter. Into a species of pure thought.[26]

---

[24] "Returning Voyagers: The Ghanaian Novel in the Nineties," *Journal of Modern African Studies* 34.1 (1996): 187. On the other hand, I do not agree with Wright's view that the novel's fantasy is inspired only by such a virtualisation of reality, as these pages evince.

[25] Quoted in *Storming the Reality Studio: A Casebook of Cyberpunk and Postmodern Science Fiction*, ed. Larry McCaffery (Durham NC/London: Duke UP, 1991): 6, 20, 25.

[26] Mike Leigh, *"Naked" and Other Screenplays* (London: Faber & Faber, 1995): 48.

The similar destiny awaiting Africa is brutally expressed in Torro's words: "We have decided that conceptually there is no difference between existence and non-existence, hence we do not consider anything wrong when you no longer exist" (166).

Major Gentl's strategy supports an epistemology which shows regard for nature. The author concentrates, among other things, on the city's architecture, which features "fruity columns," (101), while Gentl's bamboo house has "taken root and was growing heartily" (137), and termites

> just continued to change the architecture of Government House when they wanted, with their inspired saliva plus earthen engineering. And wasn't it the cheapest way of building strong mansions, using termites intelligently? And the way the biting combined the different forms of red, grey, and brown was beautiful to behold. (66)

In *Search Sweet Country*, the guava fruit appears as a recurrent metaphor. It is pondered, for instance, by Kofi Loww:

> All the stones of a guava pointed in different directions, and each stone could be subversive of love and action. And any love or power that did not have this infinite direction of seeds, this patterned way of variety, could neither fit into his heart, nor his head. Yet what did he in his withdrawn openness, in his slow explorations, have to give towards this very same variousness that he wished for? (152)

In *Woman*, the novel which represents a first step towards the literary realization of this variousness, a passing reference to the same fruit is more figurative and idiomatic: "it looks as if the lawyer has already swallowed the guava of truth" (29). In Gentl's Achimota, where "Fruit was law: [...] there was fruit in the toilets, fruit in the halls, and fruit in the aeroplanes, so that you could eat the city." Fruit becomes a part of the action: one of the elders "enjoyed the joy of ruling in very difficult times that needed much fruit and calm in equal quantities [...] O you guava government" (3;17).

The scatological dimension is another feature associated with the behaviour of the trickster Ananse. In Laing's latest novel: *"You could speak your mind koraa* [completely] *in Achimota City, and even talk to the government while sitting on the toilet"* (italics in the text, 74). His characters rejoice in anything connected with excrement – which confirms the atypical direction of his writing among anglophone African authors, for such images are generally associated with moral decay and corruption, particularly in novels by Armah and Soyinka. According to Pelton, Ananse discloses how the human mind and heart are themselves epiphanies of a calmly transcendent sacredness so boldly engaged with this world that it encompasses both nobility and messiness – feces, lies and even death.[27]

Pelton avails himself of Victor Turner's studies on shamanism, where ritual contacts with nature lead to a sort of regeneration of society.[28] When Major Gentl has to make a decision, he similarly has to "crawl to think, sharing the grounds with frogs, lizards, crow dung, cricket droppings, the shit of wise sparrows, and worm tunnels" (144). Ananse's unruliness, like Laing's disregard for all codes, is instrumental in shaping human society. His theriomorphism makes him break "through the boundaries separating nature and culture in such a way that human life is seen to transform perpetually what is given from both above and below."[29]

The magical dimension in Laing's novels has its origin in local culture. It is hardly in keeping with the dominant academic preference for migrant writers and intellectuals that inhabit the interstitial spaces between various cultures ("the truest eye may now belong to the migrant's double vision," Homi K. Bhabha writes[30]). Nor does it correspond to the myth of authenticity defined by Rushdie – one of the authors championed by Bhabha – as a "folkloristic straitjacket."[31] One cannot help considering that Laing longs for a hybrid society, and his narrative output is structured accordingly.

Laing's novels have several things in common not only with Ananse's subversive character, but also with the joyful atmosphere of carnival, as analyzed by Bakhtin. They share the urge to overturn imposed hierarchies through a dynamic and ever-changing language, and through a refusal of accepted logic, which does not amount to pure denial but ambiguously combines ordinary and extraordinary events:

> The carnivalesque parody has little in common with the modern parody, which is purely negative and formal. For the former, by denying everything, revives and renews at the same time. Generally speaking, negation pure and simple is totally unfamiliar to popular culture [...] In the imagery of popular celebrations, pure and abstract negation does not exist. Images aim at encompassing the two poles of becoming in their contradictory unity. Those

---

27 Pelton, *The Trickster in West Africa*, 4.
28 Pelton, *The Trickster in West Africa*, 33–35.
29 Pelton, *The Trickster in West Africa*, 36.
30 Homi K. Bhabha, *The Location of Culture* (London: Routledge, 1994): 5.
31 Salman Rushdie, *The Satanic Verses* (London: Viking, 1988): 52.

who get thrashed – or killed – are dressed up, blows are joyful, beginning and ending in laughter.[32]

The scatological element is one of the main sites of this dual phenomenon, which seems to denigrate the spiritual, but actually plants the seeds of renewal:

> The ambivalent character of excrement, its links with resurrection and renewal and its particular role in the victory over fear [...]. To him [Rabelais] excrement was also joyful and disenchanting matter, degrading and courteous at the same time, combining tomb and birth in their least tragic form – a form which was comic, and by no means dreadful.[33]

Bakhtin mentions the popular novel *Aucassin et Nicolette*, a medieval combination of sung lyric and recited narrative featuring a carnivalesque war similar to *Major Gentl*'s. The two protagonists arrive in a country where the king is pregnant and a battle is "fought with rotten crab-apples, eggs and fresh cheeses."[34] When Aucassin draws his sword and slays some of the enemy, the king stops him: "It is not our custom to kill each other."[35] Compare this with Major Gentl's children's war, where both sides lay down their guns and decide "to sell hard toffee [...] The sun was hidden with hundreds of toffees thrown in jubilation" (54), and with the football match between the two armies (122–26). Even carnage is described farcically:

> hundreds of his [Torro's] men perished when the branches opened fire, with the perching crows joining in and shooting with the small guns hidden in their beaks. Two dead men propped each other upright. (141)

---

[32] "la parodie carnavalesque est très eloignée de la parodie moderne purement négative et formelle; en effet, tout en niant, la première ressuscite et renouvelle tout à la fois. La négation pure et simple est de manière générale totalement étrangère à la culture populaire [...] Dans le système des images de la fête populaire, la négation pure et abstraite n'existe pas. Les images visent à englober les deux pôles du devenir dans leur unité contradictoire. Le battu (ou tué) est paré; la bastonnade est joyeuse; elle débute et se termine au milieu des rires"; Bakhtin, *L'Œuvre de François Rabelais et la culture populaire au Moyen Âge et sous le Renaissance*, tr. Andrée Robel (1965; Paris: Gallimard, 1970): 19, 20, 204; my translation.

[33] "le caractère ambivalent des excréments, leur lien avec la résurrection et la rénovation et son rôle particulier dans la victoire sur la peur [...] Pour lui [Rabelais...] les excréments étaient en outre une matière joyeuse et dégrisante, à la fois rabaissante et gentille, réunissant la tombe et la naissance dans leur forme la moins tragique, une forme comique, nullement effrayante"; *L'Œuvre de François Rabelais*, 178; my translation.

[34] *Aucassin et Nicolette* (with *The Pilgrimage of Charlemagne*), tr. Glyn S. Burgess, ed. Anne Elizabeth Cobby (Garland Library of Medieval Literature A47; New York: Garland, 1965): 160.

[35] *Aucassin et Nicolette*, 162.

In spite of its belligerent plot, *Major Gentl's* mood is gay and sparkling, unlike the epic gravity and solemnity of the novels of Okri and Cheney–Coker. Laing's approach is opposed to a more general separation of holy and comic.[36]

The idea of the carnivalesque (and Carnival more generally) seems to haunt critical discourse about magical-realist narratives, both in and beyond Africa. Brenda Cooper, for instance, compares Cheney–Coker's novel to Rabelais' narrative mode, in that both make use of a multiplicity of voices.[37] One should also mention the Trinidadian Lawrence Scott's novel, *Witchbroom* (1993), where the Caribbean carnival, with its wake of metamorphoses and role-subversions, provides a key to understanding the novel's magical realism.[38] The following general comment by Wendy B. Faris on magical-realist novels may account for this list of diverse references: "A carnivalesque spirit is common in this group of novels. Language is used extravagantly, expending its resources beyond its referential needs."[39] Another definition is given by the Guyanese writer Wilson Harris, who says that "life in its essential contradiction is art: it is the deep unconscious humour of carnival."[40]

ಞ • ಶಿ

To confirm the presence of this magical mode in African fiction, it may be useful to introduce the Mozambican writer of Portuguese origin Mia Couto. In his two collections of short stories, effectively translated by David Brookshaw,[41] the specifically local background is of fundamental importance. It consists of a Mozambique devastated by centuries of Portuguese colonialism, the liberation war resulting in the 1974 Independence, and the fifteen-year-long Civil War. In Couto's works, history does not run in any direction, but plunders and escapes, leaving behind a geographical, social, and

---

[36] Pelton, *The Trickster in West Africa*, 11.

[37] See "Syl Cheney–Coker: *The Last Harmattan of Alusine Dunbar*, and an Interview," *African Literature Association Bulletin* 20.3 (Summer 1994): 4. See also Cooper, *Magical Realism in West African Fiction* (London: Routledge, 1998), which also deals with Ben Okri and Kojo Laing as well as Cheney–Coker.

[38] Lawrence Scott, *Witchbroom* (1992; Oxford: Heinemann, 1993).

[39] Wendy B. Faris, "Sheherazade's Children," 184.

[40] Wilson Harris, *Tradition, the Writer and Society* (1967; London/Port of Spain: New Beacon, 1973): 12.

[41] Mia Couto, *Voices Made Night* (1986; Oxford: Heinemann, 1990) and *Every Man is a Race* (1989; Oxford: Heinemann, 1994), both tr. David Brookshaw.

spiritual landscape marked by a condition of deprivation almost beyond imagination (one of his characters is a fisherman hungry to the point of taking his eyes out in order to use them as bait).[42] His characters are so accustomed to the presence of death that the grief-stricken Rosalinda becomes "her own ancestor" (*Every Man is a Race*, 26).

Couto's writing is certainly not pervaded with Laing's joyous spirit and humour, nor is it limited to a naturalist, or social-realist, narrative style. He belongs to a younger generation of Mozambican writers who have all contributed to the journal *Charrua*. Dealing with the construction of a literary space in their independent country, rather than with oppressive colonization, these writers discard the combative writing of the past and seek new aesthetic forms of expression, each in his or her own way. Couto also criticizes pamphleteering literature, and his short stories were badly received for not adhering to this mainstream tradition.[43]

His writing combines an extremely spare and direct manner with a poetic vision of things, resulting in a two-pronged incisiveness close to the short stories Ben Okri wrote before his *abiku* novels.[44] As Chris Dunton remarks, "Couto's language is clear and precise and at the same time hugely resourceful. He has a way of using figurative language which drives deep into states of being."[45]

The renowned Mozambican poet José Craveirinha, who considers Couto a pivotal figure in his country's literature, has wondered whether Couto's concision comes from his long career as a journalist,[46] a profession he has exercised while working mainly as a biologist. The lyrical aspect of his writing, on the other hand, is probably due to the fact that his father was both a journalist and a poet. Couto himself began by writing poetry. Poetry

---

[42] This blood-curdling short story, "The Blind Fisherman" (*Every Man*, 51–57), looks to be an actualization of an analogous instance that I came across in a story by the American Judith Ortiz Cofer, "Arturo's Flight," where a refugee from Germany describes the Second World War as no fairy tale, because "This was more like the ones [stories] where somebody pulls their eyes out of their heads because things are so bad they might as well get even worse so that they can get better"; Cofer, *An Island Like You* (New York: Orchard, 1995): 37. Some culture's lore may well include a similar story I am unaware of.

[43] See José Ornelas, "Mia Couto no contexto da literatura pós-colonial de Moçambique," *Luso-Brazilian Review* 33.2 (Winter 1996): 41–42.

[44] See Ben Okri, *Incidents at the Shrine* (London: Heinemann, 1986), and *Stars of the New Curfew* (London: Secker & Warburg, 1988).

[45] Chris Dunton, "Butterflies of Flesh," *West Africa* 3797 (4–10 June 1990): 942.

[46] See Craveirinha's introduction to the Italian edition, *Voci all'imbrunire* (Rome: Edizioni Lavoro, 1989): xxiv.

was the most common vehicle of expression for Mozambican writers during the colonial period, because it evaded censorship more easily than prose.[47] Couto has said that he does not like the idea of separating the two: "I believe that one can write poetry in both verse and prose. As for me, I keep writing poems in prose."[48] Take, for example, the opening of the story "The Day Mabata–bata Exploded" in *Voices Made Night*:

> Suddenly, the ox exploded. It burst without so much as a moo. In the surrounding grass a rain of chunks and slices fell, as if the fruit and leaves of an ox. Its flesh turned into red butterflies. Its bones were scattered coins. Its horns were caught in some branches, swinging to and fro, imitating life in the invisibility of the wind. (17)

Couto's artistic career, starting with poetry and moving on to narrative whose language uses all the resources excluded by realist writing, resembles Laing's and Cheney–Coker's. More generally, the poetic dimension is a common trait of magical-realist novels, being a suitable way of conveying their attitude towards the magic of the real: "In an attempt to draw the reader's attention to the richness of their continent, they often poeticize it," Amaryll Chanady says of the Latin Americans.[49] Couto is explicit in this regard: "One has to take recourse to poetry in order to tell or express what happens. Reality is so magical, so lacking in rationality, that poetry suits very well."[50]

Couto's lyricism mostly reveals the hidden aspect of the miserable existences recounted in his plots, an aspect that the dominant (colonialist and, later, orthodox Marxist) ideologies have always tried to stifle. The emergence of the poetic is therefore a means of deliverance, instrumental in

---

[47] See Patrick Chabal, *Literaturas Moçambicanas: Literatura e nacionalidade* (Lisbon: Vega Editora, 1994): 65. Quoted in Ornelas, "Mia Couto no contexto," 37–38.

[48] "Je crois que l'on peut écrire de la poésie en vers et en prose. Je continue à écrire des poèmes en prose"; Bernard Magnier & Michel Laban, "Entretien avec Mia Couto," *Notre Librairie (Club des Lecteurs d'Expression Française): Littérature du Mozambique* 112 (1993): 74; my translation.

[49] Amaryll Chanady, "The Origins and Development of Magic Realism in Latin American Fiction," *Magic Realism and Literatures: Essays and Stories; Proceedings of the Conference on Magic Realist Writing in Canada University of Waterloo / Wilfrid Laurier University (May, 1985)*, ed. Peter Hinchcliffe & Ed Jewinski (Waterloo: U of Waterloo P, 1985): 52.

[50] "On doit recourir à la poésie pour raconter, pour exprimer ce qui se passe. La réalité est si magique, si peu rationelle, que la poésie convient très bien"; Mangier & Laban, "Entretien," 74.

revealing the beauty and complexity of a world buried by the workings of
history. The repeated images of water and fishermen may help clarify this:

> See the hunter there, what he does? He prepares his spear the moment he sees
> the gazelle. But the fisherman can't see the fish inside the river. The fisherman
> believes in something he can't see. (*Voices Made Night*, 24)

The language of poetry – together with mythic and magical elements – also
provides a means of introspection and social criticism, as the typical figure
of Rosa Caramela, an outcast lame hunchback and the eponymous heroine
of Couto's most touching story, shows:[51]

> The moon seemed to stick to the hunchback, like a coin to a miser's pocket.
> And she, in front of the statues, would sing in a hoarse, inhuman voice: she
> would entreat them to emerge from their stony abode. (*Every Man*, 2)

Rosa Caramela is absurdly accused of venerating the symbols of colonialism, and subsequently arrested.

In Couto's stories, magic is sometimes explained by reference to the war.
The exploding ox mentioned above, for example, has simply trodden on a
landmine. The same fate befalls a young shepherd at the end of the story,
but is signalled here by means of an image from folklore:

> Suddenly, there was an explosion and a flash which seemed to turn night into
> the middle of its day. The little cowherd swallowed all that red, the shriek of
> crackling fire. Amid the flecks of night he saw the *ndlati*, bird of lightning,
> swoop down. He tried to shout:
> "*Who are you coming to get*, ndlati?"
> [...]
> And before the bird of fire could decide, Azarias ran and embraced it in the
> passage of its flame. (*Voices*, 22)

Distortions of reality induced by war also play a prominent role in the story
"The Whales of Quissico" (*Voices*, 55–62) where the fabulous whales carrying all sorts of treasures turn out to be submarines bringing weapons for the
rebels.

More often, however, the magical cannot be interpreted by direct,
rational reference to the factual world, despite being connected with war. In
"The Stain" (*Every Man*, 107–109), a character finds an abandoned military
jacket and puts it on. He realizes after a while that a bloodstain is slowly but
steadily spreading across the fabric; when he checks his body, he is positive

---

[51] See Amaryll Chanady, *Magic Realism and the Fantastic: Resolved Versus Unresolved
Antinomy* (New York: Garland, 1985): 82.

that he is not wounded in any way, but he starts feeling weak and finally loses consciousness. He is found inexplicably dead, the clean jacket next to his corpse. In "The Talking Raven's Last Warning" (*Voices*, 7–16), a painter publicly vomits a raven whose prophetic gifts will bring destruction to the village, given its inhabitants' greed and personal motives.[52] Just as in Laing's novels, concrete daily reality forms the basis for Mia Couto's peculiar magical realism, and both authors adhere to Omotoso's criteria mentioned at the beginning.[53]

Contrary to Maya Jaggi's hypothesis, poetry and the magical in Couto seem to be a fundamental mode of finding new standpoints and new visions of the world. It must be conceded, though, that reality often represents an insurmountable obstacle: "The most harrowing thing about poverty is the ignorance it has of itself. Faced by an absence of everything," Couto writes in his foreword to *Voices*, "men abstain from dreams, depriving themselves of the desire to be others. There exists in nothingness that illusion of plenitude which causes life to stop and voices to become night."

Couto's writing attempts to recover such dreams through a mode of writing reminiscent of oral story-telling. Today, the short story is the most popular literary genre among the new generation of Mozambican writers. This resurgence of short narrative is linked to the influence of traditional folktales, as the short story is the perfect frame within which to achieve a symbiosis between the oral tradition and the written word.[54] Couto's stories often open with quotations, proverbs, verses, or exchanges of conversation with a moral, philosophizing tone. Take, for instance, the oracular beginning of "The Ex-Future Priest and His Would-Be Widow":

---

[52] Maya Jaggi affirms that Couto's magic is "shown to have a detrimental and divisive effect on society." When interviewed by the same critic, though, the author declares that "Myth has a negative aspect only when it is not adjusted to the society in which it finds itself"; "Facts and Fiction" (interview) and "Dreams of the Poor" (review of *Voices Made Night*), *New African* (May 1990): 39–40.

[53] See also Carpentier's *The Kingdom of This World*, where the protagonist Ti Noël turns into a goose and discovers a principled system based on collective needs, but he cannot be a part of it because it is not his world: "Mackandal [the fabulous hero of the slaves' revolt] had disguised himself as an animal for years to serve men, not to abjure the world of men [...] In the Kingdom of Heaven there is no grandeur to be won [...] beautiful in the midst of his misery, capable of loving in the face of afflictions and trials, man finds his greatness, his fullest measure, only in the Kingdom of This World" (tr. Harriet de Onís, 1957; London: Victor Gollancz, 1967: 148–49).

[54] Ornelas, "Mia Couto no contexto," 38, 48. Couto, who has also written two novels, is considered one of the pioneers of this recent trend, and is already included in the national literary curricula.

Life is a web weaving a spider. Whether the creature believes himself a hunter in his own home or not, it matters little. The instant turns round and he becomes the quarry in an intruder's trap. This will be proved in the following tale which occurred in real though humble surroundings.(*Voices*, 95)

His magical realism offers fresh perspectives on hidden aspects of reality, such as its beauty and poetry, but seems to lack the revitalizing function distinguishable in Laing, Cheney–Coker and Okri. This is the primary characteristic that differentiates him from his fellow African magic realists.

It is therefore symptomatic that the only short story by Couto with a really happy ending, "The Rise of João Bate–Certo," should imply utter detachment from earthly matters. João builds a high ladder (recalling Wilson Harris's "Jacob's ladder") bit by bit, until its top is no longer visible. His fellow villagers have no idea what he is doing up there every day – until he descends from the ladder with "clouds, armfuls of clouds in bunches":

With these, he filled his house, where his mother was suffering the pains of her unbirth. When she looked through the window, she seemed to see the whole planet in front of her. His mother gradually began to feel the weightlessness of childhood. One night, she gripped her son's arms and babbled:

"Tell me, my son: is it prettier up there than down here?"

He smiled awkwardly, lost for words. And, with fingers made more for smoothing wood, he closed his mother's weary eyes. That night, so people say, the only place it rained was inside the house of João Bate–Certo. (*Every Man is a Race*, 98)

ෆ • හ

Magical Realism Beyond the Wall of Apartheid?
Missing Persons by Ivan Vladislavic

———————————————————— ა

Valeria Guidotti

> A boundary is not that at which something stops but [...] from
> which *something begins its presencing.*
> (Martin Heidegger, *Poetry, Language, Thought*)[1]

S
OUTH AFRICAN LITERATURE, LIKE SHEHERAZADE, has repeatedly
been threatened by death. Critics and intellectuals, mainly from outside Africa, formerly feared that the oppressive restriction of apartheid would kill creativity; more recently they have been afraid that its
demise, with the collapse of that totalitarian system encompassing all fields,
social, political, and cultural, would have the same result.

How can South African literature survive? Where can it find new life and
sustenance? I wish I could make a definite reply to these obsessive questions: magical realism, a major component of postmodernist fiction and an
important feature of post-colonial writing, is also a well established literary
practice in post-apartheid literature. However, the transition to freedom is a
moment of "cultural uncertainty, and, most crucially, of significatory or
representational undecidability."[2] This paper will therefore simply attempt
to trace the existence of a fictional mode identifiable as magical realism in
South Africa; it will also attempt to uncover connections with and local

---

[1] Martin Heidegger, "Building, Dwelling, Thinking" in *Poetry, Language, Thought*;
quoted by Homi K. Bhabha in *The Location of Culture* (London: Routledge, 1994): 1
(author's emphasis).
[2] Bhabha, *The Location of Culture*, 35.

divergences from the paradigmatic work of that genre: *One Hundred Years of Solitude.*

Stephen Gray denies the possibility of a South African magical-realist tradition, in that he sees magical-realist literature as the manifestation of a baroque, Catholic culture which cannot take root in the white, Anglo-Saxon, Protestant culture of South Africa.[3] Ivan Vladislavic, the writer on whose collection of short stories, *Missing Persons*, my analysis will focus, says: "I am suspicious of categories like Magical Realism, I do not think of my work that way, but I wonder has any writer actually ever admitted to being a magical realist?"[4] His work, however, was immediately paired with *The Powers That Be* by Mike Nicol, and both authors have been acclaimed by reviewers as the first South African magical-realistic writers.

In addition to the inherent difficulty of defining magical realism, in South Africa the literature in question includes that written by anglophone writers, literature written by blacks, both in English and in local languages, and also works written in Afrikaans by white and coloured, and the rich and imaginative production of the Indian community.

Until recently South Africa was a divided and unnaturally fragmented nation. In spite of this, there is the basis for common literary strategies, and magical realism, "a mode suited to exploring – and transgressing – boundaries,"[5] free from conventionalism, narrowness and hate, might function as a catalyst in the development of a new, national and cross-cultural post-apartheid literature. Magical realism, then, may replenish exhausted narrative traditions, as John Barth, one of the writers from whom Vladislavic admits having drawn imaginative sustenance, has suggested.[6] Other influences on Vladislavic include Rabelais, Sterne, Swift, Stevenson, Borges, Kafka – "a large and motley bunch," as he says.[7] In my opinion, this list denotes a precise, coherent, and quite homogeneous choice.

The 'Sestigers' or dissident Afrikaner writers, who as early as the Sixties had already severed links with their 'tribe' and its ideological and cultural orthodoxy, made some original aesthetic choices. Mazisi Kunene argues that

---

[3] Conversation between the author and Professor Gray (Johannesburg, July 1996).

[4] From a letter to the author, July 1995.

[5] Lois Parkinson Zamora & Wendy B. Faris, ed., *Magical Realism: History, Theory, Community* (Durham NC/London: Duke UP, 1995): 5.

[6] See John Barth, "The Literature of Exhaustion," *Atlantic Monthly* 220.2 (August 1967): 29-34, and "The Literature of Replenishment," *Atlantic Monthly* 233.1 (January 1980): 65-71.

[7] From a letter to the author, July 1995.

some of greatest and most innovative South African writers of European origin are possibly going to emerge among the Afrikaners. [...] The Afrikaners may better resolve their problem of being Europeans in Africa and consequently fashion a literature which in spirit will be closer to Latin American literature."[8]

Realism combined with hints of magic may indeed be found in Wilma Stockenström's novel *Expedition to the Baobab Tree*, where the main character is an old female slave who tells the story of her life as she awaits death in the womb of a baobab tree, and is adored by the Bushmen as a sort of Goddess. Similarly, in his most recent novels, especially *Imaginings of Sand*, André Brink has not only adopted postmodernist writing strategies, but also plays with magical realism, as is shown by the closely interwoven, interdependent presence of the real and the marvellous in the plots.[9]

The same seamless interweaving of everyday, sometimes brutal reality with magic and mystery seems to be a distinctive feature in the works of such black writers as Joel Matlou and Zakes Mda. In Matlou's *Life at Home and Other Stories*, "autobiographical narrative intersects with the psychodrama of dreams and picaresque journeys through a semimythological universe."[10] Mda, better known as a playwright, published his first two novels, *Ways of Dying* and *She Plays with the Darkness*, in 1995: both concern the interrelation between the dismal quality of ordinary life and the mythical–magical quality of the African cultural tradition. At the very opening of *She Plays with the Darkness*, the author describes the inhabitants of a mountain village in Lesotho as follows:

> Don't be fooled by the sunshine in their faces. They are a sad people inside, tormented by the knowledge that one day the great mist will rise and suffocate them all to death. And no one can do anything about it. The mist has a mind of its own. It does what it wants to do when it wants to do it. No one can stop it. Even those who have the gift of controlling lightning and of sending it to destroy their enemies are powerless against the mist.[11]

---

[8] Mazisi Kunene, "Some Aspects of South African Literature," *World Literature Today* 70.1 (Winter 1996): 15.

[9] In my interview with Brink in Milan, on the publication of the Italian translation of *Imaginings of Sand*, March 1997, he endorsed the hypothesis that Vladislavic's work contains hints of magical realism. Furthermore, in a recent review article on Anne Landman's *The Devil's Chimney*, he seems to confirm some of the arguments already advanced in this essay about magical realism in post-apartheid South Africa. See André Brink, "A Real and Magical Devil," *Leadership Interactive* 16.2 (August 1997): 1–3.

[10] Andries W. Oliphant, "Fictions of Anticipation: Perspectives on Some Recent South African Short Stories in English," *World Literature Today* 70.1 (Winter 1996): 62.

[11] Zakes Mda, *She Plays with the Darkness* (Johannesburg: Vivlia, 1995): 1.

These magical gifts are as taken for granted as mist and death.

Thus magical realism, in a context as multicultural and multifarious as is South Africa, seems a mode suited to creating spaces for the interaction of 'difference,' for dialogue in "a world of strangers." As Zamora and Faris argue, its main achievement, a "blurring of boundaries and genres," may help accelerate the dismantling of the monolithic imperatives, both political and cultural, entrenched by the rule of apartheid. Now that political apartheid is buried, South African writers, academics, cultural workers and intellectuals are in search of other ways of coping with new democratic realities and different power relationships, as appears from the collection of interviews published in *Exchanges* and from Njabulo Ndebele's collection of essays, *Rediscovery of the Ordinary*.[12]

In the words of Stephen Slemon, magical realism's "two separate narrative modes never manage to arrange themselves into any kind of hierarchy."[13] Neither being in a subordinate relationship to the other, each can speak. This aspect has a fundamental impact on the South African literary scene, inasmuch as it confers authority, in the sense of legitimacy and authorship, on black and white writers, the silenced majority and the privileged few, for the reconstruction of a polyphonic text in the territory of the imagination. Adoption of the principle of inclusion, not only as a political but also as an aesthetic value, will allow heterogeneity and pluralism to prevail.

Thus there will always be post-apartheid writers adhering to modes of realistic, mimetic and documentary literature as well as narratives of myths and legends or postmodern metafictions. I think, though, that thanks to its subversive stance, at once therapeutic and re-creative but by no means escapist, magical realism represents a literary discourse which has an important role to play in the dismantling of worn-out, simplistic dichotomies and in the indictment of eurocentric stereotypes, as well as of political and social obsessions.

A reviewer of his first collection of short stories said of Vladislavic's writing that it "is no fodder for lazy minds."[14] This reminds me that for

---

[12] See Duncan Brown & Bruno van Dyk, ed., *Exchanges* (Pietermaritzburg: U of Natal P, 1991) and Njabulo S. Ndebele, *Rediscovery of the Ordinary* (Johannesburg: COSAW, 1991).

[13] Stephen Slemon, "Magic Realism as Post-Colonial Discourse," in *Magical Realism*, 410.

[14] Alf Wannenberg, "*Missing Persons*, Ivan Vladislavic," *New Contrast* 71 (Spring 1990): 84.

Ángel Flores magical realists do not cater to popular taste. Vladislavic's references are never easy to interpret, and he himself has never offered an explanatory key to his works, a small number so far, yet sufficient to attract critical interest. With *Missing Persons*, published in 1989, he immediately gained a reputation as one of the most talented new South African writers.[15] His stories seemed fully in touch with his time, the transition period, though not biased by its urgencies, as well as original in its choice of theme and form, deliberately opaque and stringently referential. These were stories which partook of the great revival of story-telling in those years; stories which, besides demystifying the myth of apartheid as a master narrative, reflected upon their own possible presentation and representation of South African reality, thus positing a new aesthetic discourse. Transition was here presented as a metamorphosis, not only political and existential, but also creative.

In all books there is a paragraph or just one sentence which unexpectedly discloses hidden meanings and seems to convey the full significance of the text to the reader; this sense of sudden, deep understanding may be an illusion, but literary works ultimately belong to those who read them. At the end of the short story "Journal of a Wall" is a remarkable paragraph that is epiphanic not only for the protagonist, but for the reader as well.

My analysis will focus on this story as metonymic of a possible choice on the part of the author in favour of magical realism, or at least in favour of the adoption of certain narrative strategies considered essential to that genre. Though generally associated with Latin American fiction, and geographically inscribed in that 'marvellous' subcontinent, it seems a viable alternative mode in which to attempt the description of a country, South Africa, which can no longer be represented solely according to old patterns of mimetic realism, as has been the case with other post-colonial literatures.

I cannot think of anything more trivial and less magical than the title, setting (two adjacent houses in a white residential suburb), characters (a man who lives alone and his neighbours, a married couple) or plot (the building of a wall). It is a red-brick wall, one of the many high security walls erected by the whites to protect their properties in periods of urban guerrilla warfare, in which the township dwellers defend themselves from the soldiers' tear-gas by hurling old bricks, as shown on the television (always on in both houses).

---

[15] Ivan Vladislavic, *Missing Persons* (Cape Town/Johannesburg: David Philip, 1989). Further page references are in the text.

In South Africa, white apartheid has often caused alienation and divided people of the same race. Indeed, the protagonist's attempts to communicate with the couple fail miserably, coming up against another wall, the barrier of indifference and neglect they show when he, pretending to be short of sugar, crosses the space between the two houses and hopes to be welcomed in. Deluded and hurt, he feels a violent impulse to destroy them, their home and their "damned" wall, which no longer interests him, though he continues to enter all the phases of the construction in his diary.

On the 24th of August the wall is finished:

> There he begins the last course of bricks. How bored I am with the tired repetition of gesture. How bored I am with the familiar shapes of words. How bored I am with this journal. It's just a wall.[...]And the words that go into it like bricks are as bland and heavy and worn as the metaphor itself.
> He lays the last brick. But I have the last word. (43)

The protagonist–narrator, the author's alter ego, has imagined the osmosis between wall and journal, between apartheid and social realism. The refusal of the former brings about the dismissal of the latter and the need to express "something else." This attitude reminds us of the poetics of the post-Expressionist painters. When they looked at ordinary life and everyday objects around them, their usual perception of them was displaced and transformed.[16]

The wall, now seen as a worn-out metaphor of long years of apartheid and separation, hence of creative wilderness and emotional dispossession, becomes a liminal space where different realities and diverse perceptions of the world may be introduced. The fixity of the border represented by the wall is renegotiated, with brick-words, as metaphors of weapon-laws, transcending their realistic referents in accordance with one of the strategies Keith Maillard regards as necessary for magical-realist writing: "the impulse for the writing of magic realism arises out of the desire to transcend the form of the realistic novel not as form but as expression." He clarifies his point of view as follows:

> I would argue that the impulse for magic realist writing stems from the need to convey a living experience, that the interweaving of realistic convention with magical elements is not done for its own sake but to produce that symptomatic

---

[16] The term 'magical realism' was employed in the Twenties by Franz Roh with reference to the European artistic context of that period, hence the analogy with post-Expressionist painters such as Balthus and Chagall. See Irene Guenther, "Magic Realism in the Weimar Republic," in *Magical Realism*, 34, and Tommaso Scarano's essay in this volume.

eerie shimmer which must be seen as an attempt to express what is nearly inexpressible"[17]

— or to see what is invisible, through and beyond rigid structures, I would add.

After the moment of heightened consciousness quoted above, the man continues sporadically to keep his journal up to the second of November, All Souls' Day, when the neighbours move house, taking with them all their possessions and leaving the wall, which "looked ashamed of itself" (44). Though we are not told of the anonymous protagonist's profession, from his well-developed linguistic and literary imagination, we may deduce that he is an artist and intellectual, quite the opposite of the middle-class Groenewalds, reliable but dull and conventional in their efforts to continue untroubled in their routine and to protect their life by erecting barriers not only against the Other, "the black peril," but against otherness of any kind.

While apartheid is being dismantled, law by law, the husband brings home piles of bricks to re-entrench it behind the tall, square, massive wall, with each brick in its place. The garden fence is not enough to defend his privacy, or, rather, his longing for separateness, which frustrates the neighbour's desire for community.

The man's journal is not as precise as it would have been if he had started annotating everything from the very beginning; real facts are interwoven with memory and invention, while many details of the construction of the wall escape his attention. His neighbours, on the other hand, work in a methodical, regular, and orderly fashion; she reads the manual and he diligently carries out its instructions, almost as though they were following a recipe. One night, when they have gone out, the man steals a brick from their garden, takes it home, and puts it on an embroidered cloth. It is nothing but a common red brick, but he feels it is extraordinary and full of a life of its own:

> [...] it began to look like a loaf of bread, hot from the oven steaming, fermenting inside. I could hardly sleep that night with its hard presence in the house, its bubbling and hissing. (33)

He marks its faces with a dot of white paint "to maintain some connection with it" (33), before returning it to the pile.

---

[17] Keith Maillard, "*Middlewatch* as Magic Realism," *Canadian Literature* 92 (Spring 1982): 12.

He would like the wall, mechanically built by the husband, a man without imagination, to become not a frontier, but a meeting-point, that Heideggerian "boundary from which something begins its presencing" postulated by Homi Bhabha.

In the house next-door, life unfolds monotonously and everything is in its proper place. One night, however, his own room seems to become animated and to start flying:

> Then the rafters cracked like ribs and the room began to turn. The whole place rattled and groaned, spun faster and faster, and then rose slowly like an ancient flying machine, ripping roof-tiles like fingernails, tearing the sinews of electrical wiring, bursting the veins of waterpipes, up into the night sky. (25)

This is something more than the effect of too much drinking. Defying the conventions of realistic narrative, the anthropomorphized space becomes a magic room in an enchanted house of fiction. Here Vladislavic foregrounds other ways of expressing his times.

The author's experience as editor of *Staffrider*, the literary review which for many years opposed established modes of writing and rigid distinctions between genres, thus stimulating debate on the relation between literature and the other arts, between *poiesis* and *mimesis* – the flying room, the brick wall – certainly played an important role in his cultural background. *Staffrider* has been defined as "a skilful entertainer, a bringer of messages, a useful person but [...] slightly disreputable."[18] Vladislavic's writing shares much the same characteristics: he is richly inventive and loves words – word-games, verbal free association, words disengaged from syntax. He is similar to the sightseer of another story, "Sightseeing," who travels with suitcase, walking-stick, boots, camera and pen, all "means to cover vast distances and inflict metaphor and defend himself" (17). Vast distances where reality and imagination coexist, where nature is anthropomorphized: "a rain forest of trunks, torsos, severed limbs" (18) and a kilogram of powdered milk is carried "like a Conscience" (20) or where man undergoes metamorphosis into an element of nature: "disguised as a tree, the sightseer turns breakfast into Colonialism" (20).

From whom or what must the sightseer defend himself, inflicting metaphor? Sonny, the political-activist protagonist of Nadine Gordimer's novel *My Son's Story*, says: "there is no freedom in working for freedom."[19] This is

---

18 "About *Staffrider*," in *Ten Years of Staffrider*, ed. Andries W. Oliphant & Ivan Vladislavic (Johannesburg: Ravan, 1988), no page reference.

19 Nadine Gordimer, *My Son's Story* (London: Bloomsbury, 1990): 96.

the danger Vladislavic probably sees for the South African writer: there is no freedom in writing for freedom, in the total commitment of one's creativity to the struggle for political liberation.[20]

In the post-apartheid era it is very important to liberate the language of the imagination. Peter Abrahams' cry for freedom in his autobiography *Tell Freedom*,[21] though full of pathos and commitment, has been rendered obsolete. Words as weapons and subjection to the urgency of politics and protest lead to naive narrative realism. Gabriel García Márquez himself shares this opinion:

> I have a great many reservations about what came in Latin America to be called 'committed literature,' or more precisely the novel of social protest. [...] This is mainly because I think its limited view of the world and life does not help achieve anything in political terms. Far from raising consciousness, it actually slows it down. Latin Americans expect more from a novel than an *exposé* of the oppression and injustice they all know too well."[22]

The argument that much of the literature produced in South Africa, though important because *engagé*, needs to renovate a narrative language conditioned and chained by the oppressive model of social realism, is the focus of heated debate.

The impulse to change was given by Albie Sachs, a former exile, in his essay "Preparing Ourselves for Freedom," published in the late Eighties. Because of his stature as a charismatic figure who had lost an arm in the freedom struggle, Sachs's redefinition of the concept of relevance in literature has been all the more influential. He complains about the lack of wit and playfulness caused by apartheid:

---

[20] In a conversation I had with Vladislavic, he said that when he began writing, he had a much stronger sense that he had to resist the major South African tradition, which is very political. For a long time much South African writing was concerned almost exclusively with apartheid and its political problems. He understands why this was so and he has no problem with political writing as such; but there was something limiting about it. When he first started writing, he felt a greater need to resist this and he thinks that part of that resistance was to write stories which are much less connected with the real world. There was a time in South Africa when artists, not only writers but people involved in all the arts, had a duty. There was incredibly strong pressure on artists to document and reveal what was happening under apartheid. (Johannesburg, July 1996.)

[21] Peter Abrahams, *Tell Freedom* (London: Faber & Faber, 1954).

[22] Gabriel García Márquez, *The Fragrance of Guava: Conversations with Plinio Apuleyo Mendoza*, tr. Ann Wright (London: Verso, 1983), quoted in Felicity Wood, "Why Don't South Africans like Fantasy?" *New Contrast* 79 (June 1992): 38.

Can we say that we have begun to grasp the full dimensions of the new
country and new people that is struggling to give birth to itself, or are we still
trapped in the multiple ghettoes of the apartheid imagination? [...] The first
proposition I make [...] is that our members should be banned from saying
culture is a weapon of struggle [...] A.N.C. members are full of fun and romanticism and dreams, we enjoy and wonder at the beauties of nature and the
marvels of human creation, yet if you look at most of our art and literature you
would think we were living in the greyest and most sombre of all worlds.[23]

In the words of Ari Sitas, he seems to suggest "something, perhaps, akin to
the Latin American experience of 'magical realism'" as a new way of expressing South African reality.[24]

"Is [*Missing Persons*] 'the missing link' of magic realism that Albie Sachs
found wanting in South African literature?"[25] It is certainly a work which
heralds transition towards a new textual reality and creates a new link
between word and world, or more precisely between the world of the text
and the text of the world. As Malvern van Wyk Smith argues, apartheid was
also "a social text that tried to write us all into a particular scenario."[26] The
genre of this national text may change from that of social realism to another.
For Vladislavic the new genre might be magical realism.

But the country's unity cannot be achieved by artificially imposing a new
textual space on it. Such a practice runs the risk of repeating the past. Nor
was there any national literary unity under apartheid. Perhaps the best
strategy is to encourage everybody to discover and participate in the rich
mosaic of individual heritage, capable of revitalizing what Wilson Harris
calls "the largely submerged territory of the imagination."[27] In his essay on
the subjective imagination, Harris writes:

The art of fiction as architectonic scale – as an alteration of the given novel
form of the past – involves a dialogue with values *through* appearances. [...]
The mystery of the subjective imagination lies, I believe, in an intuitive, indeed
revolutionary, grasp of a play of values as the flux of authentic change through
and beyond what is given to us and what we accept, without further thought,
as objective appearances.[28]

---

[23] Albie Sachs, "Preparing Ourselves for Freedom," in *Exchanges*, 117–18.

[24] *Exchanges*, 65.

[25] Sally-Ann Murray, "Telling Stories," *Current Writing* 3 (October 1991): 190.

[26] Malvern van Wyk Smith, "Waiting for Silence; or the Autobiography of Metafiction
in Some Recent South African Novels," *Current Writing* 3 (October 1991): 93.

[27] Wilson Harris, *The Womb of Space* (Westport CT: Greenwood, 1983): xix.

[28] Wilson Harris, *Explorations*, ed. Hena Maes-Jelinek (Mundelstrup/Sydney: Dangaroo, 1981): 65.

Vladislavic sustains a dialogue with reality and with its basic features and its values, but he no longer sees them as cultural imperatives. He interprets them according to his creative imagination, using a synaesthetic, pyrotechnical language. His fiction is inevitably trapped in the political and socials aspects of his country, but this intrusion is disguised by a narrative form which is metaphoric, ironic and demystifying. His break with tradition is dynamic, freeing unsuspected, frozen energies. In his relationship with the past he uncovers rich, vital tap-roots. He re-invents and re-imagines South Africa through its icons, its already existing symbols and official national fantasies, subordinating them to his own narrative ends.

Thus, in "Journal of a Wall," two tangible realities and banal objects, a journal and a wall, become paradigmatic: the former of a certain way of writing, the latter of a certain kind of architecture. Both are charged with meanings and associations that are part of the South African collective imagination and cultural background. For apartheid has often evoked a forbidding edifice supported by granite pillars-laws, its 'architect' the country's Prime Minister, Hendrik Verwoerd.

It is no coincidence that the first story of the collection, "The Prime Minister is Dead," centres on Verwoerd's assassination, an episode of great political and historical moment, and his burial. However, in adopting a Márquesan strategy, Vladislavic desecrates the official ceremony of the state funeral, giving the reader an alternative, carnivalesque version of the event. The coffin, fallen unnoticed from the funeral hearse, is picked up by a boy and his father, who are attending the parade, and carried to the cemetery in their wheelbarrow.

> The box was heavy. The soldiers were already half a block ahead of us. We set off in pursuit, my father pushing the wheelbarrow while I held the box steady. The crowd waved us on. Once the flag got caught under the wheel and the box was almost jerked from the barrow. My father was breathing heavily by the time we caught up with the soldiers, and adjusted our pace to the slow rhythm of the music. (8)

In another tale, "Tsafendas's Diary," the plot focuses on Verwoerd's killer. Both these stories are told from the point of view of a first-person narrator, a ten-year-old child, who moves with his parents and grandmother to a new house in a suburb of Pretoria, the same year as the assassination. "It was an ordinary place [...]. No gnomes. No crazy paving" (1). His grandmother is apparently an ordinary old woman who sits, listening to her transistor, in a rocking-chair on the front verandah, crocheting and knitting. Yet the cap she knits is a thinking-cap, which influences her nephew's apprehension of reality, disclosing its hidden aspect, in much the same way as Azaro's mask does in Ben Okri's *The Famished Road*, while the blanket she crochets is a patchwork of meat. "When the Prime Minister died he left us a compost heap on which practically anything could grow" (2). This rotten compost heap, this fermenting mixture, a key image in both stories and the most indelible in the child's memory, is a metaphor of Verwoerd's apartheid legacy, a symbol of South African reality. Here public and private interweave, linguistic inventiveness opening up eerie dimensions in a dismal world so that the reader loses the perception of a neat division between fact and fiction, farce and tragedy. In "Tsafendas's Diary" these "mysteries of meat and imagination" (92) turn to meta-narrativity, providing their own evaluation:

> 21. Granny, her body swathed in the meat-blanket, her feet sticking out like boiled hams, rocking, rocking, to the mouth of the grave. She comes and goes on the precipice. She rocks herself over the edge.
> I hear her cooking, bubbling and squeaking, in the meaty broth at the center of the earth.
> 22. I'm digging it in. I have to feed the insatiable earth. I put in bones, leaf-mulch from the gutters, vegetable peelings, blankets, papers. I soak it all down. The ink begins to run. I take up my spade and I dig it in. (98)

The disappearance from the public scene of Verwoerd and Tsafendas,[29] both of whom stand for the past, is linked to Granny's death and to the death of a certain kind of writing – biased writing which claimed that there was no history but state history, and no African past, merely generalized amnesia or official myths.

In "Journal of a Wall," the wall, though an ordinary, unpoetic object, has a precise function as a catalyst of the imagination. It is analogous to the two anchors rediscovered by Wilson Harris during an expedition up the Potaro river. It provokes "a sudden eruption of consciousness." Light, brilliancy, gloom merge, the wall becoming what Harris calls "an architecture of consciousness, the curious architecture of blocks of shadow, hinges of light."[30]

The refusal of the wall as stale metaphor of apartheid and of the journal as its monotonous and monologic counterpart, in a period of social and political transition, seems to delineate a viable alternative for the over-

---

[29] Demitrio Tsafendas, aged 80, after being in jail for more than three decades, is now at the Sterkfontein mental hospital.

[30] *Explorations*, 63.

coming of clichés and platitudes. The juxtaposition of contrasting spaces, themes and modes foregrounds the dismissal of the white writer's 'burden,' of homogenizing imperatives such as "you cannot describe sunsets or write of daffodils when people live under oppression." This slogan intrudes into the story through the man's rhetorical self-questioning:

> Is there cause for celebration? No. Is there reason for building when things are falling down? No. Is there reason for drinking beer when people are starving? Probably not. [...] Does private joy make sense in the face of public suffering? (42–43)

No, no, probably not; no answer – I see here an aesthetic choice and a critical statement against fanaticism and absolute certainties on the part of the author. In the post-apartheid era, Harris's prophecy appears far-reaching:

> With the mutilation and decline of the conquered tribe a new shaman or artist struggles to emerge who finds himself moving along the knife-edge of change. He has been, as it were, cross-fertilized by victor and victim [...].[31]

Following the South American tradition of magical realism, Vladislavic's fiction not only makes its ethical position with regard to political and social liberation very clear, it also chooses as its priority the freeing of the stunted, oppressed imagination. Thus, while the South African urban context, with its suffering and unease, provides an internal link in the stories and allows for some convincing realistic effects, the ironic lightness of his fantastic and magical touches takes the unsuspecting reader into a world where extraordinary people and events appear normal, where everyday norms of behaviour may be transgressed. It is not the 'world next door' of his novel *The Folly*, an absurd, surreal world.[32] In the world of these stories, the various facets of experience conduct a dialogue with one another, reality and magic are interwoven within the same text, and language itself becomes the privileged *locus* where identities and meanings are continually destroyed and re-created. Fragments are free and fragmentary thought encompasses all aspects of experience, whereas totalitarian thought is univocal, tautological, impoverished.

In *Missing Persons* a whole society disappears: the unimaginative, arid, bourgeois couple in "Journal of a Wall," Livingstone's companions in "Sightseeing," a terrorist in "Flashback Hotel," as well as the never-named

---

31 *Explorations*, 16.
32 Valeria Guidotti, "A House for Mr. Malgas: Postmodern Allegory in *The Folly* by Ivan Vladislavic," in *Cross-Cultural Voices*, ed. Claudio Gorlier & Isabella Zoppi (Rome: Bulzoni, 1997): 79–98.

but easily identifiable Prime Ministers of the past, Verwoerd in "The Prime Minister is Dead," and P.W. Botha (head of state in the Eighties) in "The Box." Botha is jerked "out of the box," the television set, while conceitedly addressing the nation, by Quentin the protagonist. Reduced to a mere six inches in size, he is kept prisoner in a birdcage in the spare room. Soon afterwards, his wife, some ministers (the Minister of Defence among them), supermarket managers, professors and TV announcers are also snatched away and join him there. This happens under the eyes of Mary, Quentin's wife, who does not show any wonder or surprise, but is busy complaining of the *surmenage* so many guests imply:

> Mary gave all the new people blankets and put them in the spare room. In the mornings she put in a large bowl of ProNutro; in the evenings she dished up a third plate of food and put that in the room. Every two or three days she went in with a broom and swept out the rubbish and the bodies. (58–59)

All of them reduced to Lilliputian size, the story plays with hyperbole (the exaggeration of minutiae, the miniaturizing of the gigantic) and is pervaded by the anti-bureaucratic spirit characteristic of magical realism. But Quentin is not yet satisfied: in South Africa, transition requires not only the establishment's disempowerment, but also its dismemberment. Thus, the evening after Mary leaves him because he has gone too far, Quentin

> misjudged his timing and took the torso of an opera singer. He watched the thing thumping its stumps on the carpet. Then he took a mouth out of a toothpaste ad and propped it up on a coffee table. It smiled at him. He smiled back. He speared the torso on the end of a fork and brushed it against the teeth. The lips slobbered open and the teeth began to gnash. For the hell of it he took the leg of a statue, half a building, and a cubic meter of Indian Ocean. Then he gathered it all up and went through to the spare room. (59)

These literal images of dismemberment are at the same time symbolic of the dissociation between historical truth and fictional events.

In these stories many people go missing, not because of a long-awaited and feared bloody revolution (this has, rather, taken place almost peacefully), but thanks to the liberated imagination of the author. He tells us of his times, using magical details as an "antidote to existing and exhausted modes of narration."[33]

Characters who belong to typical, everyday South African reality, who have filled many pages, whose lives have been documented by a whole corpus of committed writing – protest writing and liberal writing, often

---

[33] Zamora & Faris, 7.

"tasteless, colourless, odourless" writing – these stock characters are now given the chance to live differently, though by no means happily. They can impassively witness uncanny events as if they were ordinary. They unhesitatingly believe in the violation of natural law in the story "When My Hands Burst Into Flames," where the metaphor is literalized and sustains the plot as in many post-expressionist paintings, or in "Terminal Bar," where the country's agony is portrayed through the death throes of a creepy-crawly.

The titles of many of Vladislavic's short stories (such as "Terminal Bar," "Flashback Hotel" and "Movements") emphasize their status as threshold narratives and metaphors for the transition to the post-apartheid era. As Rosi Braidotti argues, places of transit like airports, railway-station waiting rooms, bars and hotels are liminal areas, fluid boundaries where time expands and dissolves in a timeless continuum.[34] These are public places of radical openness, where people interact though provisionally osmotic spaces which, in their anonymity, are sources of creativity, inspiration and heightened perception.

Vladislavic's tales foreground their existence as imaginative and re-creative acts rather than as mimetic and documentary re-enactments. This does not imply the absence of historical referentiality. In "We Came to the Monument," for instance, the Voortrekker Monument overlooking Pretoria is never named but is always hinted at as the shrine of the Afrikaner nation and associated with the epic of the Great Trek. The history of apartheid and its undoing is forever inscribed in the decaying friezes and sculptures of the mausoleum.

According to Stephen Slemon, one of the thematic dimensions of magical realism is "the foreshortening of history so that the time scheme of the novel metaphorically contains the long process of colonisation and its after math."[35] The atmosphere of the story is apocalyptic and rarefied, but it maintains its worldliness, enmeshed as it is in a factual net of circumstances, place and society. The historical approach has nonetheless changed. For Vladislavic, the act of writing must oppose transparency and representational strategies where outward reality cripples the "subjective imagination." The signs of apartheid, in the form of ruins, collapsed walls, broken statues, stimulate literary creativity. Thus, in "We Came to the Monument," the motif of the animated statue, generally classified as one of the main *topoi* of fantastic literature, takes on a different meaning: it opens up a dialogue

---

[34] See Rosi Braidotti, *Nomadic Subjects* (New York: Columbia UP, 1994).

[35] Slemon, "Magic Realism as Post-Colonial Discourse," 411.

with social and historical reality, unsealing the doors of a whole country to admit the "live absences" and "presences," and unfreezing the roles in which history had silenced them.[36]

In the apocalypse, the darkest side of magical realism in Brian Conniff's definition, the magical and the real are fused completely; the most improbable event is the most inevitable. Indeed, just as there are two aspects of magic, so there is another side to magical realism. García Márquez does not refuse to envisage the end of mankind, which is a scientific possibility, and magical realism can narrate such gloomy and violent events in such a way as to make apocalypse not only believable but actually unavoidable.[37]

The Monument is filled with voices from the past; its destruction has already begun in the first story, "The Prime Minister is Dead." But in the post-colonial context apocalypse implies not just destruction, but also reconstruction and liberation from violence and evil. The animated statue falls in love with a girl survivor, and this makes us suspend disbelief. We know that the statue has no hands, but it does have a heart ("a sticky heart pacing out the confines of [its] broken ribcage"; 72) and can invent a language, which is all it needs "to make a monument as quick and thickle as a kite" (69).

This story, too, then, is an example of the autotelic nature of fiction and of the mythopoetic quality of language, foregrounding meta-narrativity and the refusal of the linguistic and fictional dimensions of the text to identify with the material dimension of oppression and of apartheid. The girl and the statue find shelter in an empty niche, near the decaying bas-relief representing the signing of the treaty between Piet Retief and Dingane.

> This particular panel depicts the signing of a treaty. Two men are seated at a table. One of our early leaders sits on the left. Behind him *stand* our people, his people. Some of them hold *rifles*; all of them wear hats. Our leader looks at the man opposite him, but he appears not to see him. He looks through him to the distant mountains. Immediately behind our leader stands a woman. She too looks to the mountains. One of her hands rests on our leader's shoulder. To her left, a priest. He holds a *Bible*. He looks at the man on the other side of the table with *determined tenderness*.
>
> The enemy. He sits awkwardly on the edge of his chair. He looks like a man who has never sat in a chair before. He holds a *quill* in his left hand. He is about to make a cross on the document which our leader pushes towards him.

---

[36] Wilson Harris, "Living Absences and Presences," in *"Return" in Postcolonial Writing. A Cultural Labyrinth*, ed. Vera Mihailovich–Dickman (Cross/Cultures 12; Amsterdam & Atlanta GA: Rodopi, 1994): 2.

[37] Brian Conniff, "The Dark Side of Magical Realism: Science, Oppression and Apocalypse in *One Hundred Years of Solitude*," *Modern Fiction Studies* 36.2 (Summer 1990): 68.

He does not look at the mountains. He looks at the end of the quill. Behind him, his people *kneel*. (79; my emphases)

This emblematic relationship of subordination is charged with 'trans-locative' irony, as defined by Tony Morphet:

The best and most recent example I know of this form of work is Ivan Vladislavic's book of short stories, *Missing Persons*, where the intersections of different discourses open up not only the cross-cutting tracks of history but also the problematic relations between subjectivity and location.[38]

Is this niche, containing the vanquished, the surviving girl and the animated statue, a new literary space? Will magic eventually conquer death? Is it possible to restore the Other, with his ontology of supernatural beliefs, witchcraft, folklore, myths and magic, to history – to oppose this rich heritage to that of rationality, order, normality, thus reuniting *mirabilia* and *naturalia*, and so creating the fundamental condition for a magical-realist mode of fiction?

C3 • ಬಿ

---

[38] Tony Morphet, "Cultural Settlement: Albie Sachs, Njabulo Ndebele and the Question of Social and Cultural Imagination," *Pretext* 2.1 (Winter 1990): 103.

Wilson Harris
A Case Apart

———————— ଚ

Elsa Linguanti

> We have to seee connections we don't normally look for.[1]
>
> How does newness come into the world? How is it born? of what
> fusions, translations, conjoinings is it made?[2]

1   *Magical realism*

IN A LETTER TO MICHEL FABRE, Wilson Harris offers a definition of his understanding of magical (marvellous) realism – a definition which Fabre then quotes in "Recovering Precious Words: On Wilson Harris and the Language of Imagination," his contribution to a collection of essays on Harris with the subtitle *The Uncompromising Imagination*:

> The concept of 'marvellous realism' constitutes for me an alchemical pilgrimage [...] a ceaseless adventure within the self and without the self in nature and beings that are undervalued or that have been eclipsed or imprisoned by models of conquest.[3]

The title of the collection, taken from an essay by Desmond Hamlet, does not simply reflect the writer's integrity and his use of the imagination. For the term 'imagination' recurs in works about, and by, Harris with a frequency that is bound to confuse any researcher composing a bibliography. There is a

---

[1] Wilson Harris, "Ways to Enjoy Literature," in *"Union in Partition": Essays in Honour of Jeanne Delbaere*, ed. Gilbert Debusscher & Marc Maufort (Liège: L³ – Language and Literature, 1997): 207.

[2] Salman Rushdie, *The Satanic Verses* (London: Viking, 1988): 8.

[3] Wilson Harris: *The Uncompromising Imagination*, ed. Hena Maes–Jelinek (Mundelstrup/Sydney: Dangaroo, 1991): 48.

collection of essays by Harris called *The Womb of Space: The Cross-Cultural Imagination*, while a book of lectures and talks bears the title *The Radical Imagination*. A volume of interviews, including one with Harris, edited by Alan Burns and Charles Sugnet is called *The Imagination on Trial*, and a collection edited by Michael Gilkes is entitled *The Literate Imagination*.[4] It is also interesting to note the not infrequent connection between 'imagination' and 'alchemy': W.J. Howard is the author of a paper on "Wilson Harris and the 'Alchemical Imagination',"[5] while Hena Maes-Jelinek's publications on Harris range from "The Writer as Alchemist: The Unifying Role of Imagination in the Novels of Wilson Harris" to "Wilson Harris and the Mystery of the Universal Imagination."[6] It is clear that the imagination is here seen as the matrix of artistic production; what we are dealing with is the cognitive function of a faculty that has the task of composing and combining the data of perception. This is not the imagination understood as a means of escape or as inducive of visions, as a passive reproduction of perceptual experience, or again as a synonym of 'inspiration,' related as such to the alogical and the irrational. In our own times, Galvano Della Volpe and Gaston Bachelard have contributed to the rebirth of a sort of *logos* of the imagination: aside from the particular cognitive procedure primarily characterizing the working of the artist's mind, the imagination is here seen as an abstractive procedure, indispensable to the cognitive procedure *tout court*.[7]

Of the various adjectives used to describe his work by Harris himself or by his readers, "radical" and "uncompromising" indicate a deviation from traditional lines, and from the idea of passiveness, while "cross-cultural" and "universal" indicate a deviation from lines that can be identified with one specific cultural group or another. "Alchemical," on the other hand, evokes the Renaissance practice of transforming base into noble metals, and generally observing the changing and ceaseless meeting of forms in nature.

---

[4] Wilson Harris, *The Womb of Space: The Cross-Cultural Imagination* (Westport CT: Greenwood, 1983); *The Radical Imagination*, ed. Alan Riach & Mark Williams (Liège: L³: Language and Literature, 1992); "Wilson Harris interviewed by Alan Burns," in *The Imagination on Trial: British and American Writers Discuss Their Working Methods*, ed. Alan Burns & Charles Sugnet (London: Allison & Busby, 1981): 51–65; *The Literate Imagination: Essays on the Novels of Wilson Harris*, ed. Michael Gilkes (London: Macmillan, 1989).

[5] *Literary Half-Yearly* 11 (1970): 17–26.

[6] See *Language and Literature* 1.1 (1971): 25-34, and *International Literature in English: The Major Writers*, ed. Robert L. Ross (New York: Garland, 1990).

[7] See Galvano Della Volpe, *Critica del gusto* (Milan: Feltrinelli, 1960) and, on Bachelard, Jacques Gagey, *Gaston Bachelard ou la conversion de l'imaginaire* (Paris: Rivière, 1969) and Paul Ginestier, *La Pensée de Bachelard* (Paris: Bordas, 1968).

Alchemy was an investigation into nature and man, a conception of reality and a mode of speculation about the constitution and mysterious connections of the universe. It ceased to exist with the birth of scientific chemistry (after Bacon and Paracelsus). Now that science itself has renounced its claim to absoluteness, the idea of alchemy as a speculative practice has been revived, albeit in different terms.

Thus the pilgrimage which is an adventure (that is to say, without a fixed destination) is qualified as endless (heading, as we shall see, towards forgotten origins) and alchemical. It moves "within the self and without the self," in "nature and beings," just as alchemy did (nature and beings undervalued, imprisoned or eclipsed by models shaped by the idea of conquest).

References to alchemy in Harris's work may be connected with another Renaissance practice in which he shows an interest, the ancient mnemotechnics re-explored by Frances Yates in her book *The Art of Memory*.[8] What fascinates Harris here is the circulation of knowledge, the non-separation or non-dissociation between greatly different fields of investigation and intellectual exercise, which still obtained in the Renaissance. Yates writes that there was a time when the art of memory was connected with the history of culture "as a whole," and Harris affirms that he is fascinated by the connection between the images aroused in the memory and their spatial collocation (cf "Camillo's Theatre and the Venetian Renaissance" in Yates's book):

> The convolutions of images [...] related as diverse rooms, capacities expanding or contracting within one field of consciousness. To prise these images apart is in fact to lose the dialectical field in which they stand or move.[9]

To combine "the broken parts of an enormous heritage," to find a remedy for "the terrifying cleavage in the psyche of man"[10] is one of the tasks. The historical phase of Western culture in which "the arts" – of the trivium and the quadrivium, including the sciences – made up a single whole is considered more healthy and fertile than the rigidly monolithic conception of culture at which we have now arrived.

---

[8] Frances A. Yates, *The Art of Memory* (London: Routledge & Kegan, 1966). See also Paul Sharrad, "The Art of Memory and the Liberation of History: Wilson Harris's Witnessing of Time," in *The Writer as Historical Witness*, ed. Edwin Thumboo & Thiru Kandiah (Singapore: Singapore UP, 1995): 588–99.

[9] Harris, *Tradition, the Writer and Society* (London/Port of Spain: New Beacon, 1967): 55.

[10] Harris, *Tradition, the Writer and Society*, 57.

A propos of segmentations, Harris has the following to say about the academic world and the "tragic situation of the Humanities today":

> I find that there is something gravely lacking in the Humanities, because the real activity that should be occurring there is *not* occurring. There is a tendency to have one's field and to frame up that field in the proper way. Thus one begins, in a way, to perpetrate, at the most sophisticated level, a form of self-righteous deprivation [...] you can go into very sophisticated areas of the Humanities and find it operating there, however sophisticated is the small talk that occurs.[11]

What Frances Yates is drawing to our attention is the fact that there were once links between art and science, poetry and painting, between music and architecture. Then these links were severed in order to activate processes of experimentation. However, after dismantling the old hierarchies, it should have been necessary to visualize those relationships in a new way; and this did not happen.

What we thus have is an invocation of the non-separation of the spheres of human experience, taken, shall we say, synchronically.

○ ● ∞

In a lecture on "Magical Realism" given at the University of Aarhus, Harris gave a detailed account of an expedition up the Potaro, a tributary of the Essequibo, to measure the hydroelectric power of the waters near the Tumatumari falls. He told how the boats had to anchor in dangerous positions and how the recovery of two anchors, one hooked up to another abandoned at the same point by a similar expedition three years earlier, had produced such an intense sensation of escape from danger that the resulting discharge of mental energy had forged connections not only with the experience of three years before, but also with a constellation of antecedents, "out of the pre-Columbian mists of time." A "sudden eruption of consciousness"[12] had emerged from those two simple objects, the anchors.

One might be tempted to compare this experience to a Joycean 'epiphany,' but this is something different. Contact with origins and the willing-

---

[11] "Wilson Harris interviewed by Alan Riach," in *The Radical Imagination*, 37–38.

[12] Kirsten Holst Petersen & Anna Rutherford, "Fossil and Psyche," from Petersen & Rutherford, *Enigma of Values: An Introduction to Wilson Harris* (Mundelstrup/Sydney: Dangaroo, 1976), repr. in *The Post-Colonial Studies Reader*, ed. Bill Ashcroft, Gareth Griffiths & Helen Tiffin (London/New York: Routledge, 1995): 187. Harris's Aarhus lecture was published as "A Talk on the Subjective Imagination," *New Letters* 40 (Autumn 1973): 37–48.

ness to recover the whole of previous experience come to bear on the
physical course of the engineer who is measuring the power of the waters of
a certain basin in such a way as to constitute a tangential psychic course, in
accordance with a pattern which appears so frequently in Harris's creative
and critical texts that we are by now familiar with it (see Graph 1).[13]

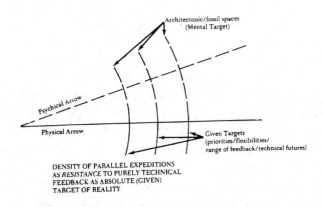

• ≈ Graph 1

A series of concentric circles is crossed by two arrows originating from the
centre. One, called the physical arrow, is a continuous line indicating objects
and fixed, material purposes which we tend to accept as genuine and worth-
while. The other one is a discontinuous line which explores fossil spaces,
residues of meaning that have lost their univocal character and are almost
devoid of any precise form.[14]

---

[13] The graph appears in the essay "Fossil and Psyche," in Wilson Harris, *Explorations*
(Mundelstrup/Sydney: Dangaroo, 1981): 71, 80, and is often reproduced in Harris's
critical writings.

[14] The temptation is also to think of Jungian archetypes; Harris comments on Jung:
"Jung never influenced me, but I had a dialogue with him. I came to him rather late and I
had become involved in these things myself, but I was alone to a large extent. I had no
one to turn to and when I came to Jung and read what he had to say about the collective
unconscious, it sustained and supported me. Because even then I was aware of the intuitive truths arising from those depths. I would not have called it the collective unconscious at that stage. Even now, I tend to hesitate: I much prefer the term universal
unconscious. [...] The word dialogue became important to me when, as a young man, I
read Martin Buber. His notion [...] was that you could have a dialogue with a stone" (*The
Radical Imagination*, 62). Again: "C.G. Jung's collective unconscious may be modified and
extended beyond the human psyche into animal species, into the rhythms of tides and

Harris's concern is no longer with a single identity – it is, rather, with the erosion of the unconscious codes constructed in what is called the "technology of realism," thus preparing, "within the self" for contact "without the self," with "nature and beings that have been undervalued, eclipsed, imprisoned" by models of the world inspired by the concept of "conquest," an arbitrary conquest of nature and of beings. The indelible but submerged traces of the imprisoned, eclipsed – because undervalued or feared, and undoubtedly forgotten – fossil identity are redeemed from oblivion.

What we have is thus an invocation of the non-separateness of the spheres of human experience, taken, shall we say, diachronically.

The model of conquest is at the basis of the fundamental binary system rejected by Harris, giving rise to the need "to cross frontiers, to break polarisations."[15] Fractures, breaks, gaps, rifts between "apparent incompatibles" govern the imagination.[16] The conquest and subjugation of nature and the conquest and subjugation of human beings have created dichotomies and binary oppositions which infect history. The imagination as an essential human capacity can cure us from the habit of thinking in manichaean terms and allow us to conceive of wholeness – as a process – instead of accepting fragmentation as an inevitable condition of humanity. Thus the "gap" is transformed into a "gateway," in an alchemical transformation of the basic elements of the colonialist vision.

2 Forms

If the novel, as Harris claims, can operate in this way and be this pilgrimage, it has to transform itself:

> The issue of form is a formidable one. Imaginative art is form, complex form. Without a change in form new content is invalid and that is why protest novels, or protest media or protest politics do little to change the texture of a civilization or alter the habits of power, or territorial imperative as it is called, in any profound way.[17]

---

rocks, the densities and transparencies of forests and waterfalls, the stars, genes, and so on"; "The Open Door," *Journal of Modern Literature* 20.1 (Summer 1996): 12.

[15] In *The Four Banks of the River of Space*, 288. In *The Carnival Trilogy* (London: Faber & Faber, 1993): *Carnival* is the first volume, *The Infinite Rehearsal* the second, and *The Four Banks of the River of Space* the third.

[16] Extracts from correspondence received by Michel Fabre from Wilson Harris, in *The Uncompromising Imagination*, 43.

[17] *The Uncompromising Imagination*, 47.

The transformation must be from a "novel of persuasion" (a novel that endorses existing conceptions of man and society) to a "novel of implosion," or "fulfilment," capable of exploring the fossil identity, the floods of time that make up the essence of beings and things, in a pilgrimage or endless alchemical adventure reaching beyond appearances.

What is not required, therefore, is 'realism': Harris works against the still dominant techniques, models and values of fictional realism:

> the novel of persuasion rests on grounds of apparent common sense; the tension which emerges is the tension of individuals on an accepted plane of society we are persuaded has an inevitable existence.[18]

That kind of novel is rejected in favour of the novel of "implosion," characterized by "a tragic centrality or a capacity for plural forms of profound identity"[19] and featuring elements of dialogue rather than persuasion, fulfilment rather than consolidation. According to Harris, the writer

> sets out again and again across a certain territory of primordial but broken recollection in search of a community whose existence he begins to discern within capacities of unique fiction.[20]

The novel must therefore not be a presentation of what is given, what we accept without further investigation as "objective appearance." This vision of reality crumbles away, together with the 'realistic' mode of so many contemporary works, which merely perpetuate the problems they purport to address. Most fiction remains trapped within the limits set for it by the ideology of the day – what Harris calls "the shallows of consciousness." Getting out of these shallows involves a complex, difficult exploration but one that must be resolutely pursued.

The traditional conception of character is thus destroyed: he/she becomes complementary to others. Characters do not stand by themselves, but in a relationship to others who echo them, but without duplicating them. They flow into each other and into the landscape, in a series of relationships and role inversions. The experiences of one character are exchanged with those of another. This mirror-play is sometimes applied to figures centuries apart. By explicitly giving his characters historical or mythical names, Harris underlines the deep relationship that unites the lives of people separated in

---

[18] In *Tradition, the Writer and Society*, 29. For an early, ground-breaking account of Harris's vision and representational originality, see Hena Maes–Jelinek, *The Naked Design: A Reading of "Palace of the Peacock"* (Mundelstrup/Sydney: Dangaroo, 1976).

[19] *Tradition, the Writer and Society*, 40.

[20] *Tradition, the Writer and Society*, 54.

space and time, but caught in the same drama of oppression, in the same need to understand, undoubtedly in the same contradictions, the same mystery. By exchanging their masks, the hidden links that connect different individuals and cultures become dramatically visible. Otherness is not outside, but deposited inside each person; for latent within each person are the persons he or she might have been.

In Harris the action is not narrated in the tenses of diegesis in accordance with the narrative tradition, but is presented almost in slow motion, or telescopically, or on a screen with special effects, and then repeated and seen from different angles and against different backgrounds, in different times, and thus made emblematic. With regard to the textual construction, internal analepsis and prolepsis serve to support the architecture. Moreover, the rhetorical phenomenon of repetition with variation is strongly present, with continual permutation of the elements that recur. The narrator does not accept the role of reader's guide. He shows himself, speaks of himself, splits into two, stresses his unreliability. He himself is on trial and often needs a guide. Narrator and reader are thus placed in the same position and depend on the same mentors.

The temporal setting is and is not today: rectilinearity is another of the conventions that are annulled. In the early novels, a sort of 'dream-time' is opposed to historical time, while the later novels present the time of memory and meditation in spatial terms. The spatial setting, or place, is the forest of Guyana, but superimposed on this are other places, as though a kind of watermark, or the same places in different periods, like multiple photographic exposures. Space annihilates time, and the primary category imposed is the womb of space, to which temporal categories and constructions are subjugated.

The reader is caught up in the fluidity that is one of the secrets of Harris's writing – continually invited to interpret and judge, but a few pages on made to doubt the validity of his/her interpretations and judgements. (One characteristic aspect of this fluidity is Harris's radical approach to intertextuality.[21]) Exposed to ambiguity and paradoxes, one is made aware of the partiality (in both senses) of one's own judgement and capacity to interpret.

---

[21] Intertextuality includes the Amerindian and African, as well as the classical and modern heritages (Faust is Quetzalcoatl, El Dorado can be equated with Ithaca). It also comprises science, in particular all the theories of our century, from quantum mechanics to chaos theory. See the interview with Riach, *The Radical Imagination*. The cross-cultural strategy which links figures in Europe with eclipsed figures in the ancient world is discussed in various essays in both *Explorations* and *The Womb of Space*.

Harris makes the reader aware of the nullity of pre-packaged, simplistic conclusions; we cannot help seeing that the act of reading and the act of writing stand in mutual relationship to each other. Reading brings with it a radical request for change, like an annunciation. It is almost like learning a new language. It requires discipline and patience, and above all a readiness to take the plunge and submit to sudden changes of direction, to face an almost tangible darkness lit up by flashes or glimpses of sense.

It is, of course, language that creates the magic. According to Harris, language contains the key to all human transformation. Language itself must therefore be transformed, its power to immobilize attitudes and opinions unmasked, and words and concepts made free to associate in new ways. Language is a system of codified representations whose effect is based on the link, but also on the radical separation, between signifier and signified. We must not allow ourselves to be imprisoned by its apparent completeness, nor should it be used as an instrument. In the experience in the forest of Guyana, Harris realized that "language began to break its contract with mere tools framed to enshrine a progressive deprivation."[22]

Harris uses language in a way that deliberately upsets its implicit correlations, especially its binary construction. He uses all the means he can find to destroy the common idea that things are what they appear to be. Signifiers are uprooted from their usual referents: terms like death, life, dream, theatre, museum, time, carnival, music may qualify anything except what they usually qualify. Everything that divides into segments is rejected. A dialectic of paired antinomies and paradoxical juxtapositions is created (fossil suns, living absences). The 'false' simile gives way to the 'true' (literalized) metaphor, and hyperbole and antonomasia are literalized. Repetitions haunt the pages: in a kind of ebb and flow ("images, [partial images] play back, one upon the other"[23]), the same words or syntagmata, slightly modified, appear several times on the same page with an effect like that of the reappearance in music of a given motif. Central metaphors are repeated from one novel to another. Some only marginally treated in one text reappear at the heart of another, thus creating a network of metaphors that include decapitation, the fall, the Gorgon, the spider, the crab, the spider's web, Penelope's web, and metaphors from the fields of architecture, music, the theatre and science.

The whole procedure tends to shake the various elements out of their immobility. It frees language from the bonds of the semantic fields to which

---

22 *The Radical Imagination,* 72.
23 *The Radical Imagination,* 34.

it usually belongs, not by altering the lexis, as Joyce does in *Finnegans Wake*, but by altering the relationships of inclusion/exclusion. The obligation of non-contradiction is negated, and only the syntactic rhythm, or cadence of the sentence, is maintained. Yet the rhythm produced is not only the result of the elegant succession of the clauses: the rhythm of the narrative is born of the way 'partial images' appear in different lights, reverberate upon one another, and overlap. The reader is caught up in the rhythm of this music and begins to perceive orchestral effects that record geological movements (the rocks as architectural tide: "within the still rock is the moving tide, and within the moving tide is the rock or stone"[24]), landscape rhythms (the music of the sun, the music of fire), and biological rhythms (hills and waves miniaturized in our bodies). In reading, he thus perceives his own heart and mind dancing to that rhythm.[25]

The work of the imagination is often represented by means of graphic forms borrowed from geometry or physics: diagrams, arrows and other forms implying not only the unsuitability and the limitation of 'received,' 'realistic' language to communicate the changing landscape of truth in man's world, but also the relationship between art and science.

3   *The Four Banks of the River of Space*

In the closing volume of the *Carnival Trilogy*, *The Four Banks of the River of Space*,[26] the interplay between the realistic background, the imaginative texturing, the unifying vision, and the range of intertextual elements produce "an astonishingly orchestrated book."[27] The succession of metaphors in the title of Harris's novel prepares the reader for the type of language he will encounter in this novel. The obscurity is perhaps more apparent than real: if the reader gives way to the rhythm of the page and its logic, he will not be disoriented by the temporal and spatial excursions, the tortuous, if lively ramifications of the metaphoric fabric, or the many digressions.

Anselm, a former engineer, returns from London in his mental theatre to the characters and the episodes of his infancy (first bank), and of his adult

---

[24] *The Radical Imagination*, 88.

[25] *The Radical Imagination*, 110.

[26] *The Four Banks of the River of Space* (London: Faber & Faber, 1990), repr. in *The Carnival Trilogy* (London: Faber & Faber, 1993). Page references to the novel in the latter trilogy-edition are in the text.

[27] Hena Maes–Jelinek, "'Unfinished Genesis': *The Four Banks of the River of Space*," in *The Uncompromising Imagination*, ed. Maes-Jelinek (Mundelstrup/Sydney: Dangaroo, 1991): 230.

life in Guyana (second bank). He is placed on trial (third bank), and together with two friends and a Macusi guide, he makes an excursion through the forest towards the waterfall and the sun rising in the transparency of suspended water-drops (fourth bank). The titles of the chapters are "The King of Thieves," "Carnival Heir of Civilizations," "The Trial," and, with a sense of finality – which at the same time entails a new beginning – "Home."

> Perhaps eve ˛ mental probe into the substance of space begins with visualizations
> of the familiar, familiar absurdity, familiar structure or shape, living waxwork
> epitaph, slow-motion joy-ride to the stars [...]. (339)

The relationships between the characters – alive and dead – are revealed by analepsis, prolepsis, focalization of memories, remembered or imaginary dialogue. They refer to Uncle Proteus, who had made his fortune in the diamond mines and squandered it all (336); his sister, Aunt Alicia, "Poverty's Queen," who had adopted Anselm, and her husband, Harold, "a womanizer" whom Anselm hated. Then there is the "porkknocker," nicknamed Black Pizarro because he is obsessed with gold, and also called the "king of thieves"; Lucius Canaima, a killer whom Anselm saw commit a crime but did not report, despite a sense of horror; Robot, a policeman and "technician of artificial intelligence" whom Anselm did not trust; the beautiful and mysterious Rose sisters, full of secrets; the English missionary couple of the El Dorado Mission House, Penelope and George Ross, who are persecuted by the ghost of her first husband, Simon, who died in Normandy during the war, after discovering his wife had been unfaithful; a Macusi woodcutter; a guide; and, lastly, the three drowned children of the Mission.

The "eclipsed" relationships, which emerge from the exertions of the memory by means of "revisionary steps," and from the re-activation of what is buried there, reveal that one of the twin Rose sisters is the real mother of Anselm, who was saved by Proteus from death when he caught Asian 'flu like his mother, who died of it. The other twin is the mother of Canaima, and the father of both children is Harold. The secret is kept until the surviving sister decides to punish Harold by revealing it to him two weeks before his death. The secret is now revealed to Anselm, and he thus learns that the two people he has always most distrusted, Harold and Canaima, are, respectively, his father and his brother.

The analogical relationships, activated by speculation and emblematization and often alluded to in the names of the characters, make of each of them a focus for an infinite number of antecedents: stories, myths and legends on the one hand, hopes and nightmares, passions and errors, contradictions and dreams that all human beings share on the other.

In the textual system, each of the characters is accompanied by emblematic objects and defining periphrases initially fixed in the reader's memory and subsequently enriched by elements which may specify, amplify and/or vary their range of application, with the result that the sphere of one character may come to include aspects belonging to another, as well as, by aggregation of *exempla*, the whole intertext.

Hence Lucius, the half-brother/cousin of Anselm (they share the same father, and their mothers are twin sisters), also called Canaima of the Macusi tribe like the Amerindian "god of retaliation, evil spirit," is always associated with a knife; Pizarro, obsessed with gold, king of thieves, with "a slab of gold"; Penelope, a queen, with her web, or with a mantle; Robot, the technological man, with a telescope; the Rose sisters with a thorn; the dead Macusi dancer with the bird's wings that quiver on the lips of the bird-mask; Aunt Alicia with a "cap," a "fossil museum," a vase decorated with historical scenes, and a theatre in which various actors perform the same role.

In the theatre of Anselm's memory, the characters evoked recite confessions, make revelations, and deliver occasional messages. Apparitions sometimes have clear outlines, and are sometimes apocalyptic in shape. They tell Anselm things that they themselves did and did not understand when they lived their lives. Illustrating sequences of his life for him, they remind Anselm of episodes that he did or did not witness. They say that they/we are not creators or masters, but guests of our lives, which are little known to us because we hardly examine them, unless we face a "regenerative process."

The I-narrator Anselm, "a good man, something of a bloody saint" (271),[28] architect, engineer, painter, lover, sculptor, government surveyor and government architect, is transformed by his experience on the banks of the river of space, first into "a spy who retraces his steps within the long Carnival day of the twentieth century (292) and then into a "'carnival heir of

---

[28] The name is that of a Benedictine monk from Aosta who took vows in 1061, became Archbishop of Canterbury in 1093, had a difficult relationship with William the Conqueror, and a better one with Henry I, on the question of royal investiture. He was canonized by Thomas à Becket and named Doctor of the Church by Clement XI. He wrote *De veritate* and other treatises. He had confidence in the ability of human reason to investigate even the divine mysteries and in the metaphysical and unitative character of being as perfection. Reason, he maintained, puts man into contact with the whole order of being and so there must be some immediate idea of God in human experience.

civilizations'" (314). He constructs his theatre ("I etched into theatre, into grassy curtains, backdrops of trees, tides, oceans"; 270), the Imaginary Theatre in which "several (all partial) performances by different actors" take place (329), and later the Imaginary "post-Christendom Cathedral" (315), which is subsequently overshadowed by a redemptive Presence:

> redemption by the overshadowing Presence I had glimpsed as intricately woven into 'living absences,' into the arts, into the sciences, into architecture. Waterfall, rainfall, riverfall. (344)

Contact with the people Anselm meets has consequences – "my self-portrait became stranger and truer. [...] Who was I?" (293) – and he perceives the "compulsions that had driven [him], the thread of the dance linking all creatures" (293). He too, by chance, becomes a killer – in throwing up into the air the knife that Canaima has thrust between his ribs, he kills a bird – and experiences the "hole of greed" when he tries to steal Proteus's rags. Faced with an "enigma of parallels" (316), "the enigma of creation" (322), "the mystery of the abyss," he is able "to *salvage* the unfathomable quantum address of every resurrection of the Imagination" (304; my emphasis). When he succeeds, it is by means of a "gathering up":

> Not simply a reconciliation of opposites. Such a formula was too uncreative or mechanical. Not just a mechanics of psyche. But a *gathering up* of all that had been experienced in every condition of existence, an accumulation of apparently imperceptible change into true change, in which nothing was lost and everything possessed an inimitable difference akin to joy. (317, my emphasis)

His progress is aided by "the flowering seed of visualised presence" (318), "the beauty of creative conscience" (317), "the shared burdens of intuitive Memory" (325). He goes through every Protean riddle of being because he has been given (by Proteus) the "riches of the Imagination" (369).

His coming to understand the story of Rose (who, handing him over to Proteus, has left him free to live) leads Anselm to accept Canaima as his brother, making it possible for him to "nurse" in his arms all his protean family:

> Harold and the Rose sisters were as much my children now as they had been my terrible parents and relations, Proteus my child as much as he had been my wild patron and uncle. (383)

In the dark courtroom of the tribunal, Anselm comes before the judge with a mind haunted by questions: "Who is my brother?" (351), "When does one's trial truly commence?" (352), "What is the law of love [...] the law of revenge?" (354), "What was Being?," "What was Presence?" (357), "What is a full life?" (362). The judge is invisible: "Was invisibility the hidden curvature of the art of God one clings to unknowingly?" (359). In the theatre of the law, there begins a

> shared trial, the trial of the self. I was on trial. Alicia was on trial. Canaima, Rose, Proteus, Harold were on trial. Nameless others. The judge was on trial. The natures of art and science, man-made order, nature-made furies or daemons were on trial. (357)

In his sentence, the judge orders him to "*Nurse the shadow of the law* [...] Build the Shadow-Organ of Home [...] Home is the turning world" (387; my emphasis).

ෂ • ೞ

The Dantesque journey starts, then, in a theatre:

> The world was a stage.[...] Unsure of my lines, my part in the play of a civilization. For play it was. Play of truth (269)

– subsequently called the "theatre of memory" (370). It proceeds towards the garden and the palace of the Rose, towards the dark courtroom of the tribunal, towards Proteus's hut (an ark, a "cardboard palace"), to build the post-Christendom Imaginary Cathedral which encloses "the Shadow and the Voice of the Presence": "Presence was the immensely and varied genius of the sacred" (357).

In the sanctuary – the woods, the waterfalls – Anselm discovers that "within my fossilisation of parent–self lay a Word [...] my bruised Word-child" (394): "a transfigurative wound [...] revives the conception of the mystery of the Word, the Word made flesh" (394), "the intimate, ultimate dance of the Word, the renewed Word, the ecstatic Word" (398).

This revival of the Word is followed by the discovery of "Dido orchid" (401–402). After the Macusi guide has opened up a passage through the forest by fire, the flower ("botanic lore transferred into the soil of the Americas") evokes

> a crucial moment in the womb of the human imagination, when the queen gives up the ghost of black or white purity and biased fossil, biased formula, on her funeral pyre in the heart of future generations. (403)

Another "jest of nature" are the eels (electric eels of the *Electrophorous electricus* species) that cause the death of the three children of the Mission:

> Electric eels are innocent monsters one suppresses in every dream narrative of the depth and its fantastic creatures. They are an organ of apparently innocent craftsmanship in nature, neither daemon nor fury. [...] They approach in a swirling current without guile, fondle fluid arm and leg, and seek to dance

with all who come close. But each stroke, each embrace, breeds shock and paralysis in those they touch. The swimmer in their embrace collapses and sinks like a stone (390); the ease with which the eel had coiled itself around them [the three children] suggested an intimacy with elements (with the fluid electricity of the elements, animal electricity, animal 'lighthouse') (412). 'Eel' or 'umbilicus' equalled 'electricity.' That was the nature of their innocent jest, innocent transgression into consuming technology, consuming spires of electricity that would pierce the heavens and rival the stars. The gift of life was a gift of terrifying responsibility. (412–13)

After witnessing a procession of "newborn, newdead population wired into a ribcage. It was the still dance of the robin and the dove, the dolphin and the whale" (416), the three friends, Anselm and the two missionaries Penelope and George Ross, are suddenly surrounded: "Surrender yourselves to your captors" (422). The "motionless subtly active" captors (417) are the electric eels, the innocent monsters that caused the death of the three children of the Mission, or perhaps the children themselves. The reader – and Anselm – discovers that Anselm is holding in his arms (and the gesture is again that of *nursing*) a child who is his brother Canaima ("I have drawn the Shadow of my brother from the river of the dead"; 419), that Penelope holds the child who was Simon before the incident that had aroused a desire in him for power, violence and cruelty (an "alternative" life that Simon did not exploit), and Ross holds a little girl who sang at the Mission.

ෆ • ℬ

The principal instruments of this textual journey are two 'scientific' elements. One is observation, the science of the engineer or of the geologist who has studied the territory, describing it and drawing it with graphs. The second is a theoretical element, which here serves as interpretative instrument: 'quantum' theory. A further element is anthropological and consists of legends, the Macusi myth about the procession of the rocks in the waterfall, an interaction, like all myths, between the constraints of observation and the potentialities of the imagination.

The graph that the geologist reads for Robot, who hopes to discover a killer's hiding-place and capture him, shows only the alternation of four tall vertical rocks and three deep passages between one rock and the next. When the water-level in the river is high, the rocks and passages are submerged, and the water thunders down from the falls. When the level is low, some areas of water remain at the bottom of the passages between the rocks, and these are represented on the graph by crosses or stars (see Graphs 2 and 3).

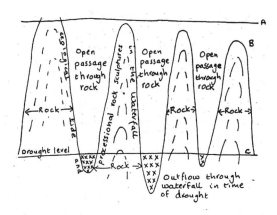

• ∽   Graph 2

According to the Macusi myth, the profiles of the rocks are sculptures that check the course of the river and form a procession of bodies inside the waterfall. The procession is awaiting the moment when the Macusi tribe will become extinct and it can revive. It thus represents the tribe's epitaph, but also, they believe, the birth of something else. The Macusi tribe have a bird's-eye view of the geology of the rocks, according to which they see the Atlantic further down, its high tides, together with the rocks, preventing the rivers from being consumed in the ocean. In short, water is preserved by means of a miraculous architecture, in an equilibrium of parallel forces, and only myth, or the arts, can approach appraisal of or gain access to the complete non-human otherness of matter: rock, wood, dust, water.

From the philosophical point of view, 'quantum' theory acts as a solvent on the rigid frame of concepts about mind and matter inherited from the nineteenth century, promoting interaction between disparate lines of thought. These include the ideas of modern physics about the mutability of matter, the "interference of possibilities," and Carl Friedrich Weizsäcker's "coexistent states" and overlapping possibilities,[29] as well as older cultural traditions, opposed to the law of *tertium non datur*, which have found expression in the concepts of natural (non-formalized) language, in myth, religion and art.

ςδ • ∽

---

[29] Werner Heisenberg, *Physics and Philosophy* (1962; Harmondsworth: Penguin, 1990): 166, 173.

Before the first bank is abandoned, the text has already effected some startling transmutations in the words of Anselm: the "king of thieves" has returned, after having "eaten of the pooled stars in the Macusi river of drought" (305), bringing with him a cup of the "diagrammatic pooled stars in or under the drought-body of the Macusi/Potaro river" (306; see Graph 2). Freed of his obsession with gold, he officiates at the funeral of the Macusi killed by Canaima and pours some of that same water over the body. This is the beginning of a series of associative and analogical shifts in semantic fields, whereby chains of signifiers proceed metonymically/metaphorically, and require a radial reading.

The song of the Macusi birdman just buried blends with the song of the three drowned children of the mission choir; the music is the voice of a flute, and the flute is "akin to a spiral or a curious ladder that runs into space" (309). Anselm and Penelope can hear

> the rhythm of the pooled stars that the king of thieves tilted upon him [the dead Macusi]. That *tilt* is important. [...] That tilt tells of a ladder. (309)[30]

The voices of the flute tell how the river of the dead, flowing beneath the visible Potaro, and the river of the living are one quantum stream possessed of four banks.

This is difficult for the reader to follow, unless preturnaturally attentive to the mystery of creation and prepared to follow traces of pre-Columbian myths. The reader notices, however, that Anselm believes he has the proof of the curve of music that ascends the ladder of space. After ten years' study, he has succeeded in drawing a graph of the relation between the level of the river and the volume of water:

Anselm's account of his graphic encoding reads as follows:

> A sufficiency of close agreement or accord between the stars permitted me to trace a stage-discharge rib or curve in the river's fluid skeleton. The eccentric stars that flew off above or below that rib provided an implicit nightsky or constellation in the river, a primitive violin in league with the diagrammatic voice of the flute, a dual bow, a heart, a head and a neck. It was but a glimpse into a library of illustrated dream within a theatre of science. (313)

---

[30] "Uprooting is what I mean by 'tilting of the field': the uprooting of certain places or objects in the field that seem immovable"; "if you can tilt the field, then you will dislodge certain objects in the field and your own prepossessions may be dislodged as well" (*The Radical Imagination*, 43, also 44, 45, 63, 74). "You can tilt the whole field of a civilization when you go to the extremities or the margin. You can tilt that field. And when you tilt the field, prepossessions are dislodged" (127).

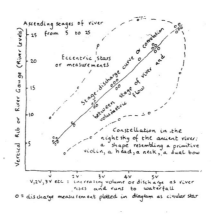

The title of the book is thus explained:

> One cannot tame the voices of the flute, voices of such uncanny lightness yet miracle of being that they are able to *tilt* the two rivers, the visible and the invisible river, into diagrammatic discourse; and in so doing to create the four banks of the river of space into a ladder upon which the curved music of the flute ascends. Those banks are dislodged into rungs in the ladder and into stepping stones into original space. (310; Graph 4)[31]

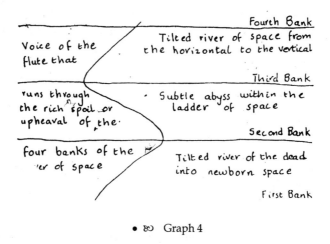

• ∞   Graph 4

---

[31] On Harris's "adjectival insistence," see Russell McDougall, "'Corporeal Music': The Scale of Myth and Adjectival Insistence in *Palace of the Peacock*," *The Uncompromising Imagination*, 92–105; also insistent is the use of the preposition 'into,' laying stress on change, on transformation, on the metamorphic nature of the very subject-matter.

We find support here for a "sacred reciprocity between art and science" (418; "Science is a species of art, after all"; 415), as demonstrated perhaps by the graphs themselves.

Among the epigraphs prefacing the volume is a passage from a book on quantum science:[32]

> Quantum reality consists of simultaneous possibilities, a 'polyhistoric' kind of being. [...] incompatible with our [...] one-track minds. If these alternative (and parallel) universes are really real and we are barred from experiencing them only by a biological accident, perhaps we can extend our senses with a sort of 'quantum microscope.' (263)

Anselm moves on quantum territory (293) and takes "memory's leap into quantum proportions" (363). "Quantum" appears to qualify the most varied semes with a frequency equal to that with which "carnival" qualifies every lexical element of *Carnival*, and there are "quantum jumps" in the meeting between the text and the reader.[33]

"Quantum" qualifies the moments of strongest transmutation: parallel or alternative existences are brought into focus with a "quantum axe" (that of the Macusi who chops down the tree with a single blow); a "quantum camera" (Anselm's, filming that scene for spectators of "quantum television," 361, 362); a "quantum knife" (that of Canaima, which also belongs to Anselm and to many other aggressors, 282). "Quantum" seems to serve to define "the genuine mystery of parallel thresholds into sustaining otherness" (316), "mystery of quantum, parallel lives, parallel formations" (318). The sharing of the role of Ulysses by many actors implies "a quantum reality that slipped forever into the future" (329). It is a synonym of the parallel/alternative, mutual, shared, reversible:

> there are alternatives. [...] Quantum parallels imply self-recognition across hard-and-fast barriers as well as subtle alternatives within a ruling frame or pattern of fate [...] the Voice [when it is heard] attached to no absolute beginning, no absolute ending, within alternatives, parallel spaces, sculptures of myth and history. (358–360)

The prevalence of intertextuality, in the form of Harris's cross-cultural-ism, feeds on the same principle. Human creativity, the metamorphic process in organic matter, and the laws of the inorganic realm may be but

---

[32] Nick Herbert, *'Quantum Reality': Beyond the New Physics* (Garden City NY: Doubleday Anchor, 1987).

[33] See the pages on Harris and modern physics in Hena Maes–Jelinek, "'Unfinished Genesis'," 230–45.

varied expressions of a universal formative process of which art, science, religion, and myth have always attempted parallel/alternative readings.[34] Quantum reality prepares for "a translation of ourselves into another level of being," "a fondest recognition of ourselves in and through others," "a testing [...] hazardous [...] miraculous community of souls" (405, 408, 407, 421).

4   A new kind of literature

This is literature as the "maximalisation of semantic incommensurability in respect of the formal means of expression."[35] Freed from the shackles of representation, the word enters into the open network of its lexical universe, re-acquires its "magic," and recovers both the "aura" that is its characteristic and the unlimited creativity of metaphor (the Prime Mover). Harris's is a form of rhetoric that says what is unspeakable but true: Anselm is invited to imagine the unimaginable, to touch the untouchable. It is a form of rhetoric capable of stating and denying everything: "It is not true, of course. Yet it is true," Anselm says at the end (420), just as Rushdie writes: "It was so, it was not so [...] it happened and it never did –maybe, then, or maybe not."[36]

This is discourse connecting with origins: "originality" is a key Harrisian word – it speaks of the beginning, of the initial stages of the mysterious existence of mankind; artistic creation is *archaic* in its relationship with Origin. It brings with it the vibration of Origin, and that same vibration is awakened in the reader. The reader's experience becomes one with that of Anselm: both experience what may be described, if not as *agnition*, at least as a sense of familiarity with the most unprecedented experiences. Both learn to react critically ("never take anything for granted") to passively received cultural formations. Both develop an unconditioned receptiveness (synapses of reception) towards pre-logical, pre-grammatical sedimented traces or fossils of visual, auditory, emotional and imaginary experiences, a receptiveness characterized by a spontaneity preceding awareness and rationality.

C8 • &

---

[34] "Gestating resources in the womb of tradition that we have bypassed or overlooked or eclipsed...." Harris sees "uncanny correspondences [...] between Maya twinships of pasts and futures and the Mathematics of Chaos. Chaos is misconceived as an anarchic phenomenon. Whereas it may be visualized as portraying an 'open' universe"; *Jonestown* (London: Faber & Faber, 1996): 5–6.

[35] George Steiner, *Real Presences: Is There Anything In What We Say?* (London: Faber & Faber, 1989): 83.

[36] Salman Rushdie, *The Satanic Verses* (London: Viking, 1988): 35.

I have no doubt that as we approach the end of the twentieth century, Harris stands as a central and emblematic as well as highly charismatic figure.

It may be said without any fear of being 'unfashionable' in this post-Logos age (a fear Harris himself does not know), that cross-culturalism, mutual relations, community, alliance with the universe and interest in the mystery of creation are the forces which will enable an oppressed and exhausted humanity to recover the human dimension. This will not be achieved by a fashionable 'traveller's ethics,' as in the best 'nomadism' (when this is not only an anarchic errantry, but a readiness to inhabit non-causality in perfect innocence, without any anticipation of sense), but by the intellectual and ethical challenge inherent in every relationship of man with man and of man with what Emmanuel Levinas calls infinity.

Furthermore, in Harris's texts I seem to hear notes that are sounded by almost all the writers discussed in the present book as 'magical realists,' as well as by other contemporary writers, mainly poets. I hear not only the need, expressed by Patrick White, to speak of the "extraordinary behind the ordinary," but also David Malouf's desire for the advent of a new man – "we are creating the lineaments of some final man." The alternative possibilities open to man and often present in Malouf's books[37] are also expressed in the lines of an Australian poet, Fay Zwicky: "remember those / who made us what we might have been."[38]

It is a question of saving something. To 'salvage,' in the sense of saving flotsam from a shipwreck and relics from the wreckage caused by our civilization, is a verb used also by the Canadian poet Robert Bringhurst – "to salvage and preserve"[39] – as well as by Fay Zwicky, in the words of Noah's wife in *Ark Poems*: "to save to save merely – no matter / what or whom – to save."[40] It is a question of salvaging lost voices, voices that speak of origin, forgotten myths and interpretations of the world thought superseded by reason and realism.

The invitation not to forget our kinship with the planet, already made in the great seventh chapter of *Under the Volcano* ("the revolving world"),[41] is also made by Harris: to listen carefully, to pay "abnormal attention" to everything that bears witness to our kinship with all there is. "The truly

---

37 *An Imaginary Life* (London: Chatto & Windus, 1978): 29.
38 *Poems 1970–1992* (St. Lucia: U of Queensland P, 1993): 232.
39 Robert Bringhurst, *Pieces of Map, Pieces of Music*, 103.
40 From "Ark Voices," in *Poems*, 83.
41 Malcolm Lowry, *Under the Volcano* (London: Jonathan Cape, 1947), 198.

attentive ear I place on the ground and to the body of the turning globe" (*Four Banks*, 312) recalls the stethoscope that Bringhurst suggests placing on the ground, while White's hopes, in *Voss*, find expression in the thoughts of Laura Trevelyan:

> Some will learn to interpret the ideas embodied in the less communicative forms of matter, such as rock, wood, metal and water. I must include water, because, of all matter, it is the most musical.[42]

"Mutual, it is all mutual" refers to more than just the telepathic communication between Voss and Laura in that book. Similarly, Malouf's Ovid writes: "I am a pool of water. A breeze shivers my surface" and "I am turning into the landscape. I feel myself sway and ripple," while in "The Crab Feast" Malouf's poetic voice says: "the crab is myself in another species."[43]

Scientific discoveries are used by Janet Frame in *The Carpathians*, where the appearance of the Gravity Star has miraculous consequences, like those Harris attributes to "'black holes of gravity' as an *extinction* of light drawn into paradoxical *genesis* of suns beyond imagined or imaginable models."[44] Malouf and Rushdie also refer to quantistic forms of reality. Bringhurst and Harris share the same view on the connection between art and science: "The arts and the sciences are in their origin one pursuit. [...] Science, like art, is founded on wonder."[45] For Malouf, too, creativity and art are "a genuine response to the miracle of life"[46] – there is creativity because there is the Other. An inrush of meaning, the aesthetic sets in motion processes of transformation. Metamorphosis comes of interaction, and the otherness which enters us makes us other.[47]

Harris sees creation as a great model underlying all human activity creative ambition, whether artistic or not – "our activity is very peculiar as if we are placed here in order to do something essentially creative."[48] He sees artists as "figures *of* and *in* creation": "Life is the miracle. Creation's the tide that runs through us into every excess" (*Four Banks*, 372). Artistic creation exists because there is a created universe and formal construction exists

---

42 Patrick White, *Voss* (1957; Harmondsworth: Penguin, 1960): 446.

43 *An Imaginary Life*, 146; *Selected Poems* (Sydney: Angus & Robertson, 1981): 99.

44 *Explorations*, 85 (my emphasis).

45 Bringhurst, *Pieces of Map, Pieces of Music*, 111.

46 *Explorations*, 84.

47 See Bringhurst's poem "The Reader," in *Pieces of Map, Pieces of Music*, 57, and "Interview with David Malouf" by Beate Josephi, in *Provisional Maps: Critical Essays on David Malouf*, ed. Amanda Nettelbeck (Nedlands: U of Western Australia, 1994).

48 *The Uncompromising Imagination*, 56.

because we have been created as forms.[49] As in the poems of Bringhurst, man's centre of identity is no more and no less than the perception of the wholly inexplicable presence, factuality, and perceptible substantiality of the created universe. It is. We are.

First and foremost, all these writers urge the "dropping of the boundaries of the self." The communion of experience in a play when several actors take a share in the performance and the role is "*shared by many actors*, broken into mutual parts" (*Four Banks*, 357) recalls the central scene of Ondaatje's *In the Skin of a Lion* and the lesson' that "the flying nun" gives to the shy, isolated Patrick.[50] The construction of a communal space and gesture – "the thread of the dance may bring us together again and again" (*Four Banks*, 276) – recalls the unforgettable final scene of Jack Hodgins's *The Resurrection of Joseph Bourne*.[51] The relationship with "the everlasting stranger within oneself" and the "self-recognition of ourselves in and through others" (*Four Banks*, 407, 408) recalls the need for "overlapping" felt by Hodgins's eponymous protagonist in *Spit Delaney's Island*,[52] or the endings of *Remembering Babylon* and *The Moor's Last Sigh*.[53] In the former, the nun who takes care of the bees and studies their language observes the tide at sunset: "As we approach prayer. As we approach knowledge. As we approach each other." The Moor's dying words constitute a testament to "our need for flowing together, for putting an end to frontiers, for the dropping of the boundaries of the self," a utopian dream that is also found in Frame's *The Carpathians*.

This is what Harris chooses to call "*coniunctio* or true marriage" or "potential for true marriage between cultures,"[54] and is what supports his great metaphor of "the seamless whole," in a "glimmering apprehension of the magic of creative nature" (*Four Banks*, 305).

∓ • ℥

---

49 George Steiner, *Real Presences*, 201.

50 Michael Ondaatje, *In the Skin of a Lion* (Toronto: McClelland & Stewart, 1987).

51 Jack Hodgins, *The Resurrection of Joseph Bourne* (Toronto: Macmillan, 1979).

52 "If people can't overlap, at least a little, how do they know each other?"; Jack Hodgins, *Spit Delaney's Island* (Toronto: Macmillan, 1976): 15. For the same metaphor in Harris, see *Tradition, the Writer and Society*, 30, 49, 51 and passim.

53 Malouf, *Remembering Babylon* (Toronto: Alfred A. Knopf, 1993): 200; Rushdie, *The Moor's Last Sigh* (London: Jonathan Cape, 1995): 433.

54 *The Womb of Space*, 34, 37, 50, 127; see also Rushdie's "cross-pollination," in *Imaginary Homelands: Essays and Criticism 1981–1991* (London: Granta, 1991): 20.

The literary adventure we may continue to call 'magical realism' is a matter of "*coniunctio* or true marriage," non-separation, or a breaking down of barriers between apparent incompatibles. What we find on the surface is a *coniunctio* of the ordinary and the extraordinary, realism and magic, the marvellous and the mundane, factual and counterfactual, thought and the imaginary, history and myth, art and science. Underlying this is the need to connect Me and the Other, nature and beings (the human world/the non-human world), my experience and other people's experiences, and in this way to fly the cage of solipsism. This is, I believe, writing about reconciliation, following estrangement and desecration.

What has given rise to this type of literature could be defined as an "explosive process" in cultural dynamics, one that takes place at the intersection of heterogeneous cultures.[55] The inrush of the extra-systemic into the system constitutes one of the fundamental sources transforming a static model into a dynamic one. The moment of explosion not only creates new possibilities: a new reality comes into being, through a seismic resemanticizing of memory (Harris's "evolutionary epicentre") permitting us to "shake the frame of dead matter" and "unlearn ways of seeing."[56] This is literature produced at one of those "moments in history when energies flow out from broken traditional patterns"[57] with different cultures, thought and imagination, art and science crossing each other in the attempt to realize an imaginative, profoundly revolutionary *coniunctio*.[58]

ଓ • ৩

---

[55] Yuri Lotman, *Cercare la strada*, ed. Maria Corti (Venice: Marsilio, 1994), and *Kul'tura I Vzryv* (Moscow: Gnosis, 1993).

[56] *The Womb of Space*, 124, 126.

[57] *Explorations*, 64.

[58] See also the conclusion of Werner Heisenberg's *Physics and Philosophy*, "The Role of Modern Physics in the Present Development of Human Thinking," 175–94.

Works Cited

&

ABRAHAMS, Peter. *Tell Freedom* (London: Faber & Faber, 1954).

AGAMBEN, Giorgio. *Mezzi senza fine* (Turin: Bollati Boringhieri, 1996).

ALAZRAKI, Jaime. *En busca del unicornio: Los cuentos de Julio Cortázar* (Madrid: Gredos, 1983).

ALEXANDER, Michael. *Mrs Frazer on the Fatal Shore* (New York: Simon & Schuster, 1971).

ALEXIS, Jacques-Stéphen. "Du réalisme merveilleux chez les Haïtiens," *Présence Africaine* 8–10 (June–November 1956): 245–71.

ANAND, Mulk Raj. *Gauri* (1960; New Delhi: Arnold–Heinemann, 1981).

ASHCROFT, Bill, Gareth GRIFFITHS & Helen TIFFIN, ed. *The Post-Colonial Studies Reader* (London/New York: Routledge, 1995).

ASTURIAS, Miguel Ángel. *Hombres de maíz*, in *Obras completas* (1949; Aguilar: Madrid 1968).

——. *Men of Maize*, tr. Gerald Martin (A Merloyd Lawrence Book; New York: Delacorte/ Seymour Lawrence, 1975).

ATWOOD, Margaret. *The Animals in That Country* (Toronto: Oxford UP, 1968).

——. *Survival* (Toronto: Anansi, 1972).

——. "MacEwen's Muse," *Canadian Literature* 45 (Summer 1970): 24–32.

——. "Canadian Monsters: Some Aspects of the Supernatural in Canadian Fiction," in STAINES, 113–30.

BACHELARD, Gaston. *The Poetics of Space*, tr. Maria Jolas (*La Poétique de l'espace*, 1958; tr. 1965; Boston MA: Beacon, 1994).

BAKER, Suzanne. "Magic Realism as a Postcolonial Strategy: *The Kadaitcha Sung*," *SPAN* 32 (1991): 55–63.

——. "Binarism and Duality, Magic Realism and Postcolonialism," *SPAN* 36 (1992): 82–87.

BAKHTIN, Mikhail M. *L'Œuvre de François Rabelais et la culture populaire au Moyen Âge et sous le Renaissance*, tr. Andrée Robel (1965; Paris: Gallimard, 1970).

——. "Forms of Time and of the Chronotope in the Novel," in Bakhtin, *The Dialogic Imagination: Four Essays*, ed. Michael Holquist, tr. Caryl Emerson (Austin: U of Texas P, 1981): 84–258.

BARBER, Karin. "Popular Arts in Africa," *African Studies Review* 30.3 (September 1987): 1–78.

BARTH, John. "The Literature of Exhaustion," *Atlantic Monthly* 220.2 (August 1967): 29–34.

——. "The Literature of Replenishment," *Atlantic Monthly* 233.1 (January 1980): 65–71.

BAUDRILLARD, Jean. *Simulacra and Simulation*, tr. Sheila Faria Glaser (*Simulacres et simulations*, 1981; Ann Arbor: U of Michigan P, 1994).

BERTINETTI, Paolo, & Claudio GORLIER, ed. *Australiana* (Rome: Bulzoni, 1982).

BHABHA, Homi K. *The Location of Culture* (London: Routledge, 1994).

BOWERING, George. "Avison's Imitation of Christ the Artist," *Canadian Literature* 54 (1972): 56–69.

BRAIDOTTI, Rosi. *Nomadic Subjects* (New York: Columbia UP, 1994).

BRINGHURST, Robert. *Pieces of Map, Pieces of Music* (Toronto: McClelland & Stewart, 1987).

——. *The Calling: Selected Poems 1970–1995* (Toronto: McClelland & Stewart, 1995).

——. *The Elements of Typographic Style* (Vancouver: Hartley & Marks, 1996).

BRINK, André. *Imaginings of Sand* (London: Secker & Warburg, 1996).

——. "A Real and Magical Devil," *Leadership Interactive* 16.2 (August 1997): 1–3.

BROWN, C. Mackenzie. *The Triumph of the Goddess* (1990; Delhi: Sri Satguru, 1992).

BROWN, Duncan, & Bruno VAN DYK, ed. *Exchanges* (Pietermaritzburg: U of Natal P, 1991).

BUBER, Martin. *To Hallow This Life*, ed. & tr. Jacob Trapp (New York: Harper, 1958).

BURNS, Alan, & Charles SUGNET, *The Imagination on Trial: British and American Writers Discuss Their Working Methods* (London: Allison & Busby, 1981).

CARPENTIER, Alejo. "De lo real maravilloso americano" (1949), in *Tientos y diferencias* (1964; Montevideo: Arca, 1973): 115–16.

——. *Los pasos perdidos* (1953; Madrid: Cátedra, 1985).

——. *The Kingdom of This World*, tr. Harriet de Onís (*El reino de este mundo*, 1949; tr. 1957; London: André Deutsch, 1976, repr. 1990).

——. *The Lost Steps*, tr. Harriet de Onís (1956; Harmondsworth: Penguin, 1968).

——. *El reino de este mundo* (1949; Barcelona: Seix Barral, 1978).

——. "On the Marvelous Real in America (1949)"; "The Baroque and the Marvelous Real" (1975), tr. Tanya Huntington & Lois Parkinson Zamora, in ZAMORA & FARIS, 75–108.

CASTORINA, Giuseppe G., & Vittoriana VILLA, ed. *La fortuna della retorica* (Chieti: Métis, 1993).

CAVELL, Richard. "Pazzi e maghi: versioni dell'artista nella narrativa canadese," *Canada: Testi e contesti*, ed. Alfredo Rizzardi (Abano Terme: Piovan, 1983): 13–30.

CHANADY, Amaryll. *Magic Realism and the Fantastic: Resolved Versus Unresolved Antinomy* (New York: Garland, 1985).

——. "The Origins and Development of Magic Realism in Latin American Fiction," in HINCHCLIFFE & JEWINSKI, 49–60.

——. "La focalizacíon como espejo de contradicciones en *El reino de este mundo*," *Revista Canadiense de Estudios Hispánicos* 12.3 (1988): 446–58.

——. "The Territorialization of the Imaginary in Latin America: Self-Affirmation and Resistance to Metropolitan Paradigms," in ZAMORA & FARIS, 125–44.

CHAUDHURI, Una. "Writing the Raj Away," *Turnstile* 2.1 (1990): 26–35.

CHENEY–COKER, Syl. *The Last Harmattan of Alusine Dunbar* (Oxford: Heinemann, 1990).

CHIAMPI, Irlemar. *El realismo maravilloso: Forma y ideología en la novela hispano-americana* (tr. from *O realismo maravilhoso: Forma y ideologia no romance hispano-americano* [1976; São Paulo: Editora Perspectiva, 1980]; Caracas: Monte Avila Editores, 1983).

CLIFFORD, James, & George MARCUS, ed. *Writing Culture* (Berkeley: U of California P, 1986).

COBBY, Anne Elizabeth, ed. *Aucassin et Nicolette* (with *The Pilgrimage of Charlemagne*), tr. Glyn S. Burgess (Garland Library of Medieval Literature A47; New York: Garland, 1965).

COFER, Judith Ortiz. *An Island Like You* (New York: Orchard, 1995).

CONCILIO, Carmen. "Topology vs Geometry: The Relational Geography of Self and Other in David Malouf's *An Imaginary Life* and *Remembering Babylon*," in ZOPPI, 736–50.

CONNIFF, Brian. "The Dark Side of Magical Realism: Science, Oppression, and Apocalypse in *One Hundred Years of Solitude*," *Modern Fiction Studies* 36:2 (Summer 1990): 167–79.

COOPER, Brenda. "Syl Cheney–Coker: *The Last Harmattan of Alusine Dunbar* and an Interview," *ALA Bulletin* 20.3 (Summer 1994): 3–17.

——. *Magical Realism in West African Fiction* (London: Routledge, 1998).

COUTO, Mia. *Voices Made Night*, tr. David Brookshaw (1986; Oxford: Heineman,1986).

——. *Every Man is a Race*, tr. David Brookshaw (1989; Oxford: Heineman, 1994).

DAKUBU, Mary Esther Kropp. "*Search Sweet Country* and the Language of Authentic Being," *Research in African Literatures* 24.1 (Spring 1993): 19–35.

DAVIES, Robertson. *Fifth Business* (1970; Harmondsworth: Penguin, 1977).

DEANDREA, Pietro. "An Interview with Ben Okri," *Africa, America, Asia, Australia* 16 (Rome: Bulzoni, 1994): 80.

——. "'New Worlds, New Wholes': Kojo Laing's Narrative Quest for Social Renewal," *African Literature Today* 20 (1996): 158–78.

DELBAERE, Jeanne. "*The Carpathians*: Memory and Survival in the Global Village," in *The Ring of Fire: Essays on Janet Frame*, ed. Delbaere (Mundelstrup/Sydney: Dangaroo, 1992): 199–208.

——. "Daphne's Metamorphoses in Janet Frame's Early Novels," *ARIEL: A Review of International English Literature* 6 (April 1975): 23–37.

——. "Magic Realism: The Energy of the Margins," in D'HAEN & BERTENS, 75–104.

——. "Psychic Realism, Mythic Realism, Grotesque Realism: Variations on Magic Realism in Contemporary Literature in English," in ZAMORA & FARIS, 249–66.

DELLA VOLPE, Galvano. *Critica del gusto* (Milan: Feltrinelli, 1960).

DEY, Esha. *The Novels of Raja Rao* (New Delhi: Prestige, 1992).

D'HAEN, Theo, & Hans BERTENS, ed. *Postmodern Fiction in Canada* (Postmodern Studies 6; Amsterdam & Atlanta GA: Rodopi/Antwerp: Restant, 1992).

DOMENICHELLI, Mario. "Il mozzo della ruota: *Noman* e *Noman's Land* di Gwendolyn MacEwen," in RIZZARDI, ed. *Moderni e Post-Moderni*, 153–63.

DREWAL, Margaret Thompson. *Yoruba Ritual: Performers, Play, Agency* (Bloomington: Indiana UP, 1992).

DUNTON, Chris. "Butterflies of Flesh," *West Africa* 3797 (4–10 June 1990): 9–42.

DUPUIS, Michel, & Albert MINGELGRÜN. "Pour une poétique du réalisme magique," in WEISGERBER, 219–32.

DRURY, Nevill. *The Shaman and the Magician: Journeys Between the Worlds* (London: Routledge, 1982).

ELIADE, Mircea. *Rites and Symbols of Initiation: The Mysteries of Birth and Rebirth* (New York: Harper & Row, 1960).

——. *Shamanism: Archaic Techniques of Ecstasy*, tr. Willard R. Trask (Bollingen Series, 76; Princeton NJ: Princeton UP, 1964).

FABRE, Michel. "Recovering Precious Words: On Wilson Harris and the Language of Imagination," in MAES–JELINEK, ed. *The Uncompromising Imagination*, 39–48.

FARIS, Wendy B. "Scheherazade's Children: Magical Realism and Postmodern Fiction," in ZAMORA & FARIS, 163–90.

FINK, Cecelia Coulas. "'If Words Won't Do, and Symbols Fail': Hodgins's Magic Reality,' *Journal of Canadian Studies – Revue d'études canadiennes* 20.2 (1985): 118–19.

FISCHER, Michael J. "Ethnicity and the Post-Modern Arts of Memory," in CLIFFORD & MARCUS, 194–233.

FLORES, Ángel. "Magical Realism in Spanish American Fiction," *Hispania* 38.2 (1955): 187–92.

FRAME, Janet. *The Edge of the Alphabet* (Christchurch: Pegasus, 1962).

——. *The Carpathians* (London: Bloomsbury, 1988).

FRASER, Robert. "Kojo Laing: Profile and Extract," *Wasafiri* 3 (Autumn 1995): 9–11.

FRIEDLANDER, Saul, ed. *Probing the Limits of Representation* (Los Angeles: U of California P, 1992).

FUNKESTEIN, Amos. "History, Counterhistory, and Narrative," in FRIEDLANDER, 66–81.

GAGEY, Jacques. *Gaston Bachelard ou la conversion de l'imaginaire* (Paris: Rivière, 1969).

GARCÍA MÁRQUEZ, Gabriel. *Cien años de soledad* (Madrid: Cátedra, 1991).

——. "Fantasía y creación artística en América Latina y el Caribe," *Texto crítico* 14 (1979): 6.

——. *The Fragrance of Guava: Conversations with Plinio Apuleyo Mendoza*, tr. Ann Wright (London: Verso, 1983).

——. *Of Love and Other Demons*, tr. Edith Grossman (*Del amor y otros demonios*, Barcelona: Mondadori/Grijalbo Comercial, 1994; New York: Random House, 1994).

GEROW, Edwin. "The Quintessential Narayan," *Literature East & West* 10.1–2 (June 1966): 1–18.

GIACOMÁN, Helmy, ed. *Homenajes a Alejo Carpentier: Variaciones interpretativas en torno a su obra* (New York: Las Américas, 1970).

GILKES, Michael, ed. *The Literate Imagination: Essays on the Novels of Wilson Harris* (London: Macmillan, 1989).

GINESTIER, Paul. *La Pensée de Bachelard* (Paris: Bordas, 1968).

GORDIMER, Nadine. *My Son's Story* (London: Bloomsbury, 1990).

GORLIER, Claudio, & Isabella ZOPPI, ed. *Cross-Cultural Voices* (Rome: Bulzoni, 1997).

GRASS, Günter, & Salman RUSHDIE. "Scrivere per un futuro" (English version 1987), in *Gli scrittori e la politica* (Milan: Linea d'ombra, 1990).

GUENTHER, Irene. "Magic Realism, New Objectivity, and the Arts during the Weimar Republic," in ZAMORA & FARIS, 33–74.

GUIDOTTI, Valeria. "A House for Mr. Malgas: Postmodern Allegory in *The Folly* by Ivan Vladislavic," in GORLIER & ZOPPI, 79–98.

GURNAH, Abdulrazak, ed. *Essays on African Writing 2: Contemporary Literature* (Oxford: Heinemann, 1995).

HALIFAX, John. *Shaman: The Wounded Healer* (New York: Crossroad, 1982).

HANSSON, Karin. *The Warped Universe: A Study of Imagery and Structure in Seven Novels by Patrick White* (Lund: CWK Gleerup, 1984).

HARIPRASANNA, A. *The World of Malgudi: A Study of R.K. Narayan's Novels* (New Delhi: Prestige, 1994).

HARRIS, Wilson. *The Carnival Trilogy* (London: Faber & Faber, 1993).

——. *Explorations: A Selection of Talks and Articles 1966–1981*, ed. & intro. Hena Maes-Jelinek (Mundelstrup/Sydney: Dangaroo, 1981).

——. *Fossil and Psyche* (Austin: U of Texas, 1974), repr. in Maes–Jelinek, ed. *Explorations*.

——. *Jonestown* (London: Faber & Faber, 1996).

——. "Leo Austin's *Poems*: A Review," *Kyk-Over-Al* 20 (November 1955): 205.

——. "Living Absences and Presences" in MIHAILOVICH–DICKMAN, 1–5.

——. "The Open Door," *Journal of Modern Literature* 20.1 (1996): 7–12.

——. *The Radical Imagination*, ed. Alan Riach & Mark Williams (Liège: L³ - Language and Literature, 1992).

——. "A Talk on the Subjective Imagination," *New Letters* 40 (Autumn 1973): 37–48.

——. *Tradition, the Writer and Society: Critical Essays* (London/Port of Spain: New Beacon, 1967).

——. "Wilson Harris interviewed by Alan Burns," in BURNS & SUGNET, 51–65.

——. "Ways to Enjoy Literature," in *"Union in Partition": Essays in Honour of Jeanne Delbaere*, ed. Gilbert Debusscher & Marc Maufort (Liège: L³ - Language and Literature, 1997): 201–208.

——. *The Womb of Space* (Westport CT: Greenwood, 1983).

HEISENBERG, Werner. *Physics and Philosophy* (1962; Harmondsworth: Penguin, 1990).

HERBERT, Nick. *'Quantum Reality': Beyond the New Physics* (Garden City NY: Doubleday Anchor, 1987).

HINCHCLIFFE, Peter, & Ed JEWINSKI, ed. *Magic Realism and Canadian Literature: Essays and Stories; Proceedings of the Conference on Magic Realist Writing in Canada, University of Waterloo/Wilfrid Laurier University (May, 1985)* (Waterloo, Ontario: U of Waterloo P, 1986).

HODGINS, Jack. *Spit Delaney's Island* (Toronto: Macmillan, 1976).

——. *The Invention of the World* (Scarborough, Ontario: Macmillan, 1977).

——. *The Resurrection of Joseph Bourne, or: A Word or Two on Those Port Annie Miracles* (Toronto: Macmillan, 1979).

HOWARD, W.J. "Wilson Harris and the 'Alchemical Imagination'," *Literary Half-Yearly* 11 (1970): 17–26.

HUGGAN, Graham. *Territorial Disputes: Maps and Mapping Strategies in Contemporary Canadian and Australian Fiction* (Toronto: U of Toronto P, 1994).

JAFFÉ, Aniela. *Apparitions* (Le Mail: Mercure de France, 1983).

JAGGI, Maya. "Facts and Fiction" (interview) and "Dreams of the Poor" (review of *Voices Made Night*), *New African* (May 1990): 39–40.

JAMESON, Fredric. "On Magic Realism in Film," *Critical Inquiry* 12.2 (1986): 301–25.

JOLLY, Roslyn. "Transformations of Caliban and Ariel: Imagination and Language in David Malouf, Margaret Atwood and Seamus Heaney," *World Literature Written in English* 26:2 (Autumn 1986): 296–330.

JUNG, Carl Gustav. *Collected Works of C.G. Jung*, ed. Sir Herbert Read, Michael Fordham, Gerhard Adler & William McGuire (Bollingen Series; Princeton NJ: Princeton UP, 1980).

——. *Letters*, ed. Gerhard Adler & Aniela Jaffé (Princeton NJ/London: Princeton UP, 2 vols., 1973–75).

KAKAR, Sudhir. *Intimate Relations: Exploring Indian Sexuality* (New Delhi: Penguin, 1989).

KENYON, Linda. "A Conversation with Robert Kroetsch," *New Quarterly* 1 (Spring 1988).

KINSLEY, David. *Hindu Goddess* (1986; Delhi: Motilal Banarsidass, 1987).

KROETSCH, Robert. *What the Crow Said* (Don Mills, Ontario: General, 1978).

KRONFELD, Chana. *Modernisms on the Margin* (Berkeley/Los Angeles: U of California P, 1996).

KUNENE, Mazisi. "Some Aspects of South African Literature," *World Literature Today* 70.1 (Winter 1996): 13–16.

LAING, Kojo. *Search Sweet Country* (London: Heinemann, 1986).

——. *Woman of the Aeroplanes* (1988, London: Picador, 1989).

——. *Major Gentl and the Achimota Wars* (Oxford: Heinemann, 1992).

LAMBERT, Alison. "The Memory Flower, the Gravity Star, and the Real World: Janet Frame's *The Carpathians*," *New Zealand Literature Today* (New Delhi: Indian Society for Commonwealth Studies, 1993): 102–20.

LEAL, Luis. "El realismo mágico en la literatura hispanoamericana," *Cuadernos Americanos* 63.4 (1967): 230–35.

LEIGH, Mike. "*Naked*" and Other Screenplays (London: Faber & Faber, 1995).

LEVI, Giovanni. "Les Usages de la biographie," *Annales ESC* 6 (novembre–décembre 1989): 1325–36.

LEVINAS, Emmanuel. *Totality and Infinity: An Essay on Exteriority*, tr. Alphonso Lingis (*Totalité et infini: Essai sur l'exteriorité*, 1961; Pittsburgh PA: Duquesne UP, 1969).

——. *Time and the Other and Additional Essays*, tr. Richard C. Cohen (*Le temps et l'autre*, 1979; Pittsburgh PA: Duquesne UP, 1987).

——. *Proper Names*, tr. Michael B. Smith (*Noms propres*, 1976; Stanford CA: Stanford UP, 1996).

LINGUANTI, Elsa. "Too Narrow a Body: Reading David Malouf," *Africa, America, Asia, Australia* 3 (1988): 19–36.

——. "Sequenze e ritmi in *A Fringe of Leaves* di Patrick White," in BERTINETTI & GORLIER, 209–21.

LOTMAN, Yuri. *Kul'tura I Vzryv* (Moscow: Gnosis, 1993).

——. *Cercare la strada*, ed. Maria Corti (Venice: Marsilio, 1994).

LYOTARD, Jean-François. "Going Back to the Return," in *The Languages of Joyce: Selected Papers from the 11th International Joyce Symposium (12–18 June 1988)*, ed. Rose Maria Bosinelli, Carla Vaglio Marengo & Christine van Bhoeemen, tr. Madeleine Burt Merlini (*L'écrit du temps*, 1988; tr. 1988; Venice, 1992): 193–210.

MCCAFFERY, Larry, ed. *Storming the Reality Studio: A Casebook of Cyberpunk and Postmodern Science Fiction* (Durham NC/London: Duke UP, 1991).

MACEWEN, Gwendolyn. *Noman* (1972, Toronto: General, 1985).

——. *Rhymes and Reasons*, ed. John Robert Colombo & Roy Bentley (Toronto: Holt, Rinehart & Winston, 1971).

MCDOUGALL, Russell. "'Corporeal Music: the Scale of Myth and Adjectival Insistence in *Palace of the Peacock*," in MAES-JELINEK, ed. *The Uncompromising Imagination*, 92–105.

MCLEOD, Marion. "Janet Frame in Reality Mode," interview, *New Zealand Listener* (24 September 1988): 25.

MCLUHAN, Marshall. "Canada: The Borderline Case," in Staines, 226–48.

MCMULLIN, Stanley. "Adam Mad in Eden: Magic Realism as Hinterland Experience," in HINCHCLIFFE & JEWINSKI, 13–22.

MAES-JELINEK, Hena. *The Naked Design: A Reading of "Palace of the Peacock"* (Mundelstrup/Sydney: Dangaroo, 1976).

——. "The Writer as Alchemist: The Unifying Role of Imagination in the Novels of Wilson Harris," *Language and Literature* 1.1 (1971): 25–34.

——, ed. *Wilson Harris: The Uncompromising Imagination* (Mundelstrup/Sydney: Dangaroo, 1991).

MAGNIER, Bernard, & Michel LABAN. "Entretien avec Mia Couto," *Notre Librairie (Club des Lecteurs d'Expression Française): Littérature du Mozambique* 112 (1993): 72–76.

MALAMOUD, Charles. *Cooking the World: Ritual and Thought in Ancient India*, tr. David White (*Cuire le monde: Rite et pensée dans l'Inde ancienne*, 1989; Delhi: Oxford UP, 1996).

MALOUF, David. *An Imaginary Life* (London: Chatto & Windus/New York, George Braziller, 1978; London: Picador, 1980).

——. *12 Edmonstone Street* (London: Chatto & Windus,1985).

——. *Remembering Babylon* (1993; London: Vintage, 1994)

——. *Selected Poems* (Sydney: Angus & Robertson, 1981).

——. *Selected Poems 1959–1989* (London: Chatto & Windus, 1994).

MAILLARD, Keith. "*Middlewatch* as Magic Realism," *Canadian Literature* 92 (Spring 1982): 10–21.

MAJA-PEARCE, Adewale. *A Mask Dancing: Nigerian Novelists of the Eighties* (London: Hans Zell, 1992).

——. "At Last, the Real Thing!," *New African* (January 1991): 43–44.

——. "Interview with Kojo Laing," *Wasafiri* 5–6 (1987) : 27–29.

MALLORY, William E., & Paul SIMPSON-HOUSLEY, ed. *Geography and Literature: A Meeting of the Disciplines* (Syracuse NY: Syracuse UP, 1987).

MÁRQUEZ RODRÍGUEZ, Alexis. *Lo barroco y lo real maravilloso en la obra de Alejo Carpentier* (Mexico City: Siglo XX, 1982).

——. "Alejo Carpentier: Teorías del barroco y del real–maravilloso," in *Ocho veces Alejo Carpentier* (Caracas: Grijalbo, 1992): 55–91.

MDA, Zakes. *She Plays with the Darkness* (Johannesburg: Vivlia, 1995).

MIHAILOVICH–DICKMAN, Vera, ed. *"Return" in Post-Colonial Writing: A Cultural Labyrinth* (Cross/Cultures 12; Amsterdam/Atlanta GA: Rodopi, 1994).

MILIANI, Domingo. *Arturo Uslar Pietri, renovador del cuento venezolano* (Caracas: Monte Avila, 1969).

MITCHELL, Kenneth. "Landscape and Literature," in Mallory & Simpson–Housley, 23–29.

MOBOLADE, Timothy. "The Concept of Abiku," *African Arts* 7.1 (Autumn 1973): 62–64.

MONEGAL, Emir Rodríguez. "Realismo mágico versus literatura fantástica: un diálogo de sordos," *Otros mundos, otros fuegos: Fantasía y realismo mágico en Iberoamérica; Proceedings of the XVI Congreso Internacional de Literatura Iberoamericana* (East Lansing, 1973; Latin American Studies Center, USA: Michigan State University, 1975): 25–37.

MORETTI, Franco. *Modern Epic: The World System from Goethe to García Márquez*, tr. Quintin Hoare (*Opere Mondo*, 1994; Turin: Einaudi, 1996).

MORPHET, Tony. "Cultural Settlement: Albie Sachs, Njabulo Ndebele and the Question of Social and Cultural Imagination," *Pretext* 2.1 (Winter 1990): 94–103.

MUKHERJEE, Meenakshi. *The Twice Born Fiction: Themes and Techniques of the Indian Novel in English* (New Delhi/London: Heinemann, 1971).

——. ed. *Considerations* (New Delhi: Allied, 1977).

MURRAY, Sally–Ann. "Telling Stories," *Current Writing* 3 (October 1991): 184–92.

MURTI, Suryanarayana K.V. *Kohinoor in the Crown: Critical Studies in Indian English Literature* (New Delhi: Sterling, 1987).

MUSGRAVE, Susan. *Songs of the Sea Witch* (Vancouver: Sono Nis, 1976).

——. "Joe Rosenblatt's Writing Caresses the Language," *Weekend Sun Saturday Review* (29 June 1996): 15.

NAIK, M.K. *Dimensions of Indian English Literature* (New Delhi: Sterling, 1984).

NANDY, Ashis. *The Intimate Enemy: Loss and Recovery of Self Under Colonialism* (Delhi: Oxford UP, 1983).

NARAYAN, R.K. *The Man-Eater of Malgudi* (1961; Harmondsworth: Penguin, 1983).

NDEBELE, Njabulo S. *Rediscovery of the Ordinary* (Johannesburg: COSAW, 1991).

NETTLEBECK, Amanda ed. *Provisional Maps: Critical Essays On David Malouf* (Nedlands: U of Western Australia, 1994).

NWANKO, Chimalun. Review of *The Last Harmattan of Alusine Dunbar*, *African Studies Review* 35.1 (1992): 134–35.

OFEIMUN, Odia. "Surrealistic Power-Play," *West Africa* 3918 (19–25 October 1992): 1794–95.

OKELY, Judith, & Helen CALLAWAY, ed. *Anthropology and Autobiography* (London: Routledge, 1992).

OKRI, Ben. *Astonishing the Gods* (London: Phoenix, 1996).

——. *Birds of Heaven* (London: Phoenix, 1996).

——. *Dangerous Love* (London: Phoenix, 1996).

——. *The Famished Road* (London: Vintage, 1992).

——. *Incidents at the Shrine* (London: Heinemann, 1986).

——. *Songs of Enchantment* (London: Vintage, 1994).

——. *Stars of the New Curfew* (London: Secker & Warburg, 1988).

OLIPHANT, Andries W. "Fictions of Anticipation: Perspectives on Some Recent South African Short Stories in English," *World Literature Today* 70.1 (Winter 1996): 59–62.

——. & Ivan VLADISLAVIC, ed. *Ten Years of "Staffrider"* (Johannesburg: Ravan, 1988).

OMOTOSO, Kole. *The Form of the African Novel* (Akure/Ibadan: Fagbamigbe, 1979).

ONDAATJE, Michael. *In the Skin of a Lion* (Toronto: McClelland & Stewart, 1987).

——, ed. *Inklake: Canadian Stories* (Toronto: Lester & Orpen Dennys, 1990).

ORNELAS, José. "Mia Couto no contexto da literatura pós-colonial de Moçambique," *Luso-Brazilian Review* 33.2 (Winter 1996): 37–52.

O'SULLIVAN, Vincent. "Exiles of the Mind: The Fictions of Janet Frame," in *The Ring of Fire: Essays on Janet Frame*, ed. Jeanne Delbaere (Mundelstrup/Sydney: Dangaroo, 1992): 24–30.

PALLAN, Rajesh K. *Myths and Symbols in Raja Rao and R.K. Narayan* (Jalandhar: ABS, 1994).

PANDEY, Sudhakar, & V.N. JHA, ed. *Glimpses of Ancient Indian Poetics* (Delhi: Sri Satguru, 1983).

PATRICK, Annie. "David Malouf the Librettist," in NETTLEBECK, 133–48.

PELTON, Robert D. *The Trickster in West Africa: A Study in Mythic Irony and Sacred Delight* (1989; Berkeley: U of California P, 1980).

PERELMAN, Chaïm, & Lucie OLBRECHTS–TYTECA. *The New Rhetoric: A Treatise on Argumentation*, tr. John Wilkinson & Purcell Weaver (*Traité de l'argumentation: La nouvelle rhétorique*, 1958; Notre Dame IN: U of Notre Dame P, 1969).

PERRY, John Weir. *Roots of Renewal in Myth and Madness* (San Francisco CA: Jossey–Bass, 1976).

PETERSEN, Kirsten Holst, & Anna RUTHERFORD. "Fossil and Psyche" [extract from Petersen & Rutherford, *Enigma of Values: An Introduction to Wilson Harris*, Mundelstrup/Sydney: Dangaroo, 1976], in ASHCROFT, GRIFFITHS & TIFFIN, 185–89.

QUAYSON, Ato. "Esoteric Webwork As Nervous System: Reading the Fantastic in Ben Okri's Writing," in GURNAH, 147–48.

RAIMONDI, Piero. "Miguel Angel Asturias," introduction to Miguel Ángel Asturias, *Opere*, ed. & tr. Raimondi (Turin: UTET, 1973): ix–lxiii.

RAO, Raja. *Kanthapura* (1936; New Delhi: Orient, 1971).

——. *On the Ganga Ghat* (New Delhi: Vision, 1989).

RICŒUR, Paul. *The Rule of Metaphor. Multi-Disciplinary Studies of the Creation of Meaning in Language*, tr. Robert Czerny, Kathleen McLaughlin & John Costello (*La Métaphore vive*, 1975; tr. 1977; Buffalo/Toronto: U of Toronto P, 1993).

RILKE, Rainer Maria. *Sämtliche Werke*, Zweiter Band (Frankfurt am Main: Insel, 1956).

RIZZARDI, Alfredo, ed. *Canada: Testi e contesti* (Abano Terme: Piovan, 1983).

——. *Moderni e Post-Moderni: Studi sul romanzo canadese del Novecento* (Abano Terme: Piovan, 1994).

ROBINSON, Jeffrey. "The Aboriginal Enigma: *Heart of Darkness*, *Voss* and *Palace of the Peacock*," *Journal of Commonwealth Literature* 20:1 (1985): 149–55.

ROBINSON, Tim. "Setting Foot on the Shores of Connemara," in *Setting Foot on the Shores of Connemara & Other Writings* (Dublin: Lilliput, 1996): 21–22.

ROH, Franz. "Realismo mágico: Problemas de la pintura más reciente," in *Revista de Occidente*, (1927).

RORTY, Richard. *Contingency, Irony and Solidarity* (Cambridge: Cambridge UP, 1989).

ROSENBLATT, Joe. *Bumblebee Dithyramb* (Erin, Ontario: Press Porcépic, 1972).

——. *Poetry Hotel*, in *Gridi nel buio: Poesie di Joe Rosenblatt*, ed. Alfredo Rizzardi (Abano: Piovan Editore, 1990): 52.

——. *Tentacled Mother/Madre Tentacolare*, ed. Alfredo Rizzardi (Abano: Piovan Editore, 1995); *Tentacled Mother* (Toronto: Exile Editions, 1996).

——. *The Voluptuous Gardner: The Collected Art and Writing by Joe Rosenblatt 1973–1996* (Erin, Ontario: Press Porcépic, 1996).

ROSS, Robert L., ed. *International Literature in English: The Major Writers* (New York: Garland, 1990).

RUSHDIE, Salman. *Grimus* (1975; New York: Penguin, 1991).

——. *Imaginary Homelands: Essays and Criticism 1981–1991* (London: Granta/Penguin, 1991).

——. *The Jaguar Smile: A Nicaraguan Journey* (London: Picador, 1987).

——. *Midnight's Children* (1980; New York: Avon, 1982).

——. *The Moor's Last Sigh* (London: Jonathan Cape, 1995).

——. *The Satanic Verses* (London: Viking, 1988).

——. *Shame* (1983; London: Picador, 1984).

SACHS, Albie. "Preparing Ourselves for Freedom" in Brown & Van Dyk, 117–18.

SAID, Edward W. *Orientalism* (1978; New York: Vintage, 1979).

SALKEY, Andrew. *Anancy's Score* (London: Bogle-L'Ouverture, 1973).

SAMUELS, Andrew, Bani SHORTER & Fred PLAUT, ed. *A Critical Dictionary of Jungian Analysis* (London/New York: Routledge, 1986).

SATTHIANANDHAN, Krupabai. *Saguna* (1985; Delhi: Oxford UP, 1998).

SCARANO, Tommaso. "Raccontare l'assurdo: Il fantastico di Silvina Ocampo, Julio Cortázar e Bioy Casares," in *Modelli, innovazioni, rifacimenti: Saggi su Borges e altri scrittori argentini* (Viareggio: Mauro Baroni Editore, 1994): 165–98.

SCOTT, Lawrence. *Witchbroom* (1992; Oxford: Heinemann, 1993).

SHARRAD, Paul. "The Art of Memory and the Liberation of History: Wilson Harris's Witnessing of Time," in *The Writer as Historical Witness*, ed. Edwin Thumboo & Thiru Kandiah (Singapore: Singapore UP, 1995): 588–99.

SLEMON, Stephen. "Magic Realism as Post-Colonial Discourse," *Canadian Literature* 116 (Spring 1988): 9–24.

SMITH, M[alvern]. van Wyk. "Waiting for Silence; or the Autobiography of Metafiction in Some Recent South African Novels," *Current Writing* 3 (October 1991): 91–104.

SPENCER, Paul. "Automythologies and the Reconstruction of Ageing," in OKELY & CALLAWAY, 50–63.

STAINES, David, ed. *The Canadian Imagination: Dimension of a Literary Culture* (Cambridge MA/London: Harvard UP, 1977).

STEINER, George. *Real Presences: Is There Anything In What We Say?* (London: Faber & Faber, 1989).

SULERI, Sara. *The Rhetoric of English India* (Chicago/London: U of Chicago P, 1992).

SWARUPANANDA, Swami, ed. *Srimad–Bhagavad–Gita: Text, Word-for-Word Translation, English Rendering, Comment and Index* (Calcutta: Avaita Ashrama, repr. 1996).

TARLEKAR, G.H. "The Merits and Demerits of Kavya, according to Bhamaha and Danddin," in PANDEY & JHA, 105–18.

TEKPETEY, Kwawisi. "The Trickster in Akan–Asante Oral Literature," *Asemka: A Bilingual Literary Journal of the University of Cape Coast* 5 (September 1979): 78–82.

TEMPLE, Richard C. *The Legends of Punjab* (1884; repr. Lahore: Allied, nd).

TULL, Herman W. *The Vedic Origins of Karma* (1989; Delhi: Sri Satguru, 1990).

USLAR PIETRI, Arturo. *Letras y hombres de Venezuela* (Mexico: Fondo de cultura económica, 1948; repr. Madrid: E.M. Edition, 1978).

——. "Realismo mágico," in *Godos, insurgentes y visionarios* (Barcelona: Seix Barral, 1986).

VARGAS LLOSA, Mario. *García Márquez: Historia de un deicidio* (Barcelona: Seix Barral, 1971).

VIVAN, Itala, ed. *Voci all'imbrunire* (Rome: Edizioni Lavoro, 1989).

VLADISLAVIC, Ivan. *Missing Persons* (Cape Town/Johannesburg: David Philip, 1989).

VON FRANZ, Marie-Louise. *Projection and Re-Collection of Jungian Psychology: Reflections of the Soul* (La Salle IL/London: Open Court, 1980).

WANNENBERG, Alf. "*Missing Persons*, Ivan Vladislavic," *New Contrast* 71 (Spring 1990): 82–84.

WEISGERBER, Jean. *Le réalisme magique: Roman, peinture et cinema* (Lausanne: Editions de l'Âge d'Homme, 1987).

WESTON, Anita. "The Feasibility of the Chutnification of History: Rhetoric as Referent in the Magic-Realism of Salman Rushdie," in CASTORINA & VILLA, 498–504.

WHITE, Patrick. *Flaws in the Glass. A Self-Portrait* (Harmondsworth: Penguin, 1981).

——. "The Prodigal Son" (1958), in *Patrick White Speaks* (London: Jonathan Cape, 1990): 15–16.

——. *Riders in the Chariot* (1961; Harmondsworth: Penguin, 1974).

——. *Voss* (1957; Harmondsworth: Penguin, 1960).

WILKINSON, Jane, ed. *Talking with African Writers* (London: James Currey, 1992).

WILLIAMS, Mark. "Containing Continents: The Moralized Landscapes of Conrad, Greene, White and Harris," *Kunapipi* 7:1 (1985): 34–45.

——. & Alan RIACH. "Reading Wilson Harris," in MAES-JELINEK, ed. *The Uncompromising Imagination*, 51–60.

WILSON, Rawdon. "The Metamorphoses of Fictional Space: Magical Realism," in ZAMORA & FARIS, 209–34.

WOOD, Felicity. "Why Don't South Africans like Fantasy?" *New Contrast* 79 (June 1992): 33–39.

WRIGHT, Derek "Returning Voyagers: The Ghanaian Novel in the Nineties," *Journal of Modern African Studies* 34.1 (1996): 179–92.

YATES, Frances A. *The Art of Memory* (London: Routledge & Kegan Paul, 1966).

YEATS, W.B.. *The Collected Poems of W.B. Yeats* (London: Macmillan, 1955).

——. *Essays and Introductions* (London: Macmillan, 1961).

ZAMBARE, V.T. "Aprastuta prasamsa and Vyajastuti: Is the 'prasuta' relevant, conveyed by 'Vyanjana, word-power of suggestion,' or by 'Laksana, word-power of figuration'?," in PANDEY & JHA, 97–104.

ZAMORA, Lois Parkinson, & Wendy B. FARIS, ed. *Magical Realism: Theory, History, Community* (Durham NC/London: Duke UP, 1995).

ZOPPI, Isabella, ed. *Routes of the Roots: Geography and Literature in the English Speaking Countries* (Rome: Bulzoni, 1998).

ZWICKY, Fay. *Poems 1970–1992* (St. Lucia: U of Queensland P, 1993).

ဢ • ဢ

Contributors

———————————— ∞

SHAUL BASSI took his PhD at the University of Pisa with a thesis on Othello's ethnicity. He has published essays and reviews on Indian Literature, particularly on Indian poetry and on Salman Rushdie. He has recently edited a translation of Indian poetry into Italian, *Poeti Indiani del '900* (Venice: Supernova, 1998).

PAOLO BERTINETTI is Professor of English Literature at the University of Turin. He has edited the translation into Italian of a collection of Caribbean short stories, and has published essays and reviews on colonial and post-colonial African, Caribbean, Indian and Australian Literature. He was the Italian Representative Member of the Board of EASA from 1996 to1997.

LUCA BIAGIOTTI has a post-doctoral fellowship in English literature at the University of Pisa, where he took his PhD with a thesis on the transformation of *Romeo and Juliet* in the versions by Otway, Cibber and Garrick. He has published essays on Canadian literature, particularly on Jack Hodgins and Robert Kroetsch.

LUCIA BOLDRINI is a lecturer in English literature at Goldsmiths' College, University of London. She is the author of *Fictional Biographies of Historical Characters: (Auto)biography, Subjectivity, Theory in the Contemporary English Novel* (1998). She is currently editing the collection *James Joyce's Medieval Cultures* for the European Joyce Studies series (Rodopi, Amsterdam).

ROBERT BRINGHURST is a poet and free-lance writer living in Vancouver, British Columbia. He is author of the following collections of poems: *Bergschrund* (1973), *The Beauty of the Weapons* (1982), *Pieces of Map, Pieces of Music* (1987), *The Calling* (1995).

FRANCESCO CASOTTI is an associate professor of English literature at the University of Pisa. He has written extensively on Dickens and has published essays on Canadian and Australian writers.

CARMEN CONCILIO has a permanent research fellowship in English literature and new literatures in English at the University of Turin. She has translated J.M. Coetzee's *Age of Iron* (1995) into Italian and has published essays and reviews on Coetzee, Wilson Harris, David Malouf, Patrick White and other post-colonial writers.

PIETRO DEANDREA took his PhD at the University of Bologna with a thesis on the metamorphoses of genre in anglophone West African literature. He has translated novels by André Brink, Buchi Emecheta and Ben Okri into Italian, has published essays on Ben Okri, Kojo Laing, Mohammed ben Abdallah, and on Ghanaian poetry.

CARMEN DELL'AVERSANO has a permanent research fellowship in English literature at the University of Pisa. She is author of a book on David Malouf's *An Imaginary Life* (1996) and has published essays on Salman Rushdie.

VALERIA GUIDOTTI is an assistant professor of literatures of the English-speaking countries at the University of Turin. She has published essays on South African literature, particularly on Miriam Tlali, Ivan Vladislavic and André Brink.

ELSA LINGUANTI is a professor of English literature at the University of Pisa. She has published extensively on colonial and post-colonial literatures.

ALESSANDRO MONTI is a professor of English at the University of Turin. He has published on Indian literature and on Indian English as a specific language. He has translated Raja Rao's *Kanthapura* and Kipling's *The Jungle Books* into Italian, and is the author of a critical monograph, *Durga Marga*, on contemporary Indian fiction in English.

RENATO OLIVA is a professor of English literature at the University of Turin. He has published essays on literature and psychoanalysis and on African and Indian literature.

ALFREDO RIZZARDI is a professor of English literature at the University of Bologna. He has promoted the study of Canadian poetry in Italy, translating the work of many Canadian poets into Italian and publishing numerous essays on Canadian literature.

BIANCAMARIA RIZZARDI PERUTELLI has a permanent research fellowship in English literature at the University of Pisa. She has written on British women writers, and has translated Canadian poets into Italian, as well as publishing essays on Canadian writers.

TOMMASO SCARANO is professor of Spanish-American literature at the University of Pisa. He has published extensively on García Márquez, Juan Rulfo, Julio Cortázar, Adolfo Bioy Casares and particularly on Jorge Luis Borges.

ISABELLA ZOPPI is a researcher in anglophone literatures at the Centre for the Study of the Literatures and Cultures of Emerging Areas (CNR), in Turin. She has published essays and reviews on Caribbean, African and Canadian writers and has co-edited the volume *Cross-Cultural Voices: Investigation into the Post-Colonial* (Rome: Bulzoni, 1996), as well as editing the volume *Routes of the Roots: Geography and Literature in the English-Speaking Countries* (Rome: Bulzoni, 1998).

ఴ • ఴ

Cross Cultures

Vol. 1: CRISIS AND CREATIVITY IN THE NEW LITERATURES IN ENGLISH. Ed. by Geoffrey Davis and Hena Maes-Jelinek. 1989. 541 pp. ISBN: 90-5183-135-8   Bound Hfl. 150.-/US-$ 83.-

Vol. 2: CRISIS AND CREATIVITY IN THE NEW LITERATURES IN ENGLISH: CANADA. Ed. by Geoffrey Davis. Amsterdam/Atlanta, GA 1990. 253 pp. ISBN: 90-5183-136-6   Hfl. 70.-/US-$ 38.50

Vol. 3: ALBERT GÉRARD: Contexts of African Literature. 1990. 169 pp. ISBN: 90-5183-196-X   Hfl. 50.-/US-$ 27.50

Vol. 4: CHANTAL ZABUS: The African Palimpsest: Indigenization of Language in the West African Europhone Novel. 1991. 224 pp. ISBN: 90-5183-197-8   Hfl. 70.-/US-$ 38.50

Vol. 5: GORDON COLLIER: The Rocks and Sticks of Words. Style, Discourse and Narrative Structure in the Fiction of Patrick White. 1992. xi,499 pp. ISBN: 90-5183-393-8   Bound Hfl. 150.-/US-$ 83.-

Vol. 6: US / THEM. Translation, Transcription and Identity in Post-Colonial Literary Cultures. Ed. by Gordon Collier. ix,416 pp. ISBN: 90-5183-394-6   Bound Hfl. 125,-/US-$ 69.-

Vol. 7: RE-SITING QUEEN'S ENGLISH. TEXT AND TRADITION IN POST-COLONIAL LITERATURES. Essays Presented to John Pengweme Matthews. Ed. by Gillian Whitlock and Helen Tiffin. 1992. vii,203pp. ISBN: 90-5183-395-4   Hfl. 60.-/US-$ 33.-

Vol. 8: THE POLITICS OF ART: ELI MANDEL'S POETRY AND CRITICISM. Ed. by Ed Jewinski and Andrew Stubbs. 1992. xviii,156 pp. ISBN: 90-5183-404-7   Hfl. 55.-/US-$ 30.50

Vol. 9: IMAGINATION AND THE CREATIVE IMPULSE IN THE NEW LITERATURES IN ENGLISH. Ed. by M.-T. Bindella and G.V. Davis. 297 pp. ISBN: 90-5183-310-5   Hfl. 90,-/US-$ 49.50

Vol. 10: CHRISTIAN HABEKOST: Verbal Riddim. The Politics and Aesthetics of African-Caribbean Dub Poetry. Amsterdam/Atlanta, GA 1993. 262 pp. ISBN: 90-5183-549-3   Hfl. 75,-/US-$ 41.50

Vol. 11: MAJOR MINORITIES. ENGLISH LITERATURES IN TRANSIT Ed.by Raoul Granqvist.Amsterdam/Atlanta, GA 1993. 198 pp. ISBN: 90-5183-559-0   Hfl. 60,-/US-$ 33.-

Vol. 12: "RETURNS" IN POST-COLONIAL WRITING. A Cultural Labyrinth. Ed. by Vera Mihailovich-Dickman. Amsterdam/Atlanta, GA 1994. XV,173 pp. ISBN: 90-5183-648-1   Hfl. 60,-/US-$ 33.-

Vol. 13: HILDEGARD KUESTER: The Crafting of Chaos. Narrative Structure in Margaret Laurence's The Stone Angel and The Diviners. Amsterdam/Atlanta, GA 1994. 212 pp. ISBN: 90-5183-743-7   Hfl. 60,-/US-$ 33.-

Vol. 14: BERNTH LINDFORS: Comparative Approaches to African Literatures. Amsterdam/Atlanta, GA 1994. 160 pp. ISBN: 90-5183-616-3   Hfl. 48,-/US-$ 26.50

Vol. 15: PETER HORN: Writing my Reading. Essays on Literary Politics in South Africa. Amsterdam/Atlanta, GA 1994. XI,172 pp. ISBN: 90-5183-723-2   Hfl. 55,-/US-$ 30.50

Vol. 16: READING RUSHDIE. PERSPECTIVES ON THE FICTION OF SALMAN RUSHDIE. Ed. by M.D. Fletcher. Amsterdam/Atlanta, GA 1994. 400 pp.
ISBN: 90-5183-742-9   Bound Hfl. 160,-/US-$ 88.50
ISBN: 90-5183-765-8   Paper Hfl. 50,-/US-$ 27.50

Vol. 17: CHRISTIANE FIOUPOU: La Route. Réalité et représentation dans l'œuvre de Wole Soyinka. Amsterdam/Atlanta, GA 1994. 390 pp. ISBN: 90-5183-731-3   Hfl. 120,-/US-$ 66.50

Vol. 18: DAVID FAUSETT: Images of the Antipodes in the Eighteenth Century. A Study in Stereotyping. Amsterdam/Atlanta, GA 1995. VIII,231 pp. ISBN: 90-5183-814-X   Hfl. 75,-/US-$ 41.50

Vol. 19: THE GUISES OF CANADIAN DIVERSITY / LES MASQUES DE LA DIVERSITÉ CANADIENNE. New European Perspectives/Nouvelles perspectives européennes. Ed. by Serge Jaumain & Marc Maufort. Amsterdam/Atlanta, GA 1995. 288 pp.
ISBN: 90-5183-879-4   Bound Hfl. 140,-/US-$ 77.50
ISBN: 90-5183-863-8   Paper Hfl. 45,-/US-$ 25.-

Vol. 20: A TALENT(ED) DIGGER. Creations, Cameos, and Essays in honour of Anna Rutherford. Ed. by Hena Maes-Jelinek, Gordon Collier, Geoffrey V. Davis. Amsterdam/Atlanta, GA 1996. XIX,519 pp. ISBN: 90-5183-964-2   Bound Hfl. 250,-/US-$ 135.-
ISBN: 90-5183-953-7   Paper Hfl. 55,-/US-$ 30.50

Vol. 21: ALBERT GÉRARD: Afrique plurielle. Études de littérature comparée. Amsterdam/Atlanta, GA 1996. 199 pp.

ISBN: 90-5183-972-3   Hfl. 60,-/US-$ 33

Vol. 22: "AND THE BIRDS BEGAN TO SING". Religion ar Literature in Post-Colonial Cultures. Ed. by Jamie S. Sco Amsterdam/Atlanta, GA 1996. XXVII,327 pp.
ISBN: 90-5183-984-7   Bound Hfl. 175,-/US-$ 9;
ISBN: 90-5183-967-7   Paper Hfl. 45,-/US-$ 2!

Vol. 23: DEFINING NEW IDIOMS AND ALTERNATIVE FORMS C EXPRESSION. Ed. by Eckhard Breitinger. Asnel Papers 1 Amsterdam/Atlanta, GA 1996. XXVI,282 pp.
ISBN: 90-420-0021-X   Bound Hfl. 150,-/US-$ 83
ISBN: 90-420-0013-9   Paper Hfl. 45,-/US-$ 25

Vol. 24: JANE PLASTOW: African Theatre and Politics. Th evolution of theatre in Ethiopia, Tanzania and Zimbabwe. comparative study. Amsterdam/Atlanta, GA 1996. XIV,286 pp.
ISBN: 90-420-0042-2   Bound Hfl. 150,-/US-$ 8:
ISBN: 90-420-0038-4   Paper Hfl. 45,-/US-$ 2!

Vol. 25: DIFFERENCE AND COMMUNITY. Canadian and Europea Cultural Perspectives. Ed. by Peter Easingwood, Konrad Gros Lynette Hunter. Amsterdam/Atlanta, GA 1996. XIII,267 pp.
ISBN: 90-420-0046-5   Bound Hfl. 140,-/US-$ 77.!
ISBN: 90-420-0050-3   Paper Hfl. 40,-/US-$ 22

Vol. 26: FUSION OF CULTURES? Ed. by Peter O. Stummer ar Christopher Balme. Amsterdam/Atlanta, GA 1996. XII,332 p ASNEL Papers 2
ISBN: 90-420-0044-9   Bound Hfl. 175,-/US-$ 97
ISBN: 90-420-0043-0   Paper Hfl. 50,-/US-$ 27.!

Vol. 27: SUE KOSSEW: Pen and Power. A Post-Colonial Reading J.M. Coetzee and André Brink. Amsterdam/Atlanta, GA 1996. IX,2! pp. ISBN: 90-420-0097-X   Bound Hfl. 130,-/US-$ 72
ISBN: 90-420-0000-5   Paper Hfl. 35,-/US-$ 19

Vol. 28: ARATJARA: Aboriginal Culture and Literature in Australi Ed. by Dieter Riemenschneider and Geoffrey V. Davi Amsterdam/Atlanta, GA 1997. XVI,234 pp.
ISBN: 90-420-0151-8   Bound Hfl. 125,-/US-$ 69
ISBN: 90-420-0132-1   Paper Hfl. 35,-/US-$ 19

Vol. 29: BARBARA WILLIAMS: In Other Words. Interviews wi Australian Poets. Amsterdam/Atlanta, GA 1998. XLIII,280 pp.
ISBN: 90-420-0287-5   Bound Hfl. 150,-/US-$ 83
ISBN: 90-420-0277-8   Paper Hfl. 50,-/US-$ 27.!

Vol. 30: (UN)WRITING EMPIRE.   Ed. by Theo D'hae Amsterdam/Atlanta, GA 1998. 321 pp.
ISBN: 90-420-0471-1   Bound Hfl. 160,-/US-$ 88.!
ISBN: 90-420-0461-4   Paper Hfl. 45,-/US-$ 25

Vol. 31: ANTONELLA SARTI: Spiritcarvers. Interviews with eightee writers from New Zealand. Amsterdam/Atlanta, GA 1998. XIV,2; pp. ISBN: 90-420-0713-3   Bound Hfl. 120,-/US-$ 66.!
ISBN: 90-420-0703-6   Paper Hfl. 35,-/US-$ 19

Vol. 32: ACROSS THE LINES. Intertextuality and Transcultur Communication in the New Literatures in English. Ed. by Wolfgar Klooss. ASNEL Papers 3. Amsterdam/Atlanta, GA 1998. XI,304 p
ISBN: 90-420-0733-8   Bound Hfl. 150,-/US-$ 83
ISBN: 90-420-0723-0   Paper Hfl. 45,-/US-$ 25

Vol. 33: THE BODY IN THE LIBRARY. Ed. by Leigh Dale ar Simon Ryan. Amsterdam/Atlanta, GA 1998. VII,272 pp.
ISBN: 90-420-0753-2   Bound Hfl. 140,-/US-$ 77.!
ISBN: 90-420-0743-5   Paper Hfl. 40,-/US-$ 22

Vol. 34: ANDRÉ VIOLA, JACQUELINE BARDOLPH AND DENI! COUSSY: New Fiction in English from Africa. West, East, ar South. Amsterdam/Atlanta, GA 1998. X,244 pp.
ISBN: 90-420-0773-7   Bound Hfl. 125,-/US-$ 69
ISBN: 90-420-0763-X   Paper Hfl. 35,-/US-$ 19

Vol. 35: PIERRE FRANÇOIS: Inlets of the Soul. Contempora Fiction in English and the Myth of the Fall. Amsterdam/Atlanta, G 1999. IX,321 pp.
ISBN: 90-420-0446-0   Bound Hfl. 140,-/US-$ 77.!
ISBN: 90-420-0436-3   Paper Hfl. 50,-/US-$ 27.!